Snow White with the Red Hair

SORATA AKI

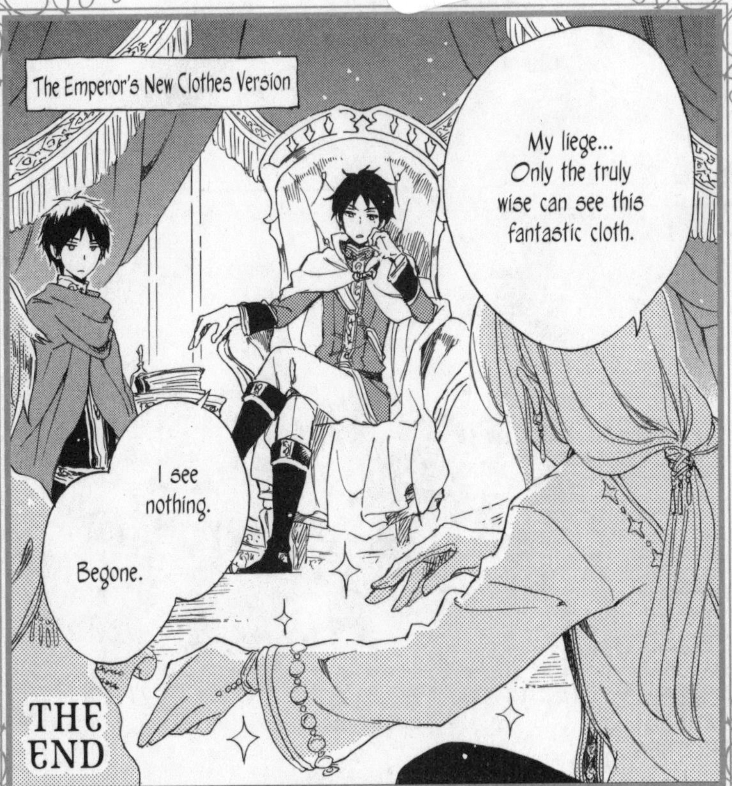
The Emperor's New Clothes Version
My liege... Only the truly wise can see this fantastic cloth.
I see nothing.
Begone.
THE END

VOLUME 12
TABLE of CONTENTS

Snow white with the red hair

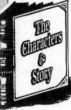

The Characters & Story

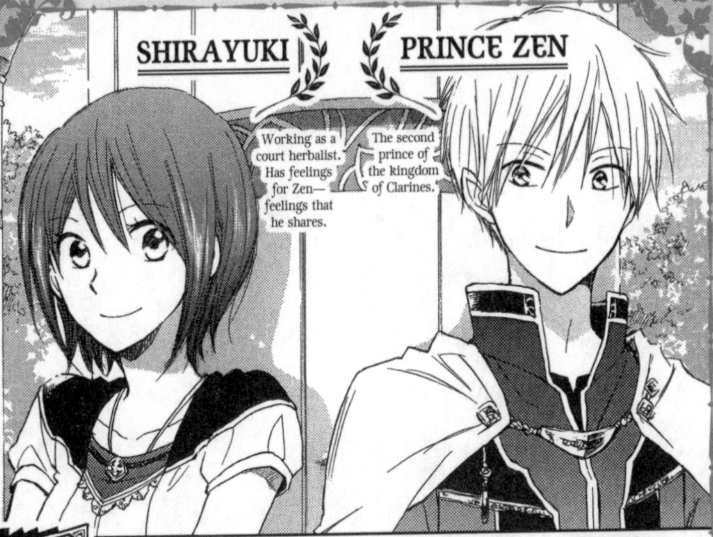

SHIRAYUKI

Working as a court herbalist. Has feelings for Zen—feelings that he shares.

PRINCE ZEN

The second prince of the kingdom of Clarines.

PRINCE IZANA

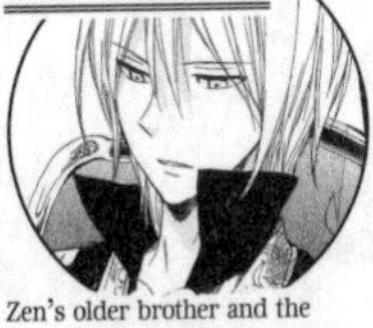

Zen's older brother and the crown prince of the kingdom. Keeping a close eye on Shirayuki and Zen's relationship...

MITSUHIDE & KIKI

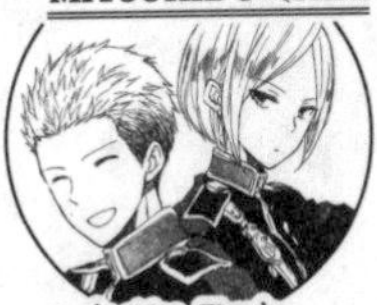

Zen's aides. They're good friends who share a strong bond.

OBI

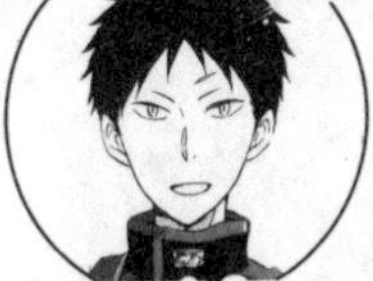

Former assassin. Currently, Zen's underling. Served as Shirayuki's bodyguard for part of her stay in Lilias.

Shirayuki was born with beautiful hair as red as apples, but when her rare hair earns her unwanted attention from the notorious prince Raj, she's forced to flee her home. A young man named Zen helps her in the forest of the neighboring kingdom, Clarines, and it turns out he is that kingdom's second prince! Shirayuki decides to accompany Zen back to Wistal, the capital city of Clarines.

Shirayuki has met all manner of people since becoming a court herbalist, and her relationship with Zen continues to grow, as the two have finally made their feelings known to each other.

After her work trip to Lilias, Shirayuki finally gets used to life as a full-fledged court herbalist.

Meanwhile, when Izana orders Zen to go on a date for the purposes of royal courtship, Zen pulls out the ace up his sleeve—none other than Kiki! Their little performance is good enough for Izana, who then grants Zen an entire wing of the palace and permission to house his aides and Shirayuki.

Shirayuki's life inside the palace has begun, and though some envious types resent her presence, she remains undaunted as she ingratiates herself with palace staff.

Elsewhere, Izana receives a letter from the sovereign of Clarines. In short, she'll be returning to the capital to make Izana the next king!

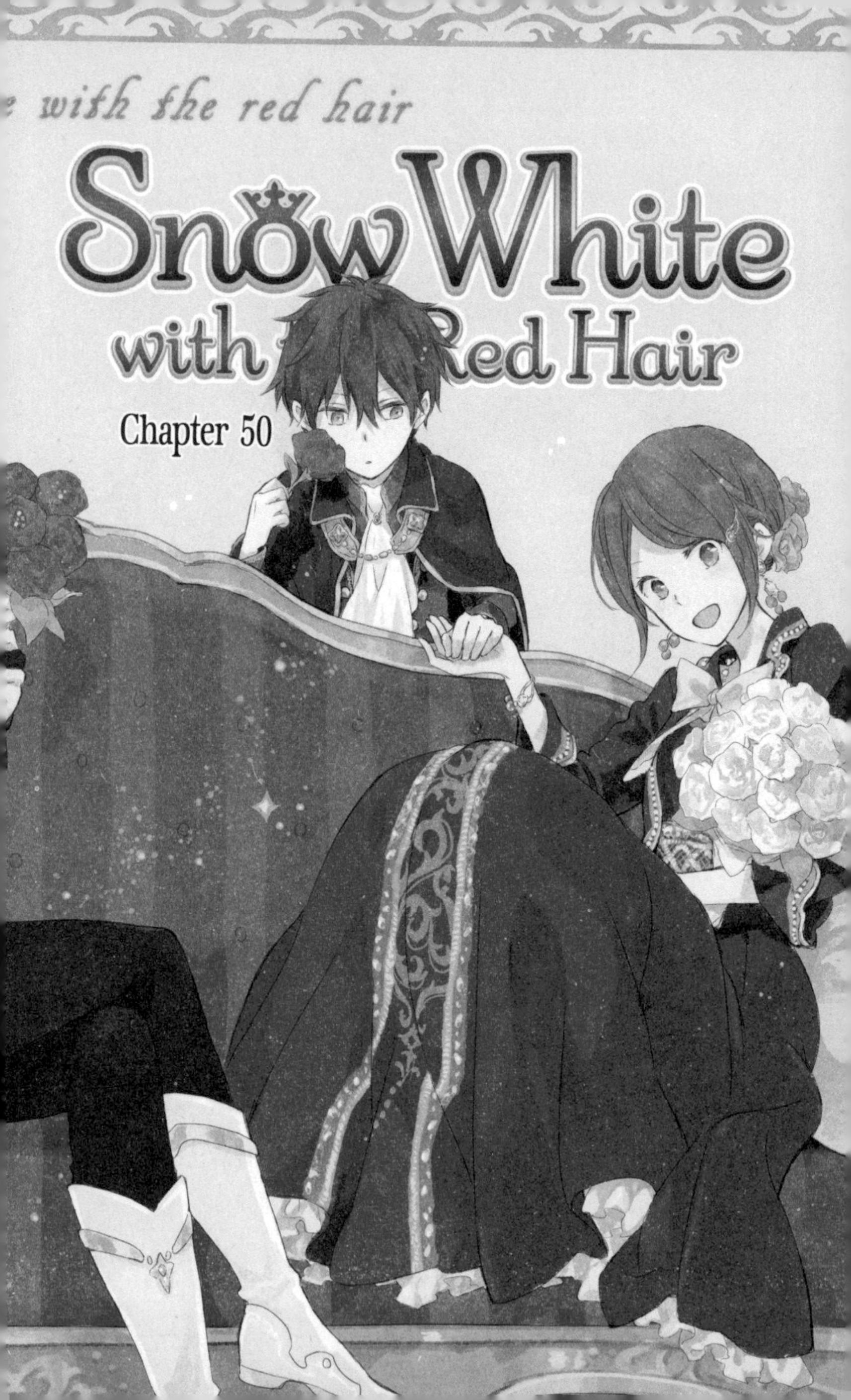
with the red hair
Snow White
with Red Hair
Chapter 50

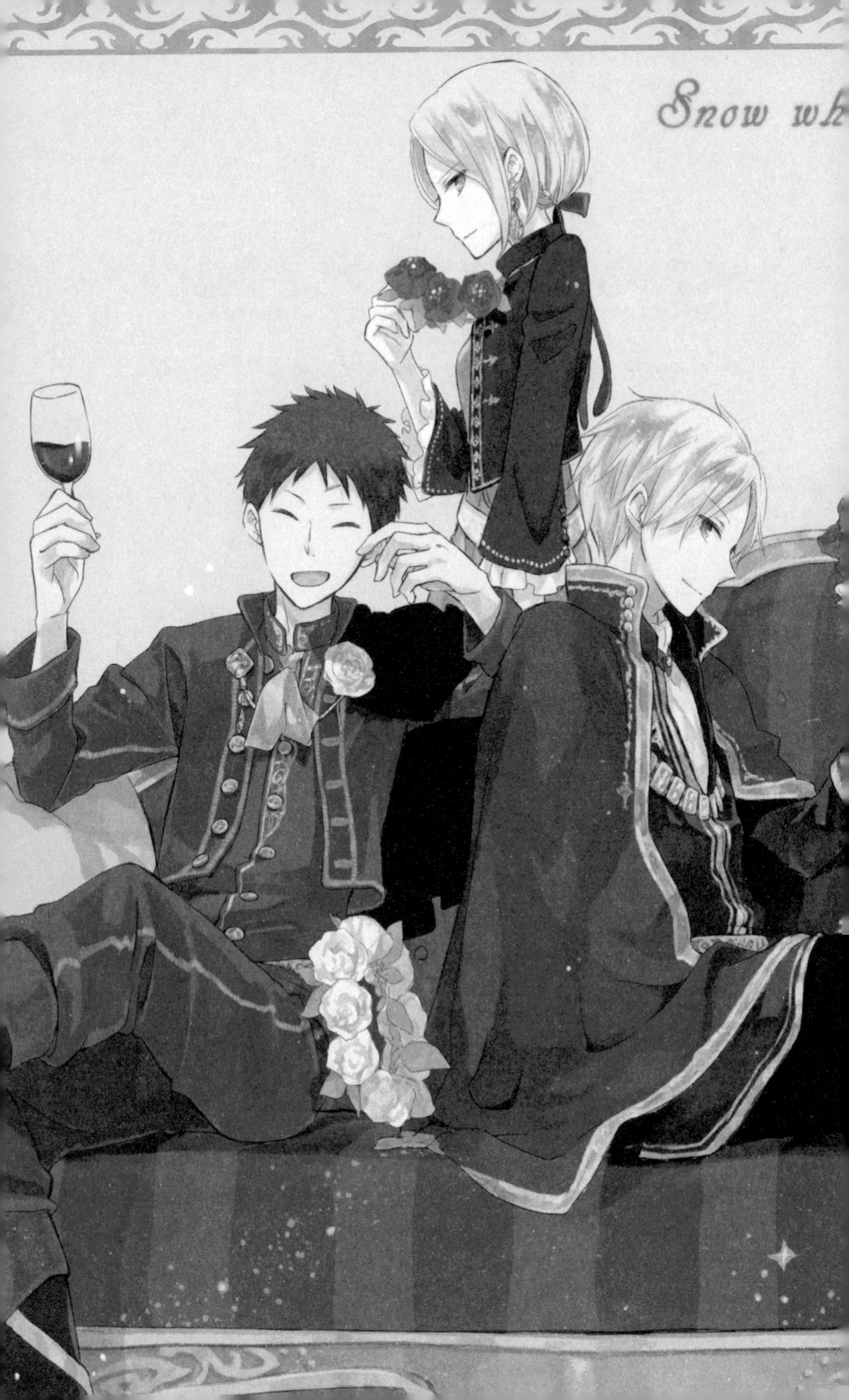
Snow wh

The title page spread for chapter 50 features the winners of the character popularity poll we held in celebration of reaching 50 chapters.

I decided to draw the top five, which is why Ryu is there. Congrats, Ryu!

And thank you to everyone who voted!

6th Place →

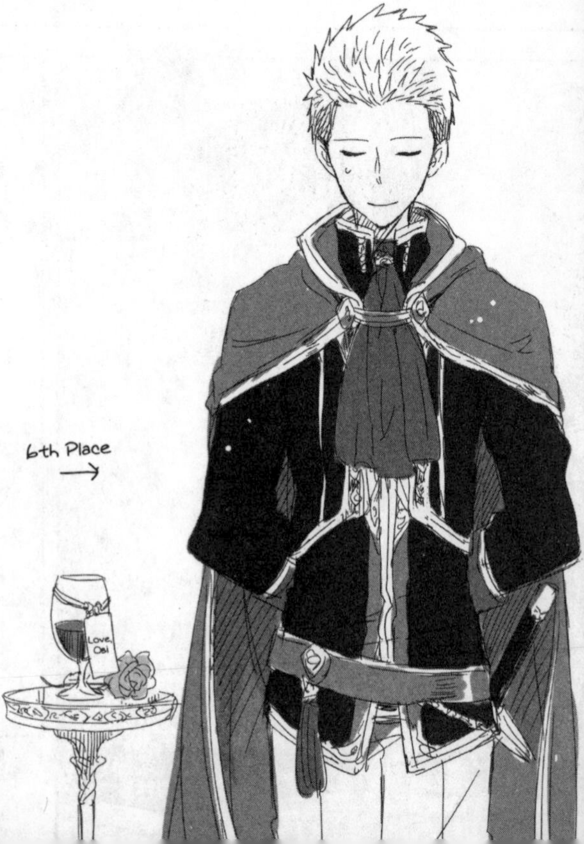
Love, Obi

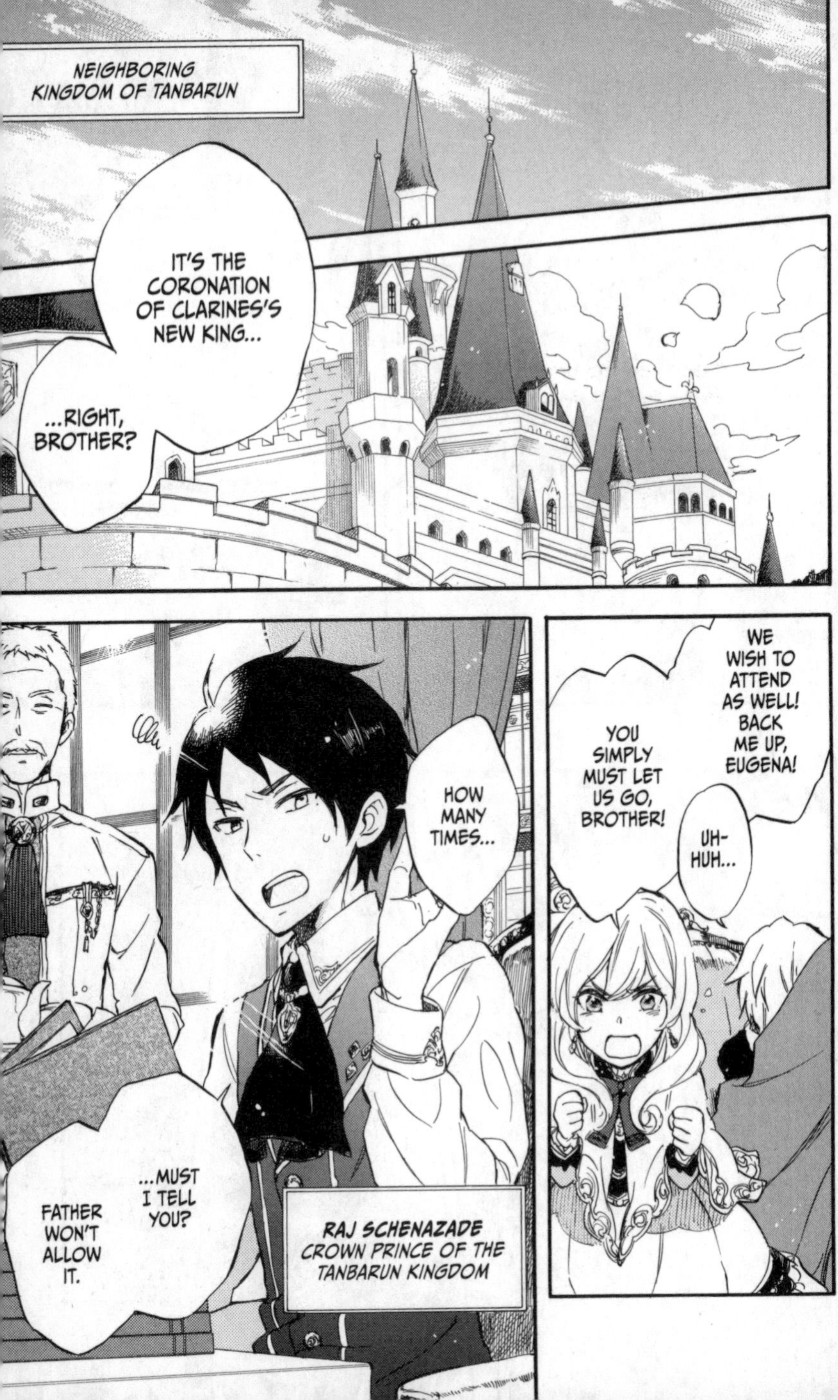
NEIGHBORING KINGDOM OF TANBARUN
IT'S THE CORONATION OF CLARINES'S NEW KING...
...RIGHT, BROTHER?
WE WISH TO ATTEND AS WELL! BACK ME UP, EUGENA!
YOU SIMPLY MUST LET US GO, BROTHER!
UH-HUH...
HOW MANY TIMES...
...MUST I TELL YOU?
FATHER WON'T ALLOW IT.
RAJ SCHENAZADE CROWN PRINCE OF THE TANBARUN KINGDOM

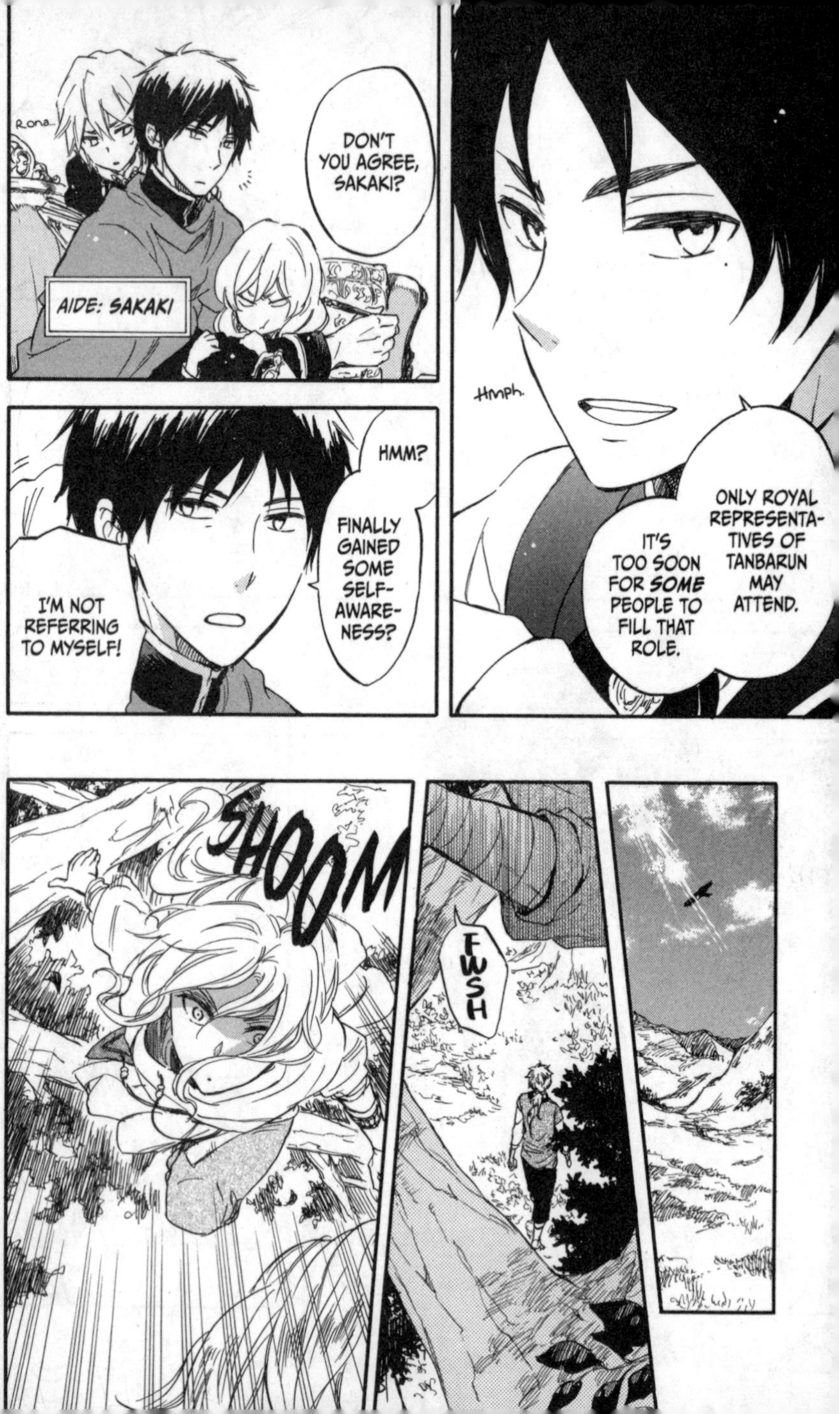
Hmph.
ONLY ROYAL REPRESENTATIVES OF TANBARUN MAY ATTEND.
IT'S TOO SOON FOR SOME PEOPLE TO FILL THAT ROLE.
Rona...
DON'T YOU AGREE, SAKAKI?
AIDE: SAKAKI
HMM?
FINALLY GAINED SOME SELF-AWARENESS?
I'M NOT REFERRING TO MYSELF!
FWSH
SHOOM

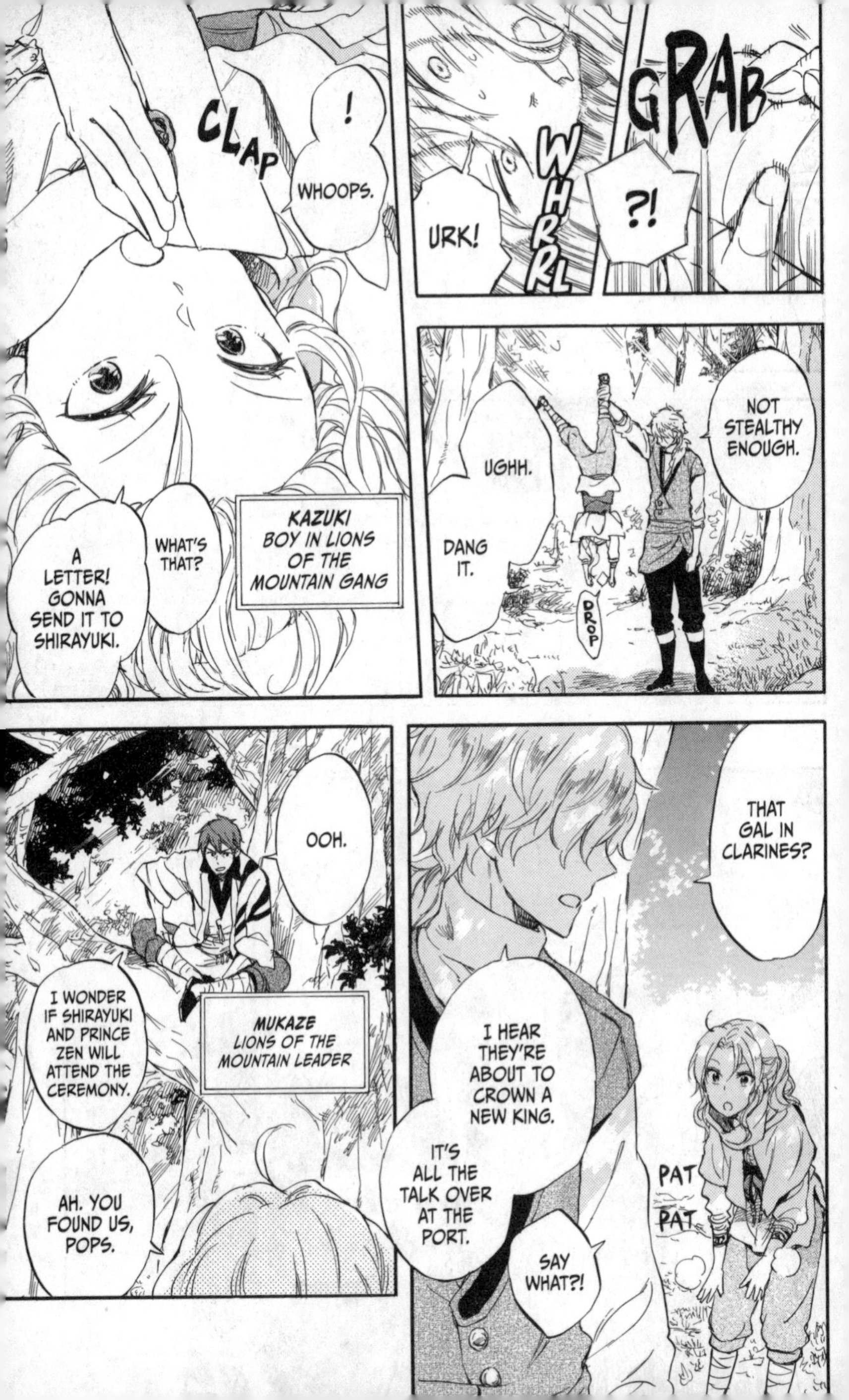
GRAB
?!
WHRRL
URK!
NOT STEALTHY ENOUGH.
UGHH.
DANG IT.
DROP
!
CLAP
WHOOPS.
KAZUKI
BOY IN LIONS OF THE MOUNTAIN GANG
WHAT'S THAT?
A LETTER! GONNA SEND IT TO SHIRAYUKI.
THAT GAL IN CLARINES?
I HEAR THEY'RE ABOUT TO CROWN A NEW KING.
IT'S ALL THE TALK OVER AT THE PORT.
PAT PAT
SAY WHAT?!
OOH.
MUKAZE
LIONS OF THE MOUNTAIN LEADER
I WONDER IF SHIRAYUKI AND PRINCE ZEN WILL ATTEND THE CEREMONY.
AH. YOU FOUND US, POPS.

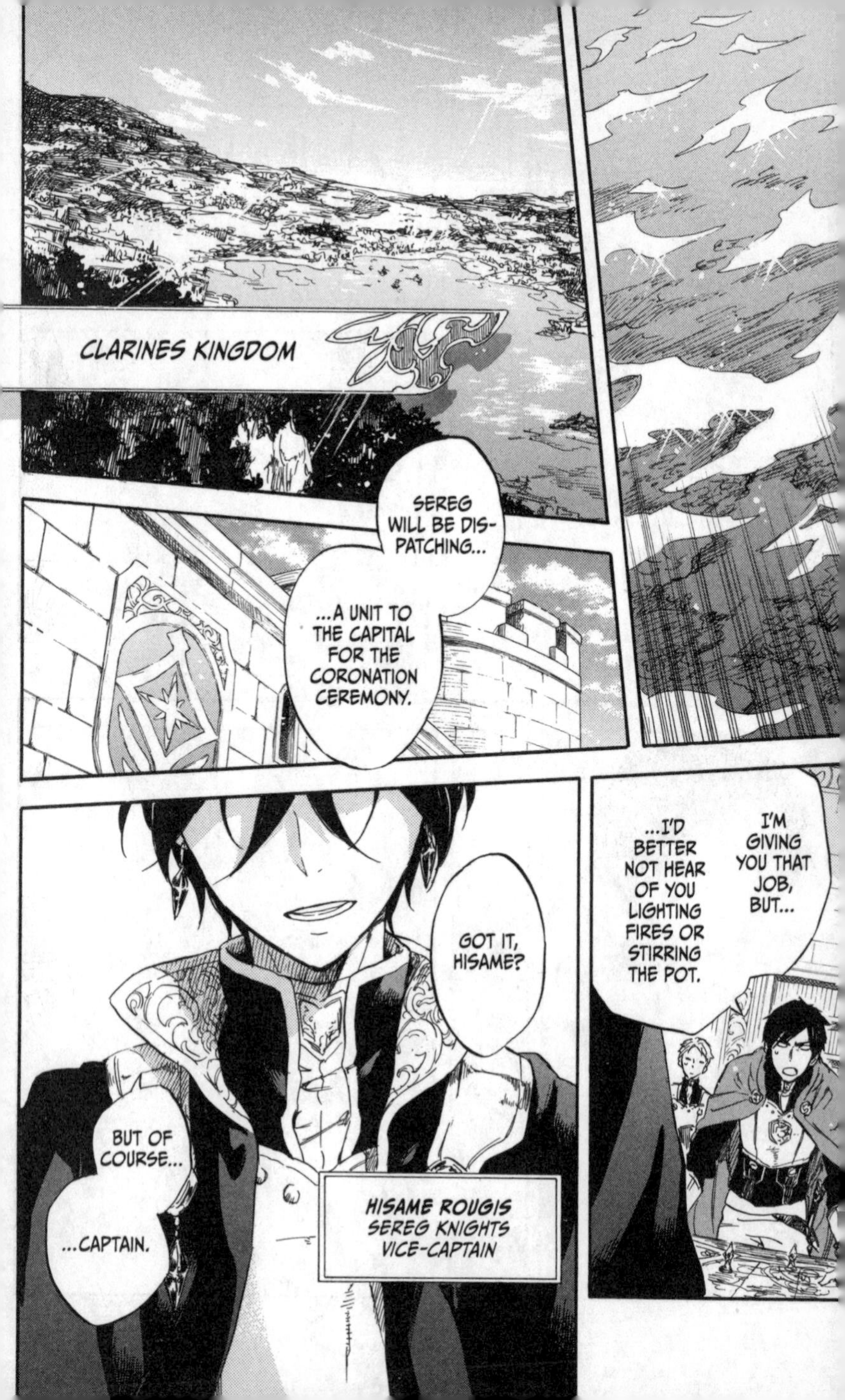
CLARINES KINGDOM
SEREG WILL BE DIS-PATCHING...
...A UNIT TO THE CAPITAL FOR THE CORONATION CEREMONY.
I'M GIVING YOU THAT JOB, BUT...
...I'D BETTER NOT HEAR OF YOU LIGHTING FIRES OR STIRRING THE POT.
GOT IT, HISAME?
BUT OF COURSE...
HISAME ROUGIS SEREG KNIGHTS VICE-CAPTAIN
...CAPTAIN.

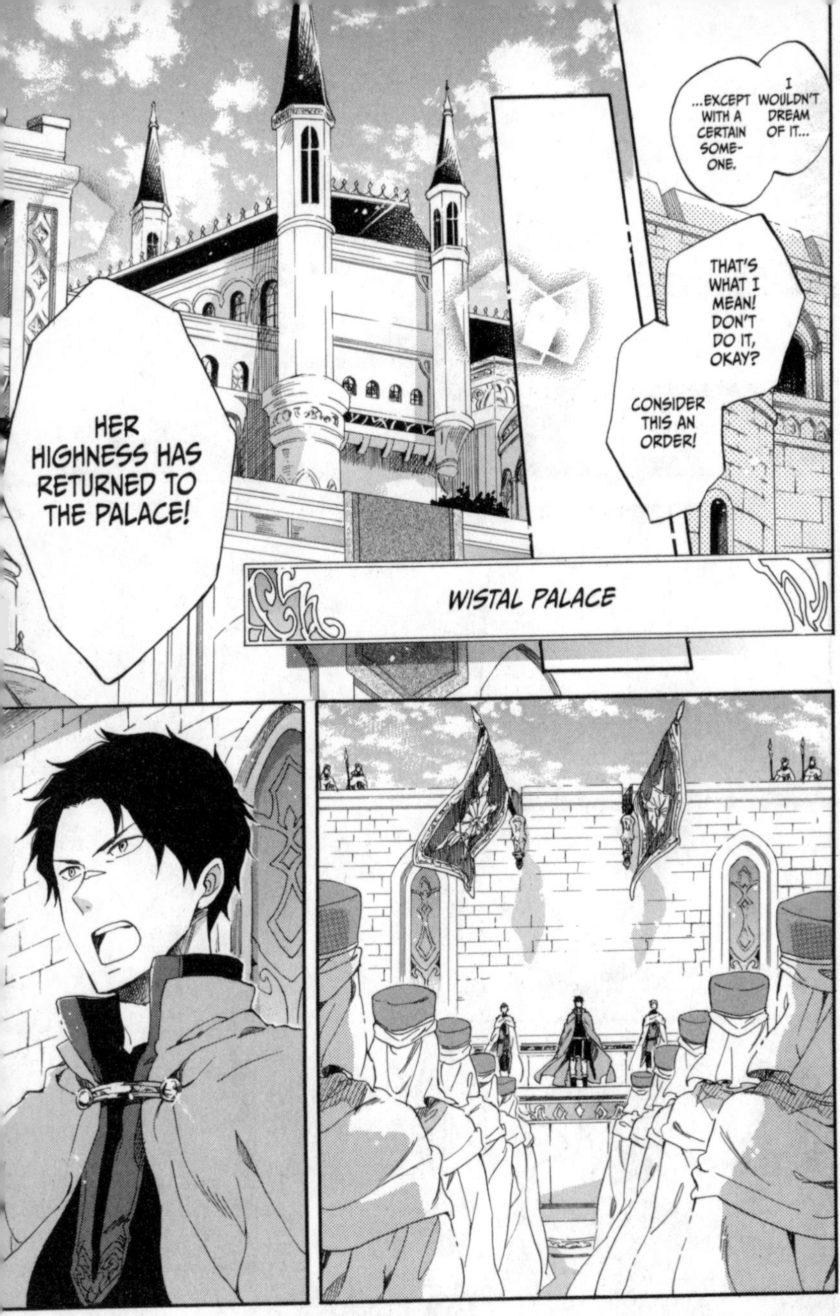
I WOULDN'T DREAM OF IT...
...EXCEPT WITH A CERTAIN SOME-ONE.
THAT'S WHAT I MEAN! DON'T DO IT, OKAY?
CONSIDER THIS AN ORDER!
WISTAL PALACE
HER HIGHNESS HAS RETURNED TO THE PALACE!

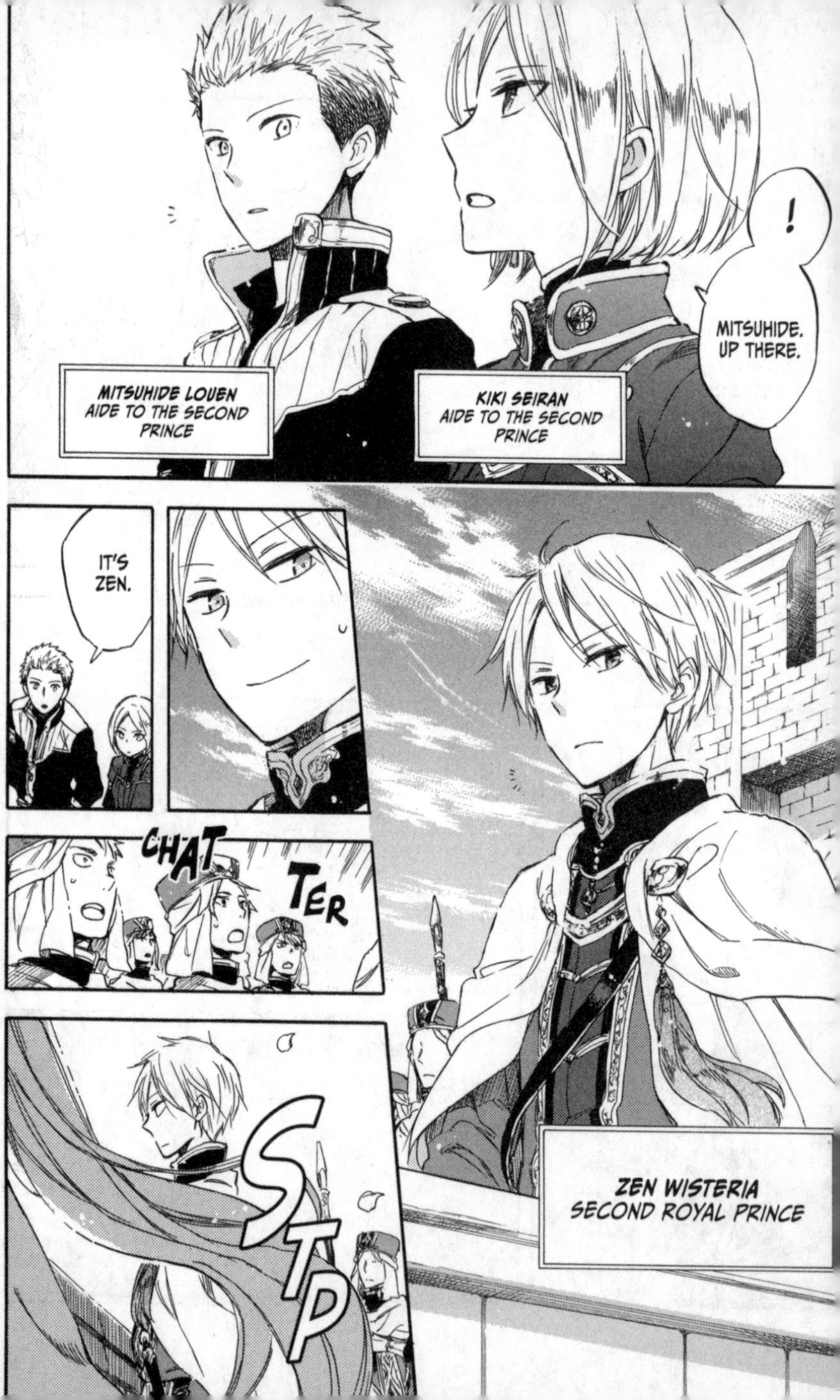
!
MITSUHIDE. UP THERE.
KIKI SEIRAN AIDE TO THE SECOND PRINCE
MITSUHIDE LOUEN AIDE TO THE SECOND PRINCE
ZEN WISTERIA SECOND ROYAL PRINCE
IT'S ZEN.
CHAT TER
STP

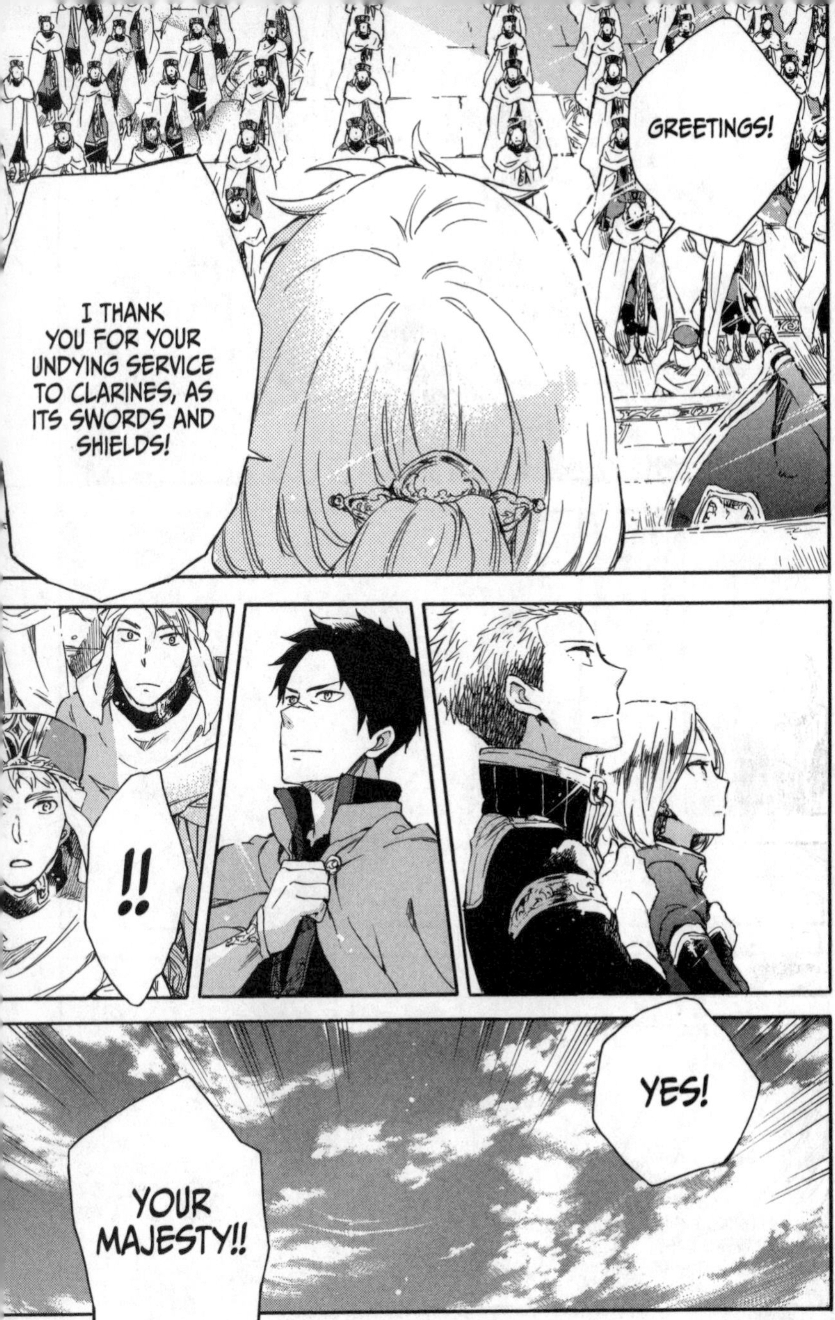
GREETINGS!
I THANK YOU FOR YOUR UNDYING SERVICE TO CLARINES, AS ITS SWORDS AND SHIELDS!
!!
YES!
YOUR MAJESTY!!

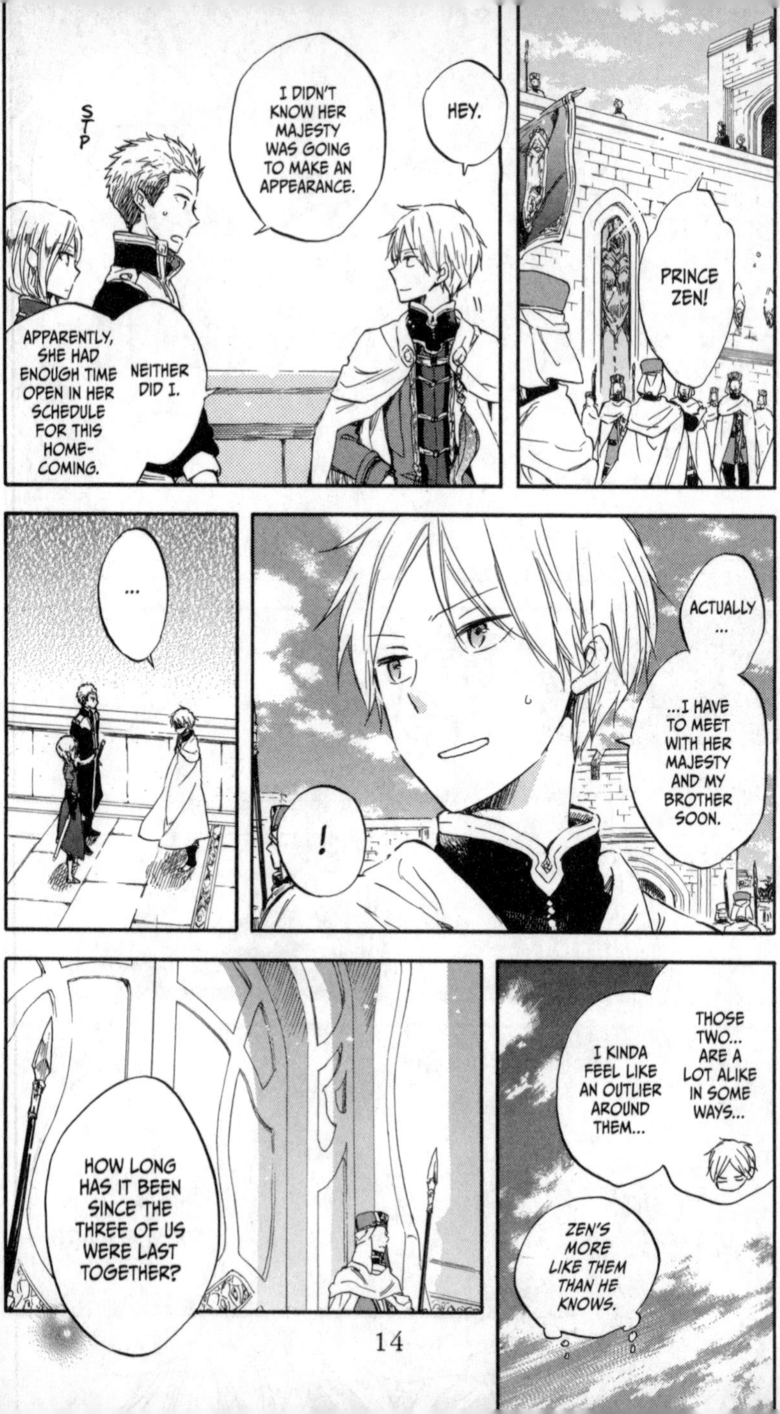
PRINCE ZEN!
HEY.
I DIDN'T KNOW HER MAJESTY WAS GOING TO MAKE AN APPEARANCE.
STP
NEITHER DID I.
APPARENTLY, SHE HAD ENOUGH TIME OPEN IN HER SCHEDULE FOR THIS HOME-COMING.
ACTUALLY...
...I HAVE TO MEET WITH HER MAJESTY AND MY BROTHER SOON.
!
...
THOSE TWO... ARE A LOT ALIKE IN SOME WAYS...
I KINDA FEEL LIKE AN OUTLIER AROUND THEM...
ZEN'S MORE LIKE THEM THAN HE KNOWS.
HOW LONG HAS IT BEEN SINCE THE THREE OF US WERE LAST TOGETHER?

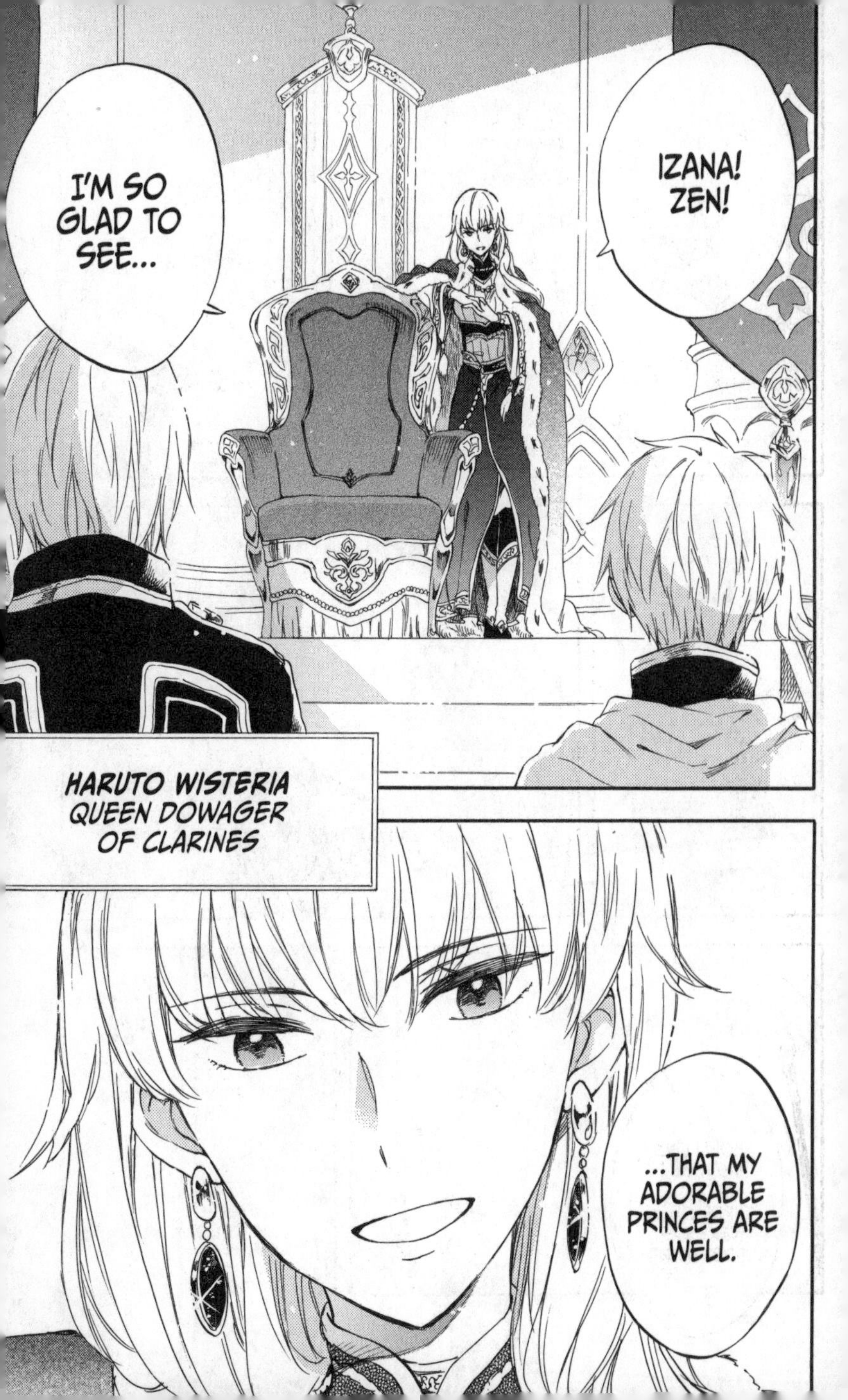
IZANA! ZEN!
I'M SO GLAD TO SEE...
HARUTO WISTERIA QUEEN DOWAGER OF CLARINES
...THAT MY ADORABLE PRINCES ARE WELL.

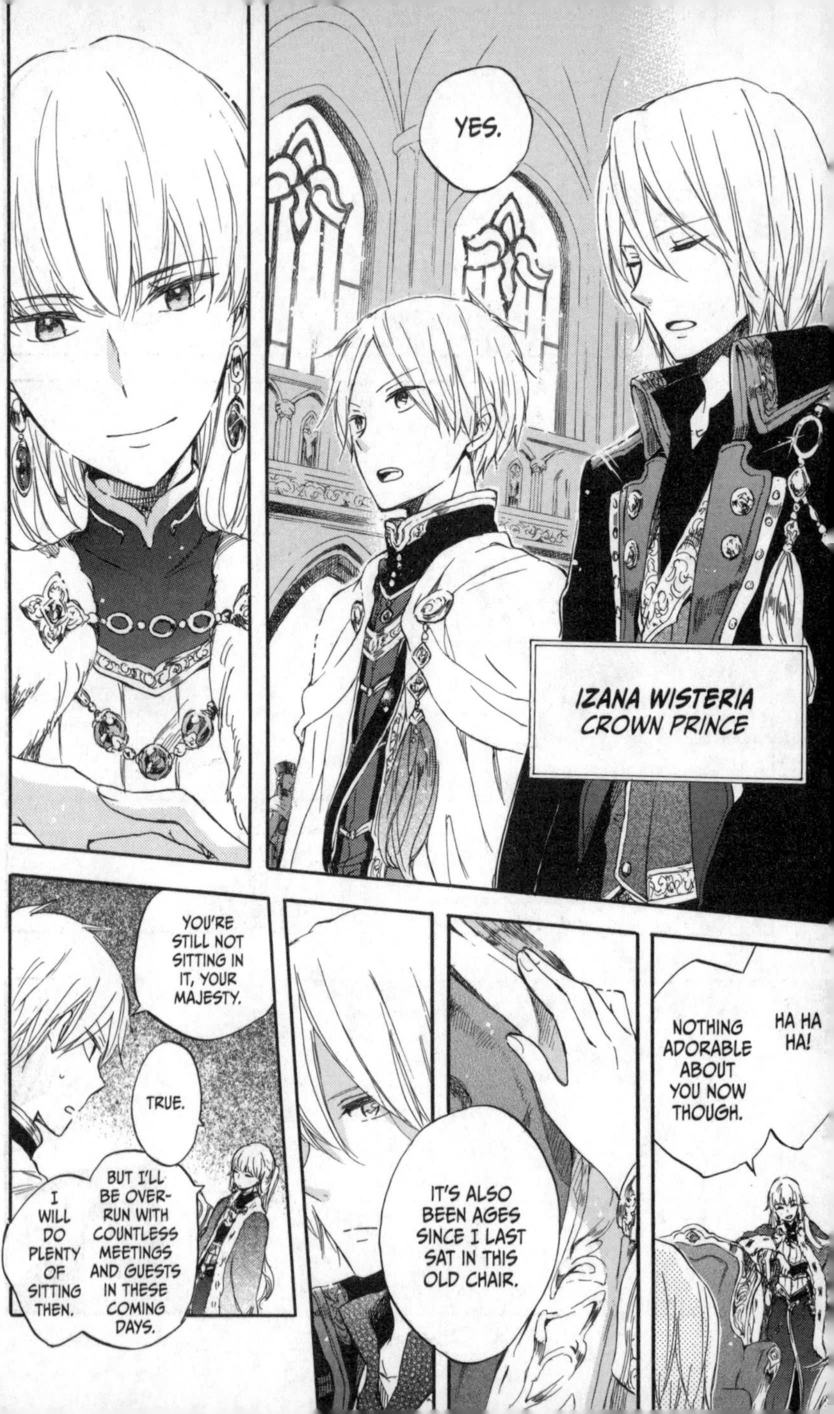
YES.
IZANA WISTERIA
CROWN PRINCE
HA HA HA!
NOTHING ADORABLE ABOUT YOU NOW THOUGH.
IT'S ALSO BEEN AGES SINCE I LAST SAT IN THIS OLD CHAIR.
YOU'RE STILL NOT SITTING IN IT, YOUR MAJESTY.
TRUE.
BUT I'LL BE OVER-RUN WITH COUNTLESS MEETINGS AND GUESTS IN THESE COMING DAYS.
I WILL DO PLENTY OF SITTING THEN.

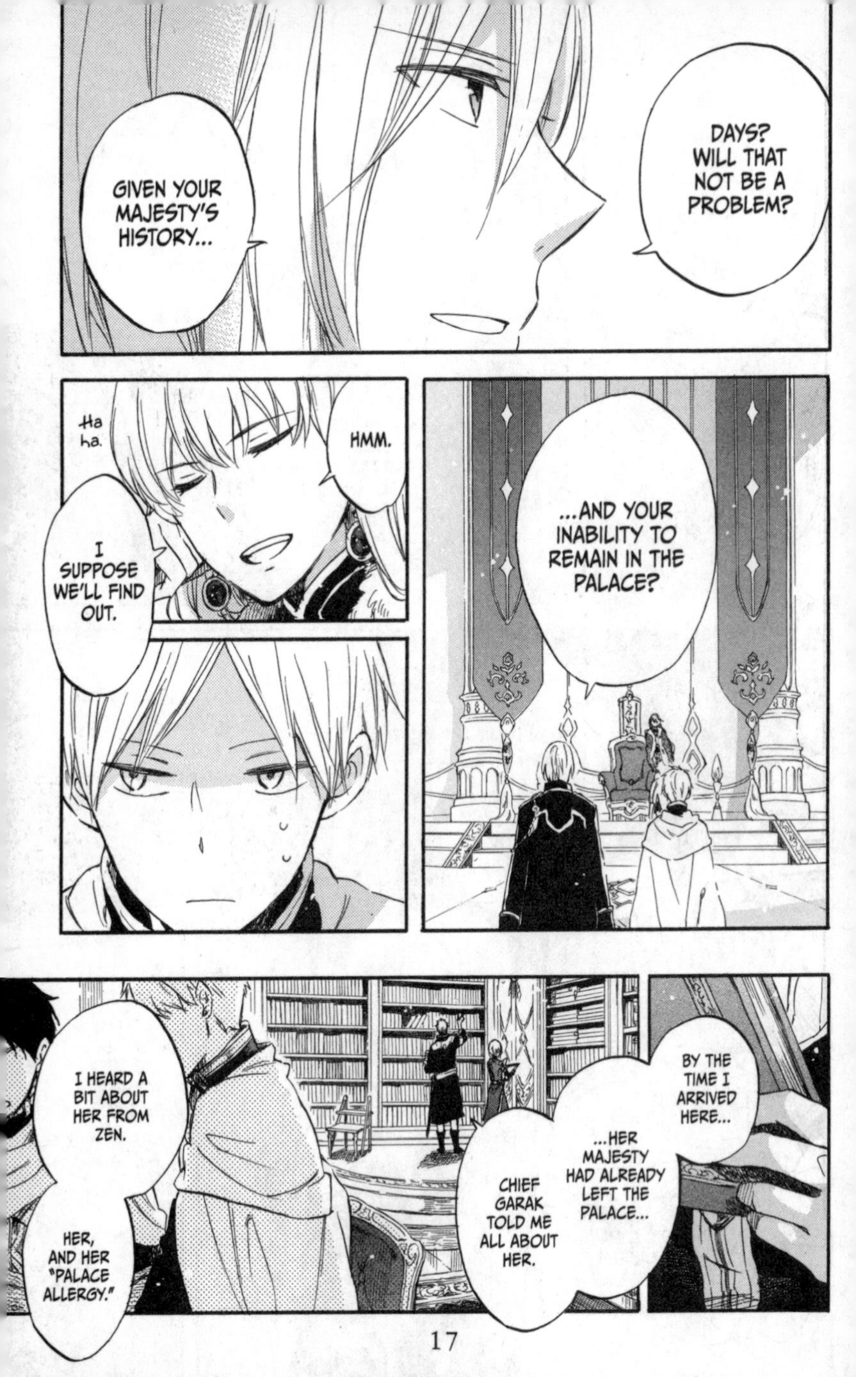
DAYS? WILL THAT NOT BE A PROBLEM?
GIVEN YOUR MAJESTY'S HISTORY...
...AND YOUR INABILITY TO REMAIN IN THE PALACE?
HMM.
Ha ha.
I SUPPOSE WE'LL FIND OUT.
BY THE TIME I ARRIVED HERE...
...HER MAJESTY HAD ALREADY LEFT THE PALACE...
CHIEF GARAK TOLD ME ALL ABOUT HER.
I HEARD A BIT ABOUT HER FROM ZEN.
HER, AND HER "PALACE ALLERGY."

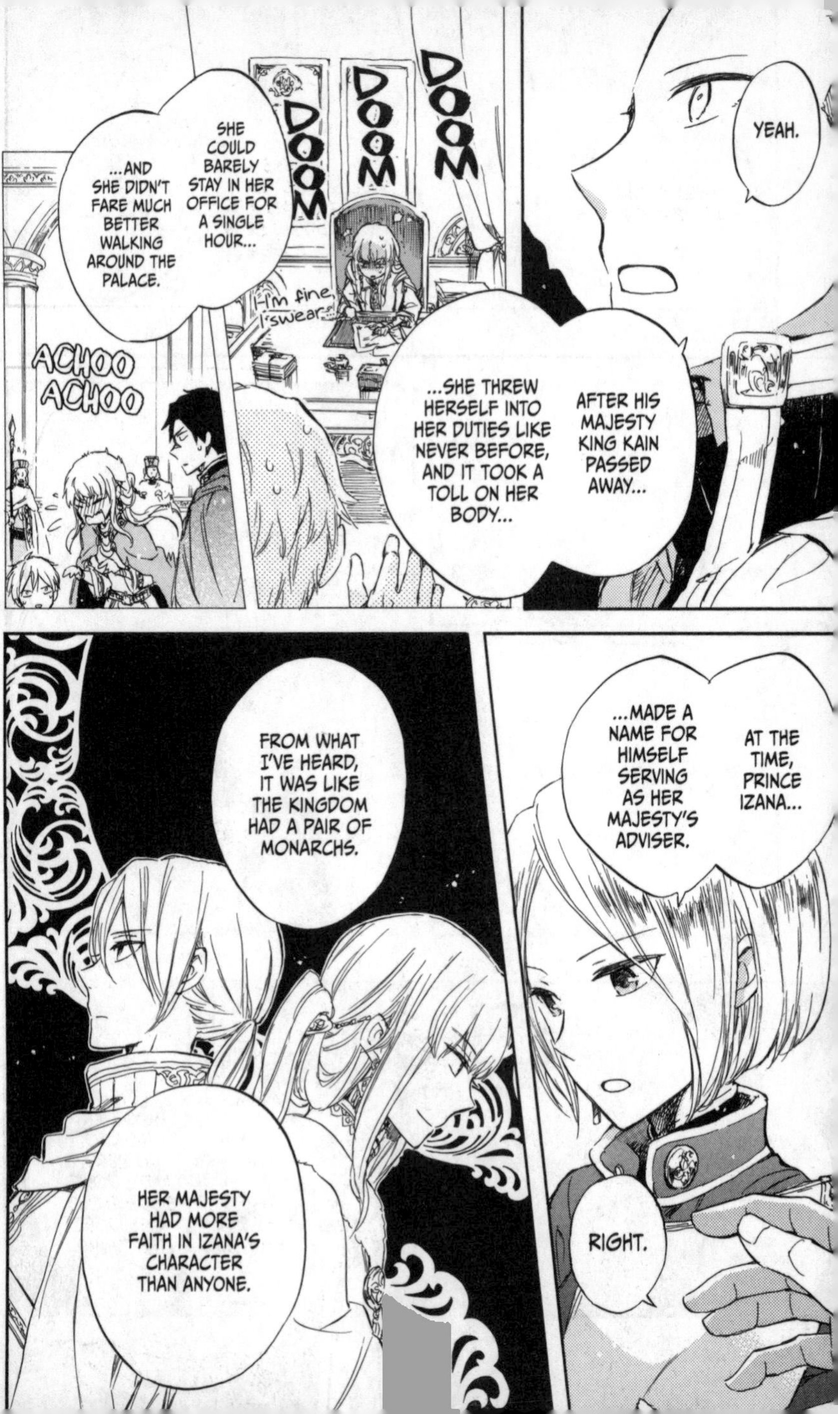
YEAH.
AFTER HIS MAJESTY KING KAIN PASSED AWAY...
...SHE THREW HERSELF INTO HER DUTIES LIKE NEVER BEFORE, AND IT TOOK A TOLL ON HER BODY...
DOOM
DOOM
DOOM
I'm fine, I swear...
SHE COULD BARELY STAY IN HER OFFICE FOR A SINGLE HOUR...
...AND SHE DIDN'T FARE MUCH BETTER WALKING AROUND THE PALACE.
ACHOO ACHOO
AT THE TIME, PRINCE IZANA...
...MADE A NAME FOR HIMSELF SERVING AS HER MAJESTY'S ADVISER.
RIGHT.
FROM WHAT I'VE HEARD, IT WAS LIKE THE KINGDOM HAD A PAIR OF MONARCHS.
HER MAJESTY HAD MORE FAITH IN IZANA'S CHARACTER THAN ANYONE.

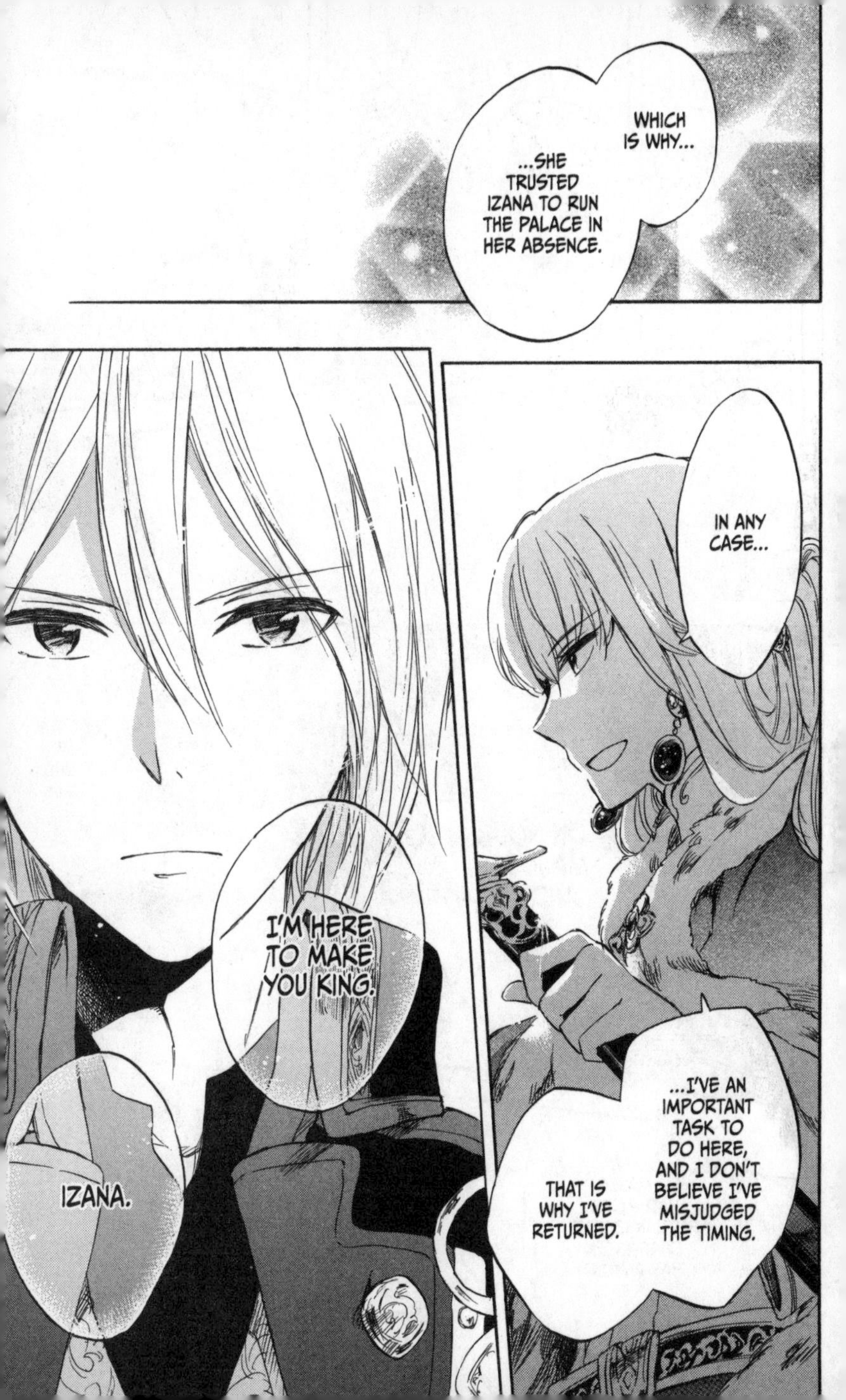
WHICH IS WHY...
...SHE TRUSTED IZANA TO RUN THE PALACE IN HER ABSENCE.
IN ANY CASE...
...I'VE AN IMPORTANT TASK TO DO HERE, AND I DON'T BELIEVE I'VE MISJUDGED THE TIMING.
THAT IS WHY I'VE RETURNED.
I'M HERE TO MAKE YOU KING.
IZANA.

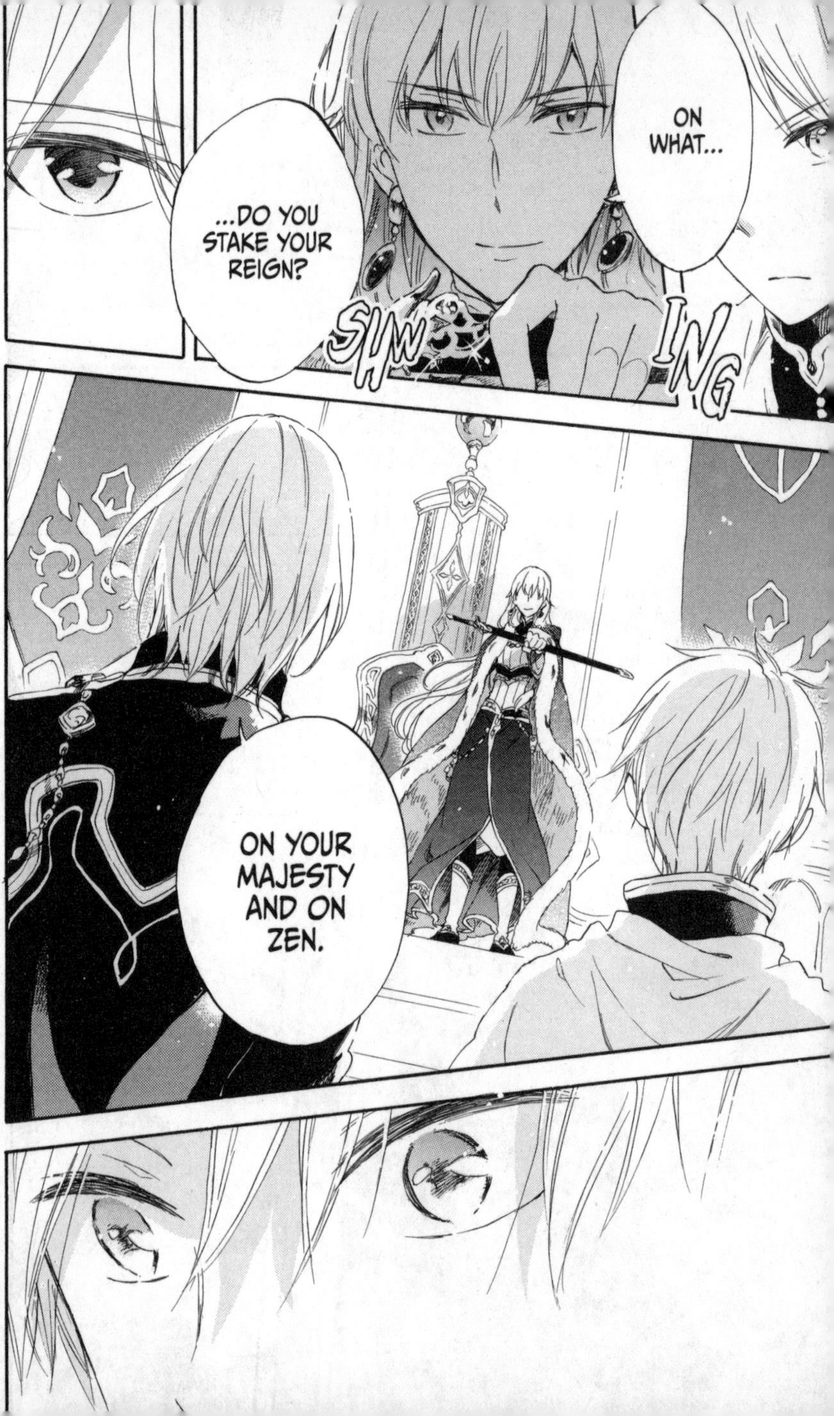
ON WHAT...
...DO YOU STAKE YOUR REIGN?
SHWING
ON YOUR MAJESTY AND ON ZEN.

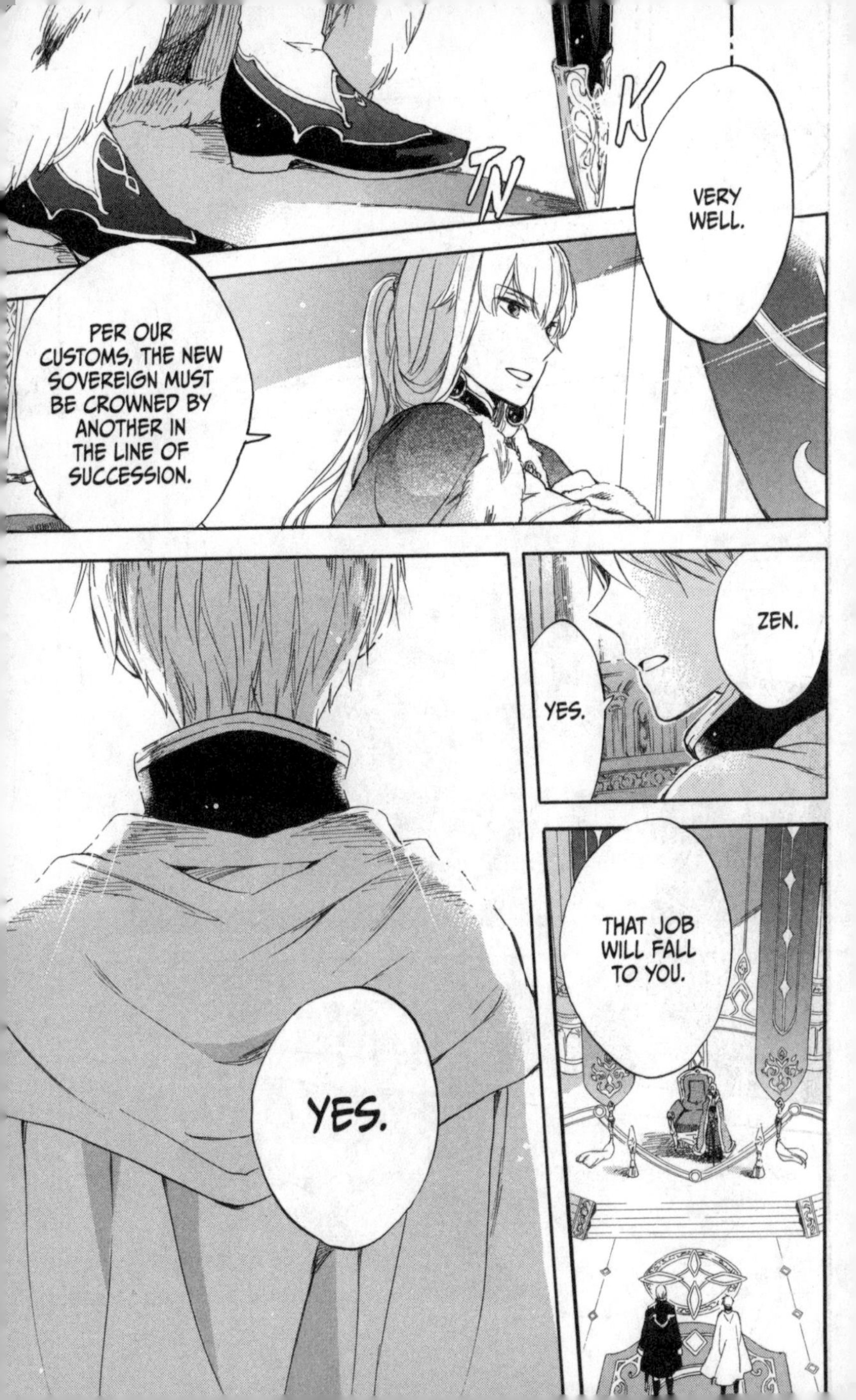
TNK
VERY WELL.
PER OUR CUSTOMS, THE NEW SOVEREIGN MUST BE CROWNED BY ANOTHER IN THE LINE OF SUCCESSION.
ZEN.
YES.
THAT JOB WILL FALL TO YOU.
YES.

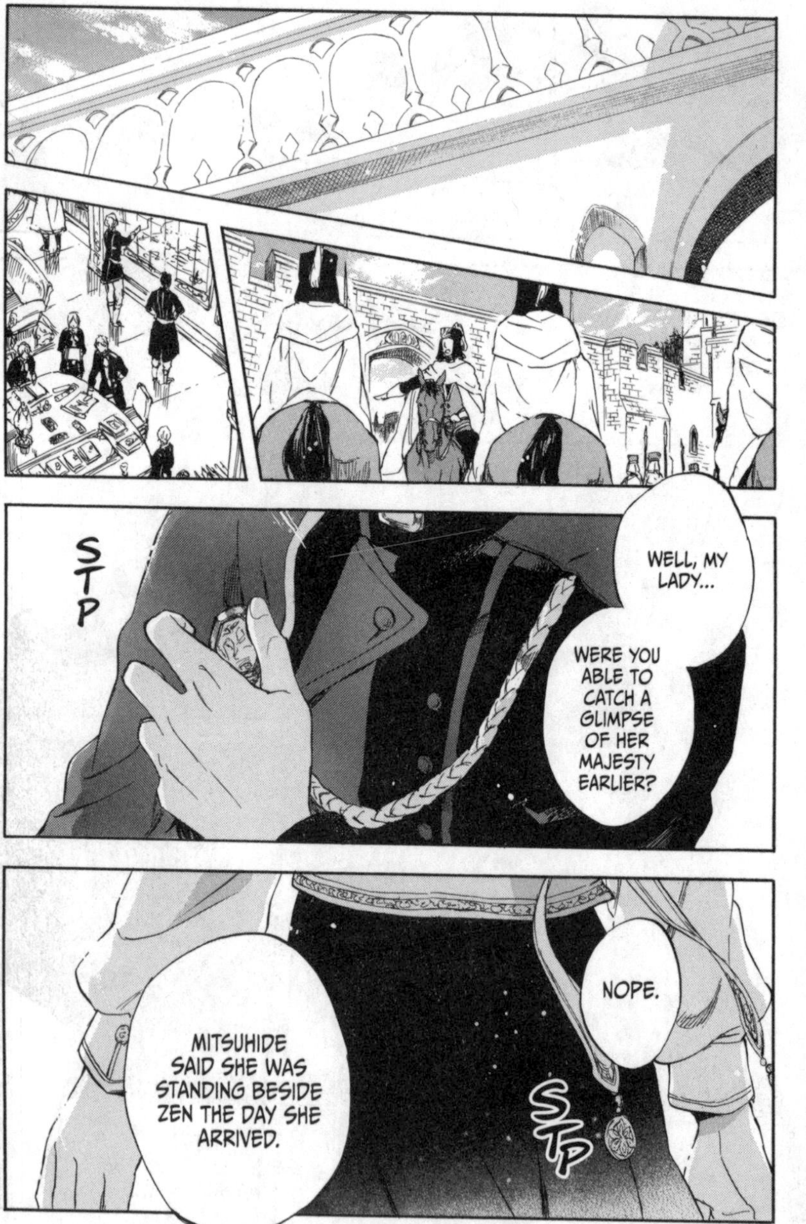
WELL, MY LADY...
WERE YOU ABLE TO CATCH A GLIMPSE OF HER MAJESTY EARLIER?
STP
NOPE.
MITSUHIDE SAID SHE WAS STANDING BESIDE ZEN THE DAY SHE ARRIVED.
STP

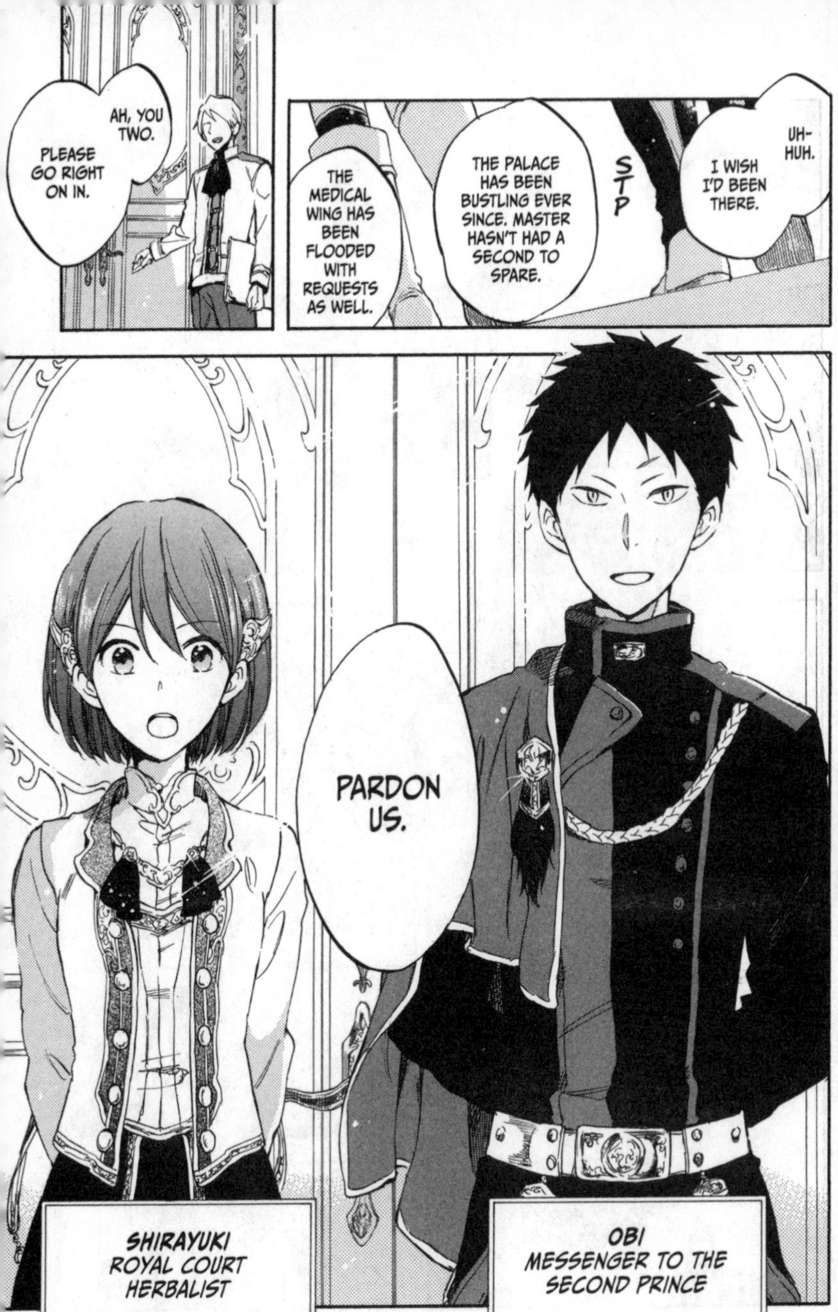
UH-HUH.
I WISH I'D BEEN THERE.
STP
THE PALACE HAS BEEN BUSTLING EVER SINCE. MASTER HASN'T HAD A SECOND TO SPARE.
THE MEDICAL WING HAS BEEN FLOODED WITH REQUESTS AS WELL.
AH, YOU TWO.
PLEASE GO RIGHT ON IN.
OBI MESSENGER TO THE SECOND PRINCE
PARDON US.
SHIRAYUKI ROYAL COURT HERBALIST

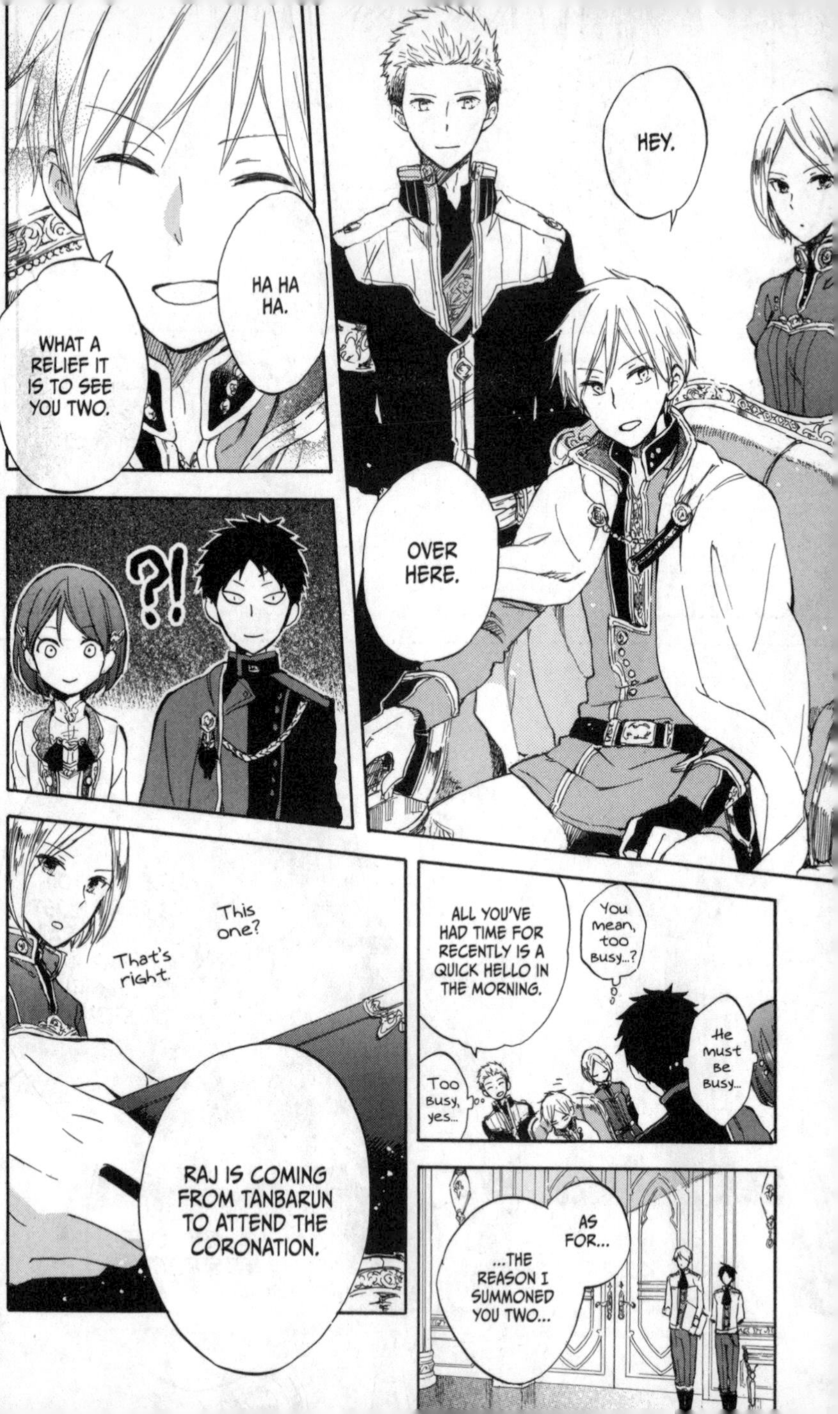
HEY.
OVER HERE.
HA HA HA.
WHAT A RELIEF IT IS TO SEE YOU TWO.
?!
ALL YOU'VE HAD TIME FOR RECENTLY IS A QUICK HELLO IN THE MORNING.
You mean, too busy...?
He must be busy...
Too busy, yes...
AS FOR...
...THE REASON I SUMMONED YOU TWO...
This one?
That's right.
RAJ IS COMING FROM TANBARUN TO ATTEND THE CORONATION.

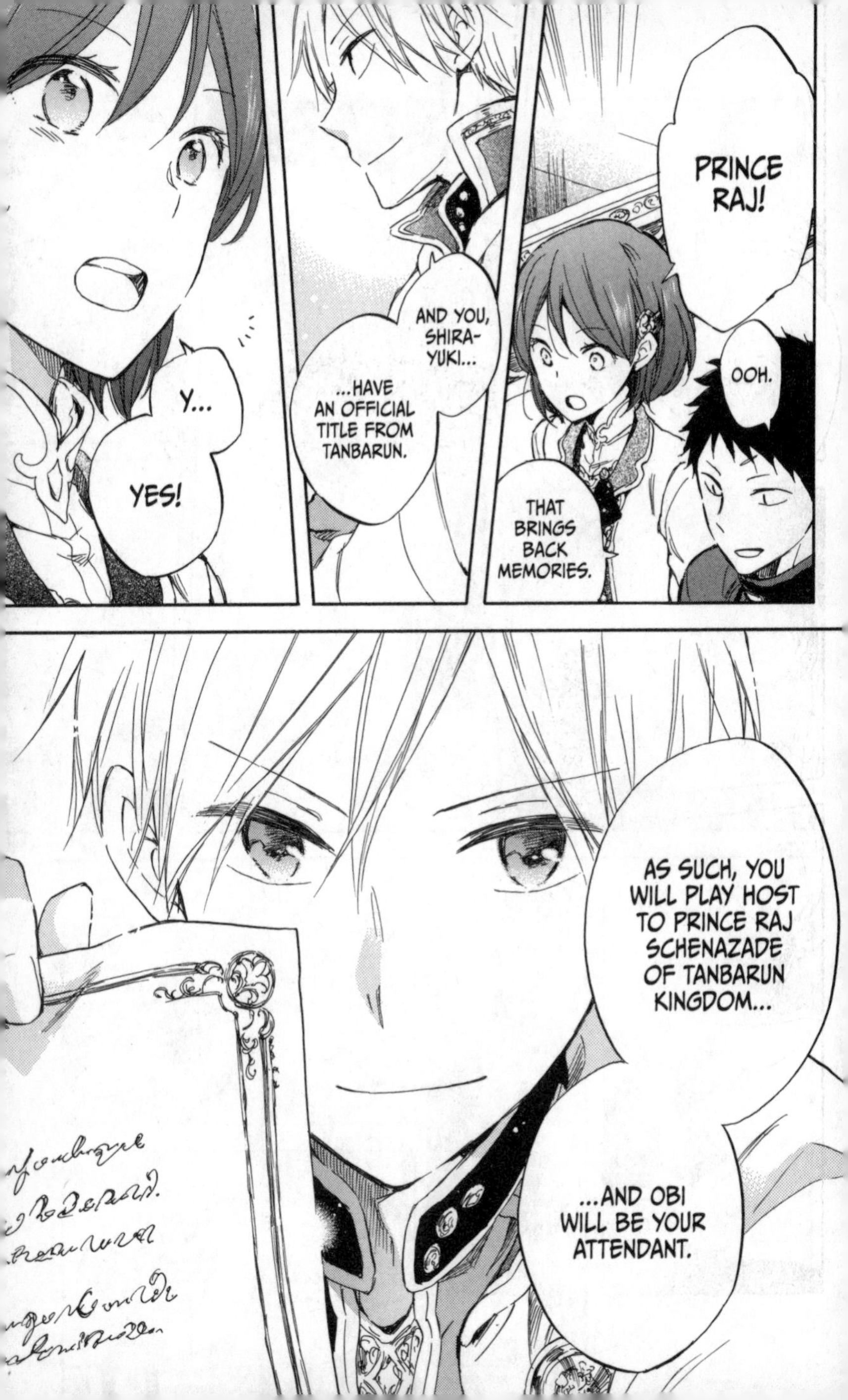
PRINCE RAJ!
OOH.
THAT BRINGS BACK MEMORIES.
AND YOU, SHIRA-YUKI...
...HAVE AN OFFICIAL TITLE FROM TANBARUN.
Y...
YES!
AS SUCH, YOU WILL PLAY HOST TO PRINCE RAJ SCHENAZADE OF TANBARUN KINGDOM...
...AND OBI WILL BE YOUR ATTENDANT.

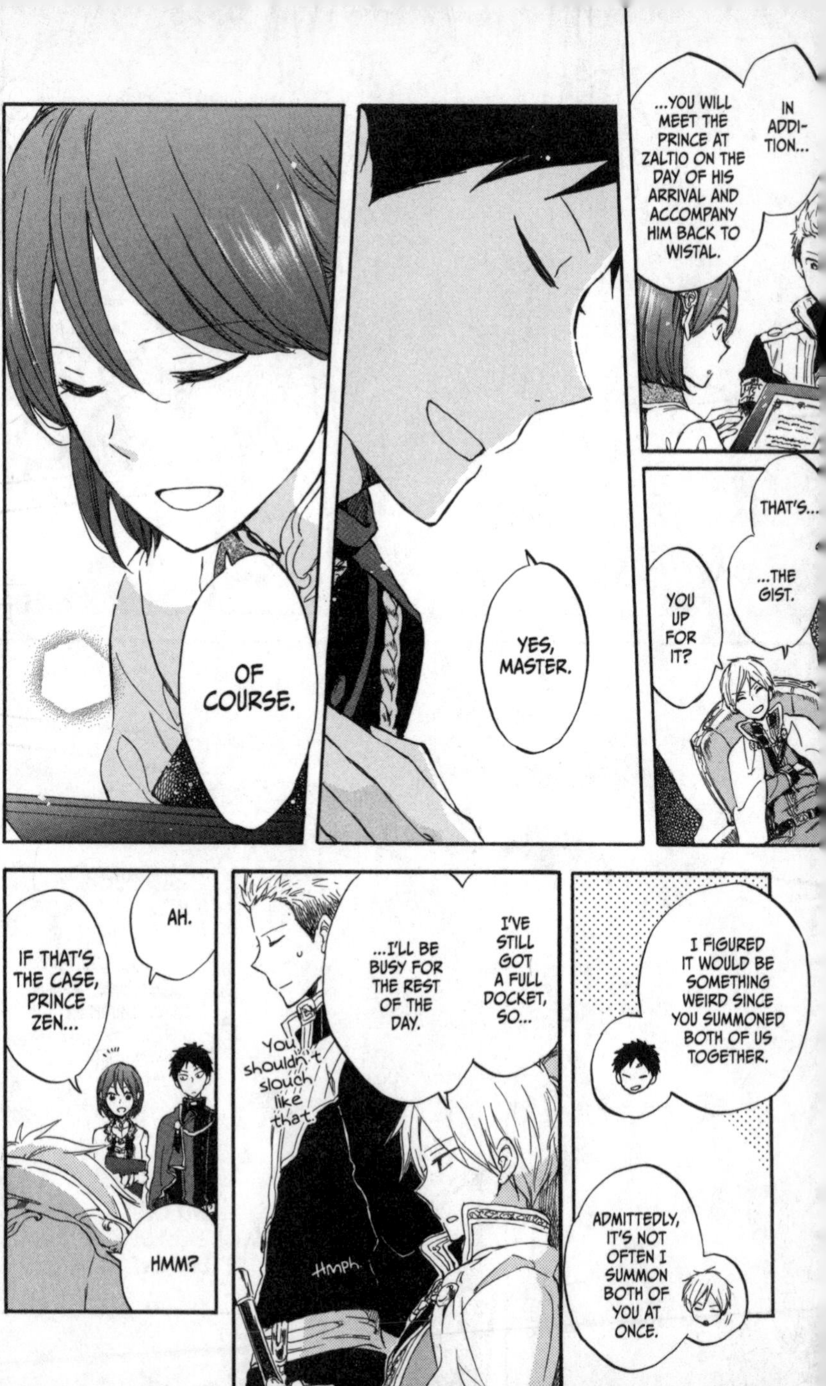
IN ADDITION...
...YOU WILL MEET THE PRINCE AT ZALTIO ON THE DAY OF HIS ARRIVAL AND ACCOMPANY HIM BACK TO WISTAL.
THAT'S...
...THE GIST.
YOU UP FOR IT?
YES, MASTER.
OF COURSE.
I FIGURED IT WOULD BE SOMETHING WEIRD SINCE YOU SUMMONED BOTH OF US TOGETHER.
ADMITTEDLY, IT'S NOT OFTEN I SUMMON BOTH OF YOU AT ONCE.
I'VE STILL GOT A FULL DOCKET, SO...
...I'LL BE BUSY FOR THE REST OF THE DAY.
You shouldn't slouch like that.
Hmph.
AH.
IF THAT'S THE CASE, PRINCE ZEN...
HMM?

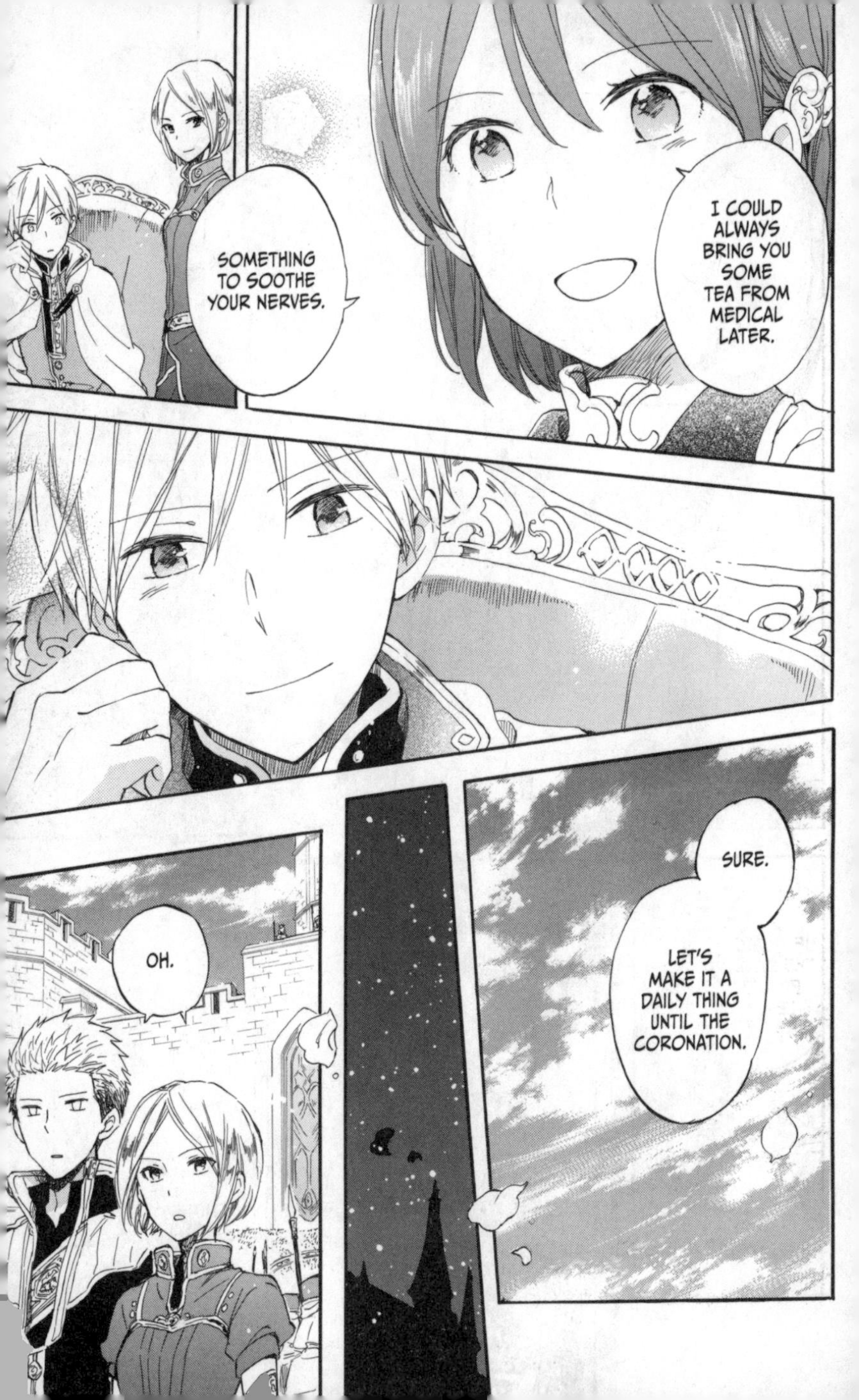
I COULD ALWAYS BRING YOU SOME TEA FROM MEDICAL LATER.
SOMETHING TO SOOTHE YOUR NERVES.
SURE.
LET'S MAKE IT A DAILY THING UNTIL THE CORONATION.
OH.

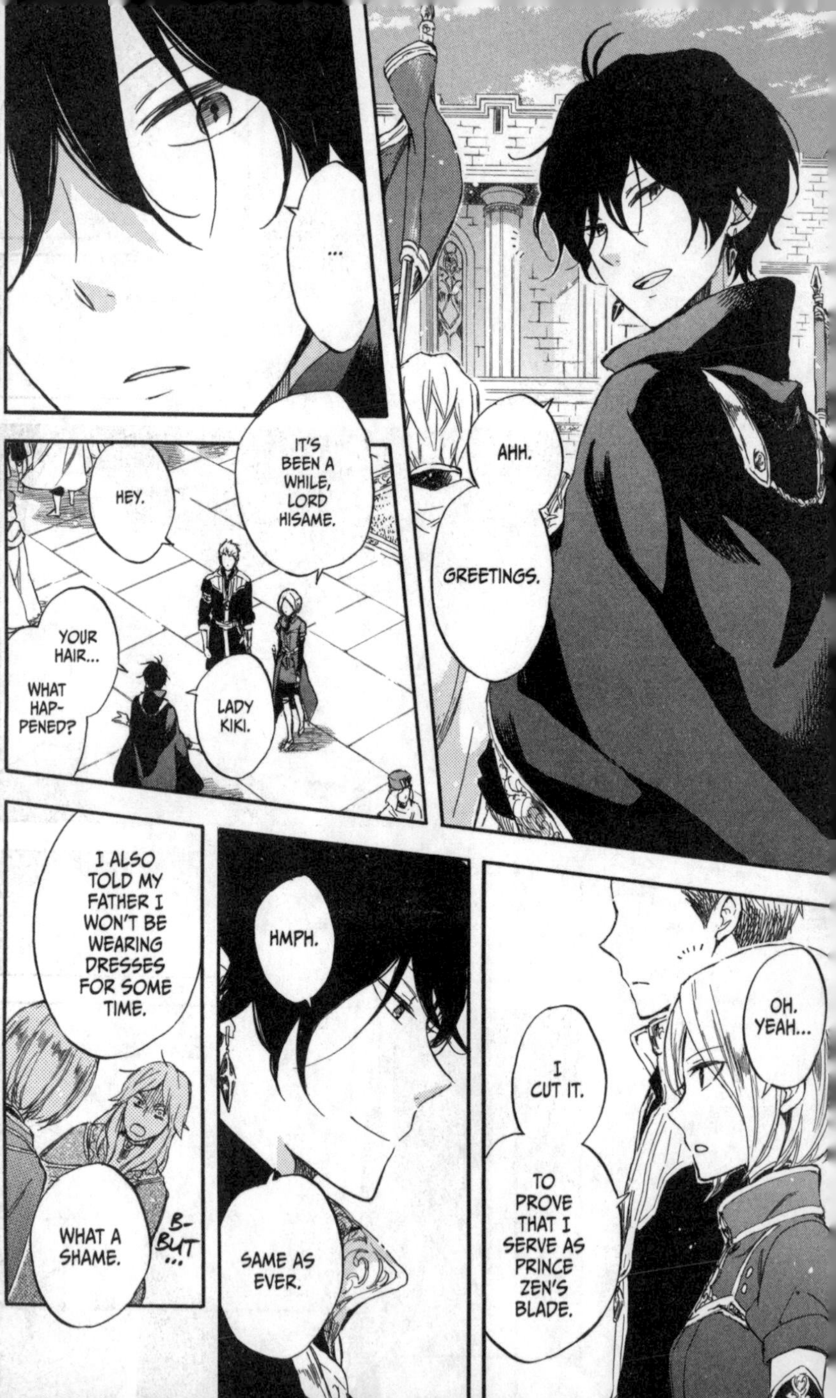

AHH.
GREETINGS.
...
IT'S BEEN A WHILE, LORD HISAME.
HEY.
LADY KIKI.
YOUR HAIR...
WHAT HAP-PENED?
OH. YEAH...
I CUT IT.
TO PROVE THAT I SERVE AS PRINCE ZEN'S BLADE.
HMPH.
SAME AS EVER.
I ALSO TOLD MY FATHER I WON'T BE WEARING DRESSES FOR SOME TIME.
B-BUT...
WHAT A SHAME.

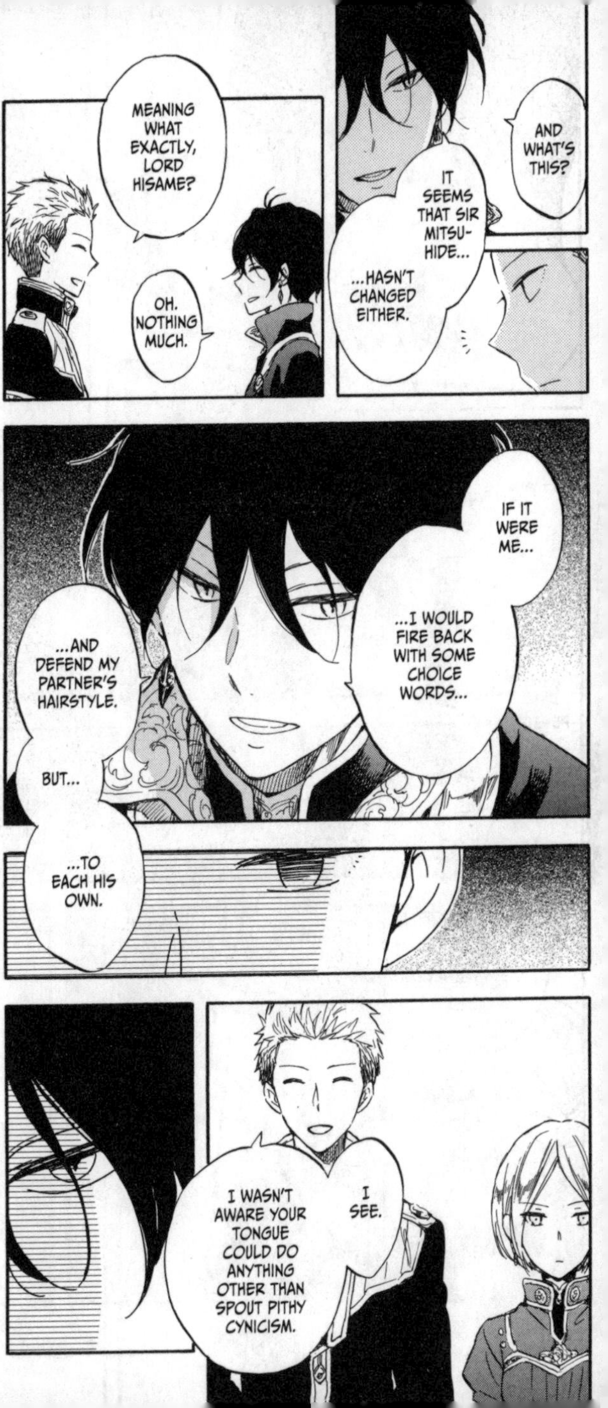
AND WHAT'S THIS?
IT SEEMS THAT SIR MITSU-HIDE...
...HASN'T CHANGED EITHER.
MEANING WHAT EXACTLY, LORD HISAME?
OH. NOTHING MUCH.
IF IT WERE ME...
...I WOULD FIRE BACK WITH SOME CHOICE WORDS...
...AND DEFEND MY PARTNER'S HAIRSTYLE.
BUT...
...TO EACH HIS OWN.
I SEE.
I WASN'T AWARE YOUR TONGUE COULD DO ANYTHING OTHER THAN SPOUT PITHY CYNICISM.

GREETINGS

Hello! Thank you for picking up volume 12 of Snow White with the Red Hair!

Finally, at long last, the day has come...

The person gracing the cover this time is...

That's right! It's Zen's big bro!

It took so long for him to appear on the cover—even though he's been around since volume 2 and played a bigger role in the Lilias arc than Zen did!

That's just how he is. He makes us wait.

But you can count on Zen to give it his all in volume 12, so let's dive in.

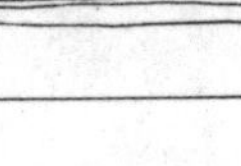
SHWNG

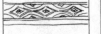

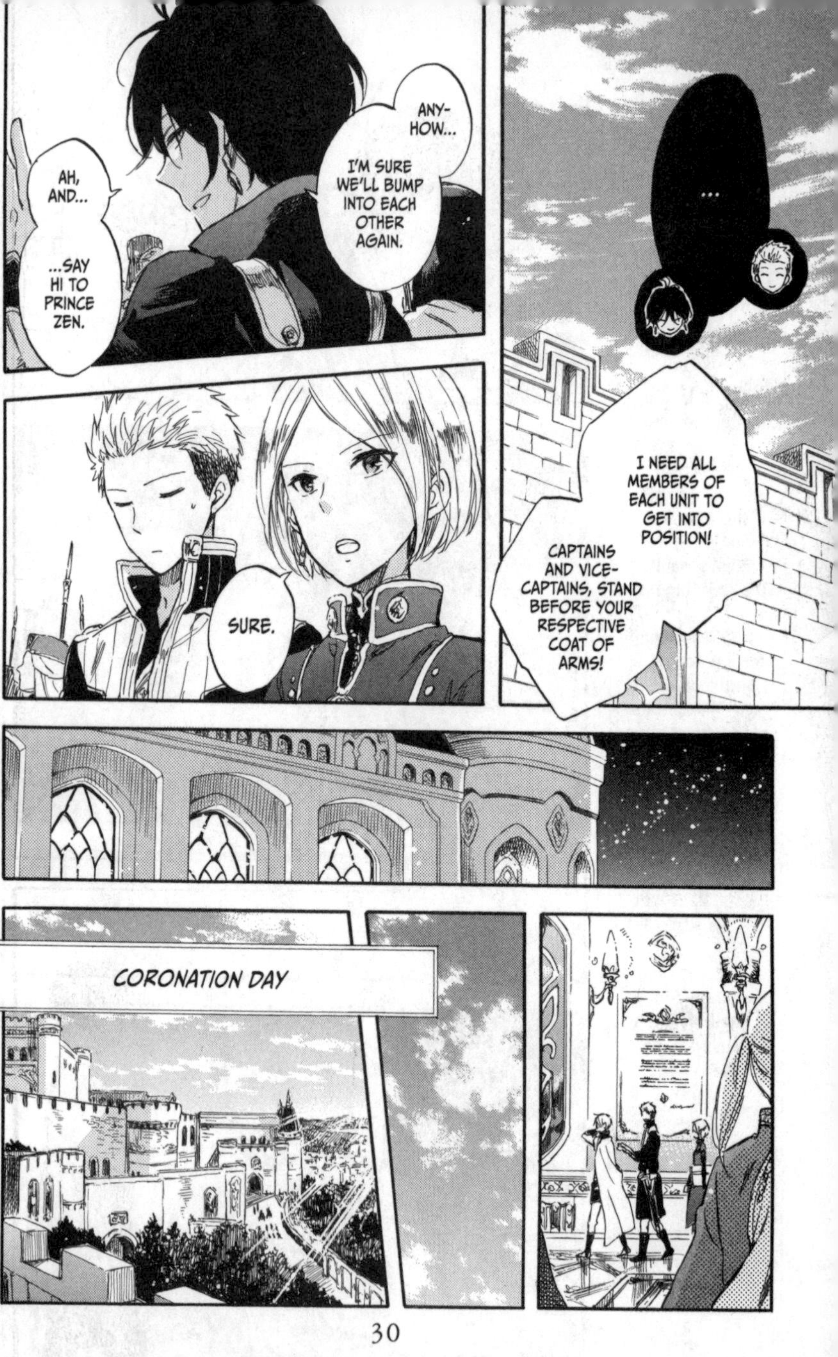
...
I NEED ALL MEMBERS OF EACH UNIT TO GET INTO POSITION!
CAPTAINS AND VICE-CAPTAINS, STAND BEFORE YOUR RESPECTIVE COAT OF ARMS!
ANY-HOW...
I'M SURE WE'LL BUMP INTO EACH OTHER AGAIN.
AH, AND...
...SAY HI TO PRINCE ZEN.
SURE.
CORONATION DAY

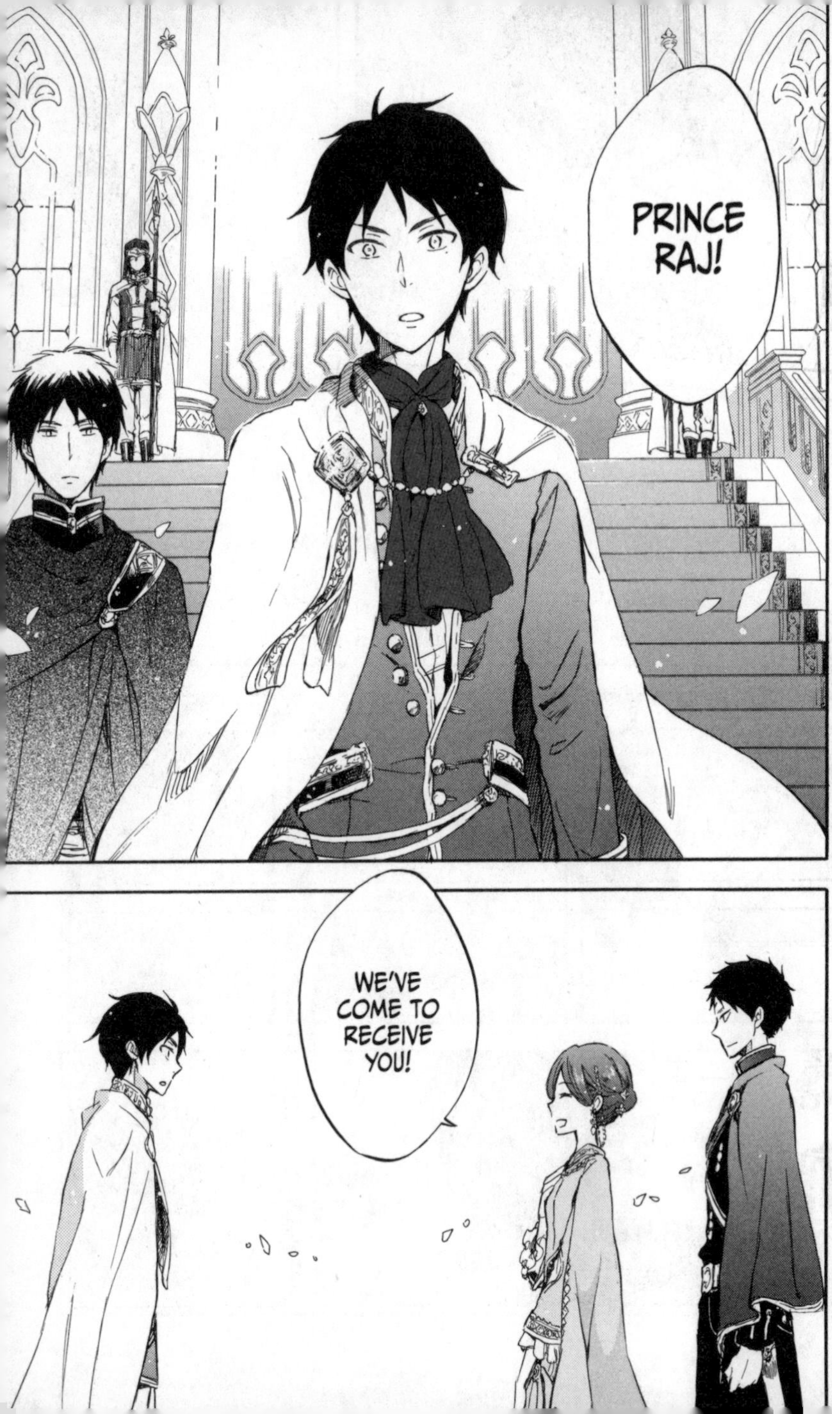
PRINCE RAJ!
WE'VE COME TO RECEIVE YOU!

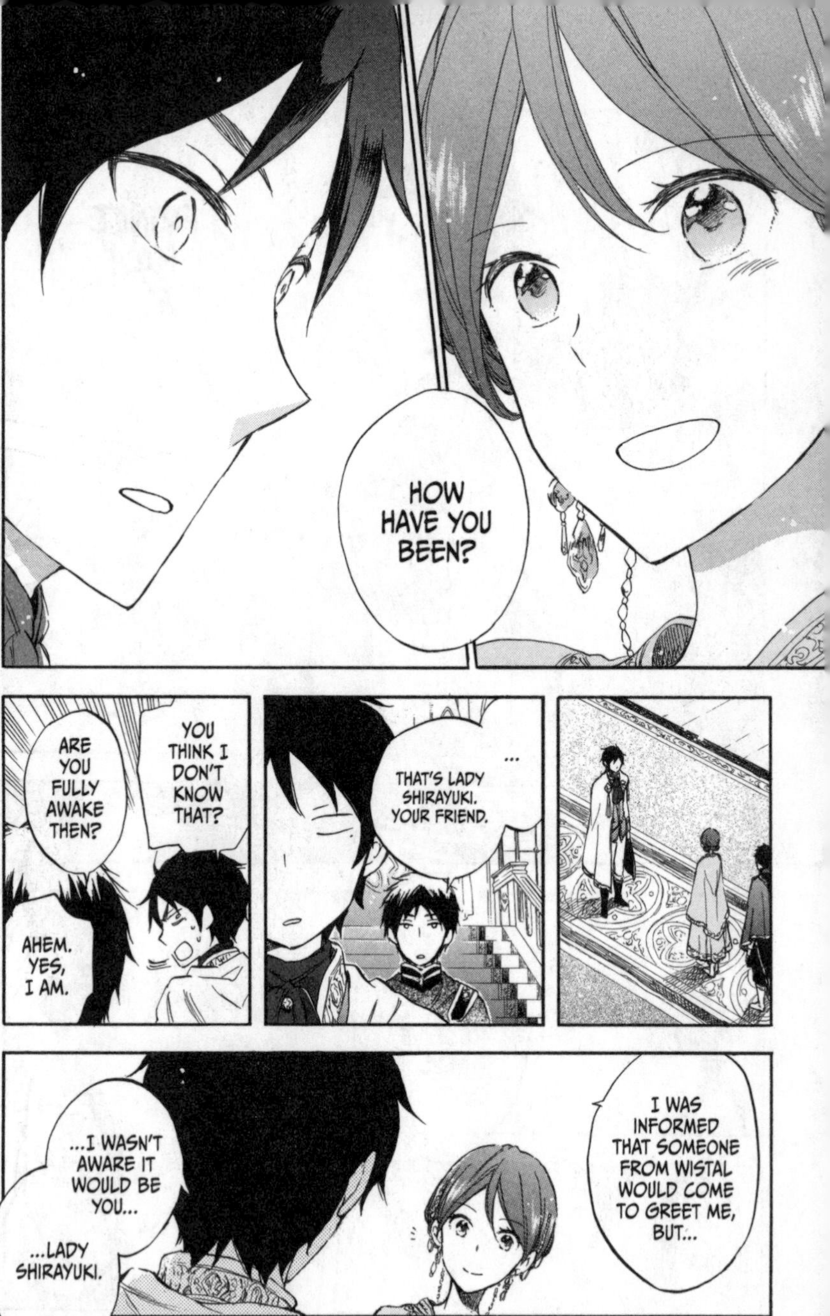
HOW HAVE YOU BEEN?
...
THAT'S LADY SHIRAYUKI. YOUR FRIEND.
YOU THINK I DON'T KNOW THAT?
ARE YOU FULLY AWAKE THEN?
AHEM. YES, I AM.
I WAS INFORMED THAT SOMEONE FROM WISTAL WOULD COME TO GREET ME, BUT...
...I WASN'T AWARE IT WOULD BE YOU...
...LADY SHIRAYUKI.

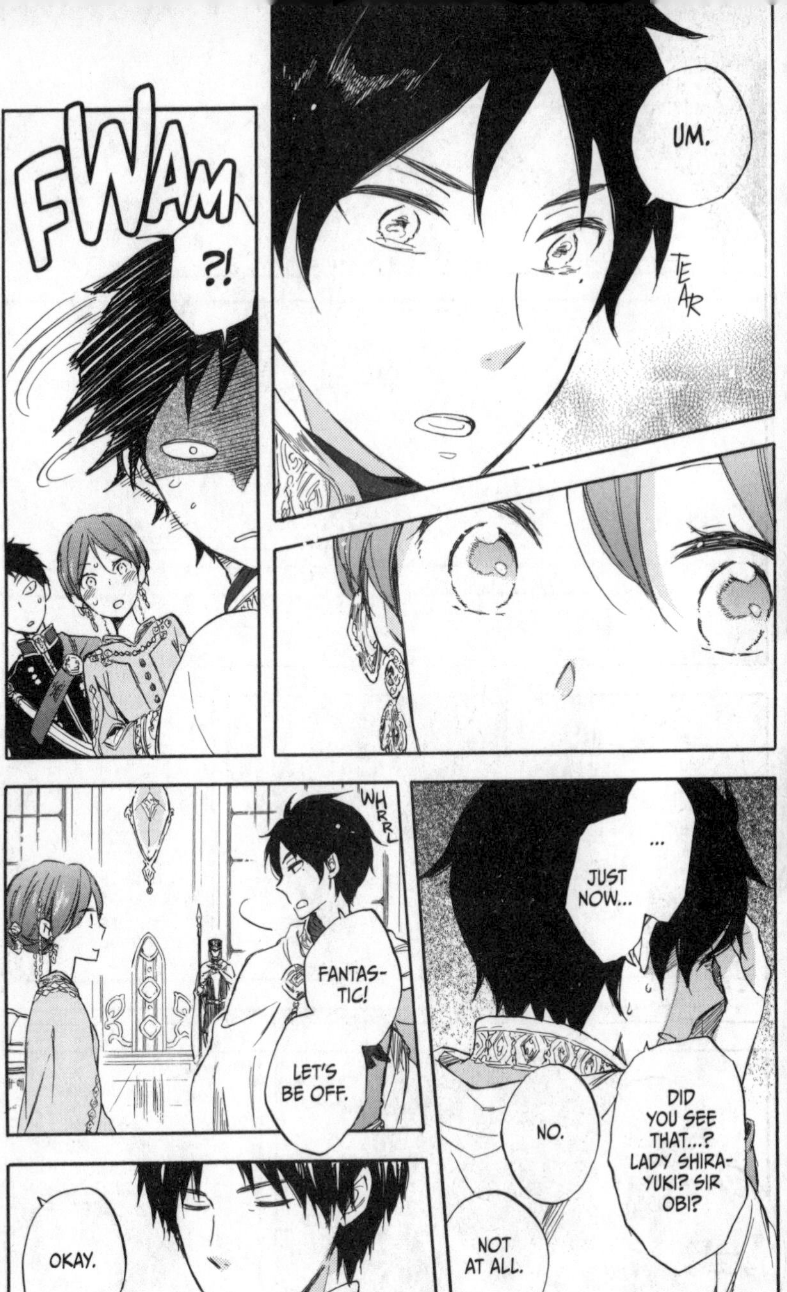
UM.
TEAR
FWAM
?!
... JUST NOW...
DID YOU SEE THAT...? LADY SHIRA-YUKI? SIR OBI?
NO.
NOT AT ALL.
WHRRL
FANTAS-TIC!
LET'S BE OFF.
OKAY.

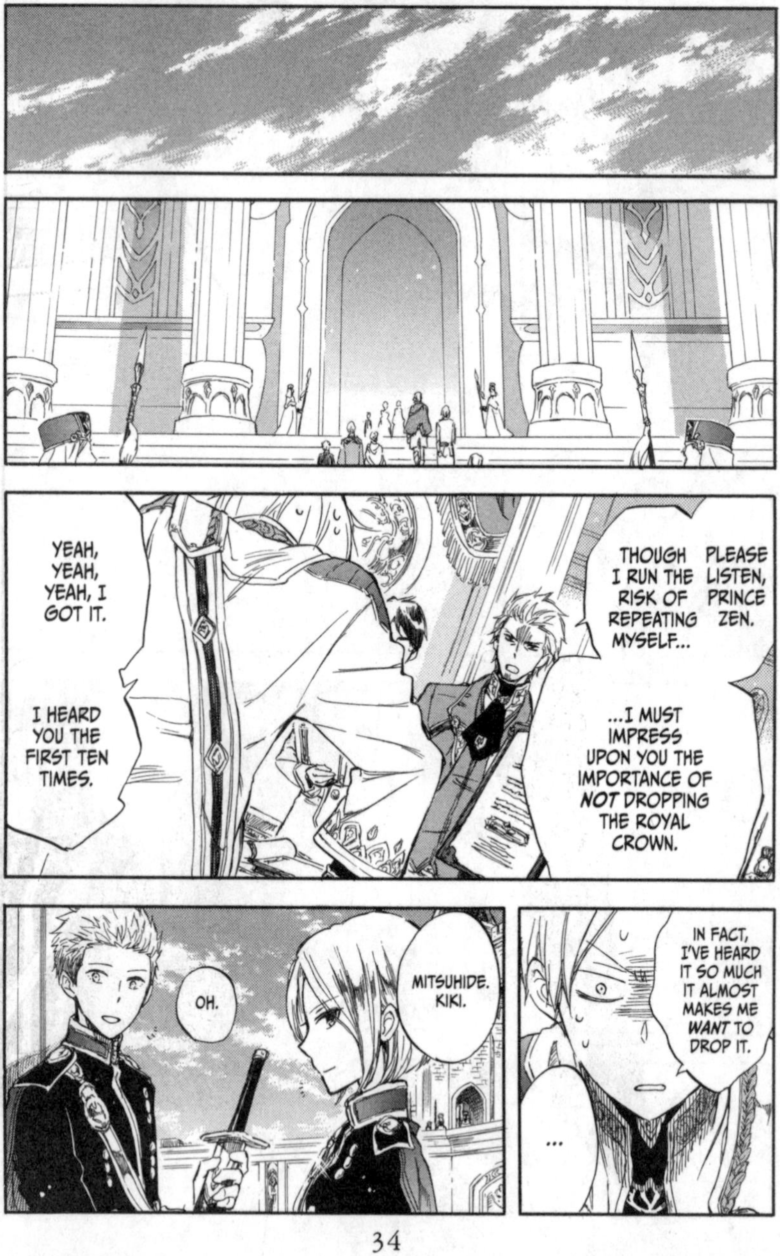
PLEASE LISTEN, PRINCE ZEN.
THOUGH I RUN THE RISK OF REPEATING MYSELF...
...I MUST IMPRESS UPON YOU THE IMPORTANCE OF *NOT* DROPPING THE ROYAL CROWN.
YEAH, YEAH, YEAH, I GOT IT.
I HEARD YOU THE FIRST TEN TIMES.
IN FACT, I'VE HEARD IT SO MUCH IT ALMOST MAKES ME *WANT* TO DROP IT.
...
MITSUHIDE. KIKI.
OH.

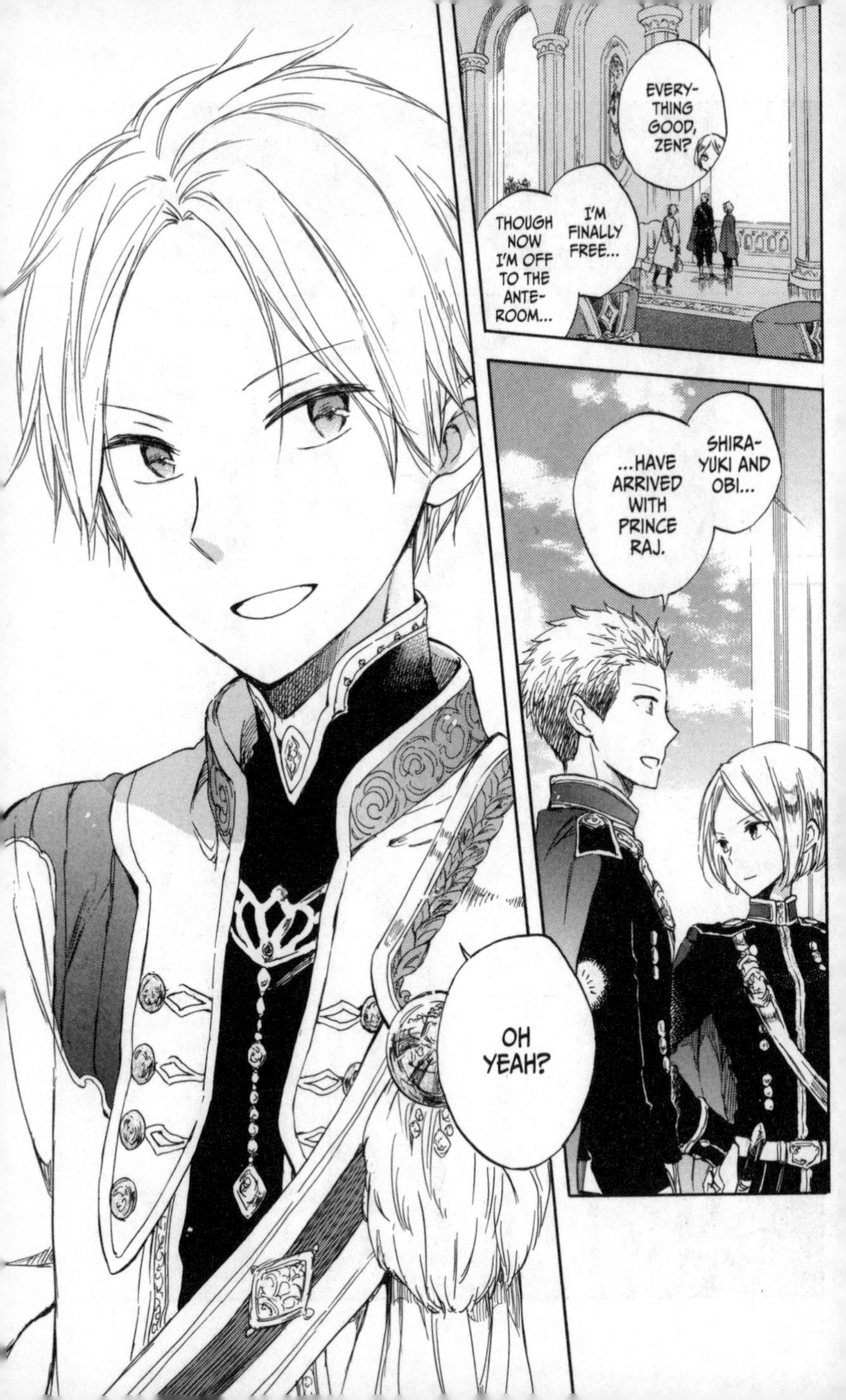
EVERYTHING GOOD, ZEN?
I'M FINALLY FREE...
THOUGH NOW I'M OFF TO THE ANTEROOM...
SHIRAYUKI AND OBI...
...HAVE ARRIVED WITH PRINCE RAJ.
OH YEAH?

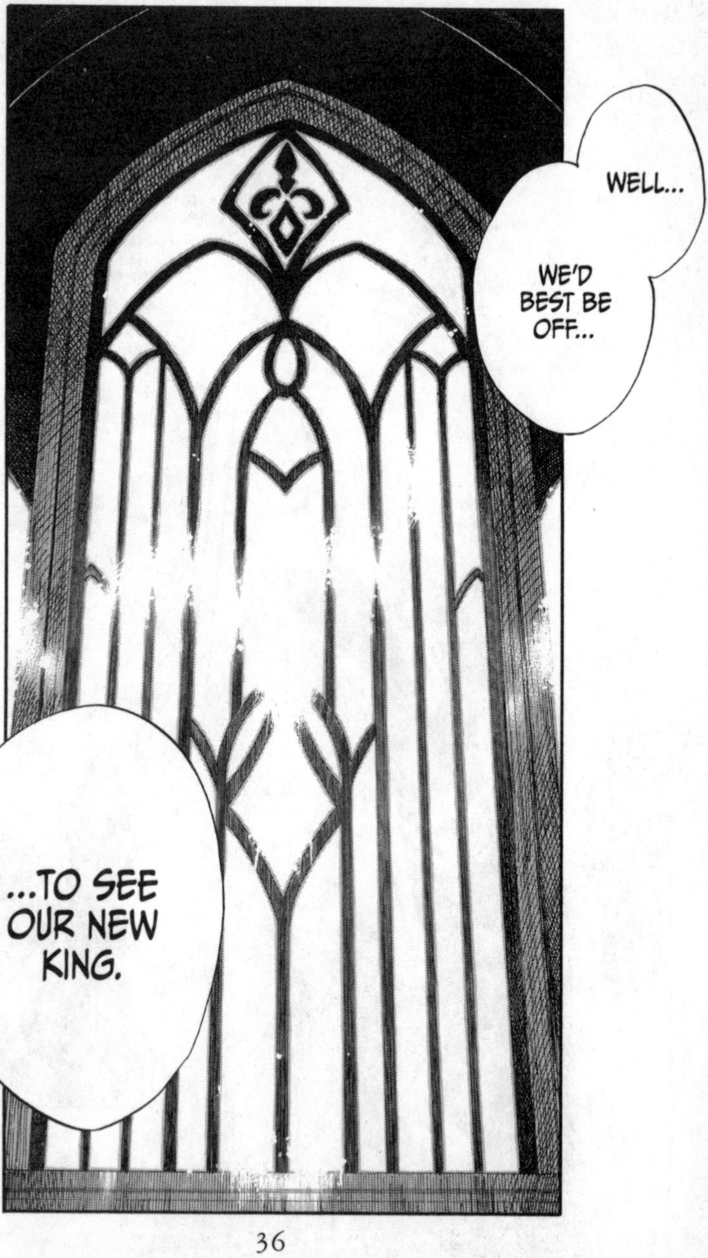
WELL...
WE'D BEST BE OFF...
...TO SEE OUR NEW KING.

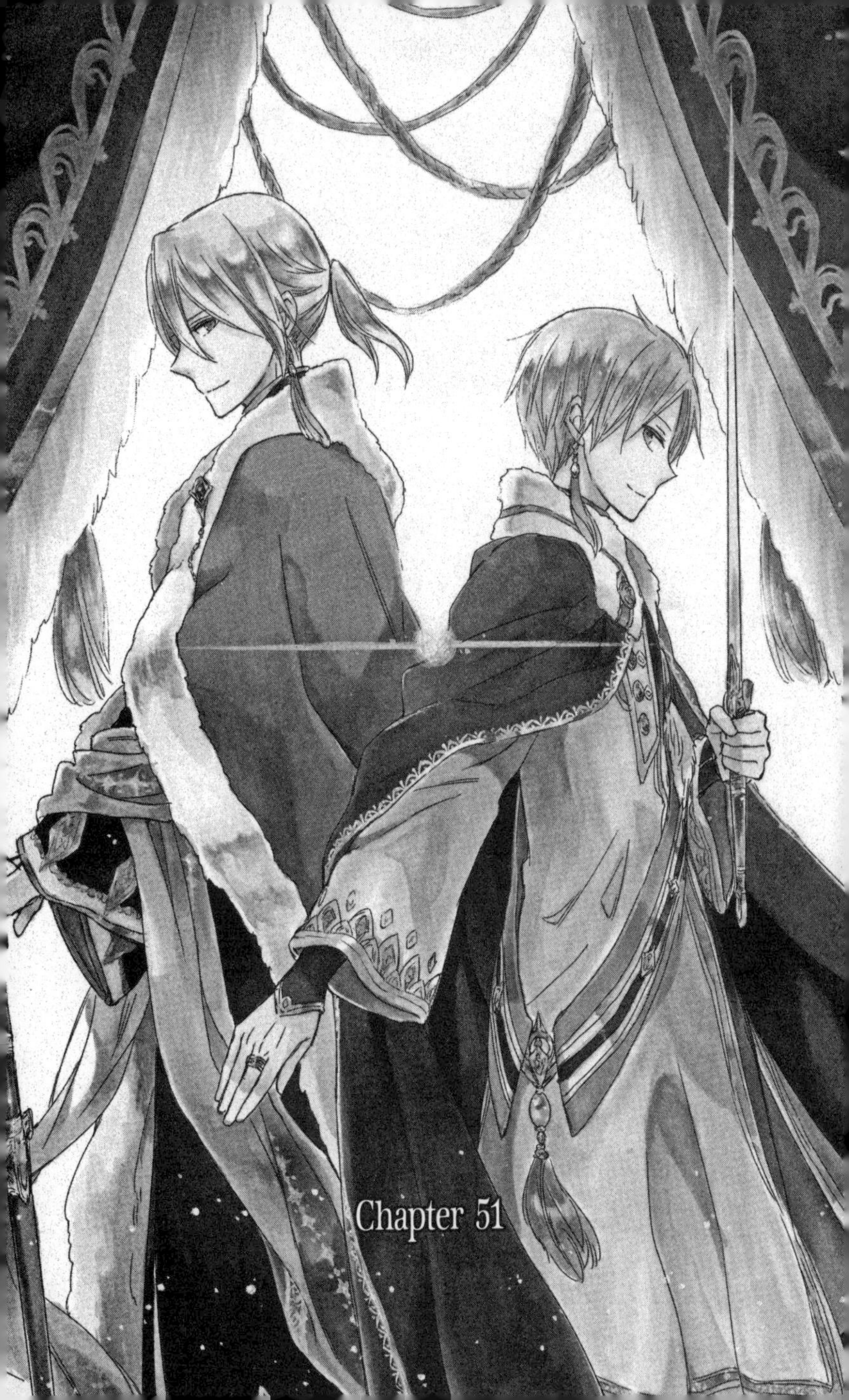
Chapter 51

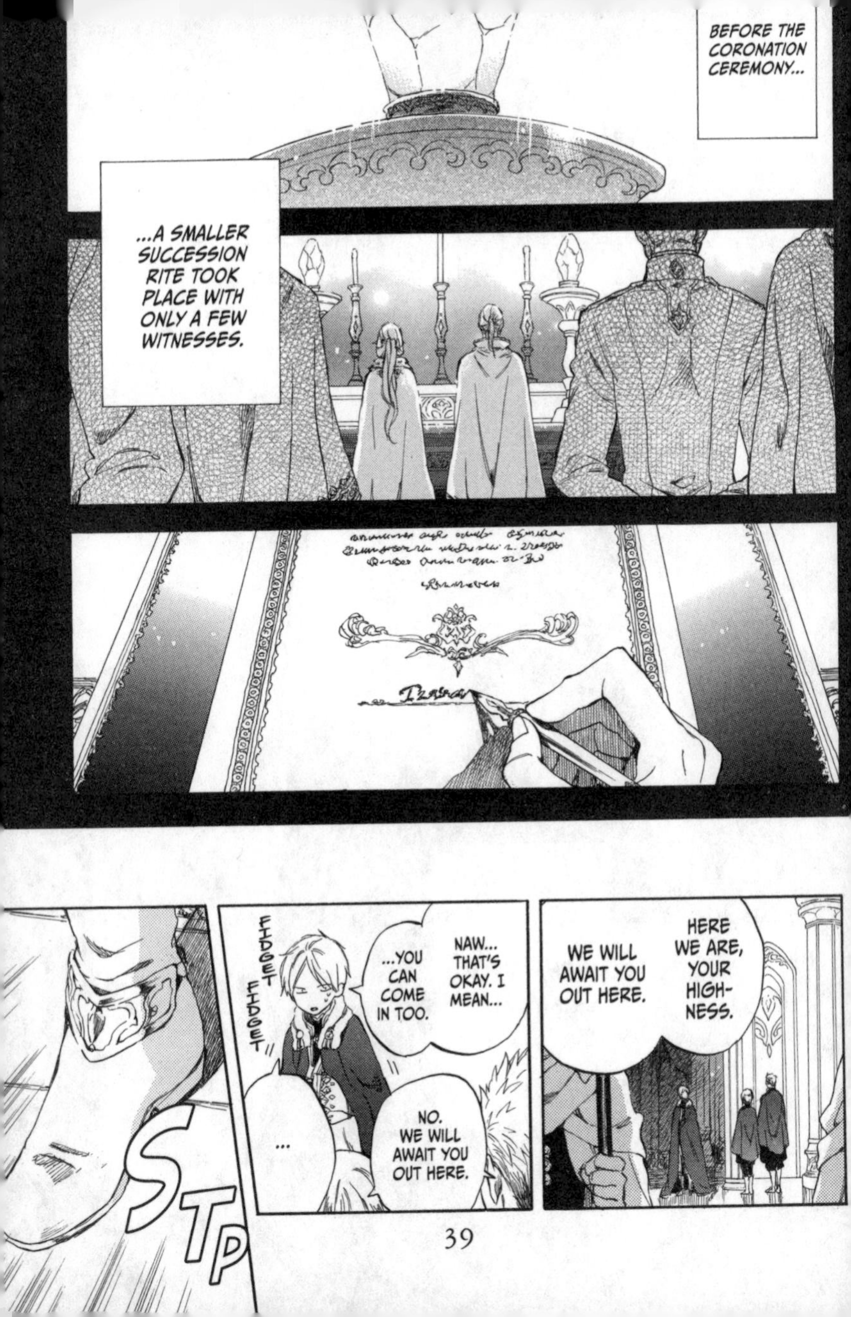
BEFORE THE CORONATION CEREMONY...
...A SMALLER SUCCESSION RITE TOOK PLACE WITH ONLY A FEW WITNESSES.
HERE WE ARE, YOUR HIGH-NESS.
WE WILL AWAIT YOU OUT HERE.
NAW... THAT'S OKAY. I MEAN...
...YOU CAN COME IN TOO.
FIDGET FIDGET
NO. WE WILL AWAIT YOU OUT HERE.
...
STP

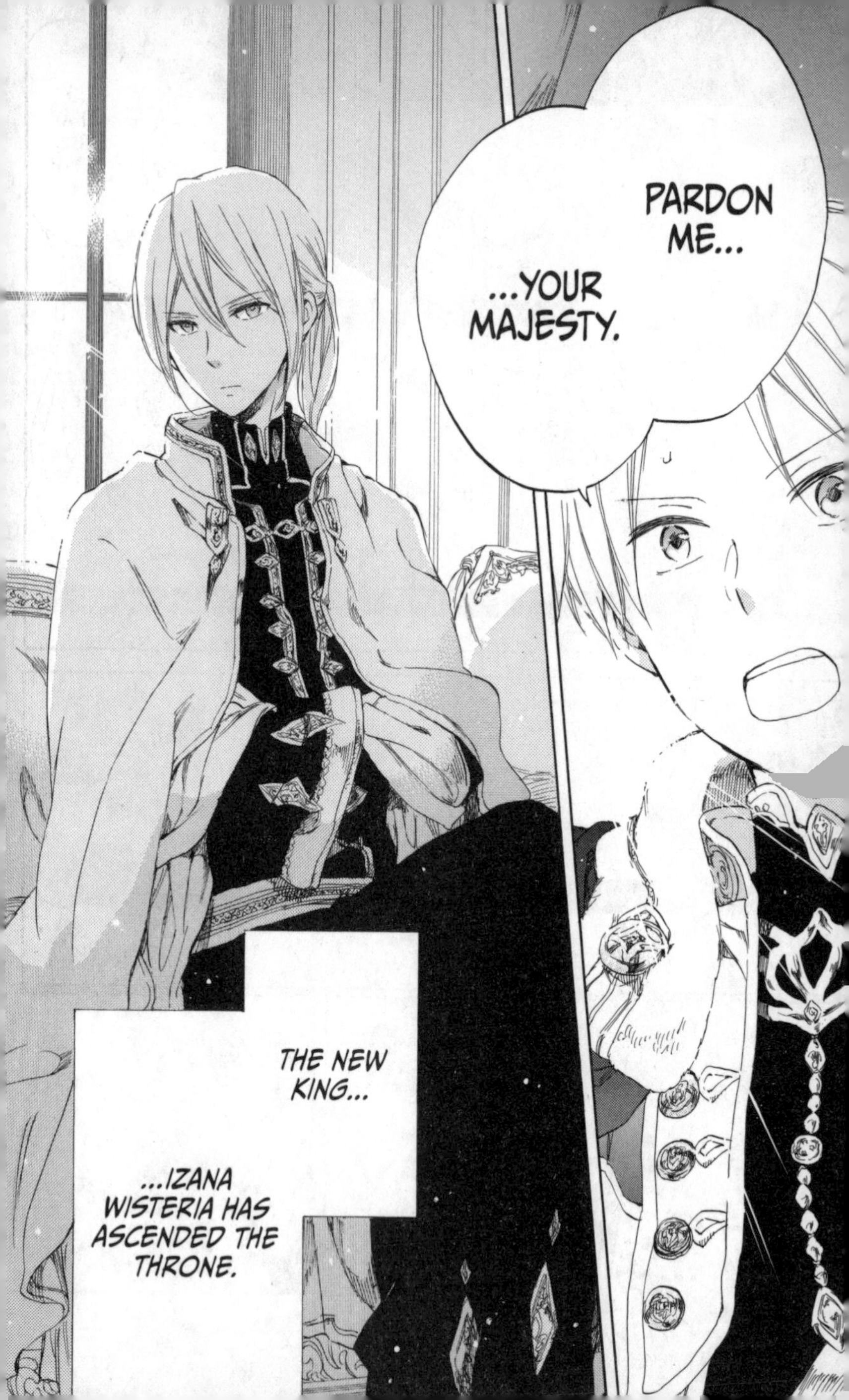
PARDON ME...
...YOUR MAJESTY.
THE NEW KING...
...IZANA WISTERIA HAS ASCENDED THE THRONE.

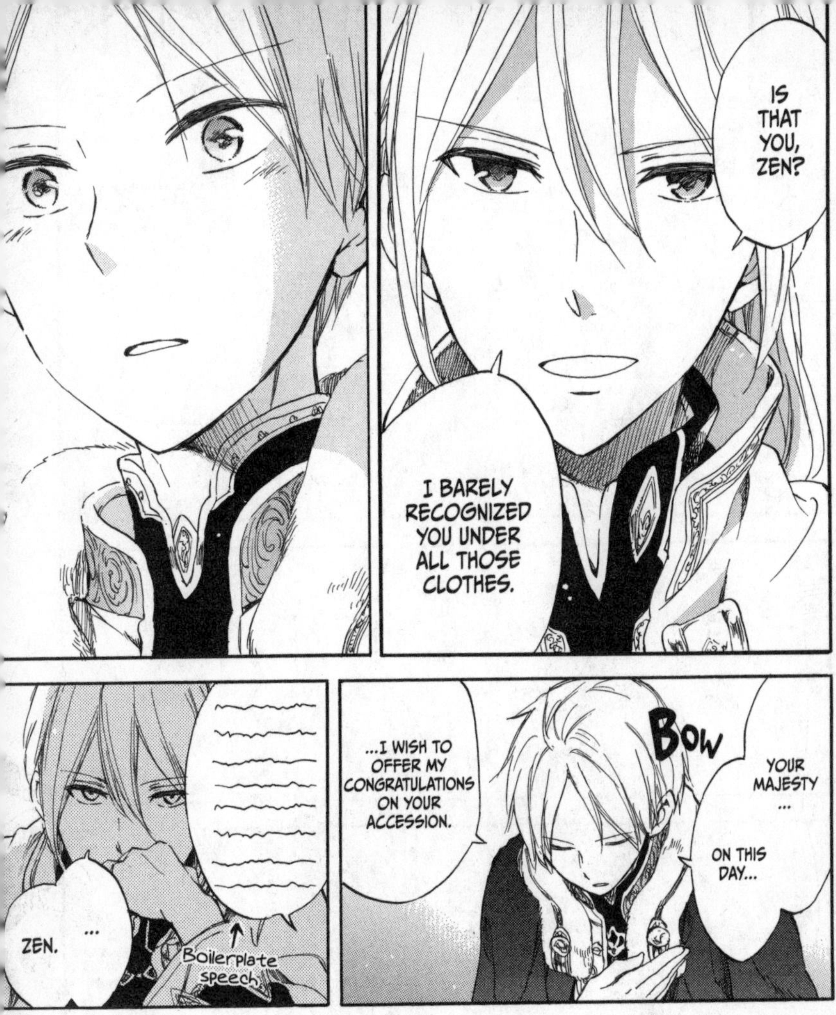
IS THAT YOU, ZEN?
I BARELY RECOGNIZED YOU UNDER ALL THOSE CLOTHES.
BOW
YOUR MAJESTY ...
ON THIS DAY...
...I WISH TO OFFER MY CONGRATULATIONS ON YOUR ACCESSION.
Boilerplate speech
...
ZEN.

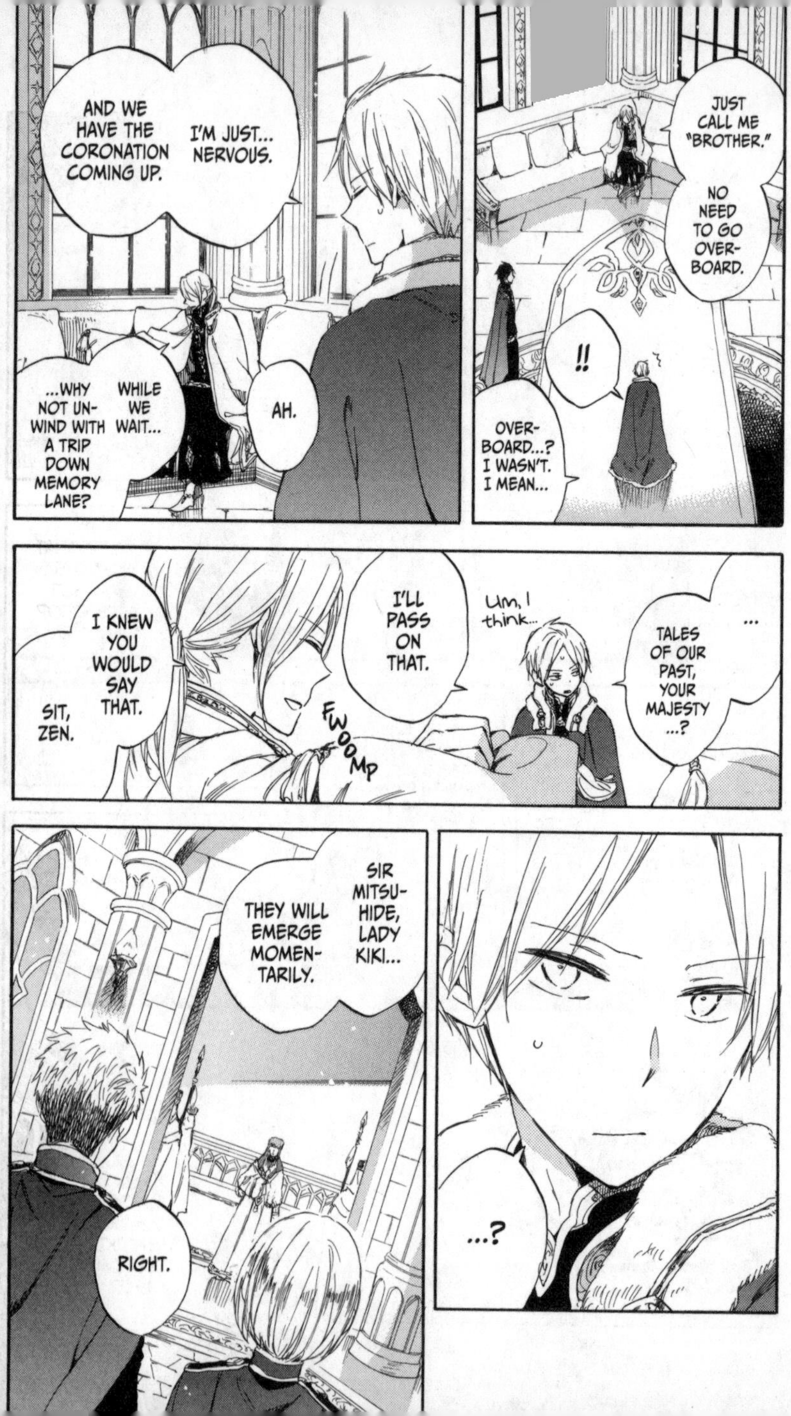
JUST CALL ME "BROTHER."
NO NEED TO GO OVERBOARD.
!!
OVER-BOARD...? I WASN'T. I MEAN...
I'M JUST... NERVOUS.
AND WE HAVE THE CORONATION COMING UP.
AH.
WHILE WE WAIT...
...WHY NOT UNWIND WITH A TRIP DOWN MEMORY LANE?
...
TALES OF OUR PAST, YOUR MAJESTY ...?
Um, I think...
I'LL PASS ON THAT.
FWOOMP
I KNEW YOU WOULD SAY THAT.
SIT, ZEN.
...?
SIR MITSUHIDE, LADY KIKI...
THEY WILL EMERGE MOMENTARILY.
RIGHT.

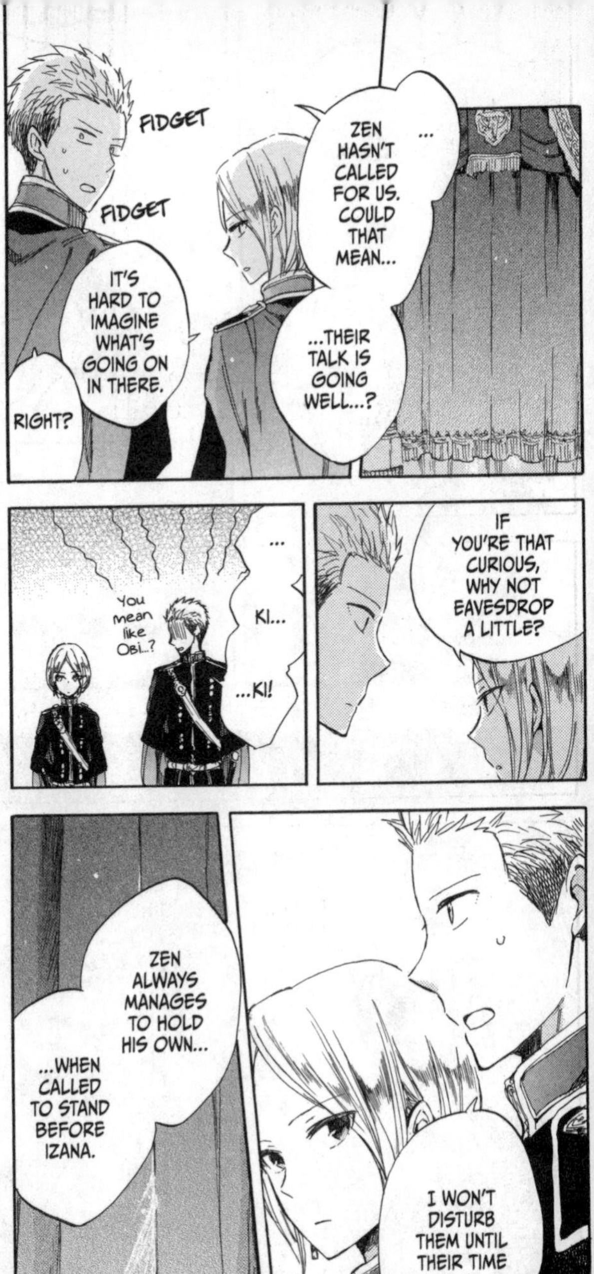
...
ZEN HASN'T CALLED FOR US. COULD THAT MEAN...
...THEIR TALK IS GOING WELL...?
FIDGET
FIDGET
IT'S HARD TO IMAGINE WHAT'S GOING ON IN THERE.
RIGHT?
IF YOU'RE THAT CURIOUS, WHY NOT EAVESDROP A LITTLE?
...
KI...
...KI!
You mean like Obi..?
I WON'T DISTURB THEM UNTIL THEIR TIME IS UP.
ZEN ALWAYS MANAGES TO HOLD HIS OWN...
...WHEN CALLED TO STAND BEFORE IZANA.

2

We ran a character popularity poll!

And here are the results!

Drumroll, please!

1st: Shirayuki—1,105 votes

2nd: Zen—854 votes

3rd: Obi—726 votes

4th: Kiki—461 votes

5th: Ryu—255 votes

And here's 6th through 10th!

6th: Mitsuhide—199 votes

I wish I could give you one more vote.

7th: Izana—190 votes

8th: Garak—41 votes

9th: Raj—33 votes

10th: Haruka—16 votes

We also had a "favorite duo" category.

1st: Shirayuki and Zen—238 votes

2nd: Mitsuhide and Kiki—173 votes

3rd: Shirayuki and Obi—64 votes

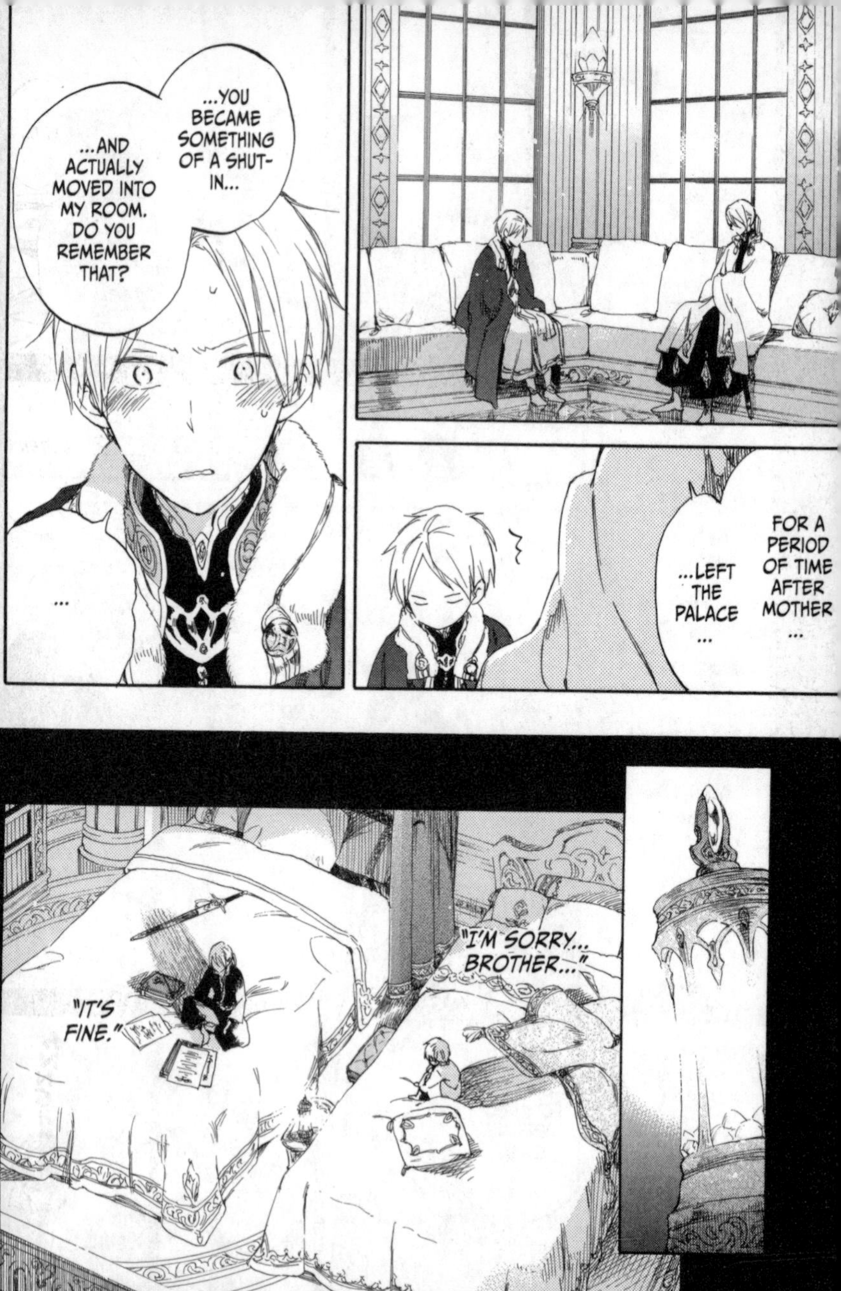
FOR A PERIOD OF TIME AFTER MOTHER ...
...LEFT THE PALACE ...
...YOU BECAME SOMETHING OF A SHUT-IN...
...AND ACTUALLY MOVED INTO MY ROOM. DO YOU REMEMBER THAT?
...
"I'M SORRY... BROTHER..."
"IT'S FINE."

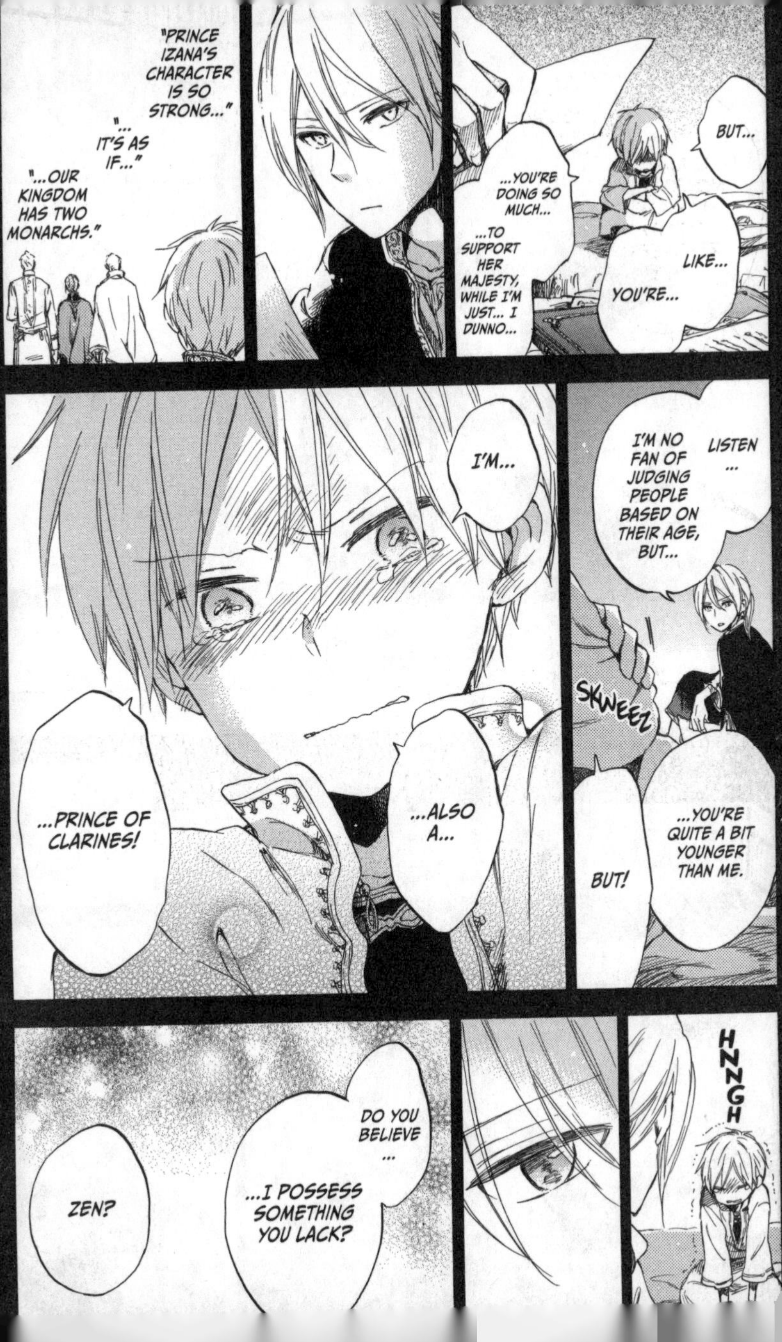
BUT...
LIKE... YOU'RE...
...YOU'RE DOING SO MUCH...
...TO SUPPORT HER MAJESTY, WHILE I'M JUST... I DUNNO...
"PRINCE IZANA'S CHARACTER IS SO STRONG..."
"...IT'S AS IF..."
"...OUR KINGDOM HAS TWO MONARCHS."
LISTEN...
I'M NO FAN OF JUDGING PEOPLE BASED ON THEIR AGE, BUT...
SKWEEZ
...YOU'RE QUITE A BIT YOUNGER THAN ME.
BUT!
I'M...
...ALSO A...
...PRINCE OF CLARINES!
HNNGH
DO YOU BELIEVE...
...I POSSESS SOMETHING YOU LACK?
ZEN?

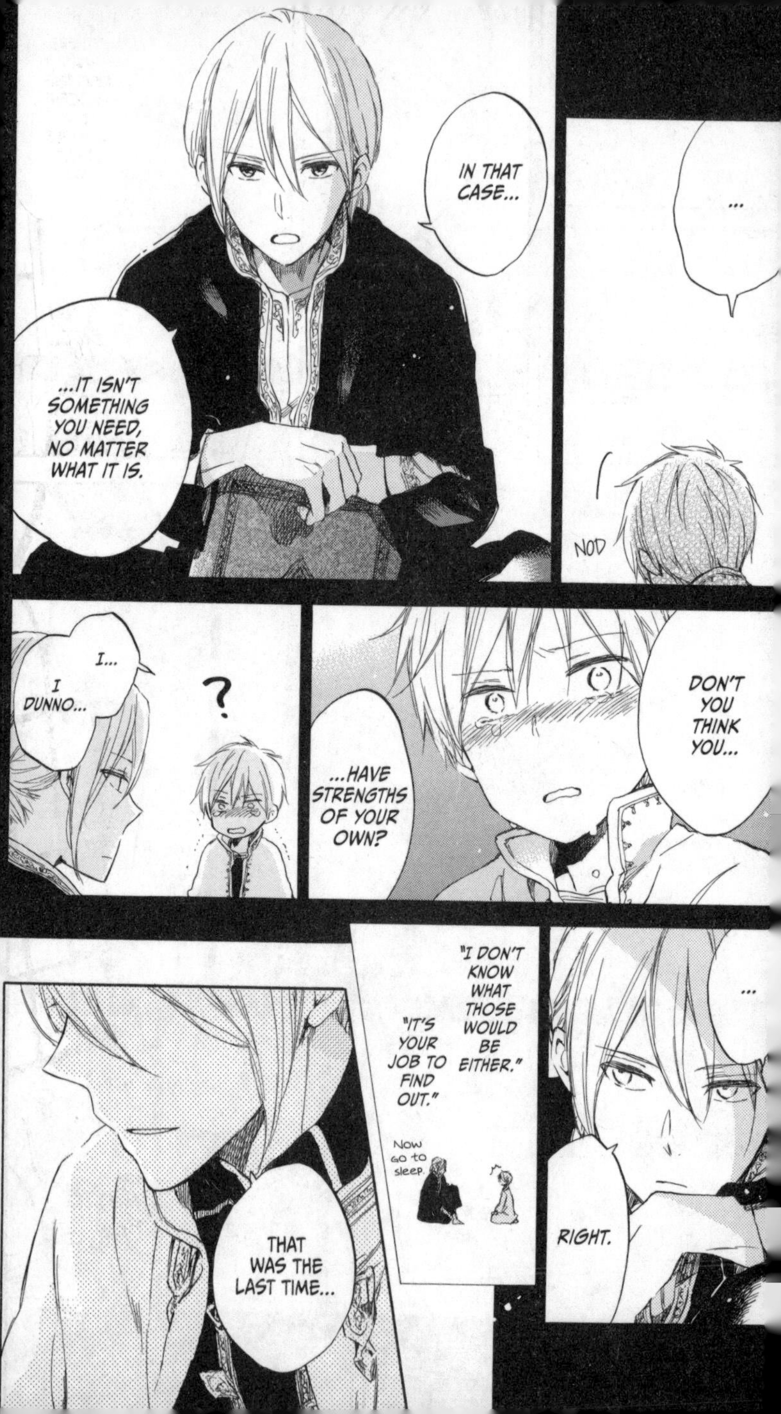
...
NOD
IN THAT CASE...
...IT ISN'T SOMETHING YOU NEED, NO MATTER WHAT IT IS.
DON'T YOU THINK YOU...
...HAVE STRENGTHS OF YOUR OWN?
?
I...
I DUNNO...
...
RIGHT.
"I DON'T KNOW WHAT THOSE WOULD BE EITHER."
"IT'S YOUR JOB TO FIND OUT."
Now go to sleep.
THAT WAS THE LAST TIME...

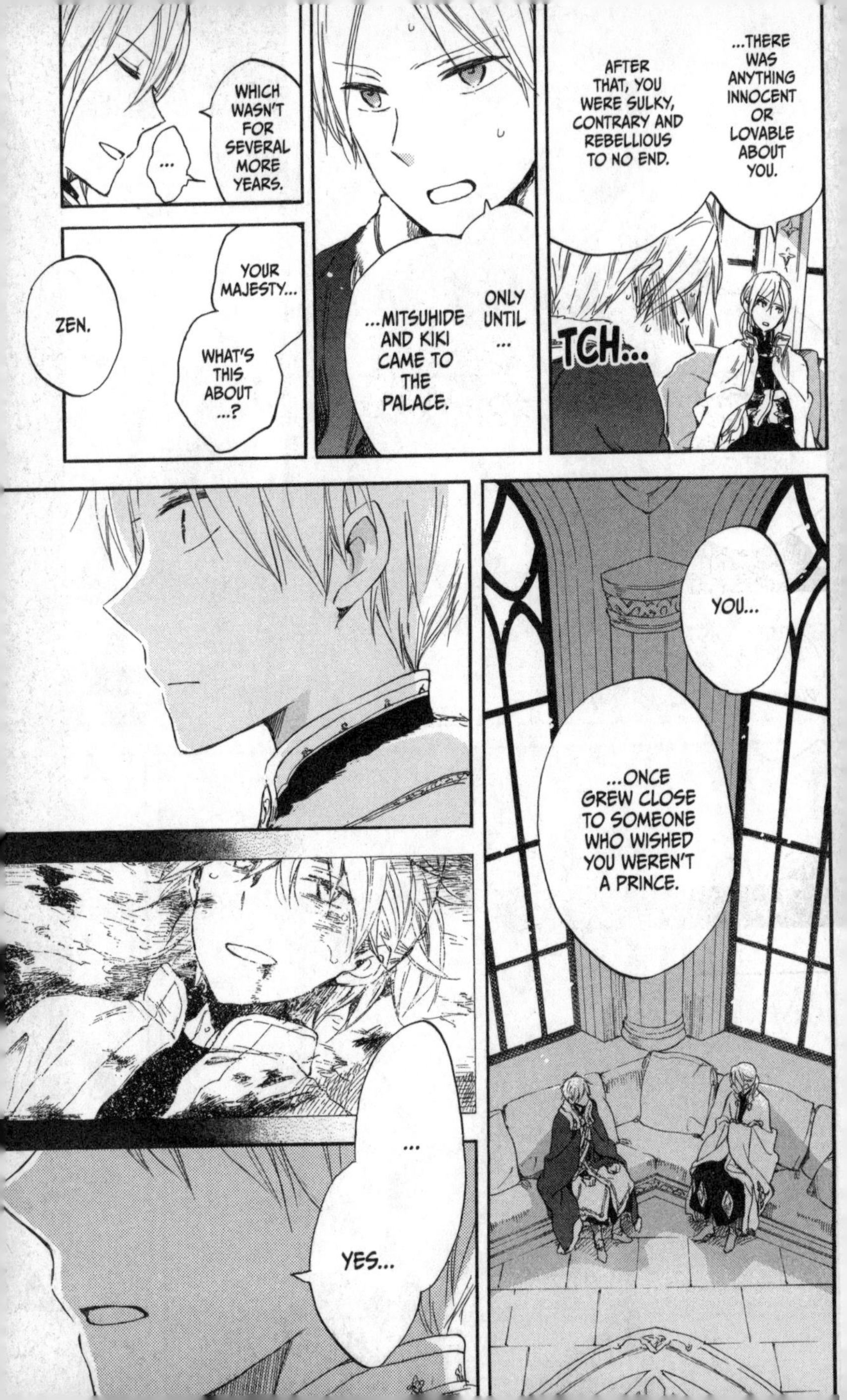
...THERE WAS ANYTHING INNOCENT OR LOVABLE ABOUT YOU.
AFTER THAT, YOU WERE SULKY, CONTRARY AND REBELLIOUS TO NO END.
TCH...
ONLY UNTIL...
...MITSUHIDE AND KIKI CAME TO THE PALACE.
WHICH WASN'T FOR SEVERAL MORE YEARS.
...
YOUR MAJESTY...
WHAT'S THIS ABOUT...?
ZEN.
YOU...
...ONCE GREW CLOSE TO SOMEONE WHO WISHED YOU WEREN'T A PRINCE.
...
YES...

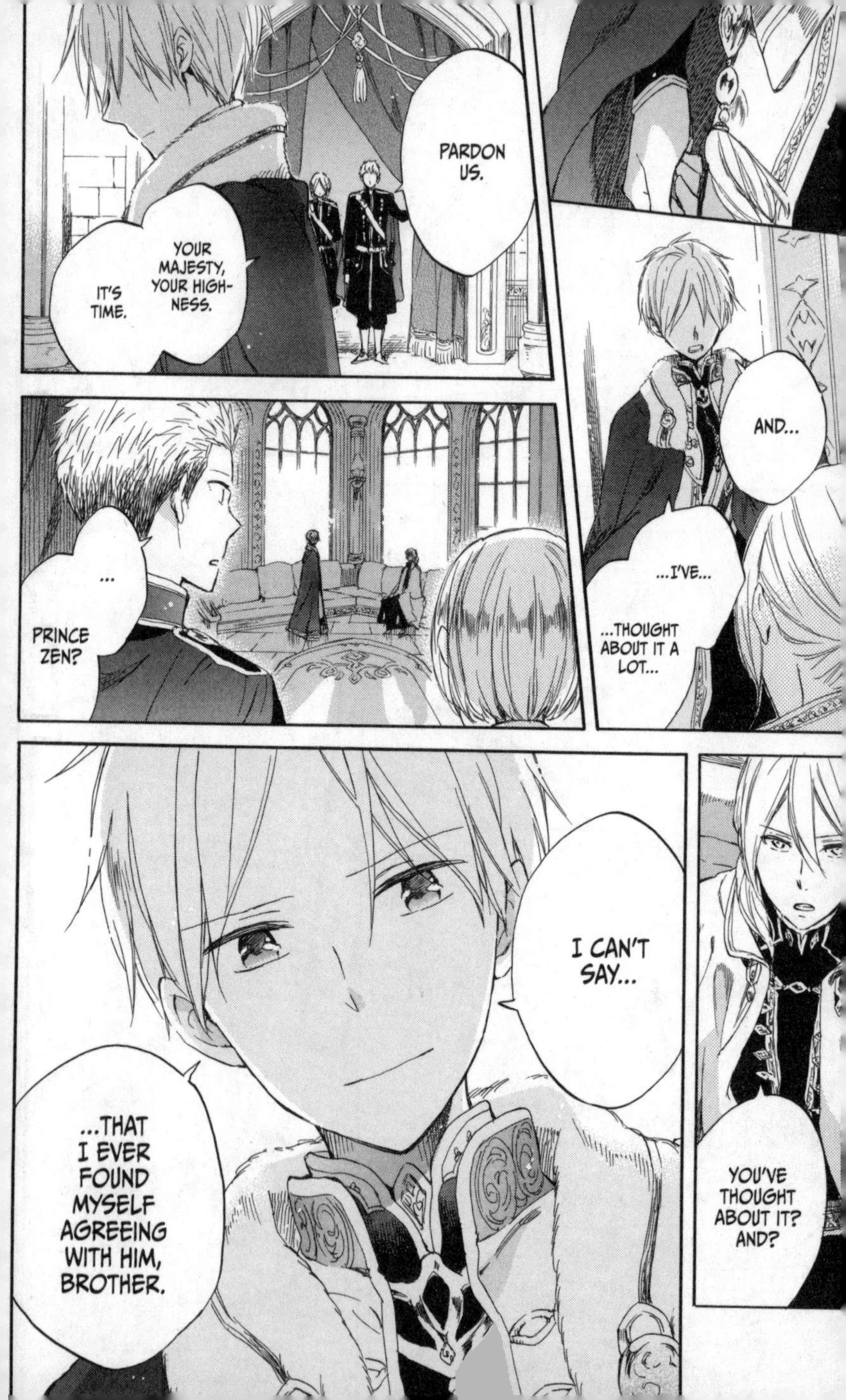
PARDON US.
YOUR MAJESTY, YOUR HIGH-NESS.
IT'S TIME.
AND...
...I'VE...
...THOUGHT ABOUT IT A LOT...
...
PRINCE ZEN?
YOU'VE THOUGHT ABOUT IT? AND?
I CAN'T SAY...
...THAT I EVER FOUND MYSELF AGREEING WITH HIM, BROTHER.

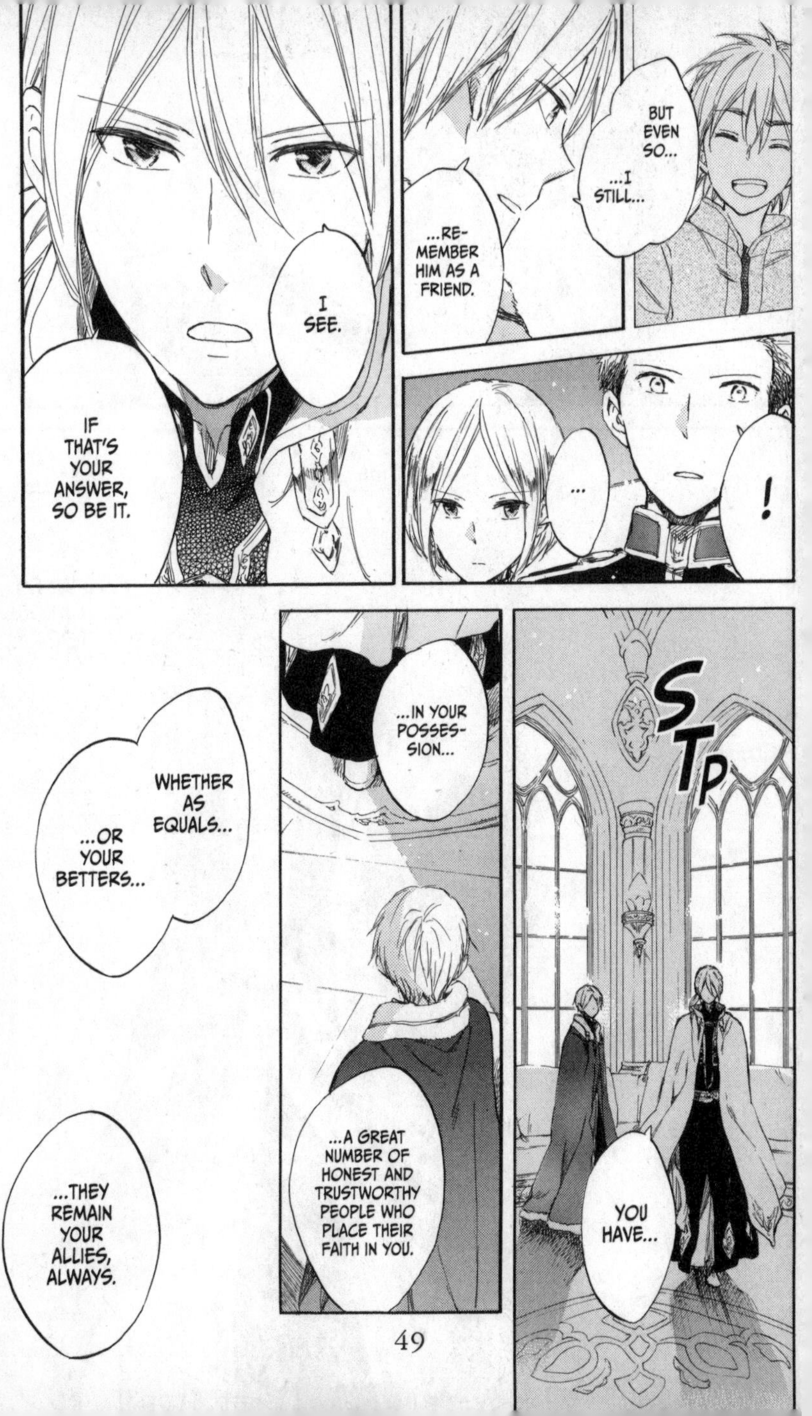
BUT EVEN SO...
...I STILL...
...RE-MEMBER HIM AS A FRIEND.
!
...
I SEE.
IF THAT'S YOUR ANSWER, SO BE IT.
STP
YOU HAVE...
...IN YOUR POSSES-SION...
...A GREAT NUMBER OF HONEST AND TRUSTWORTHY PEOPLE WHO PLACE THEIR FAITH IN YOU.
WHETHER AS EQUALS...
...OR YOUR BETTERS...
...THEY REMAIN YOUR ALLIES, ALWAYS.

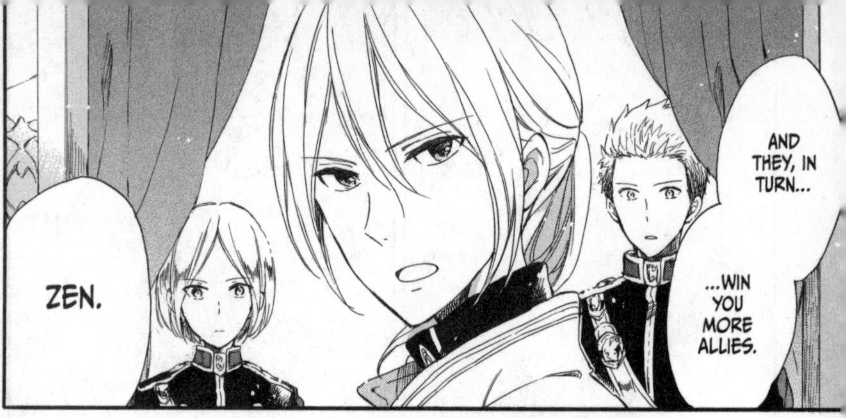
AND THEY, IN TURN...
...WIN YOU MORE ALLIES.
ZEN.
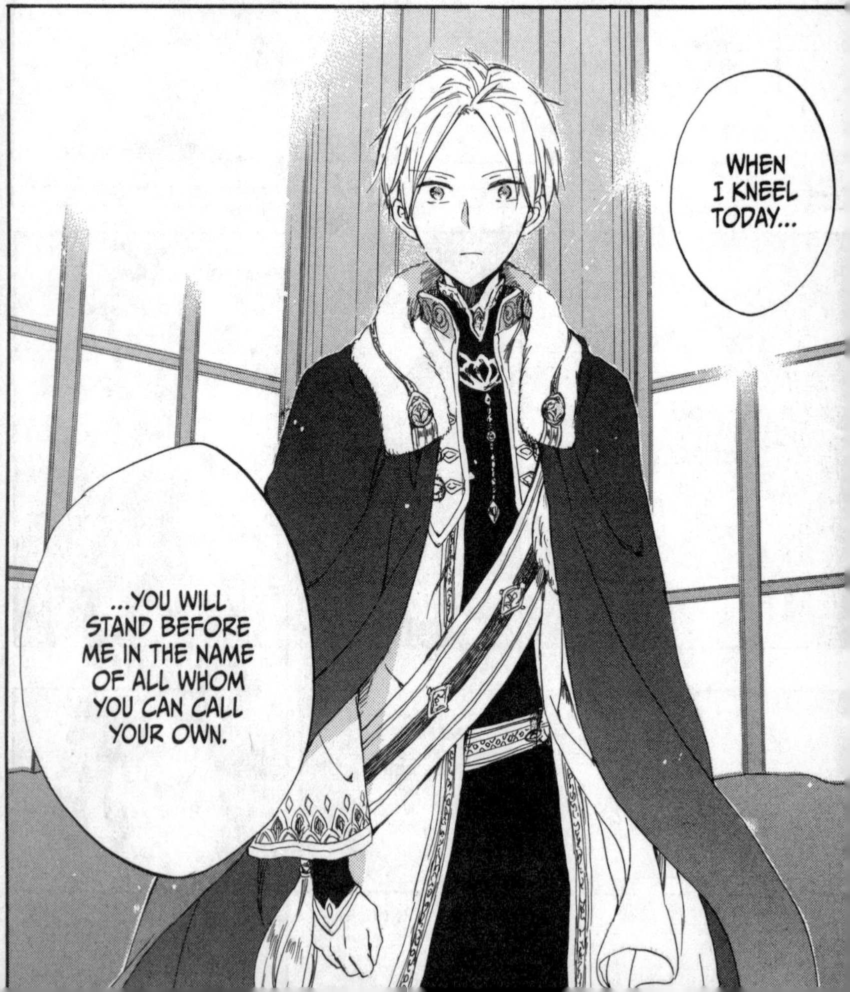
WHEN I KNEEL TODAY...
...YOU WILL STAND BEFORE ME IN THE NAME OF ALL WHOM YOU CAN CALL YOUR OWN.

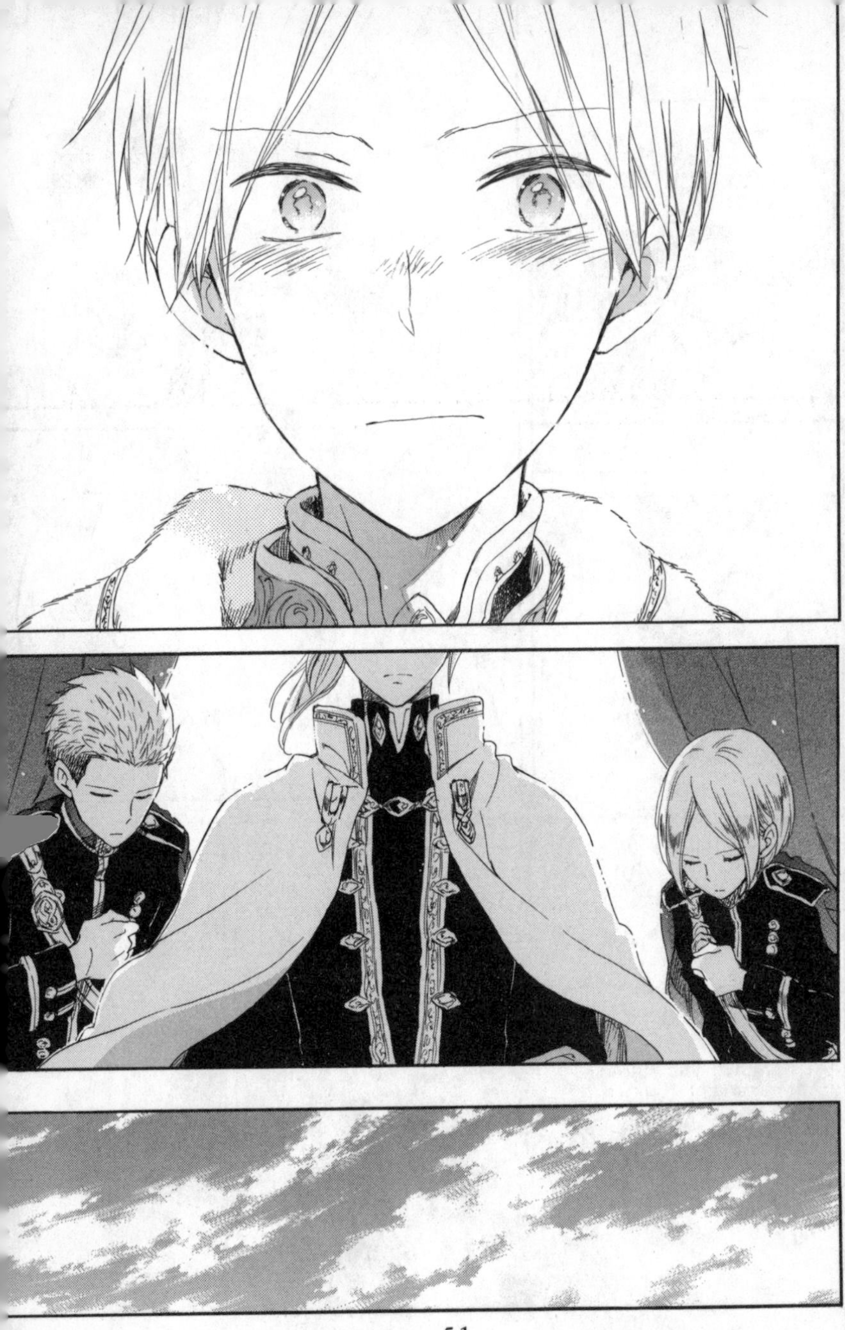

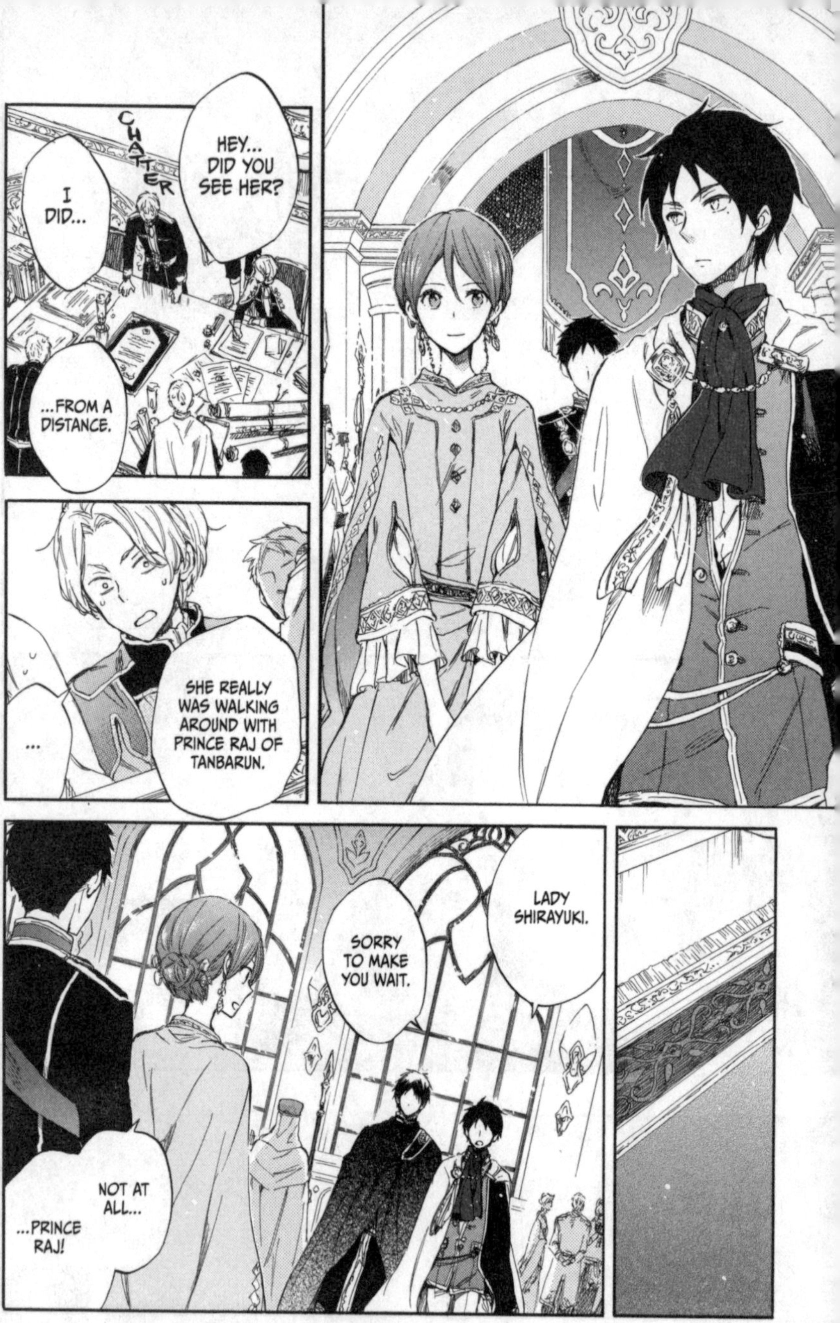
HEY... DID YOU SEE HER?
CHATTER
I DID...
...FROM A DISTANCE.
SHE REALLY WAS WALKING AROUND WITH PRINCE RAJ OF TANBARUN.
...
LADY SHIRAYUKI.
SORRY TO MAKE YOU WAIT.
NOT AT ALL...
...PRINCE RAJ!

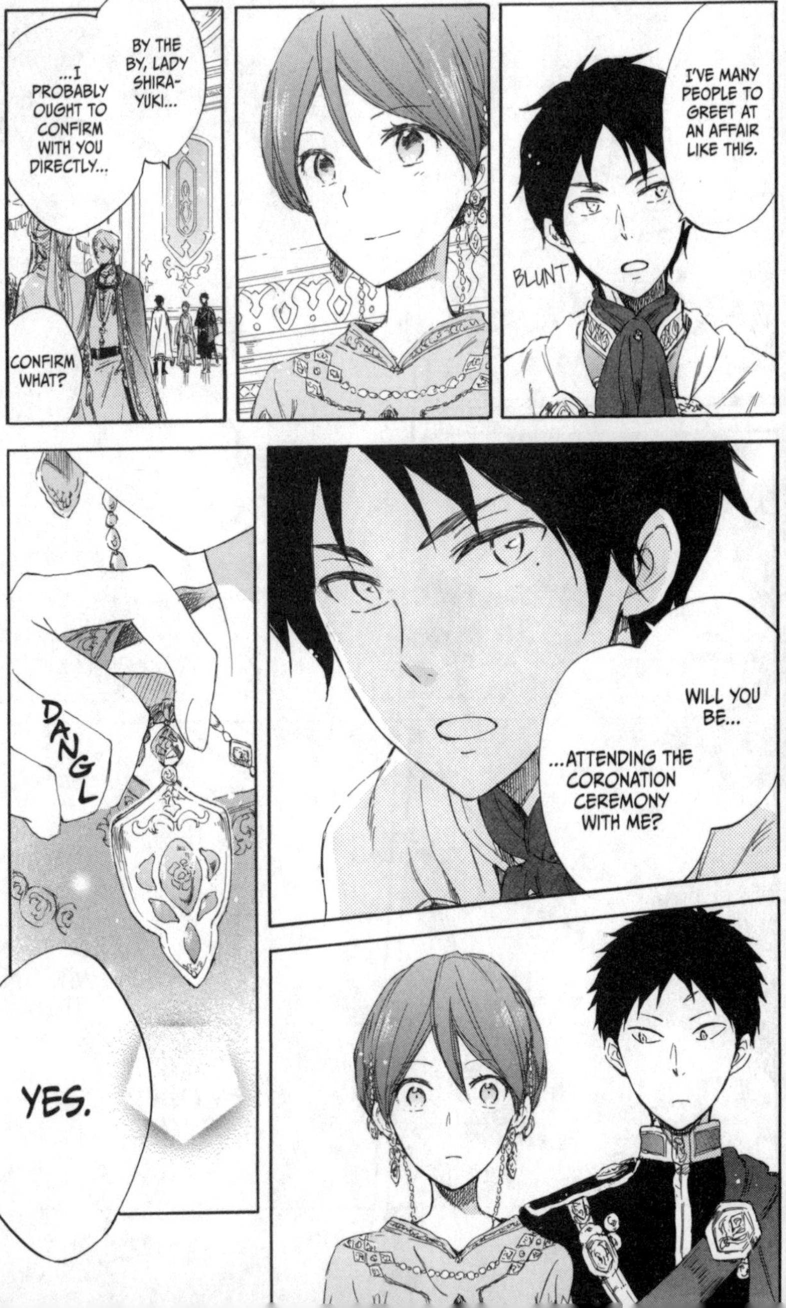
I'VE MANY PEOPLE TO GREET AT AN AFFAIR LIKE THIS.
BLUNT
BY THE BY, LADY SHIRA-YUKI...
...I PROBABLY OUGHT TO CONFIRM WITH YOU DIRECTLY...
CONFIRM WHAT?
WILL YOU BE...
...ATTENDING THE CORONATION CEREMONY WITH ME?
DANGL
YES.

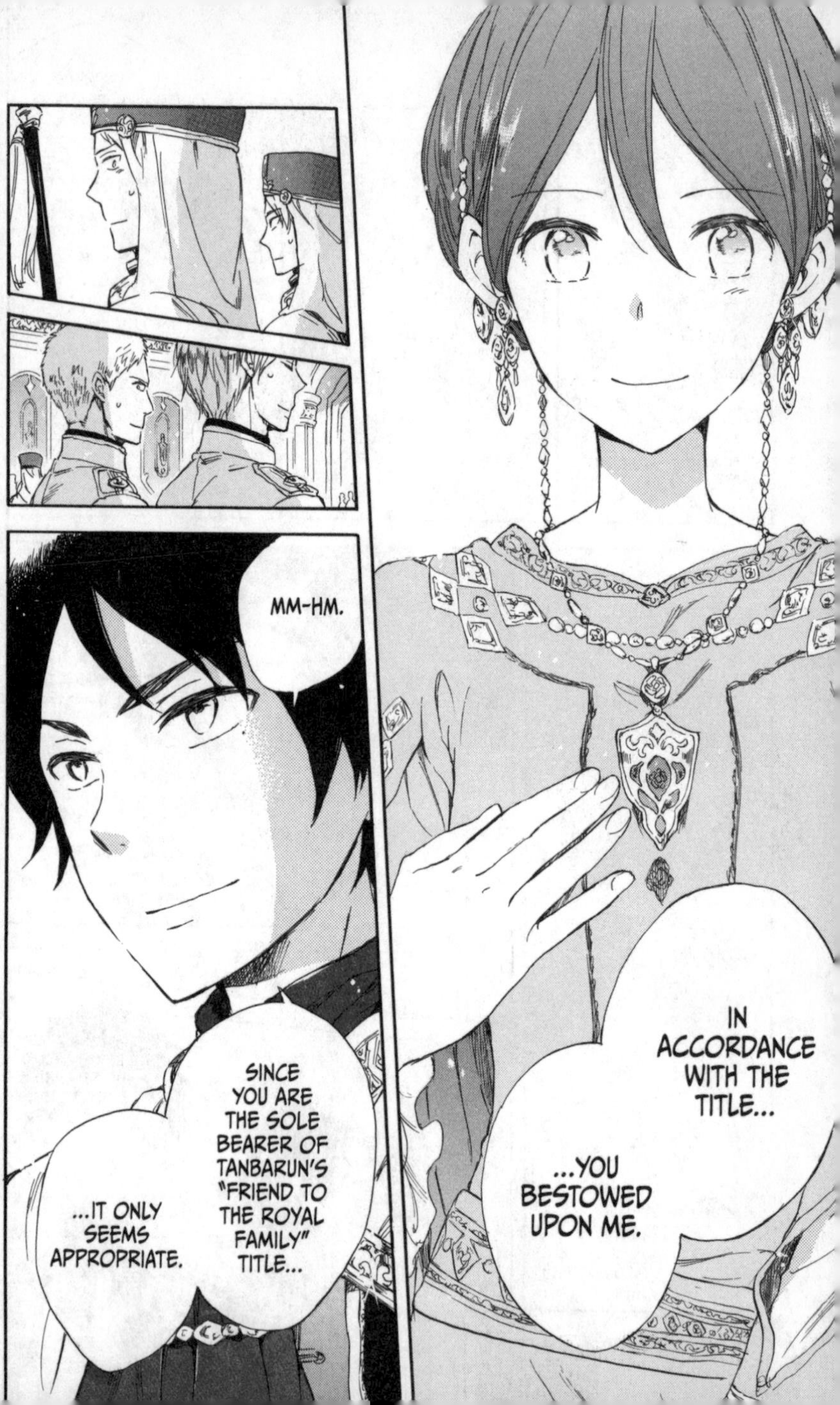
IN ACCORDANCE WITH THE TITLE...
...YOU BESTOWED UPON ME.
MM-HM.
SINCE YOU ARE THE SOLE BEARER OF TANBARUN'S "FRIEND TO THE ROYAL FAMILY" TITLE...
...IT ONLY SEEMS APPROPRIATE.

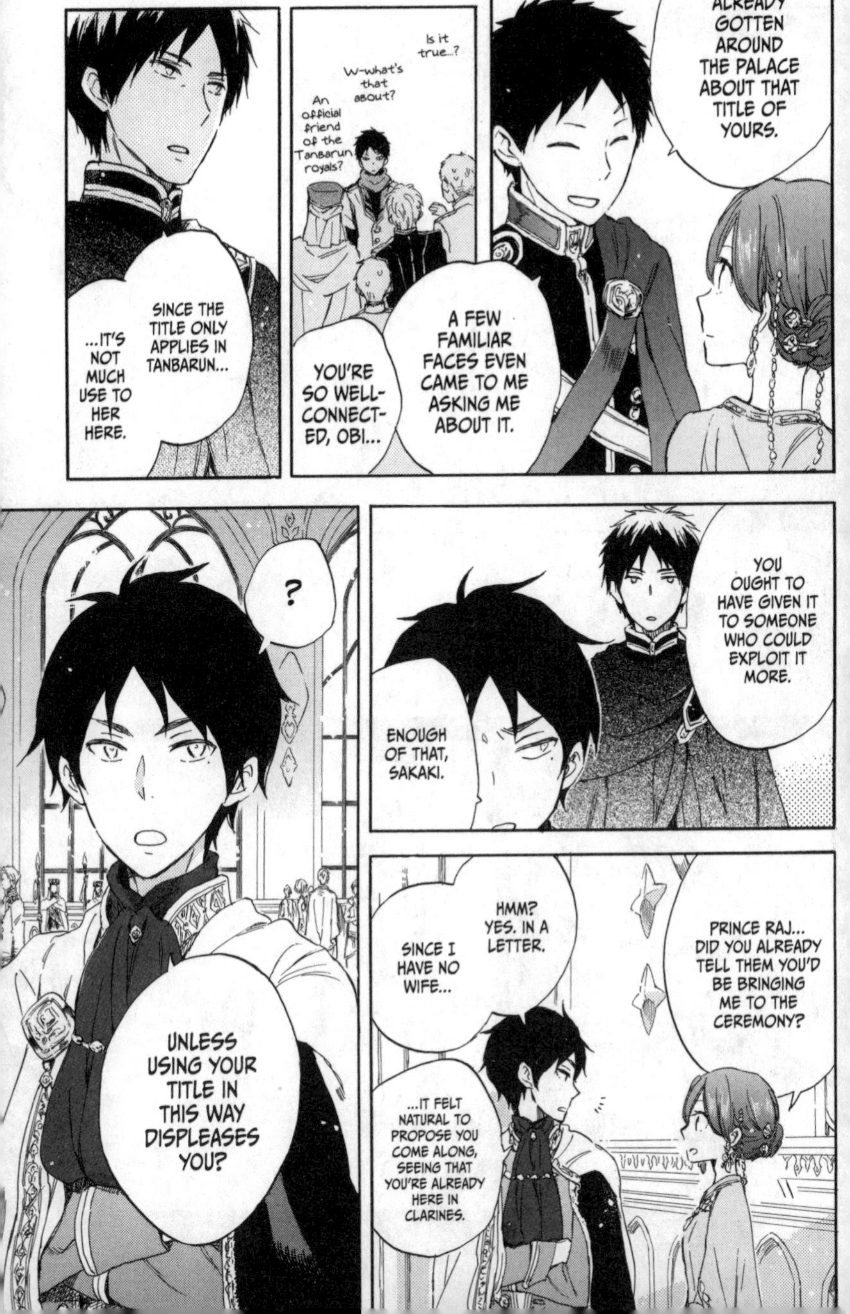
WORD'S ALREADY GOTTEN AROUND THE PALACE ABOUT THAT TITLE OF YOURS.
A FEW FAMILIAR FACES EVEN CAME TO ME ASKING ME ABOUT IT.
Is it true...?
W-what's that about?
An official friend of the Tanbarun royals?
YOU'RE SO WELL-CONNECTED, OBI...
SINCE THE TITLE ONLY APPLIES IN TANBARUN...
...IT'S NOT MUCH USE TO HER HERE.
YOU OUGHT TO HAVE GIVEN IT TO SOMEONE WHO COULD EXPLOIT IT MORE.
ENOUGH OF THAT, SAKAKI.
PRINCE RAJ... DID YOU ALREADY TELL THEM YOU'D BE BRINGING ME TO THE CEREMONY?
HMM? YES. IN A LETTER.
SINCE I HAVE NO WIFE...
...IT FELT NATURAL TO PROPOSE YOU COME ALONG, SEEING THAT YOU'RE ALREADY HERE IN CLARINES.
?
UNLESS USING YOUR TITLE IN THIS WAY DISPLEASES YOU?

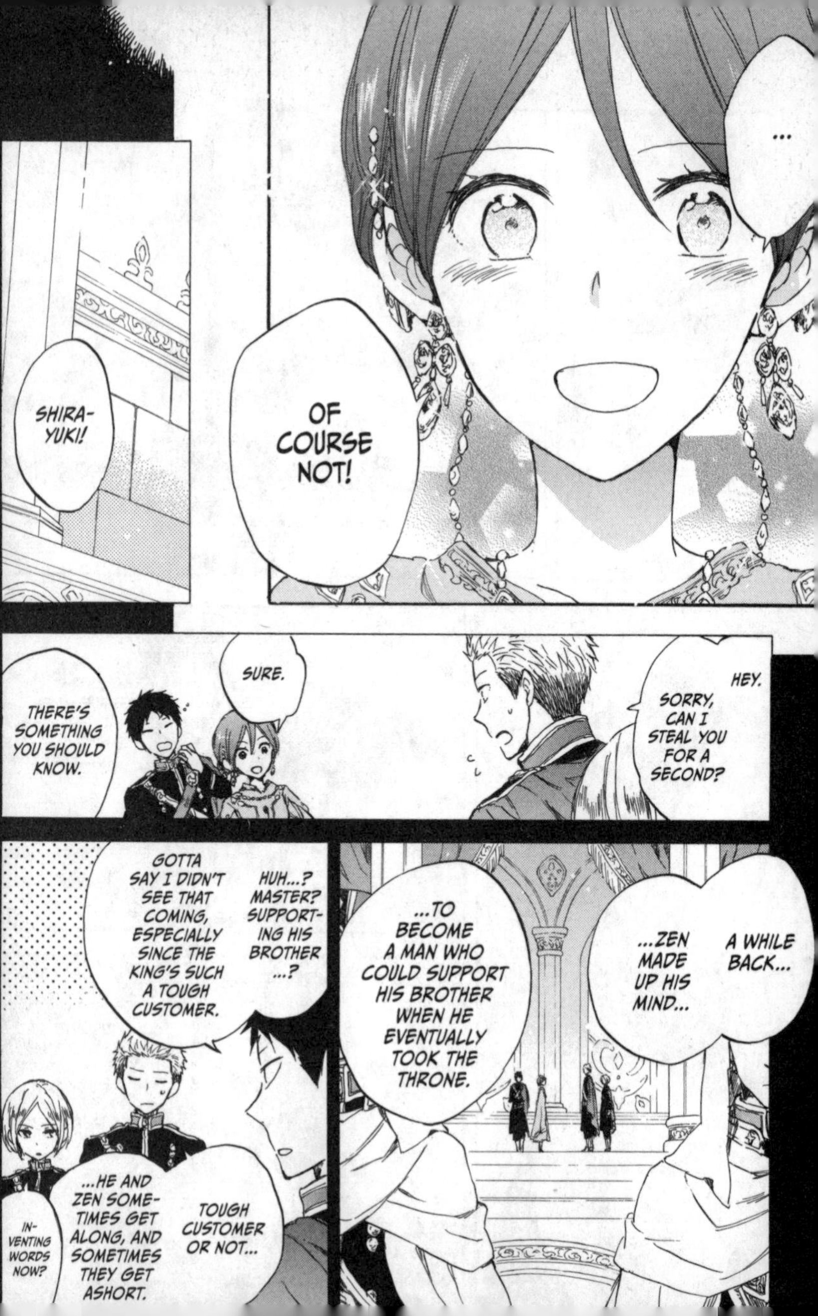
...
OF COURSE NOT!
SHIRA-YUKI!
HEY.
SORRY, CAN I STEAL YOU FOR A SECOND?
SURE.
THERE'S SOMETHING YOU SHOULD KNOW.
A WHILE BACK...
...ZEN MADE UP HIS MIND...
...TO BECOME A MAN WHO COULD SUPPORT HIS BROTHER WHEN HE EVENTUALLY TOOK THE THRONE.
HUH...? MASTER? SUPPORT-ING HIS BROTHER ...?
GOTTA SAY I DIDN'T SEE THAT COMING, ESPECIALLY SINCE THE KING'S SUCH A TOUGH CUSTOMER.
TOUGH CUSTOMER OR NOT...
...HE AND ZEN SOME-TIMES GET ALONG, AND SOMETIMES THEY GET ASHORT.
IN-VENTING WORDS NOW?

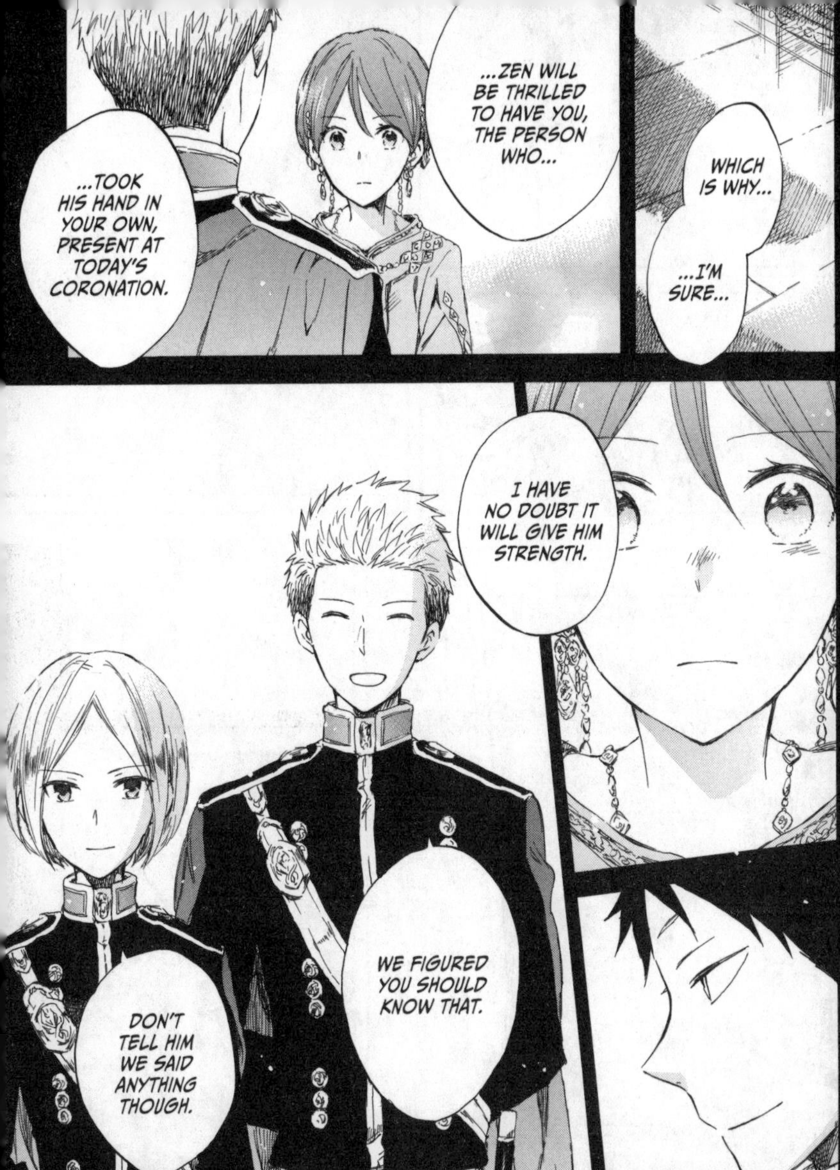
WHICH IS WHY...
...I'M SURE...
...ZEN WILL BE THRILLED TO HAVE YOU, THE PERSON WHO...
...TOOK HIS HAND IN YOUR OWN, PRESENT AT TODAY'S CORONATION.
I HAVE NO DOUBT IT WILL GIVE HIM STRENGTH.
WE FIGURED YOU SHOULD KNOW THAT.
DON'T TELL HIM WE SAID ANYTHING THOUGH.

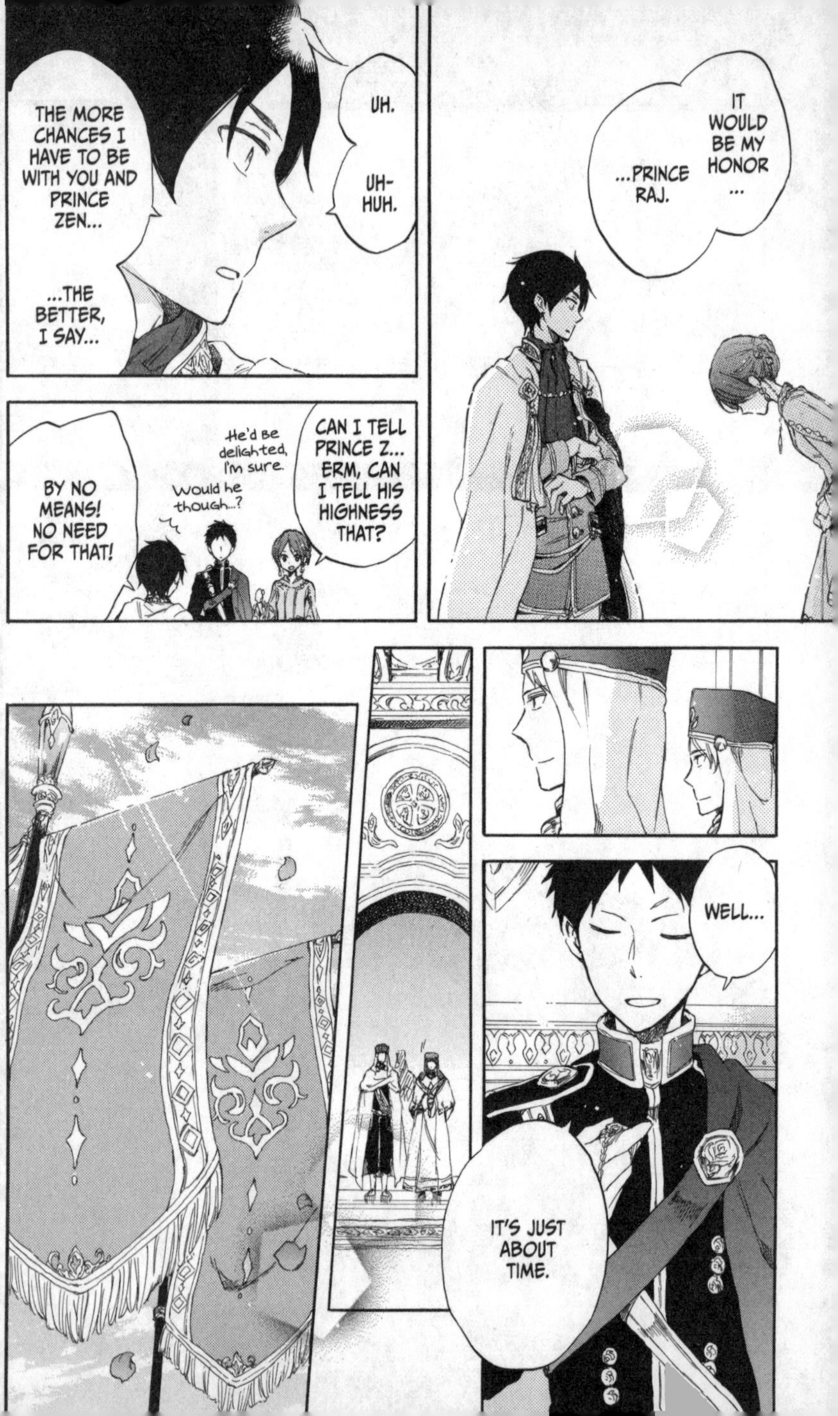
IT WOULD BE MY HONOR ...
...PRINCE RAJ.
UH.
UH-HUH.
THE MORE CHANCES I HAVE TO BE WITH YOU AND PRINCE ZEN...
...THE BETTER, I SAY...
CAN I TELL PRINCE Z... ERM, CAN I TELL HIS HIGHNESS THAT?
He'd be delighted, I'm sure.
Would he though...?
BY NO MEANS! NO NEED FOR THAT!
WELL...
IT'S JUST ABOUT TIME.

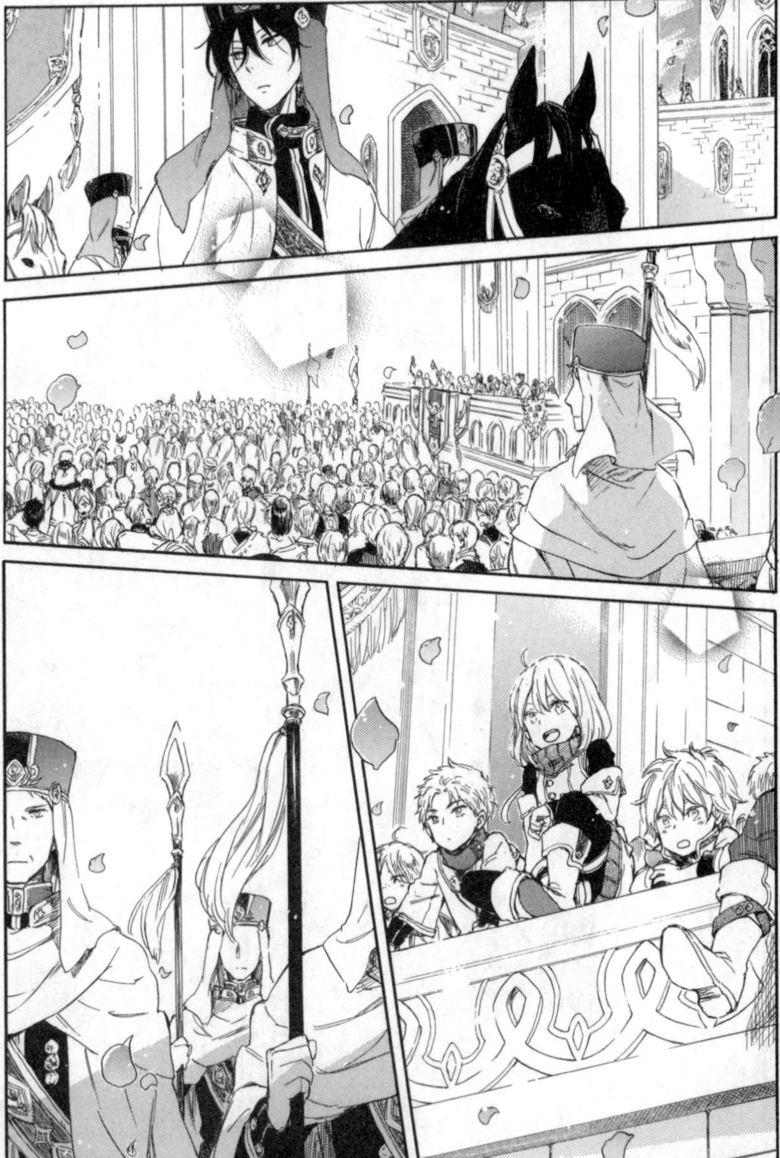

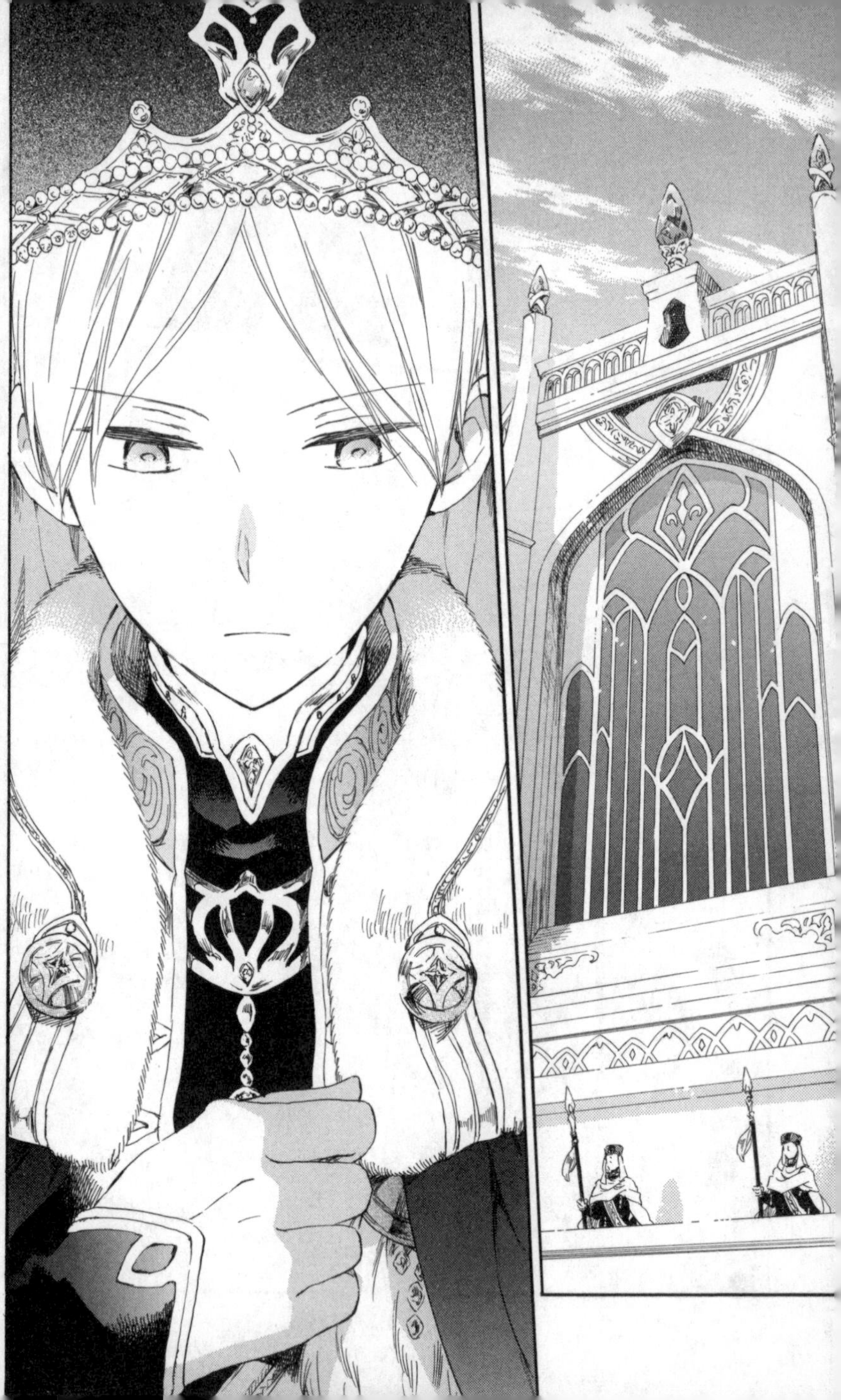

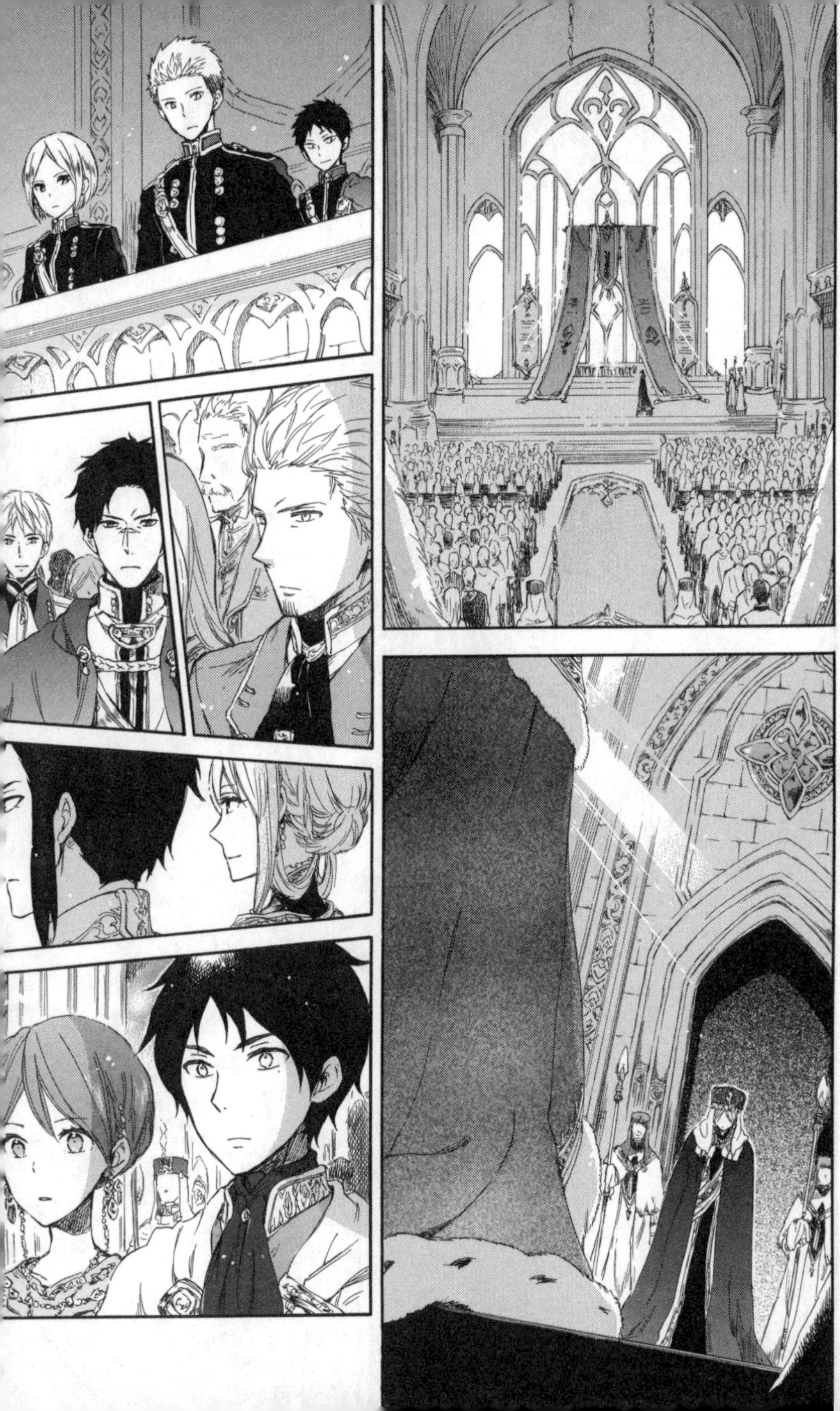

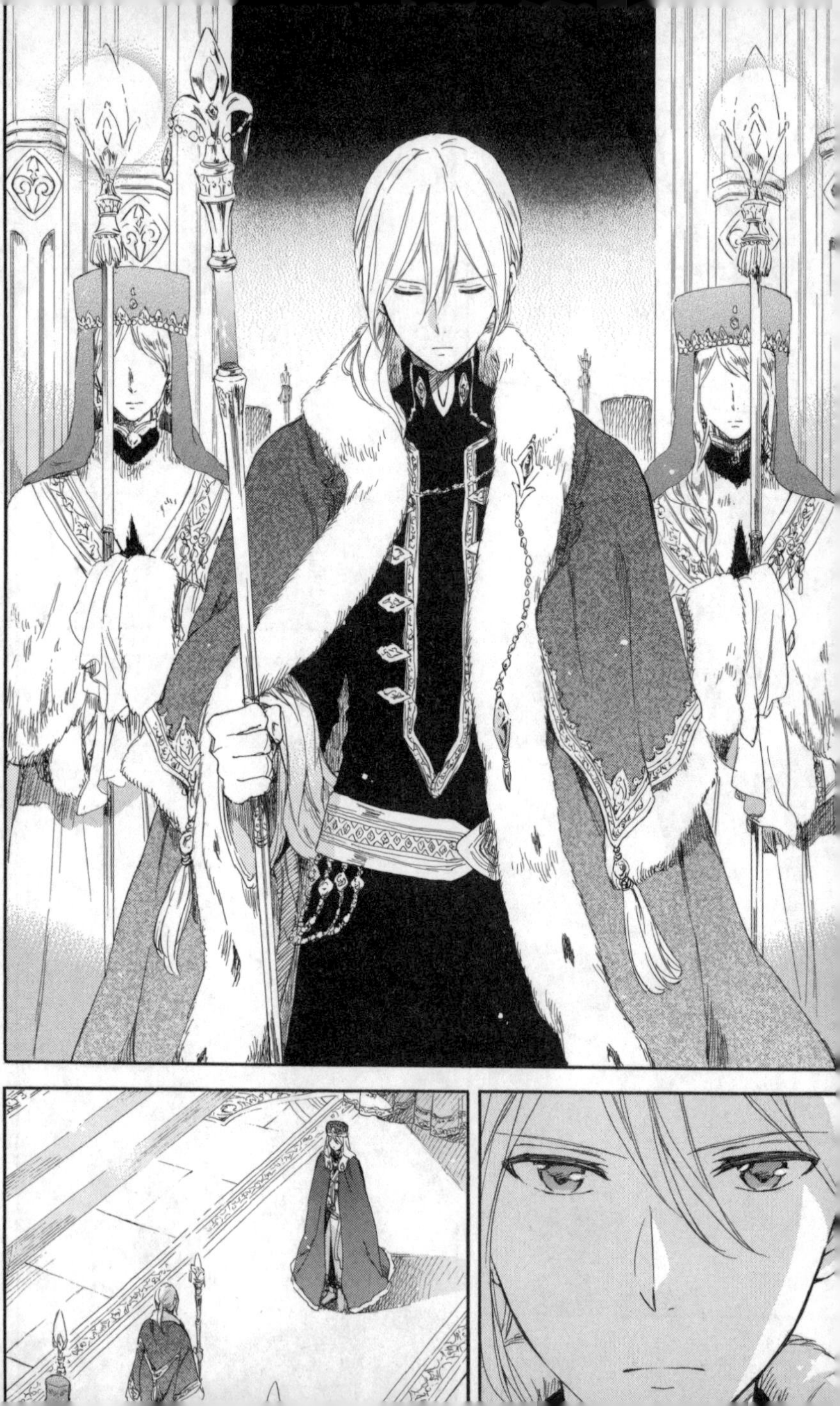

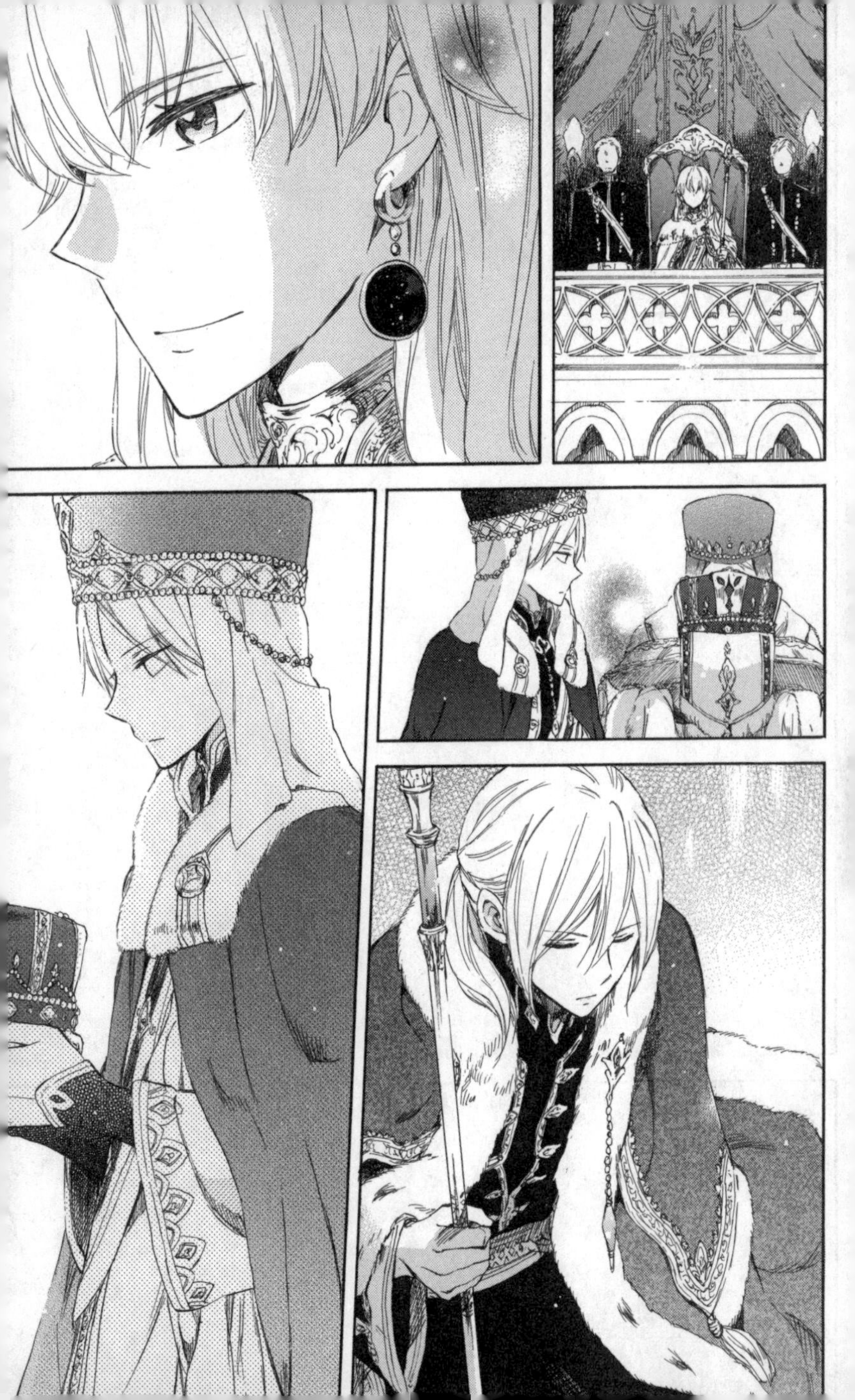

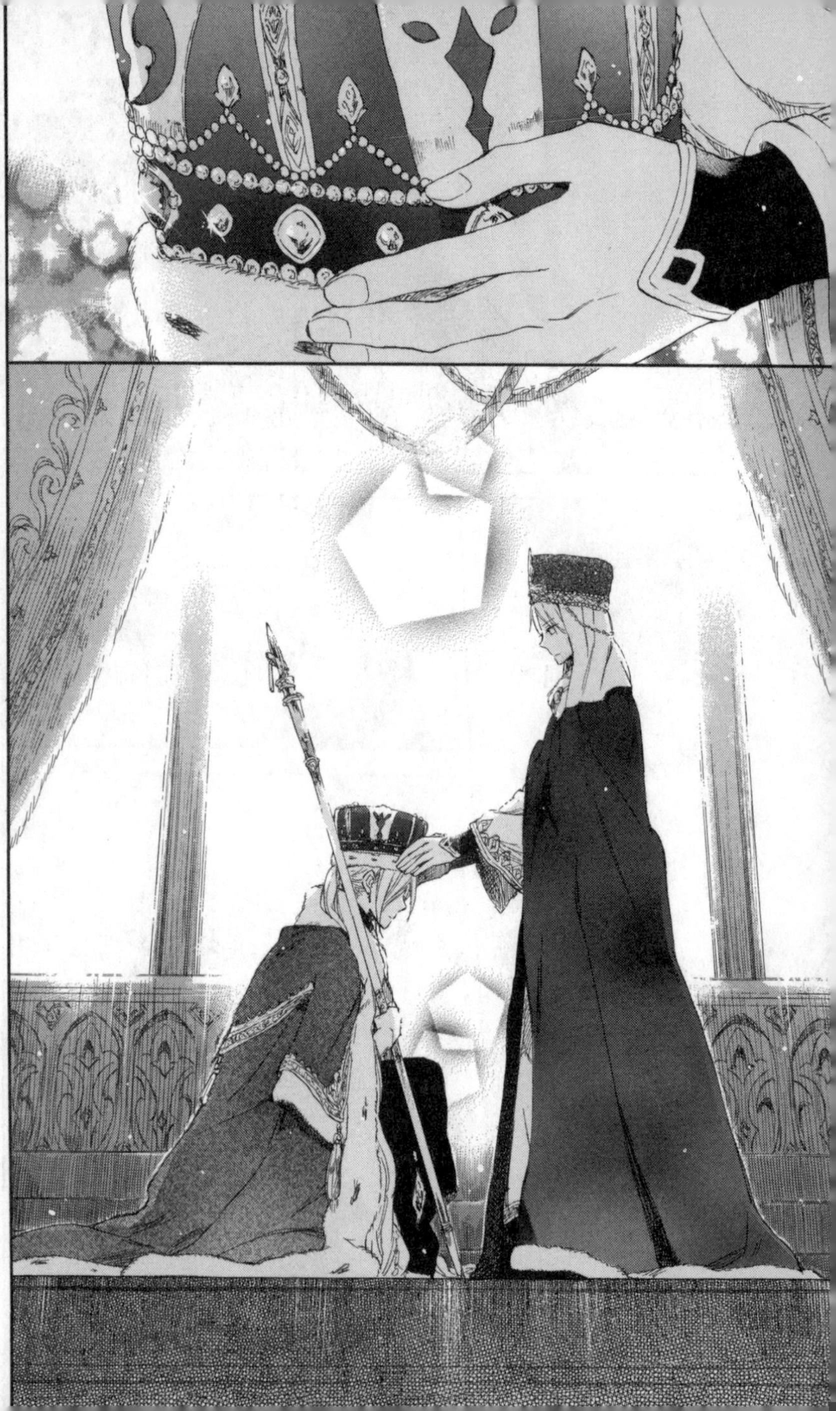

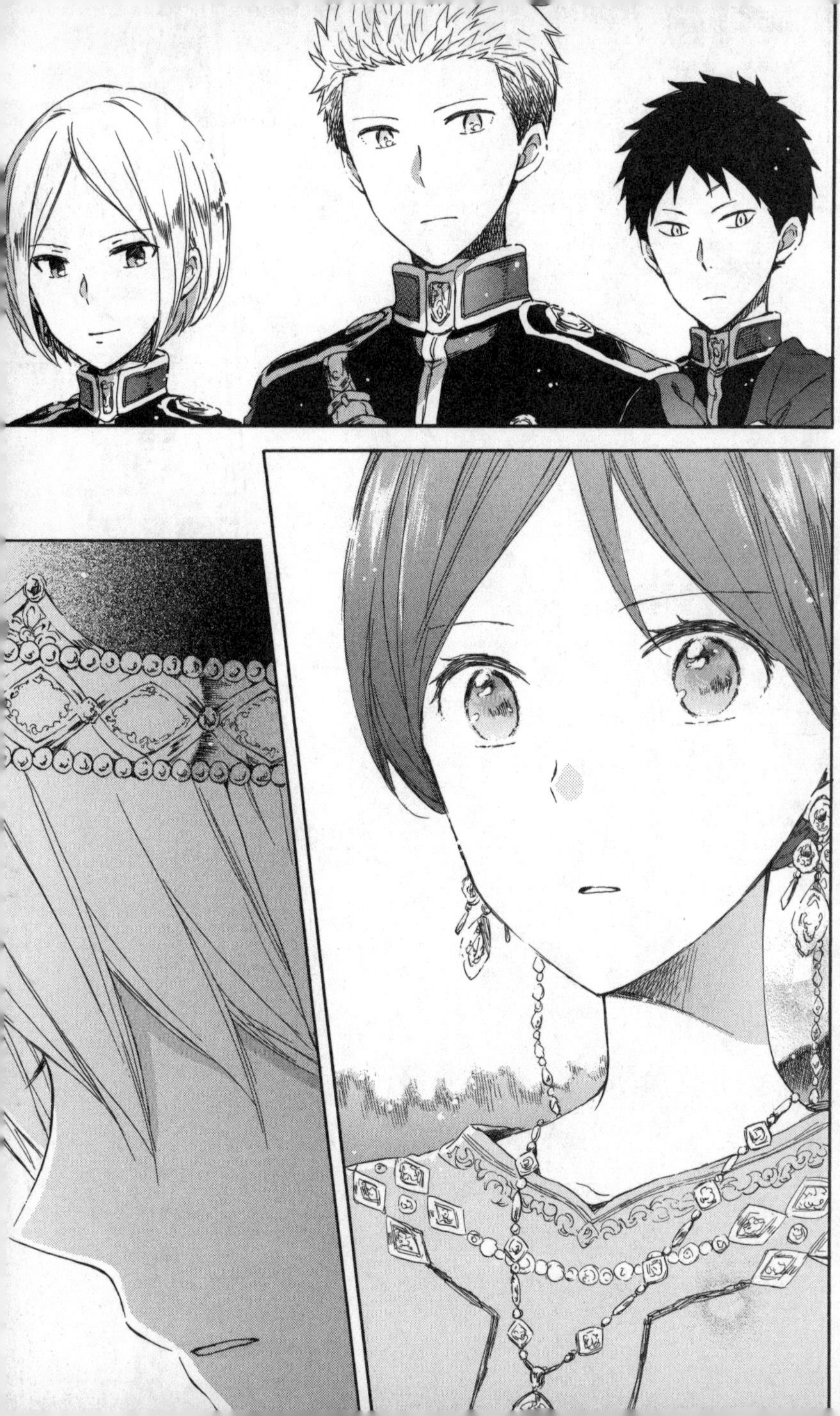

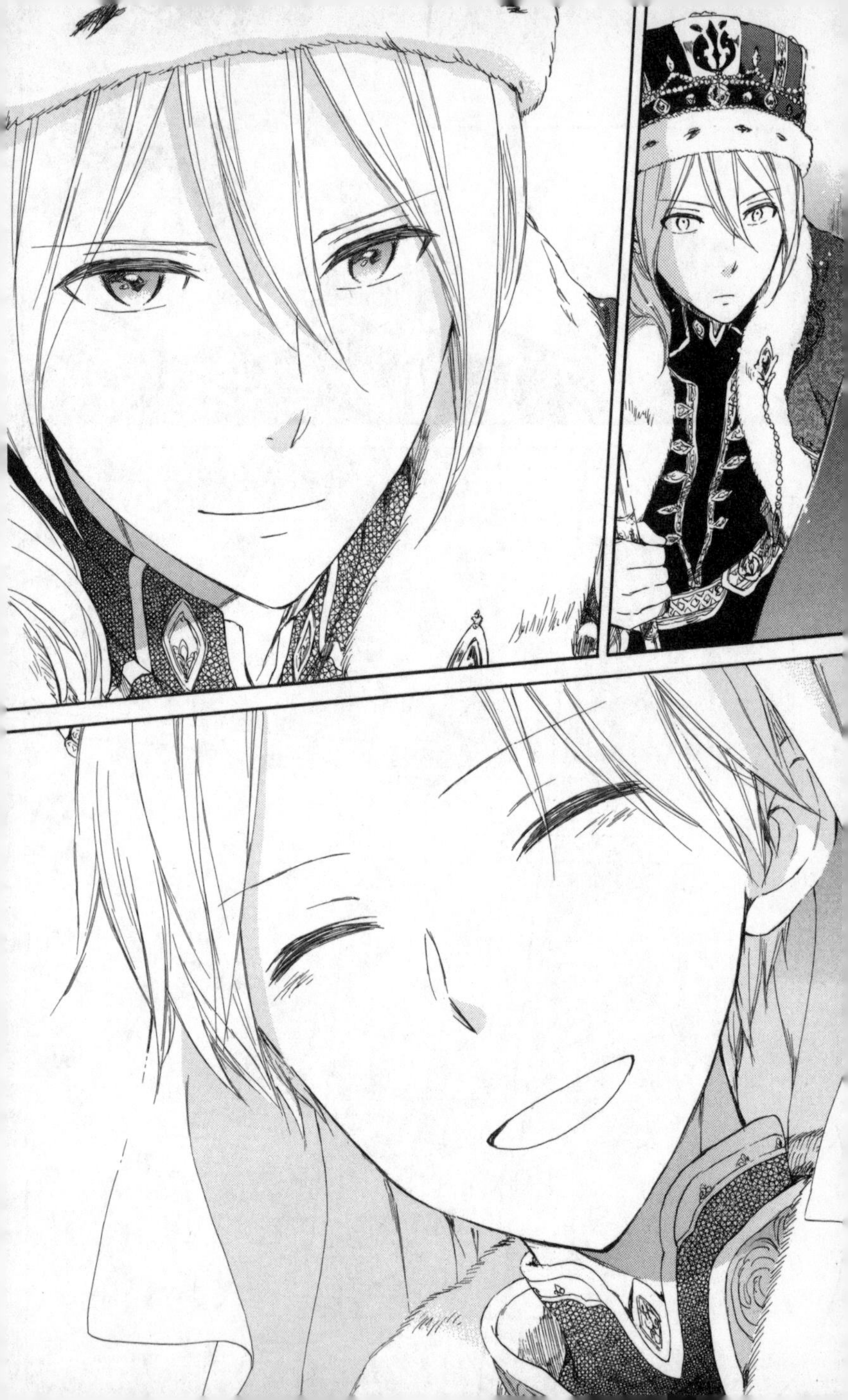

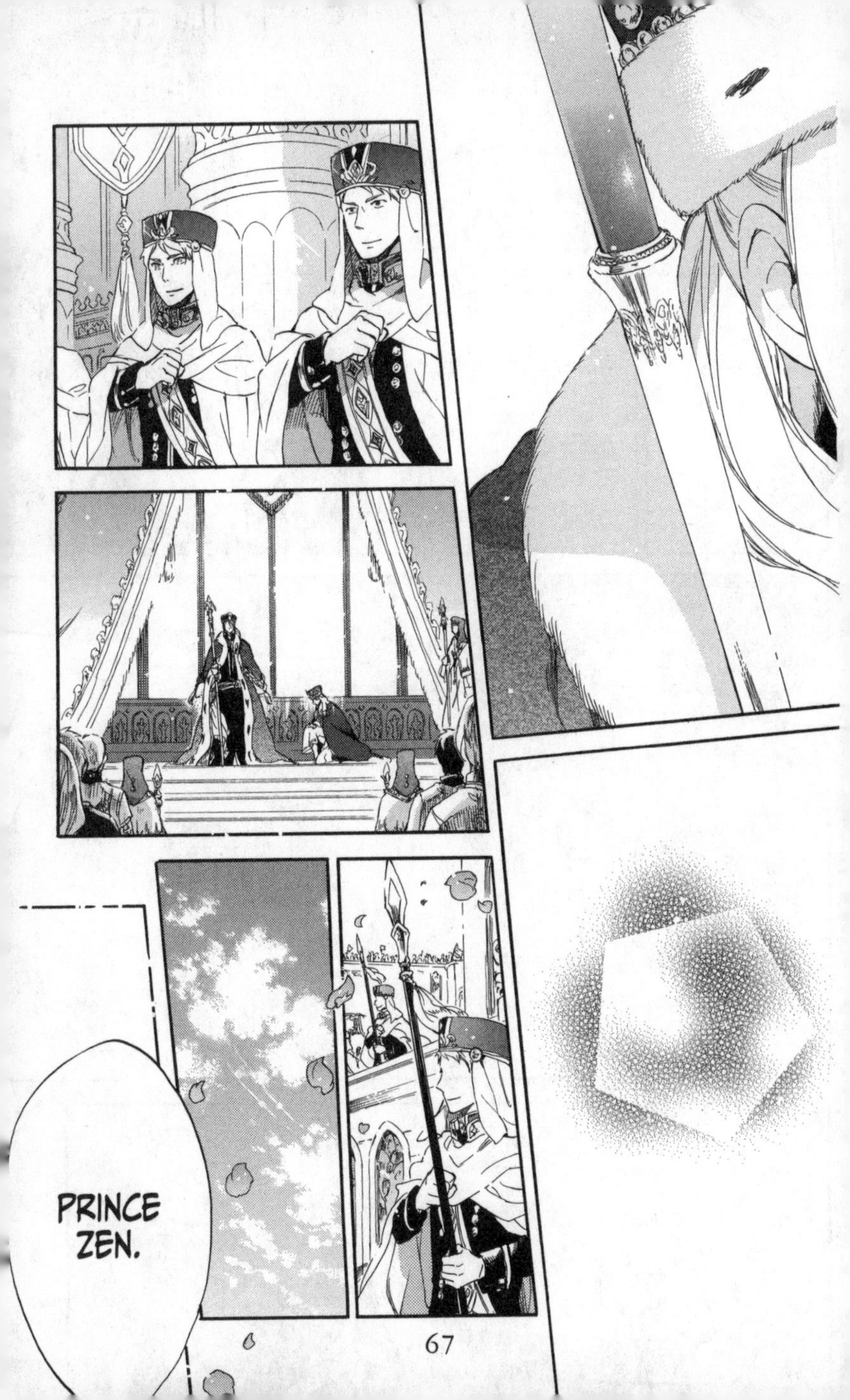
PRINCE ZEN.

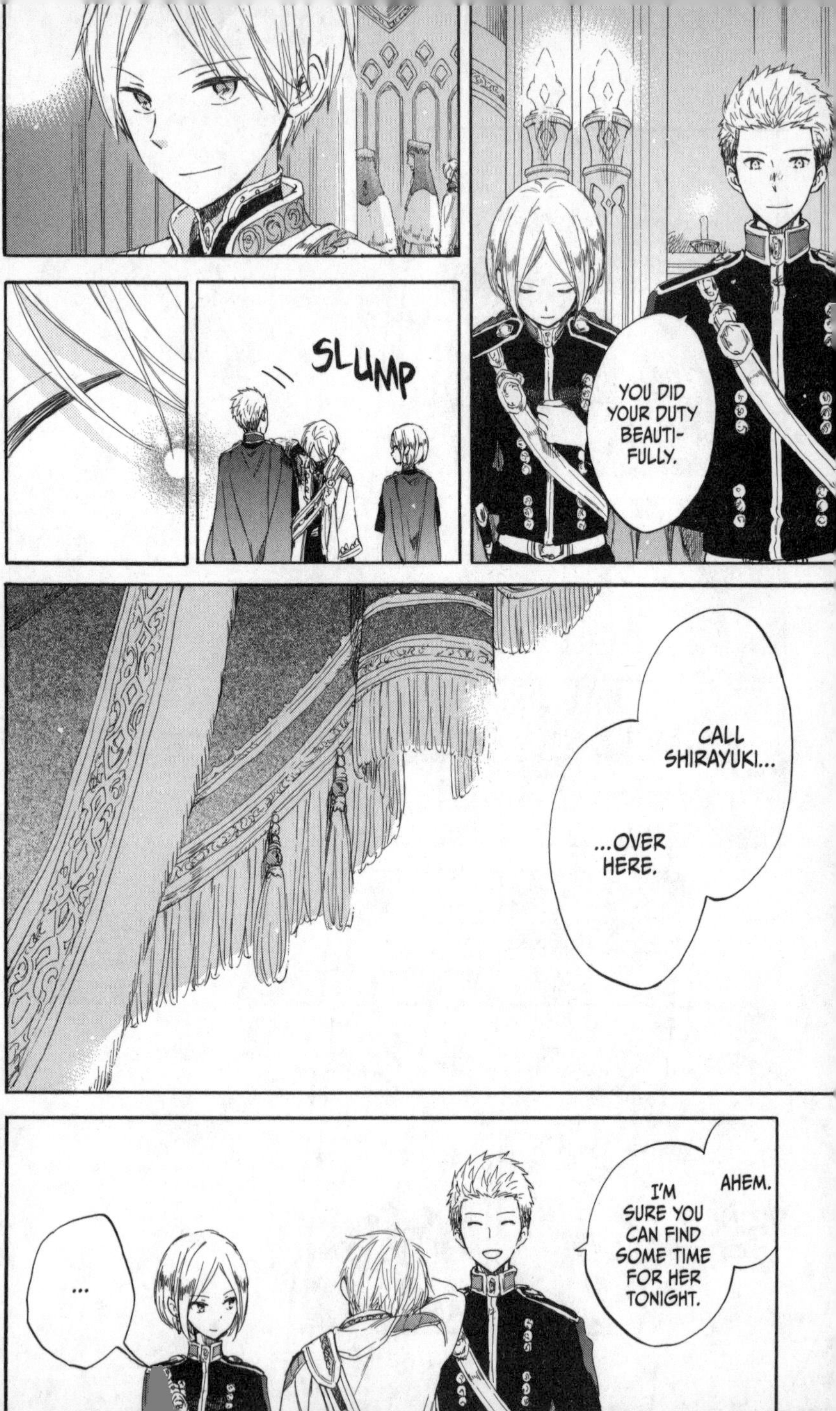
YOU DID YOUR DUTY BEAUTI- FULLY.
SLUMP
CALL SHIRAYUKI...
...OVER HERE.
AHEM.
I'M SURE YOU CAN FIND SOME TIME FOR HER TONIGHT.
...

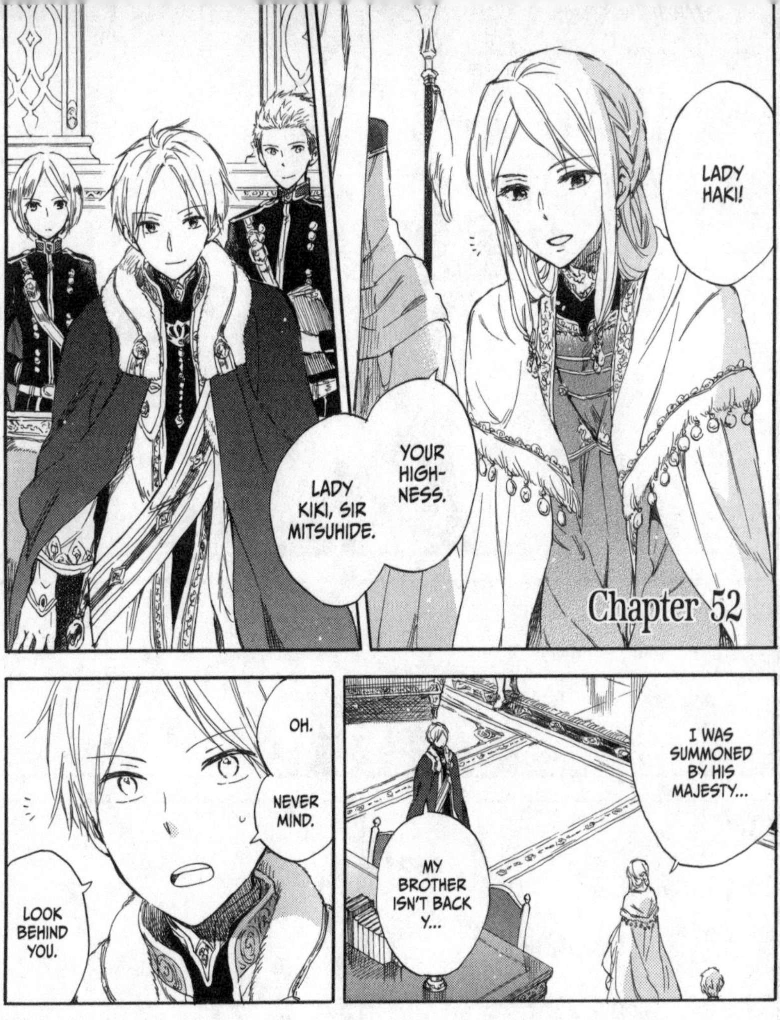
Chapter 52
LADY HAKI!
YOUR HIGHNESS.
LADY KIKI, SIR MITSUHIDE.
I WAS SUMMONED BY HIS MAJESTY...
MY BROTHER ISN'T BACK Y...
OH.
NEVER MIND.
LOOK BEHIND YOU.

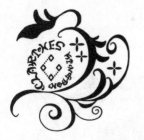

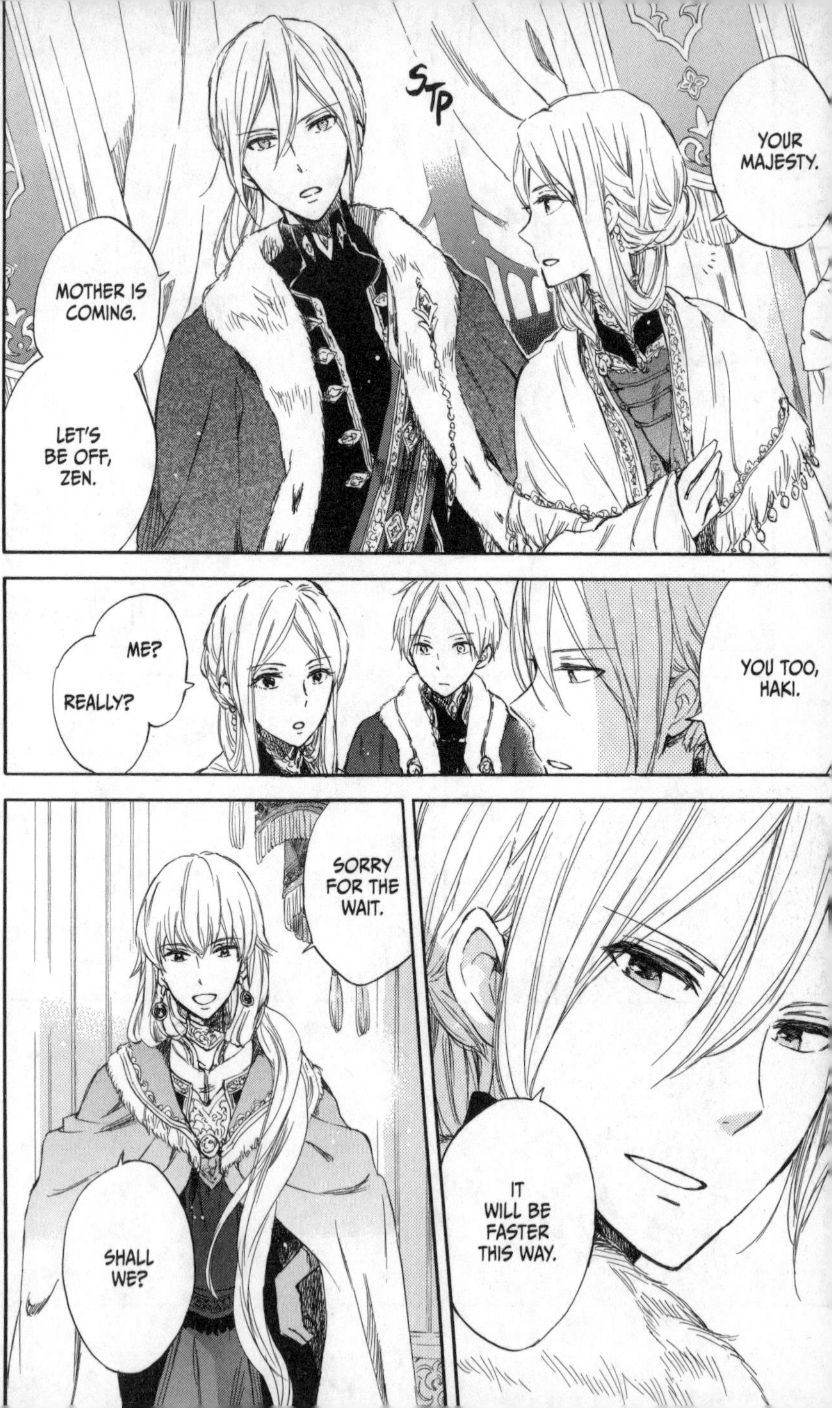
YOUR MAJESTY.
STP
MOTHER IS COMING.
LET'S BE OFF, ZEN.
YOU TOO, HAKI.
ME?
REALLY?
IT WILL BE FASTER THIS WAY.
SORRY FOR THE WAIT.
SHALL WE?

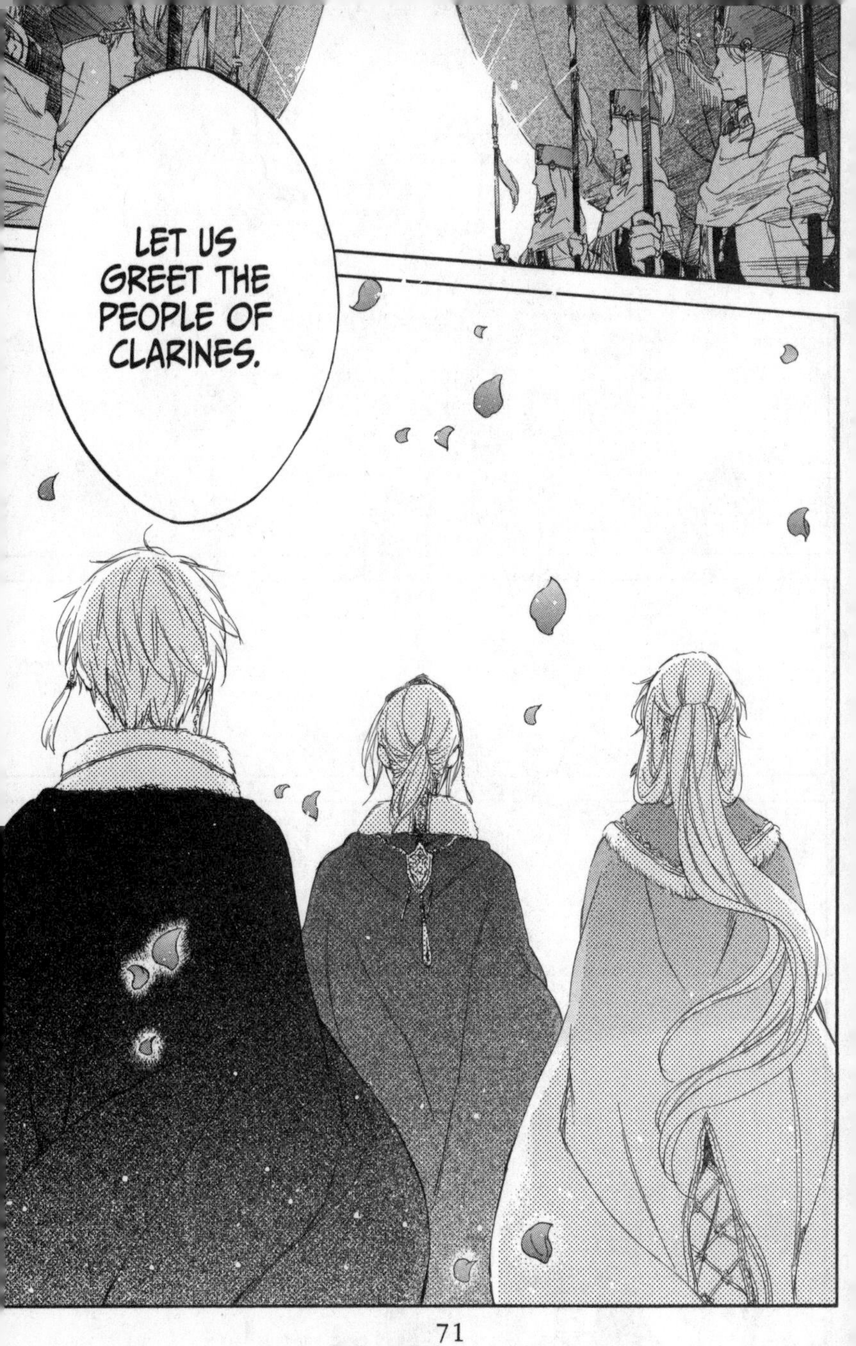
LET US GREET THE PEOPLE OF CLARINES.

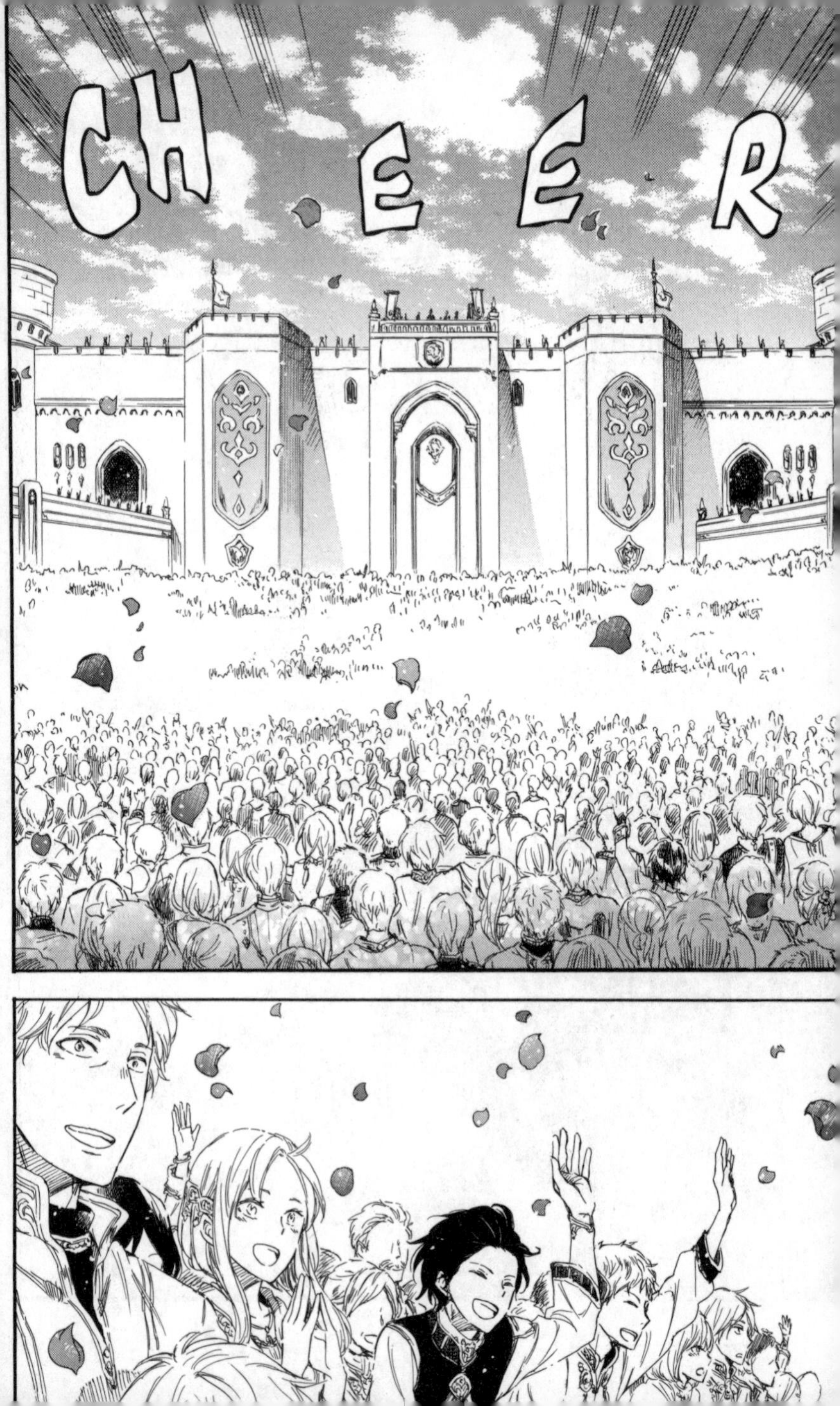
CHEER

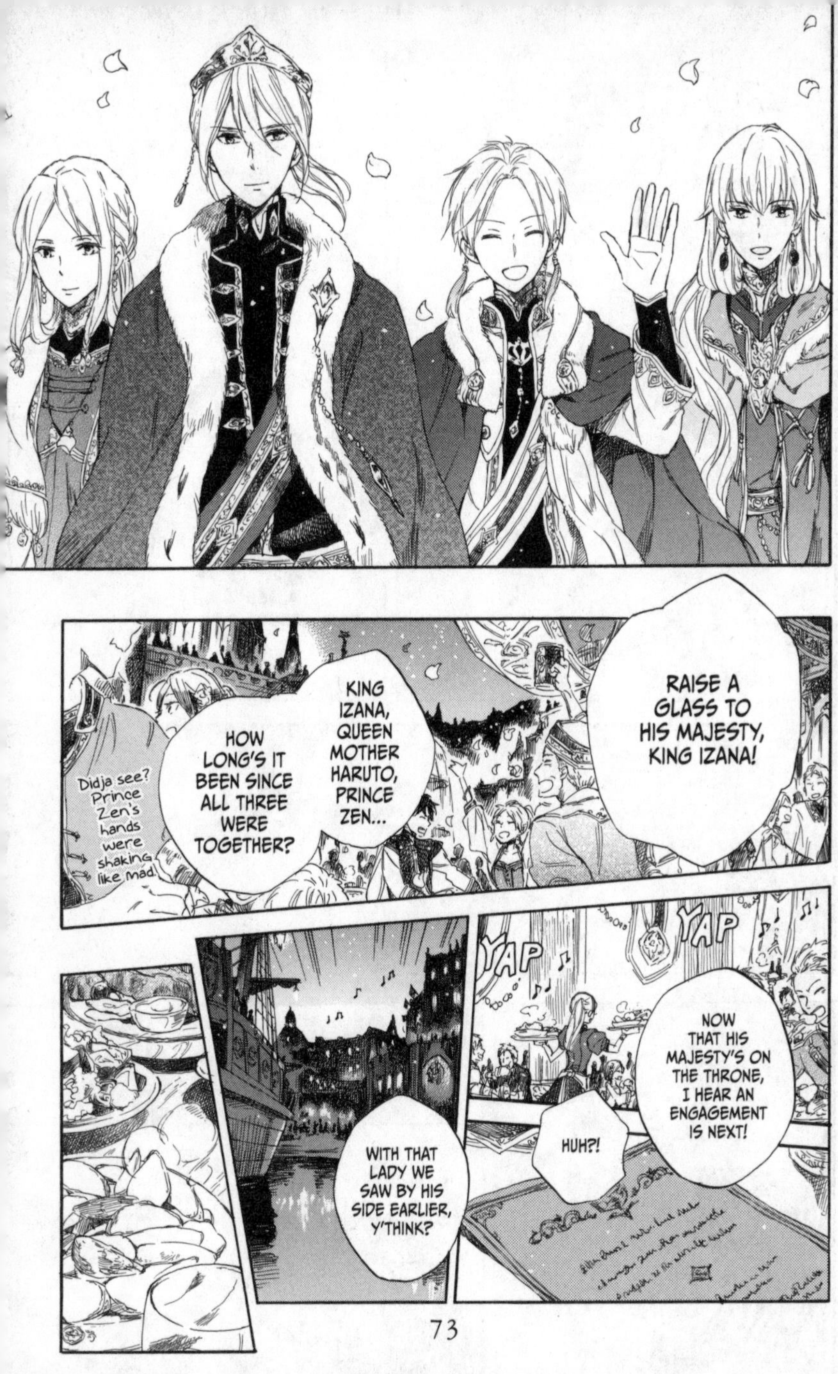
RAISE A GLASS TO HIS MAJESTY, KING IZANA!
KING IZANA, QUEEN MOTHER HARUTO, PRINCE ZEN...
HOW LONG'S IT BEEN SINCE ALL THREE WERE TOGETHER?
Didja see? Prince Zen's hands were shaking like mad.
YAP
YAP
NOW THAT HIS MAJESTY'S ON THE THRONE, I HEAR AN ENGAGEMENT IS NEXT!
HUH?!
WITH THAT LADY WE SAW BY HIS SIDE EARLIER, Y'THINK?

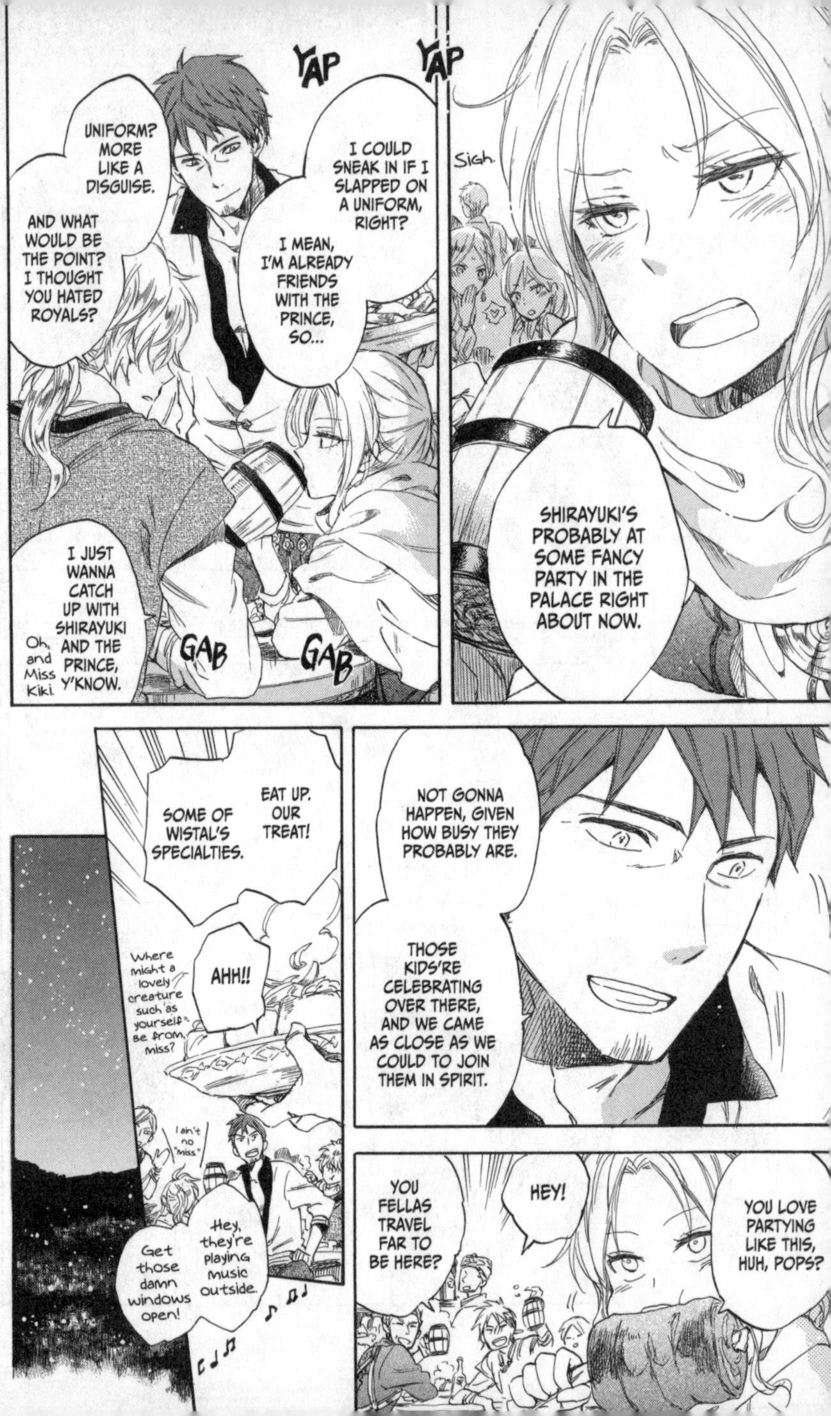
Sigh.
SHIRAYUKI'S PROBABLY AT SOME FANCY PARTY IN THE PALACE RIGHT ABOUT NOW.
YAP YAP
I COULD SNEAK IN IF I SLAPPED ON A UNIFORM, RIGHT?
I MEAN, I'M ALREADY FRIENDS WITH THE PRINCE, SO...
UNIFORM? MORE LIKE A DISGUISE.
AND WHAT WOULD BE THE POINT? I THOUGHT YOU HATED ROYALS?
I JUST WANNA CATCH UP WITH SHIRAYUKI AND THE PRINCE, Y'KNOW.
Oh, and Miss Kiki.
GAB GAB
NOT GONNA HAPPEN, GIVEN HOW BUSY THEY PROBABLY ARE.
THOSE KIDS'RE CELEBRATING OVER THERE, AND WE CAME AS CLOSE AS WE COULD TO JOIN THEM IN SPIRIT.
YOU LOVE PARTYING LIKE THIS, HUH, POPS?
HEY!
YOU FELLAS TRAVEL FAR TO BE HERE?
EAT UP. OUR TREAT!
SOME OF WISTAL'S SPECIALTIES.
AHH!!
Where might a lovely creature such as yourself be from, miss?
I ain't no "miss."
Hey, they're playing music outside.
Get those damn windows open!

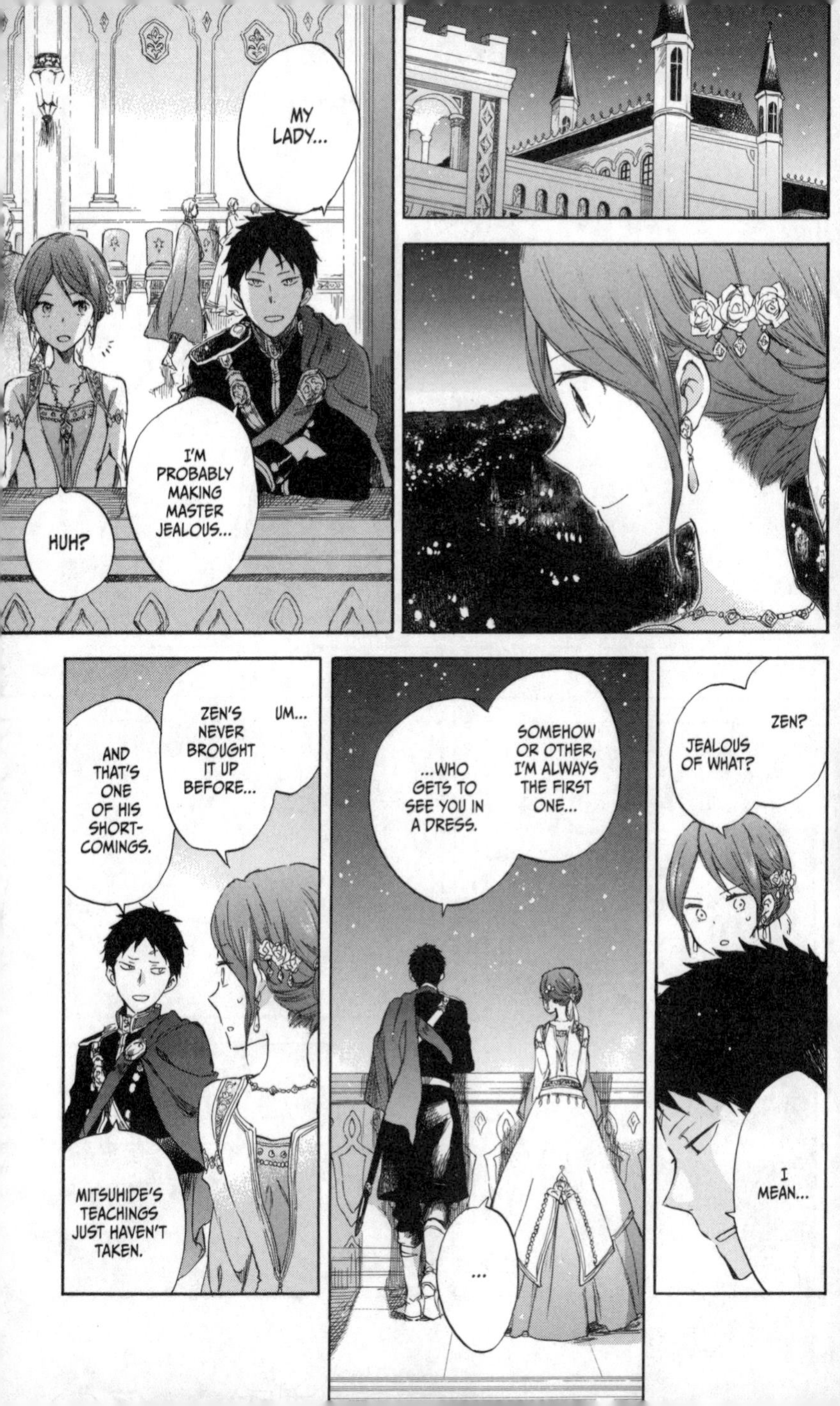
MY LADY...
I'M PROBABLY MAKING MASTER JEALOUS...
HUH?
ZEN?
JEALOUS OF WHAT?
I MEAN...
SOMEHOW OR OTHER, I'M ALWAYS THE FIRST ONE...
...WHO GETS TO SEE YOU IN A DRESS.
...
UM...
ZEN'S NEVER BROUGHT IT UP BEFORE...
AND THAT'S ONE OF HIS SHORT-COMINGS.
MITSUHIDE'S TEACHINGS JUST HAVEN'T TAKEN.

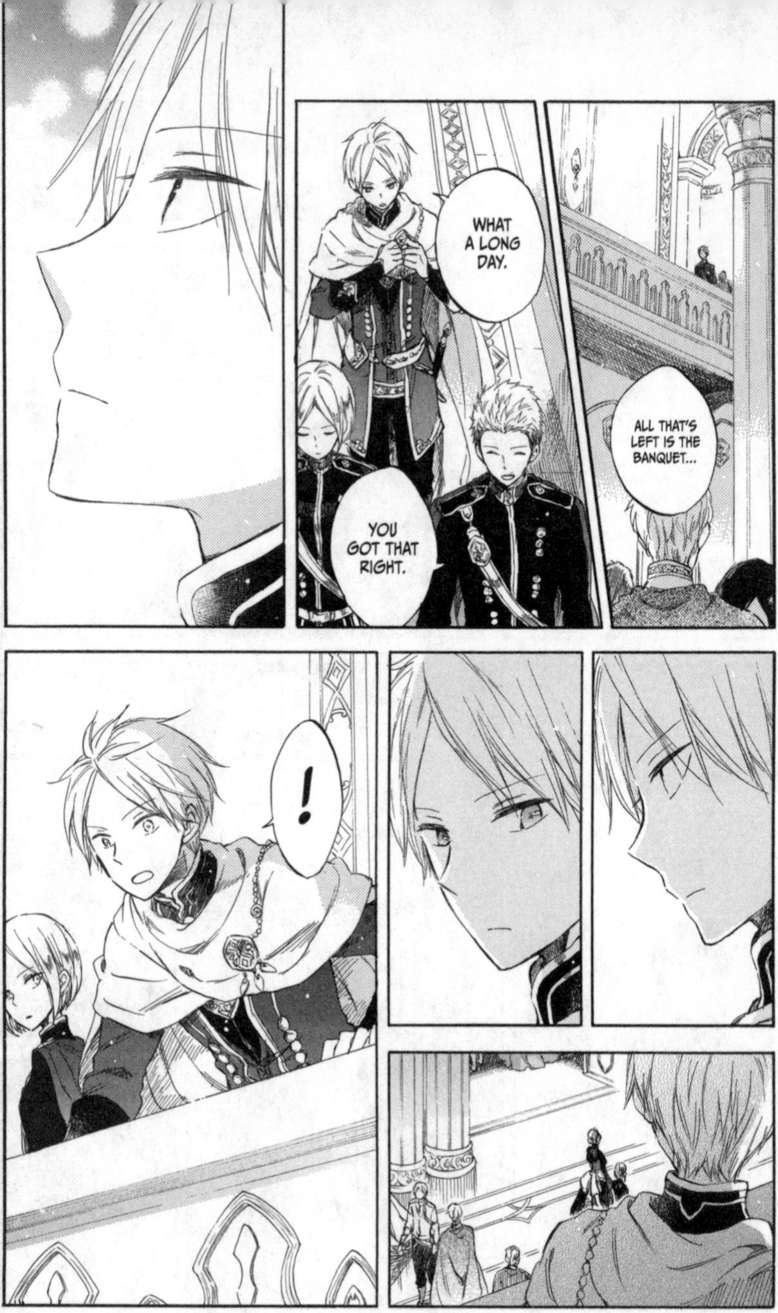
ALL THAT'S LEFT IS THE BANQUET...
WHAT A LONG DAY.
YOU GOT THAT RIGHT.
!

What is it?

MY LADY?

I THOUGHT I JUST HEARD...

...A "PLINK."

AH.

AH.

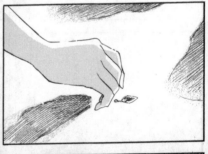

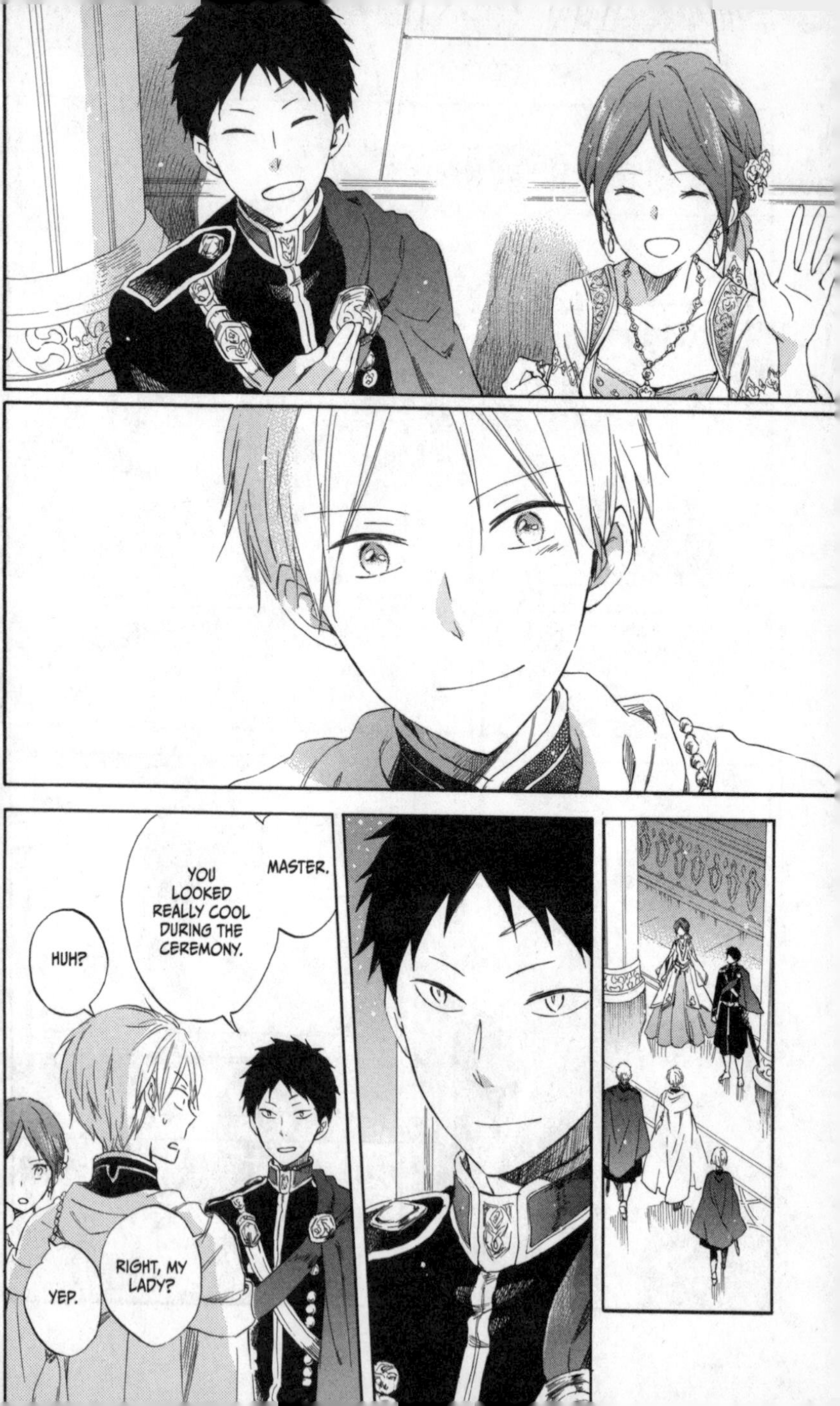
MASTER.
YOU LOOKED REALLY COOL DURING THE CEREMONY.
HUH?
RIGHT, MY LADY?
YEP.

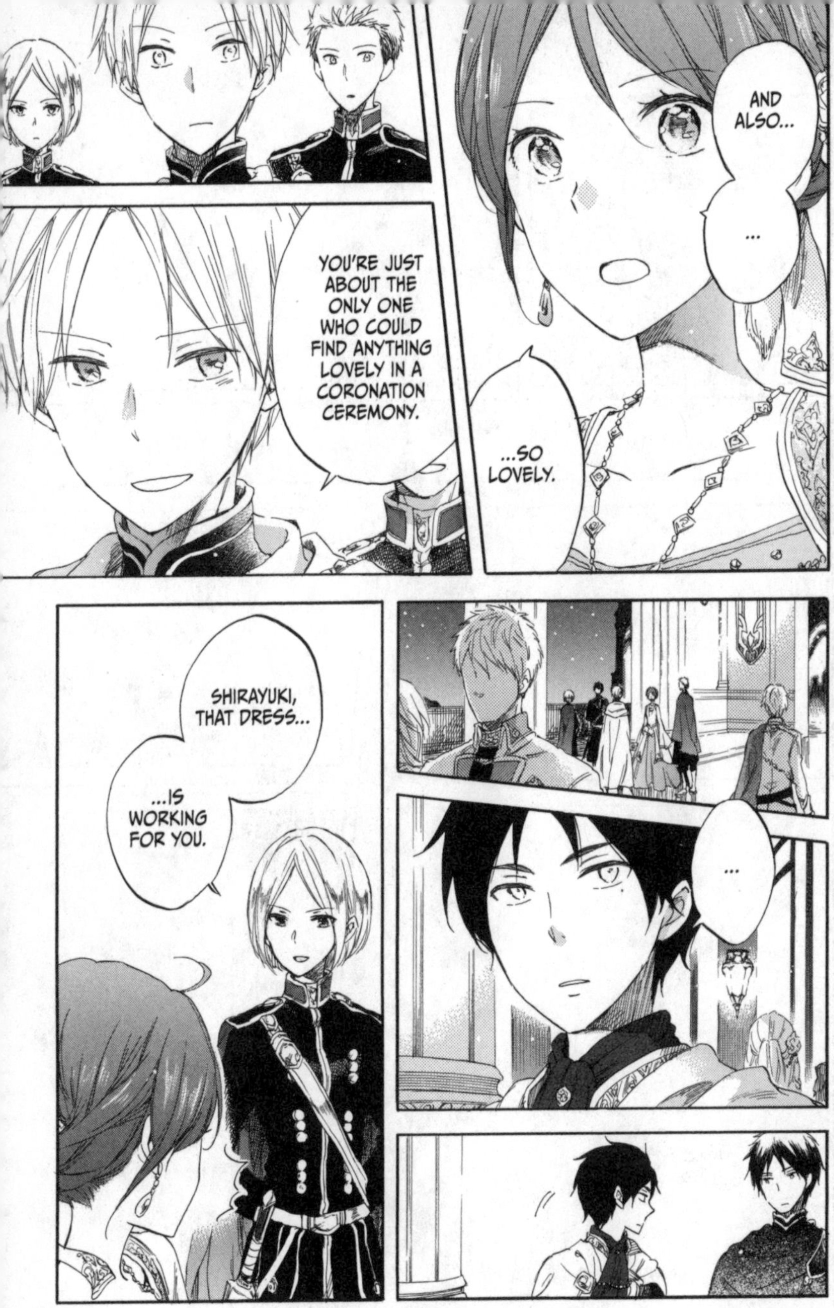
AND ALSO...
...
...SO LOVELY.
YOU'RE JUST ABOUT THE ONLY ONE WHO COULD FIND ANYTHING LOVELY IN A CORONATION CEREMONY.
...
SHIRAYUKI, THAT DRESS...
...IS WORKING FOR YOU.

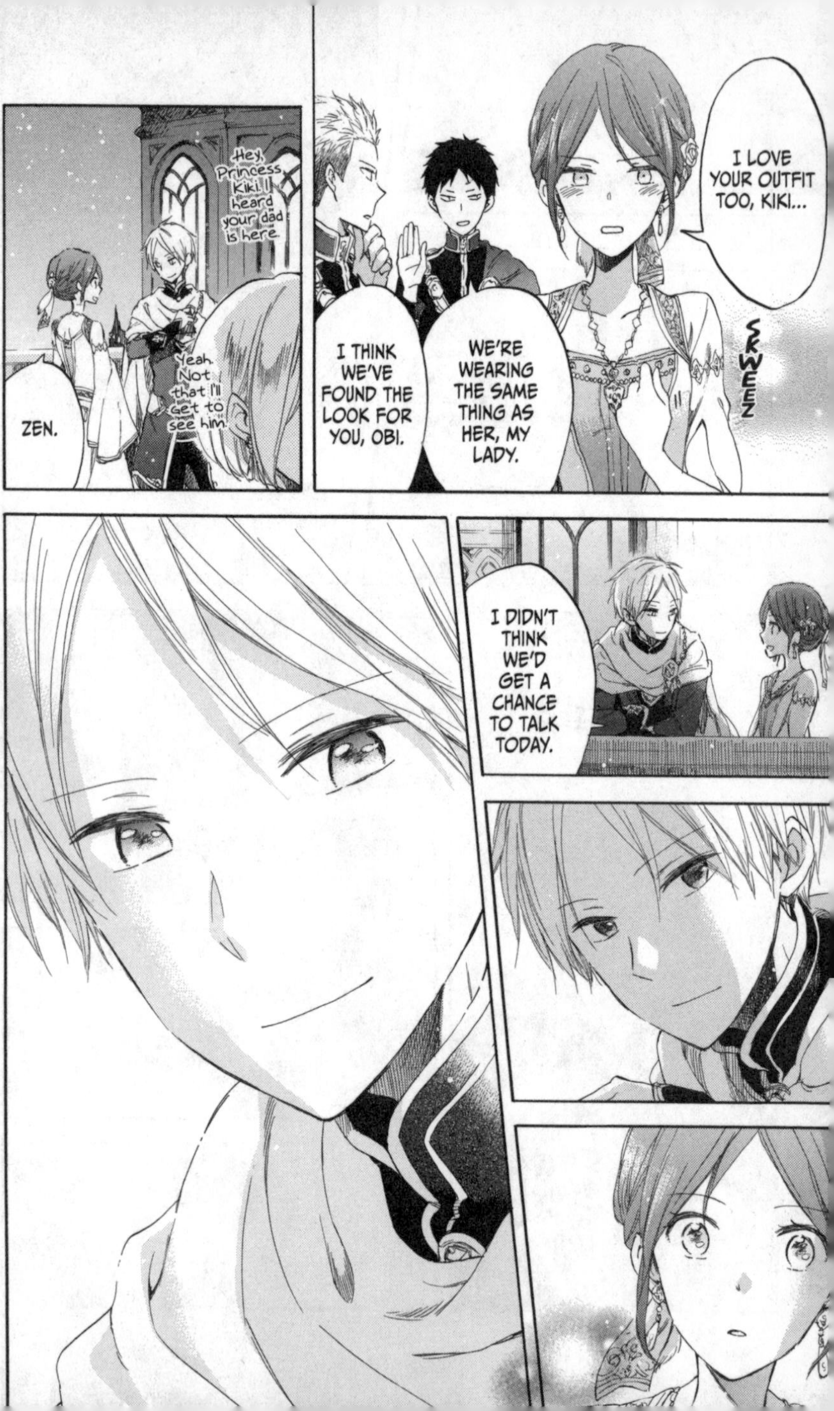
I LOVE YOUR OUTFIT TOO, KIKI...
SKWEEZ
WE'RE WEARING THE SAME THING AS HER, MY LADY.
I THINK WE'VE FOUND THE LOOK FOR YOU, OBI.
Hey, Princess, Kiki. I heard your dad is here.
Yeah. Not that I'll get to see him.
ZEN.
I DIDN'T THINK WE'D GET A CHANCE TO TALK TODAY.

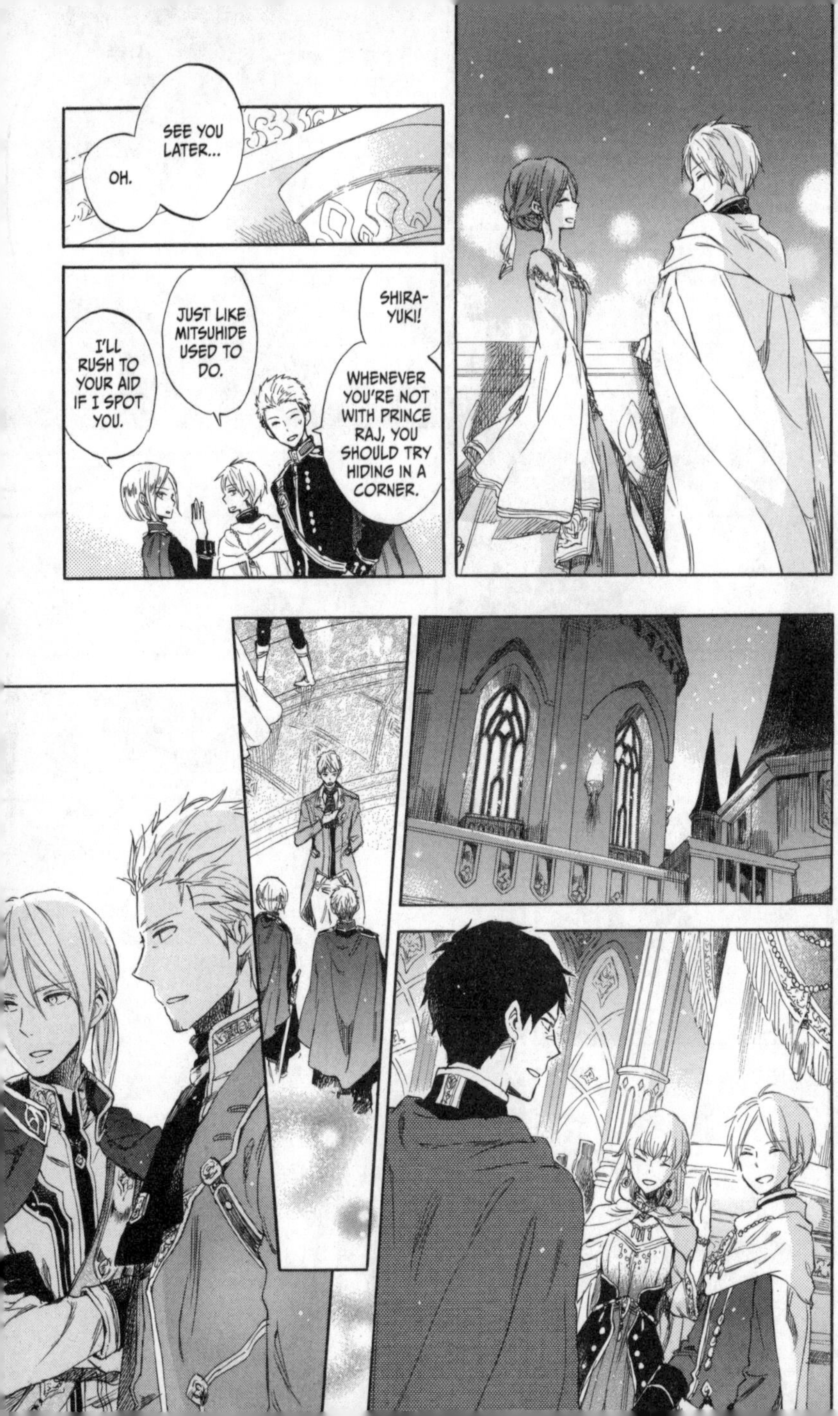
SEE YOU LATER...
OH.
SHIRA-YUKI!
WHENEVER YOU'RE NOT WITH PRINCE RAJ, YOU SHOULD TRY HIDING IN A CORNER.
JUST LIKE MITSUHIDE USED TO DO.
I'LL RUSH TO YOUR AID IF I SPOT YOU.

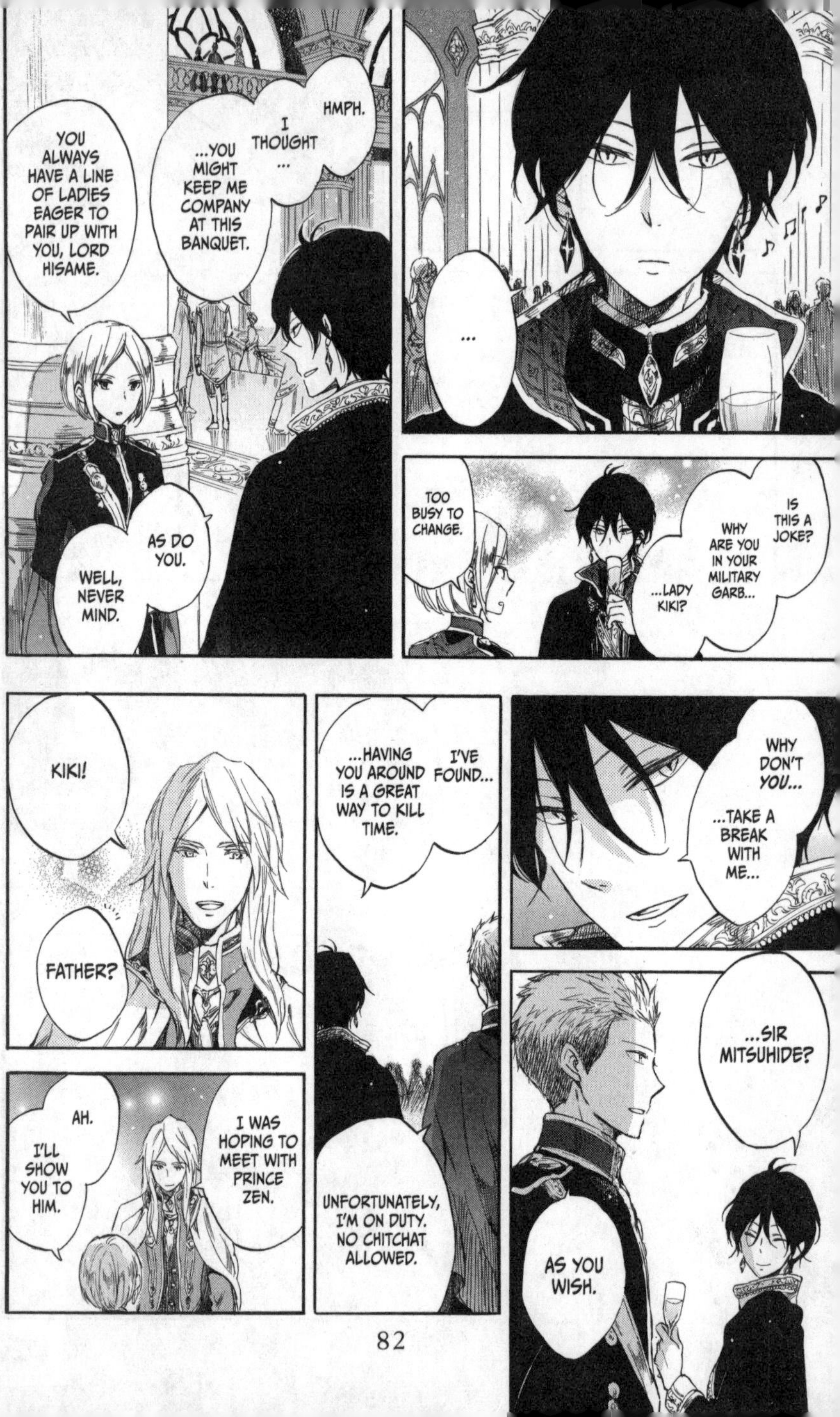
...
IS THIS A JOKE?
WHY ARE YOU IN YOUR MILITARY GARB...
...LADY KIKI?
TOO BUSY TO CHANGE.
HMPH.
I THOUGHT...
...YOU MIGHT KEEP ME COMPANY AT THIS BANQUET.
YOU ALWAYS HAVE A LINE OF LADIES EAGER TO PAIR UP WITH YOU, LORD HISAME.
AS DO YOU.
WELL, NEVER MIND.
WHY DON'T YOU...
...TAKE A BREAK WITH ME...
...SIR MITSUHIDE?
AS YOU WISH.
I'VE FOUND...
...HAVING YOU AROUND IS A GREAT WAY TO KILL TIME.
UNFORTUNATELY, I'M ON DUTY. NO CHITCHAT ALLOWED.
KIKI!
FATHER?
I WAS HOPING TO MEET WITH PRINCE ZEN.
AH.
I'LL SHOW YOU TO HIM.

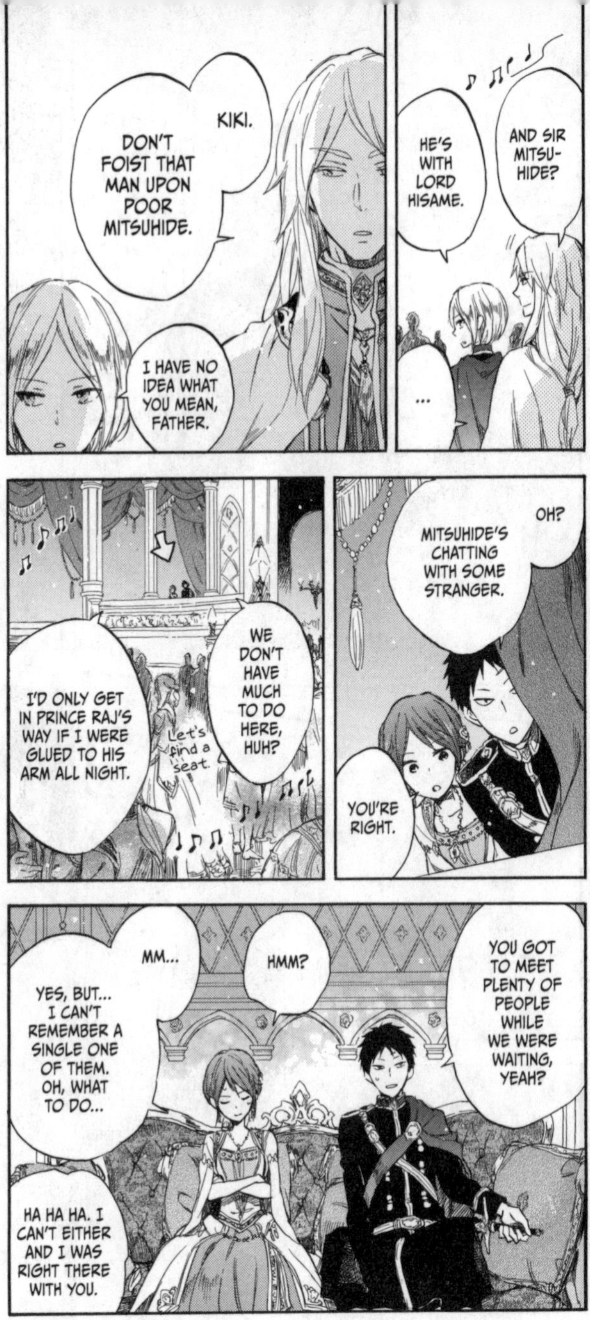
AND SIR MITSUHIDE?
HE'S WITH LORD HISAME.
...
KIKI.
DON'T FOIST THAT MAN UPON POOR MITSUHIDE.
I HAVE NO IDEA WHAT YOU MEAN, FATHER.
OH?
MITSUHIDE'S CHATTING WITH SOME STRANGER.
YOU'RE RIGHT.
WE DON'T HAVE MUCH TO DO HERE, HUH?
I'D ONLY GET IN PRINCE RAJ'S WAY IF I WERE GLUED TO HIS ARM ALL NIGHT.
Let's find a seat.
YOU GOT TO MEET PLENTY OF PEOPLE WHILE WE WERE WAITING, YEAH?
HMM?
MM...
YES, BUT... I CAN'T REMEMBER A SINGLE ONE OF THEM. OH, WHAT TO DO...
HA HA HA. I CAN'T EITHER AND I WAS RIGHT THERE WITH YOU.

3

Writing about my travels is usually the easiest way to fill these sidebars, but I haven't gone on any trips recently. What do I do now? Let's see...

I could talk about how I ate some pumpkin tempura at an udon restaurant the other day. And how it was so incredibly delicious, it made all the other pumpkin tempura I've ever had seem flavorless by comparison... Should I go with that story...?

The tempura dipping sauce was also yummy!

I'll just stick to talking about the chapters in this volume!

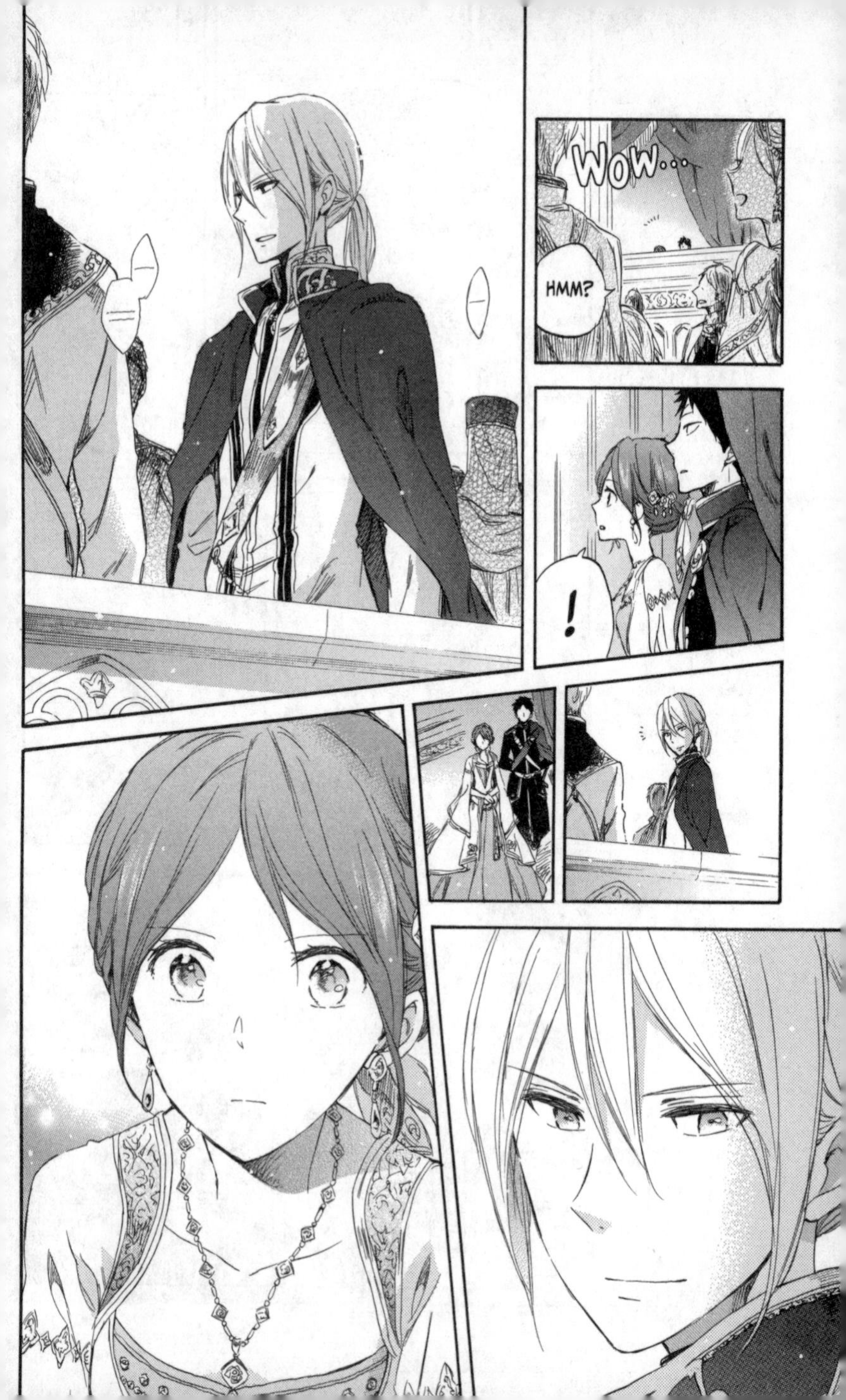
WOW...
HMM?
!

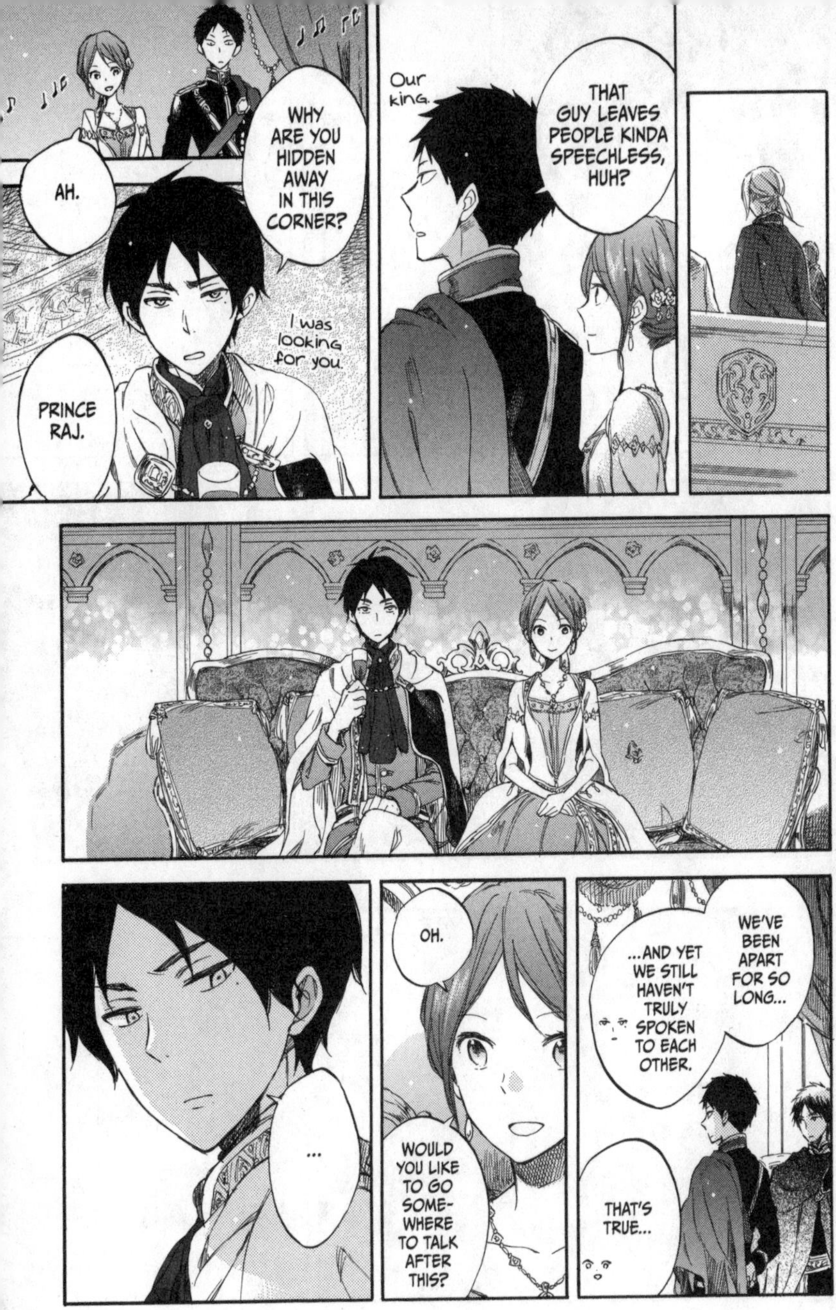
THAT GUY LEAVES PEOPLE KINDA SPEECHLESS, HUH?
Our king.
WHY ARE YOU HIDDEN AWAY IN THIS CORNER?
AH.
I was looking for you.
PRINCE RAJ.
WE'VE BEEN APART FOR SO LONG...
...AND YET WE STILL HAVEN'T TRULY SPOKEN TO EACH OTHER.
THAT'S TRUE...
OH.
WOULD YOU LIKE TO GO SOME-WHERE TO TALK AFTER THIS?
...

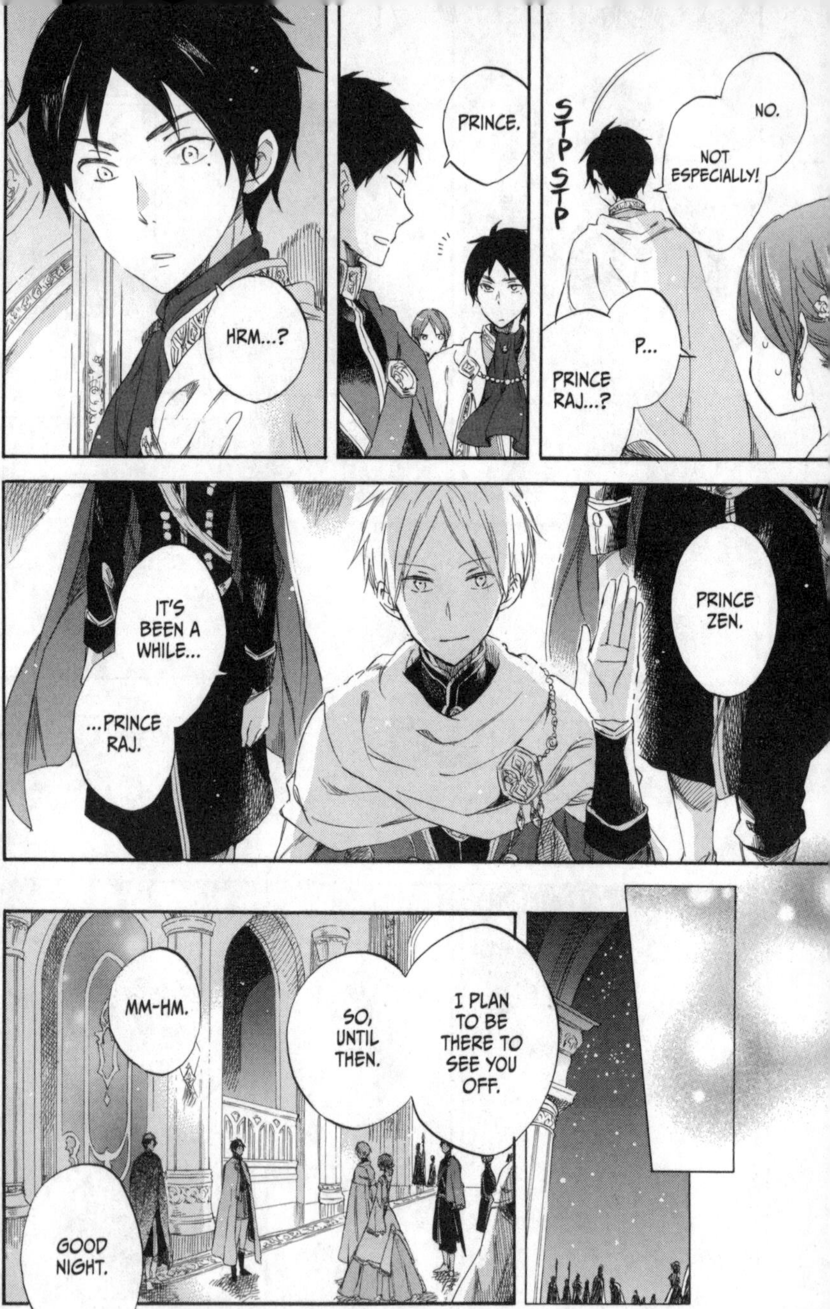
NO.
NOT ESPECIALLY!
STP STP
P... PRINCE RAJ...?
PRINCE.
HRM...?
PRINCE ZEN.
IT'S BEEN A WHILE...
...PRINCE RAJ.
I PLAN TO BE THERE TO SEE YOU OFF.
SO, UNTIL THEN.
MM-HM.
GOOD NIGHT.

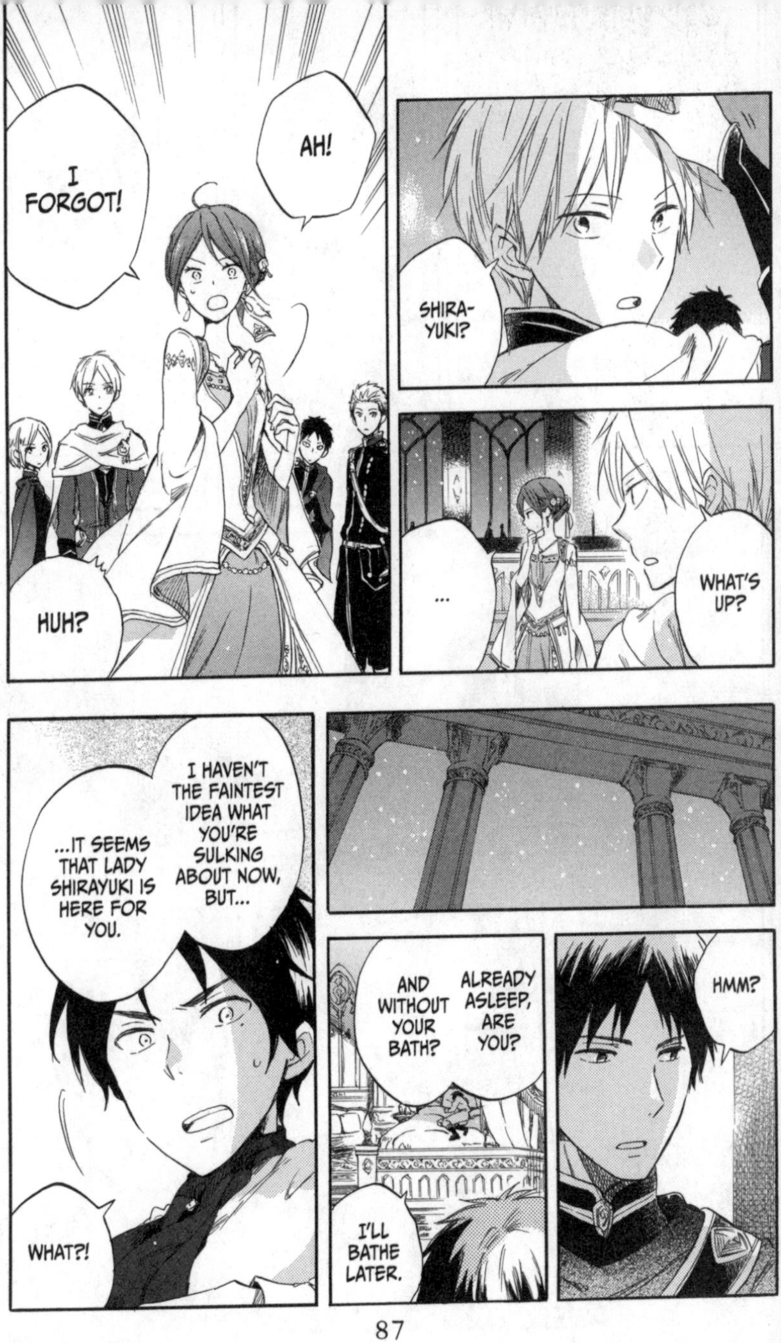
SHIRA-YUKI?
WHAT'S UP?
...
AH!
I FORGOT!
HUH?
HMM?
ALREADY ASLEEP, ARE YOU?
AND WITHOUT YOUR BATH?
I'LL BATHE LATER.
I HAVEN'T THE FAINTEST IDEA WHAT YOU'RE SULKING ABOUT NOW, BUT...
...IT SEEMS THAT LADY SHIRAYUKI IS HERE FOR YOU.
WHAT?!

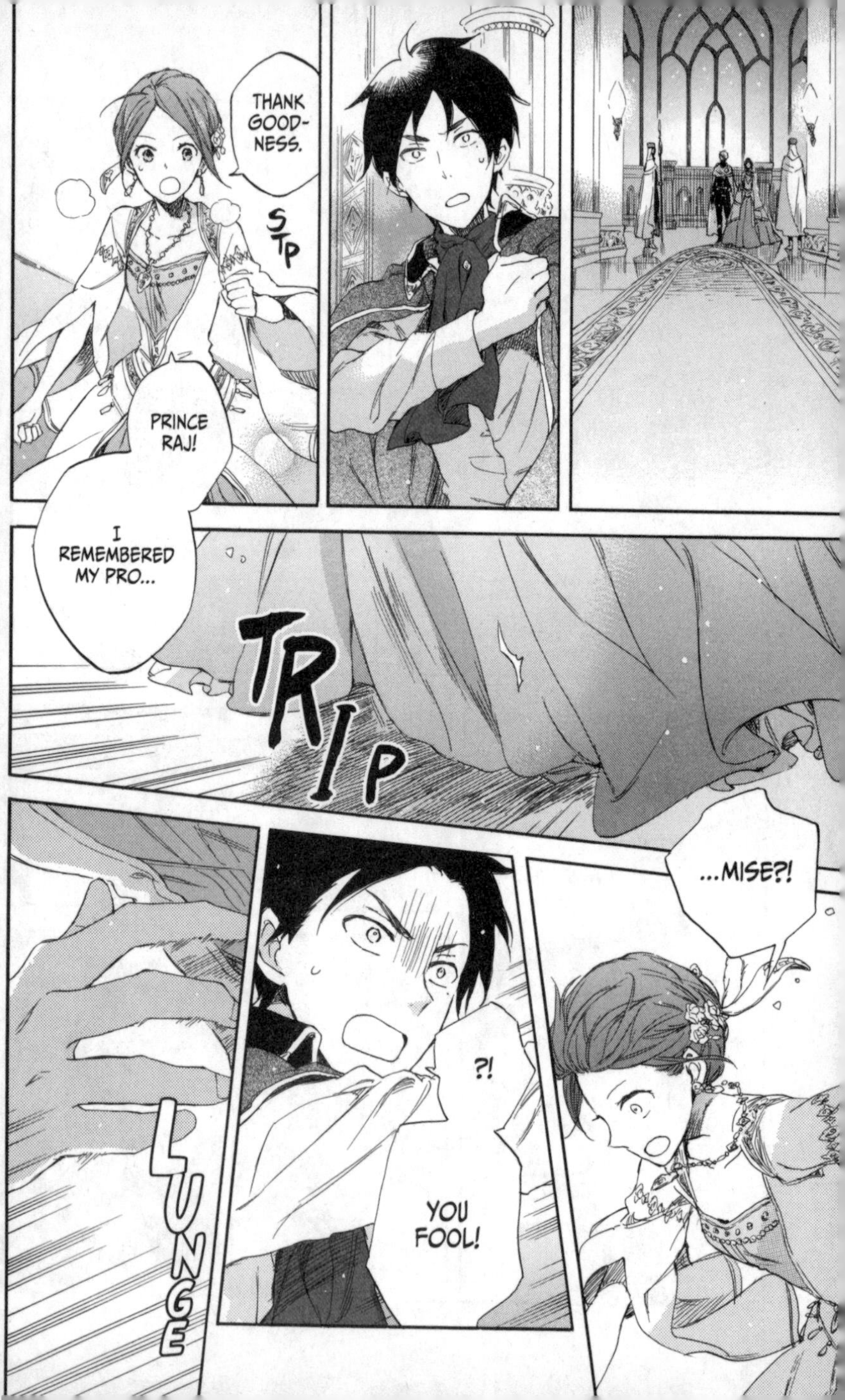
THANK GOODNESS.
STP
PRINCE RAJ!
I REMEMBERED MY PRO...
TRIP
...MISE?!
?!
YOU FOOL!
LUNGE

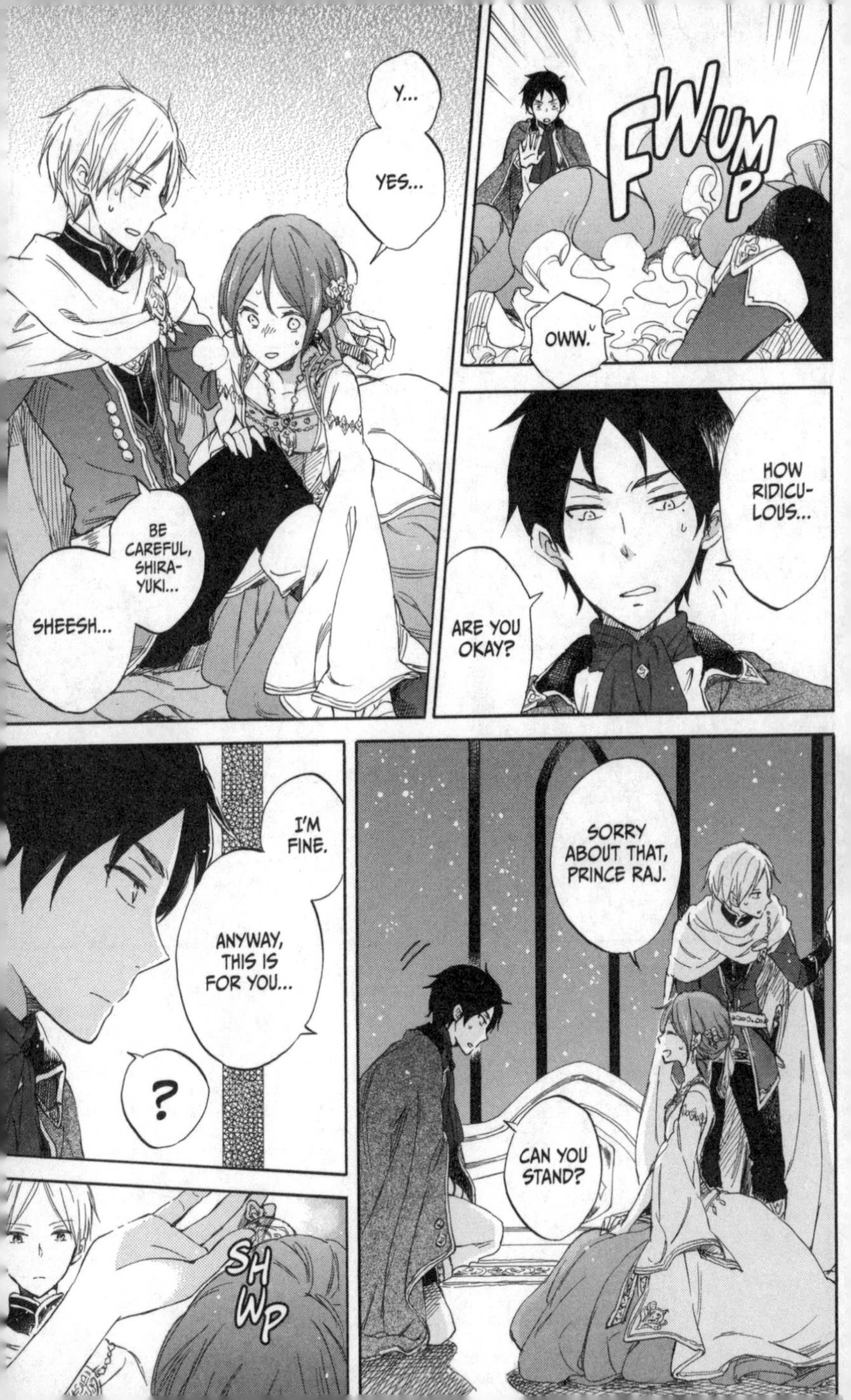
FWUMP
OWW.
HOW RIDICULOUS...
ARE YOU OKAY?
Y...
YES...
BE CAREFUL, SHIRAYUKI...
SHEESH...
SORRY ABOUT THAT, PRINCE RAJ.
CAN YOU STAND?
I'M FINE.
ANYWAY, THIS IS FOR YOU...
?
SHWP

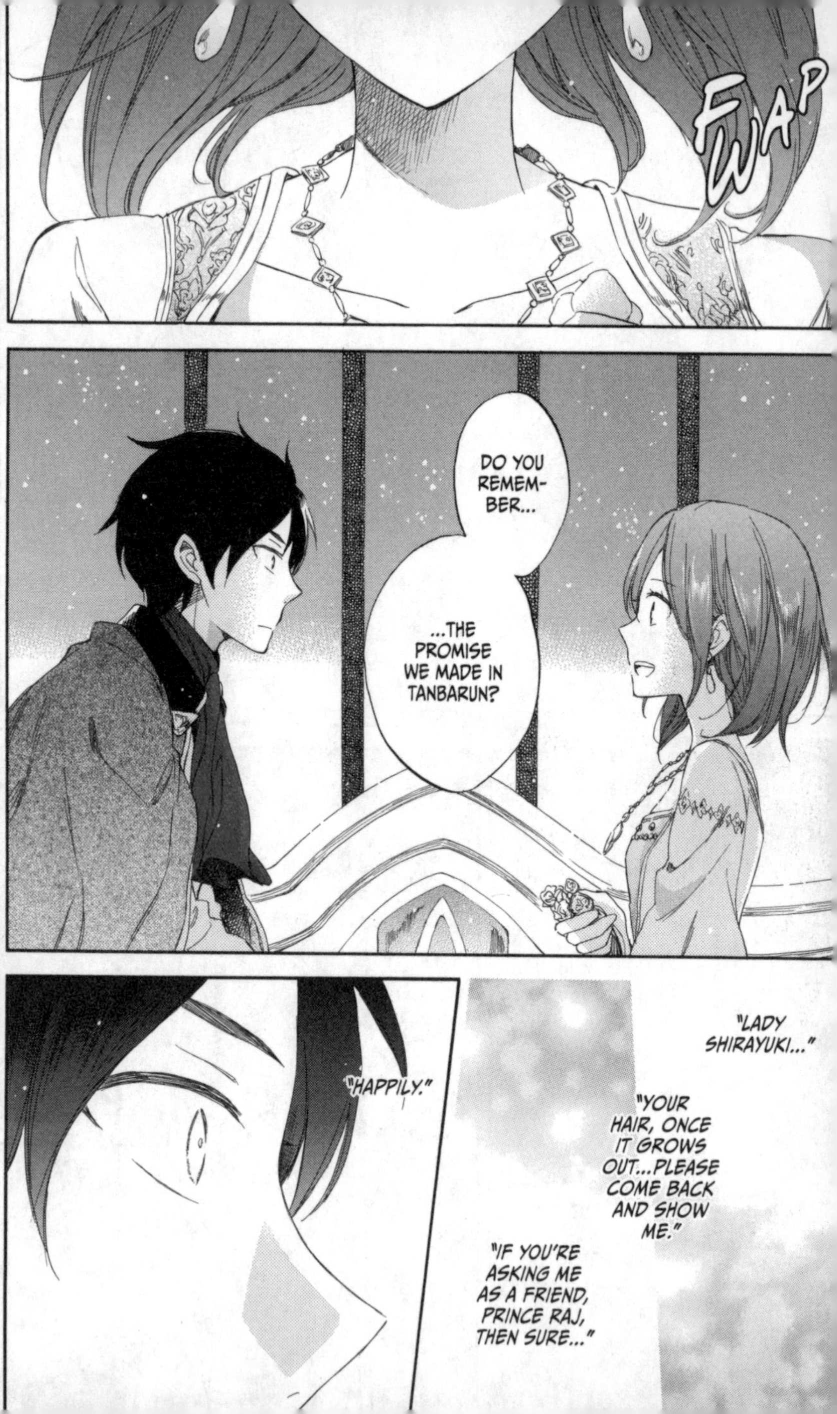
FWAP
DO YOU REMEMBER...
...THE PROMISE WE MADE IN TANBARUN?
"LADY SHIRAYUKI..."
"YOUR HAIR, ONCE IT GROWS OUT...PLEASE COME BACK AND SHOW ME."
"IF YOU'RE ASKING ME AS A FRIEND, PRINCE RAJ, THEN SURE..."
"HAPPILY."

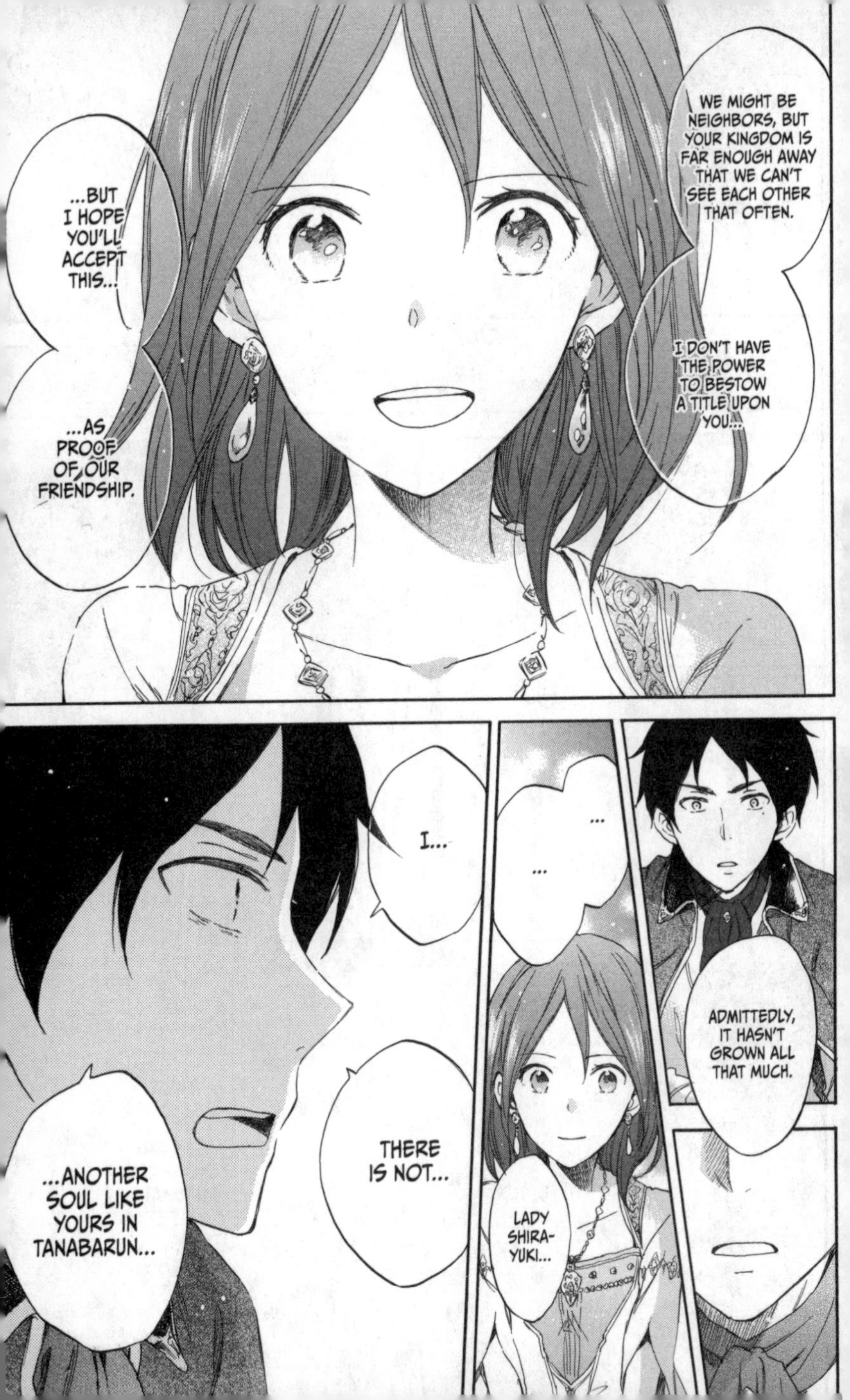
WE MIGHT BE NEIGHBORS, BUT YOUR KINGDOM IS FAR ENOUGH AWAY THAT WE CAN'T SEE EACH OTHER THAT OFTEN.
I DON'T HAVE THE POWER TO BESTOW A TITLE UPON YOU...
...BUT I HOPE YOU'LL ACCEPT THIS...
...AS PROOF OF OUR FRIENDSHIP.
ADMITTEDLY, IT HASN'T GROWN ALL THAT MUCH.
...
...
LADY SHIRA-YUKI...
I...
THERE IS NOT...
...ANOTHER SOUL LIKE YOURS IN TANABARUN...

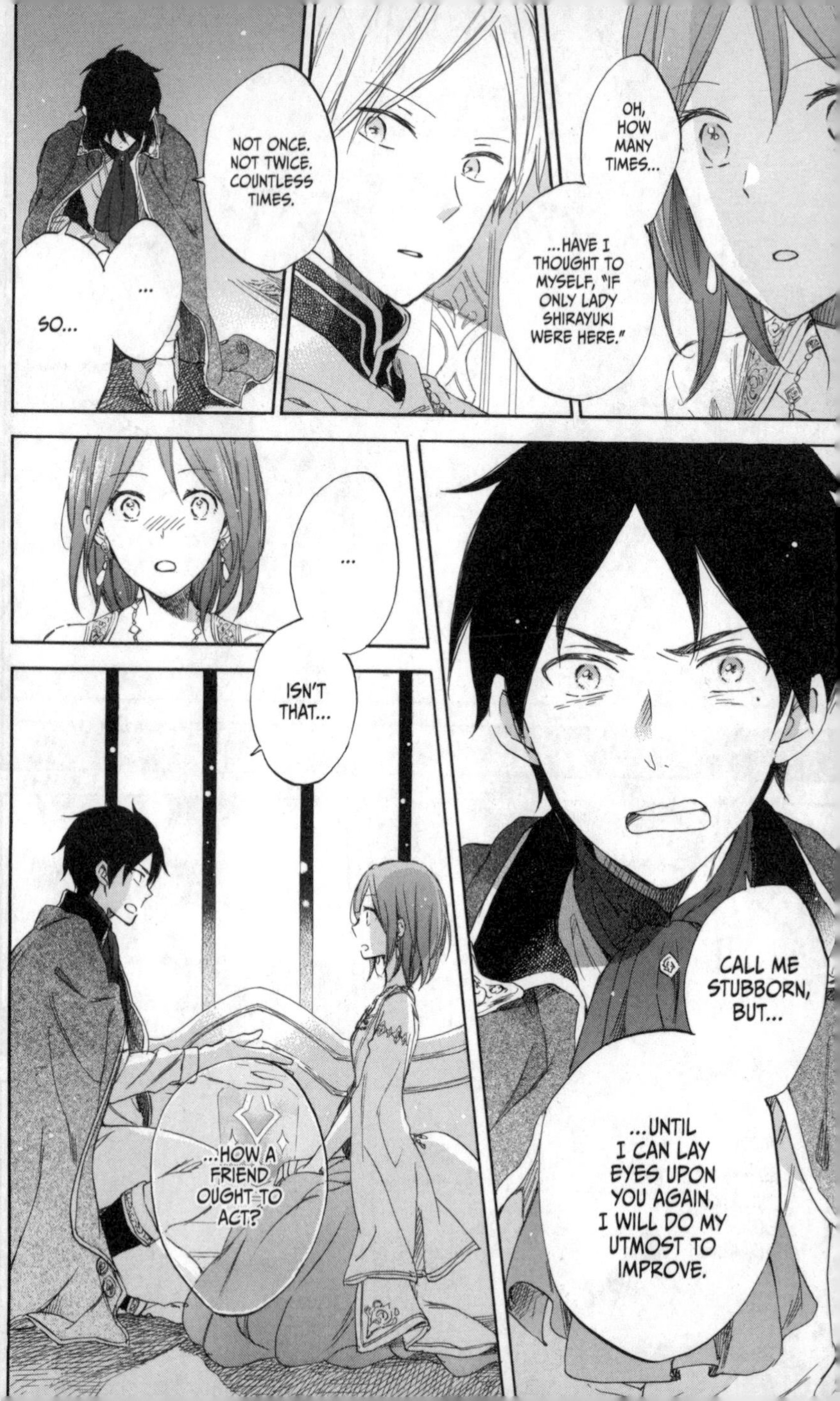
OH, HOW MANY TIMES...
...HAVE I THOUGHT TO MYSELF, "IF ONLY LADY SHIRAYUKI WERE HERE."
NOT ONCE. NOT TWICE. COUNTLESS TIMES.
...
SO...
CALL ME STUBBORN, BUT...
...UNTIL I CAN LAY EYES UPON YOU AGAIN, I WILL DO MY UTMOST TO IMPROVE.
...
ISN'T THAT...
...HOW A FRIEND OUGHT TO ACT?

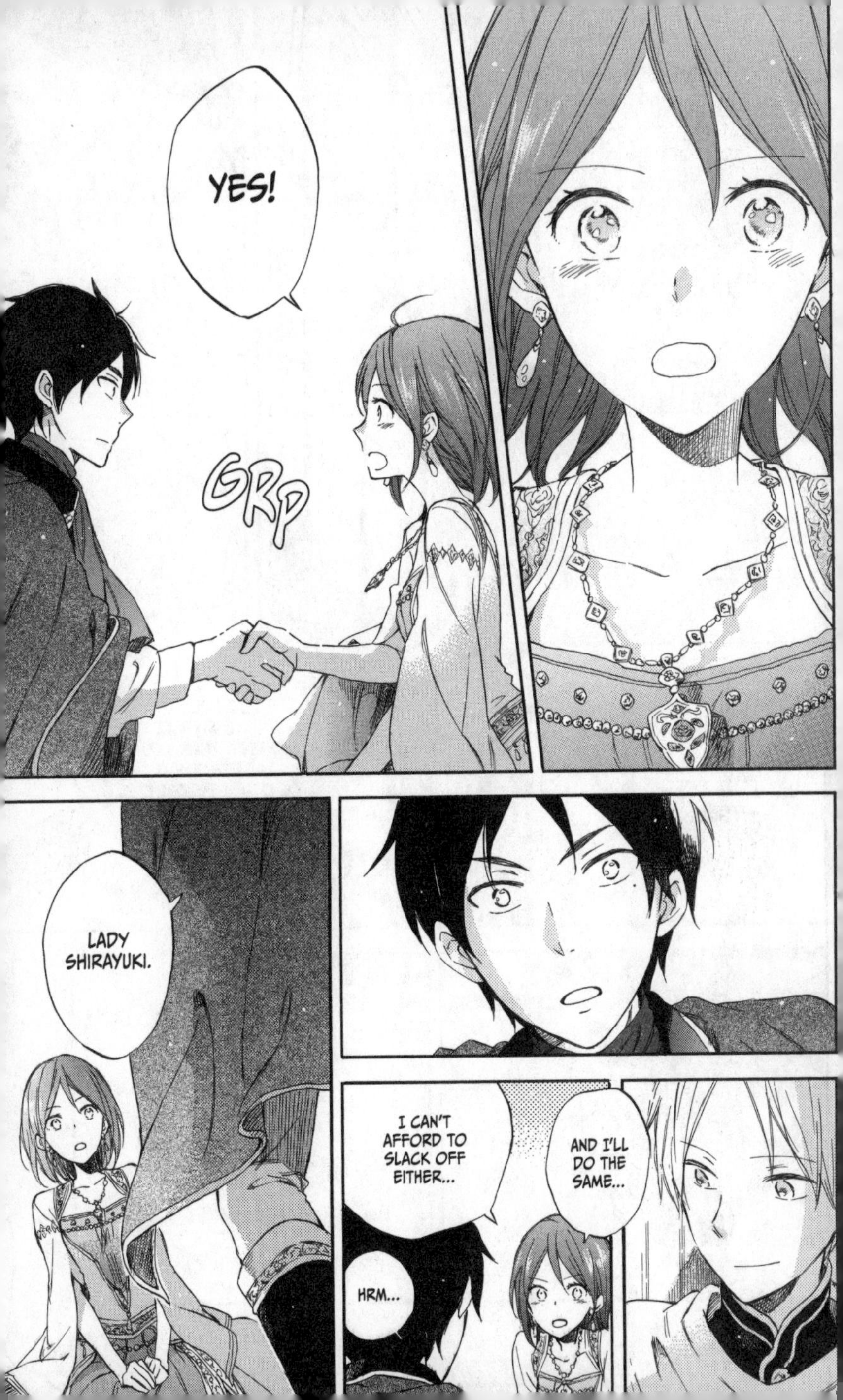
YES!
GRP
AND I'LL DO THE SAME...
I CAN'T AFFORD TO SLACK OFF EITHER...
HRM...
LADY SHIRAYUKI.

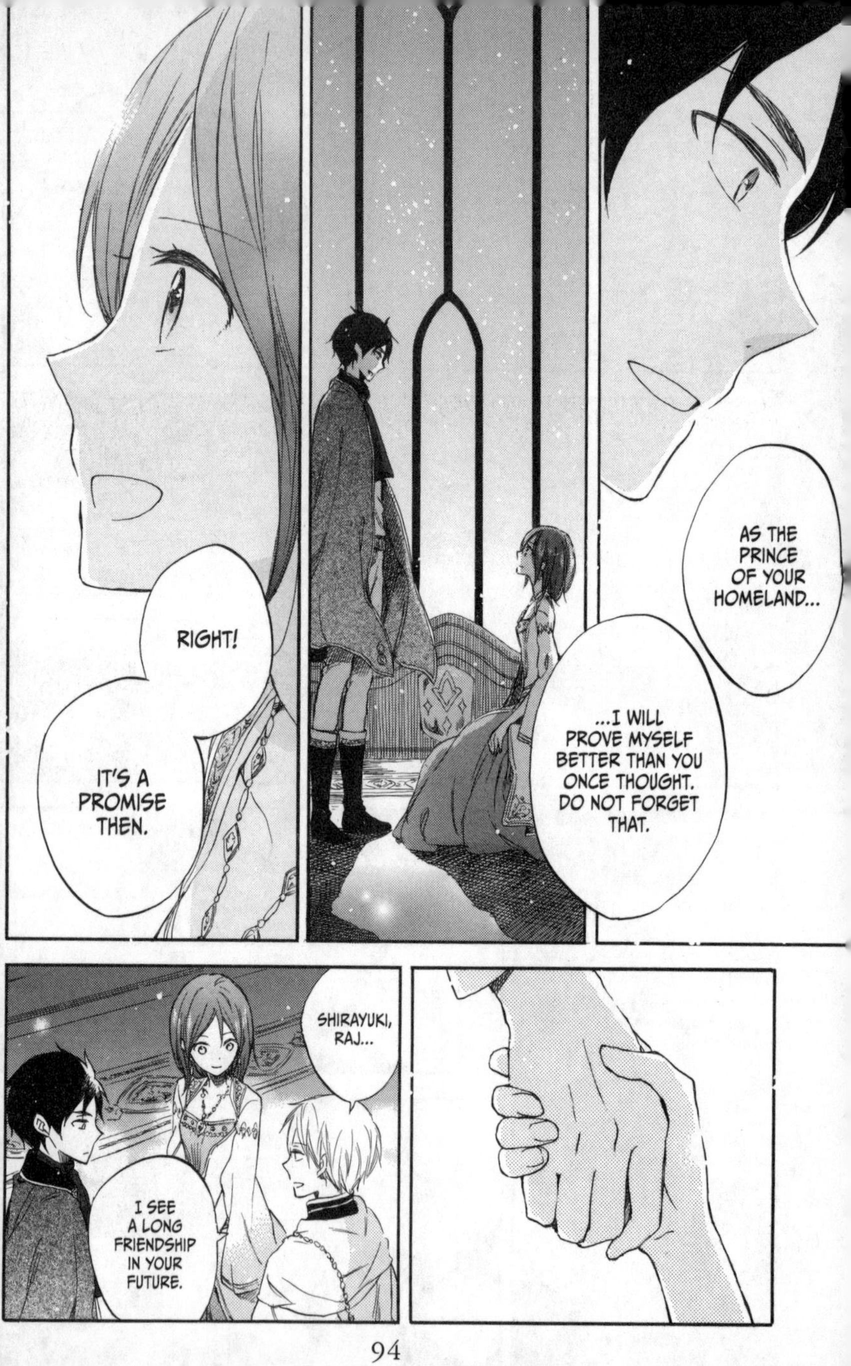
AS THE PRINCE OF YOUR HOMELAND...
...I WILL PROVE MYSELF BETTER THAN YOU ONCE THOUGHT. DO NOT FORGET THAT.
RIGHT!
IT'S A PROMISE THEN.
SHIRAYUKI, RAJ...
I SEE A LONG FRIENDSHIP IN YOUR FUTURE.

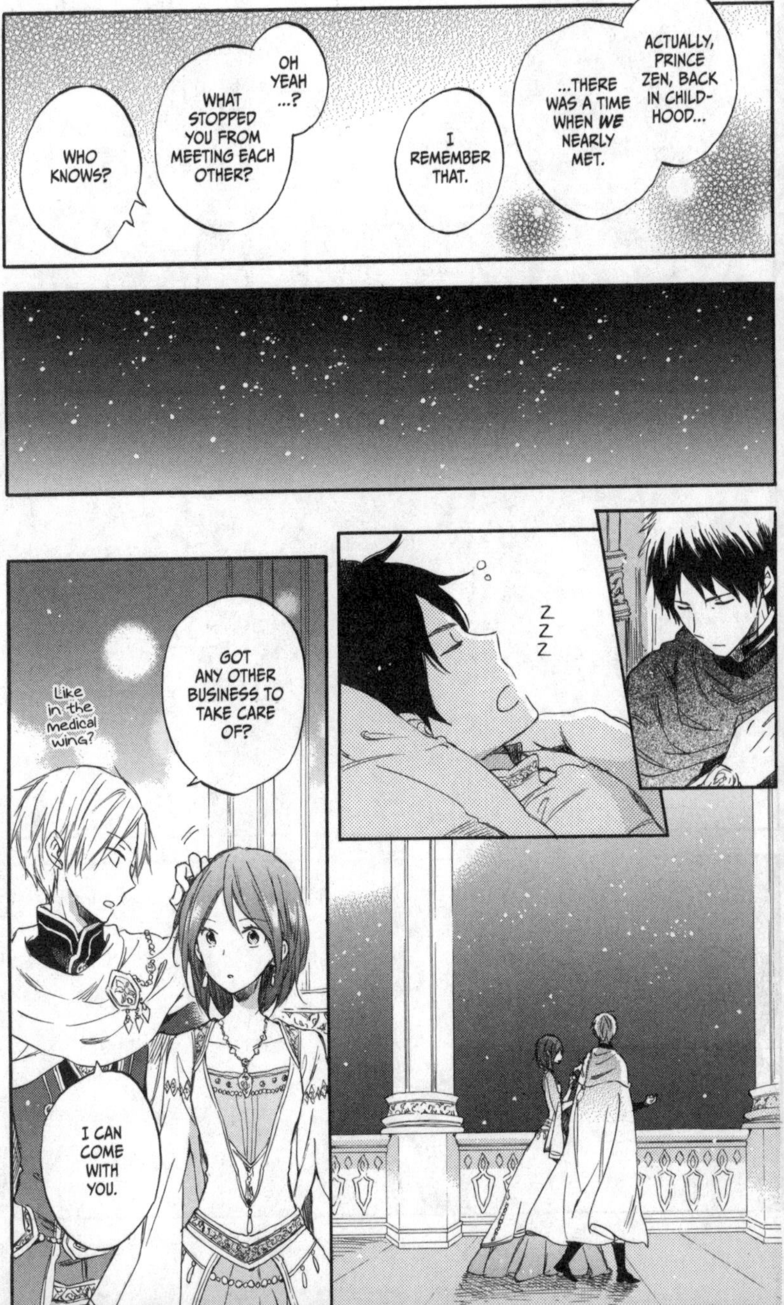
ACTUALLY, PRINCE ZEN, BACK IN CHILDHOOD...
...THERE WAS A TIME WHEN WE NEARLY MET.
I REMEMBER THAT.
OH YEAH ...?
WHAT STOPPED YOU FROM MEETING EACH OTHER?
WHO KNOWS?
ZZZ
GOT ANY OTHER BUSINESS TO TAKE CARE OF?
Like in the medical wing?
I CAN COME WITH YOU.

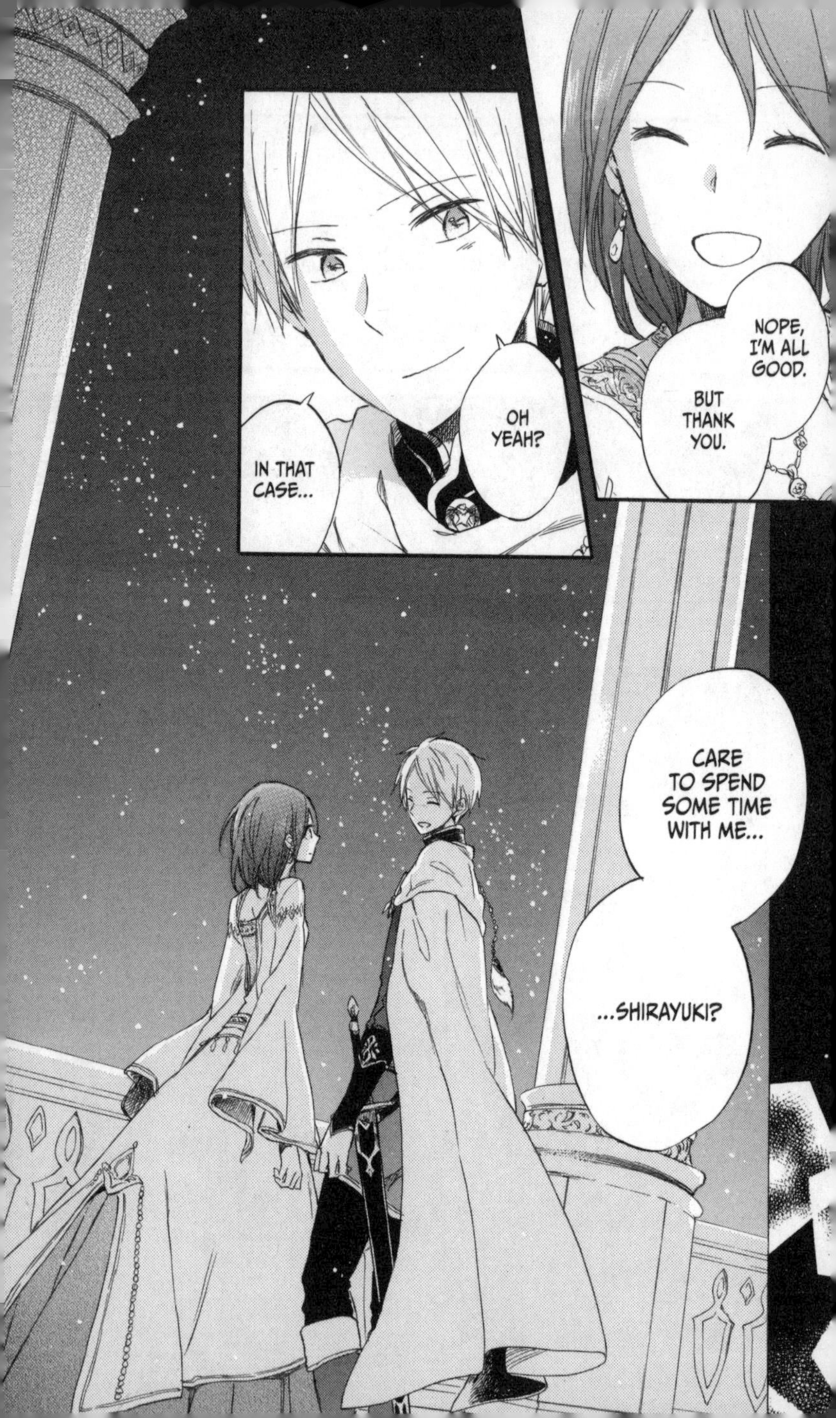
NOPE, I'M ALL GOOD.
BUT THANK YOU.
OH YEAH?
IN THAT CASE...
CARE TO SPEND SOME TIME WITH ME...
...SHIRAYUKI?

Chapter 53

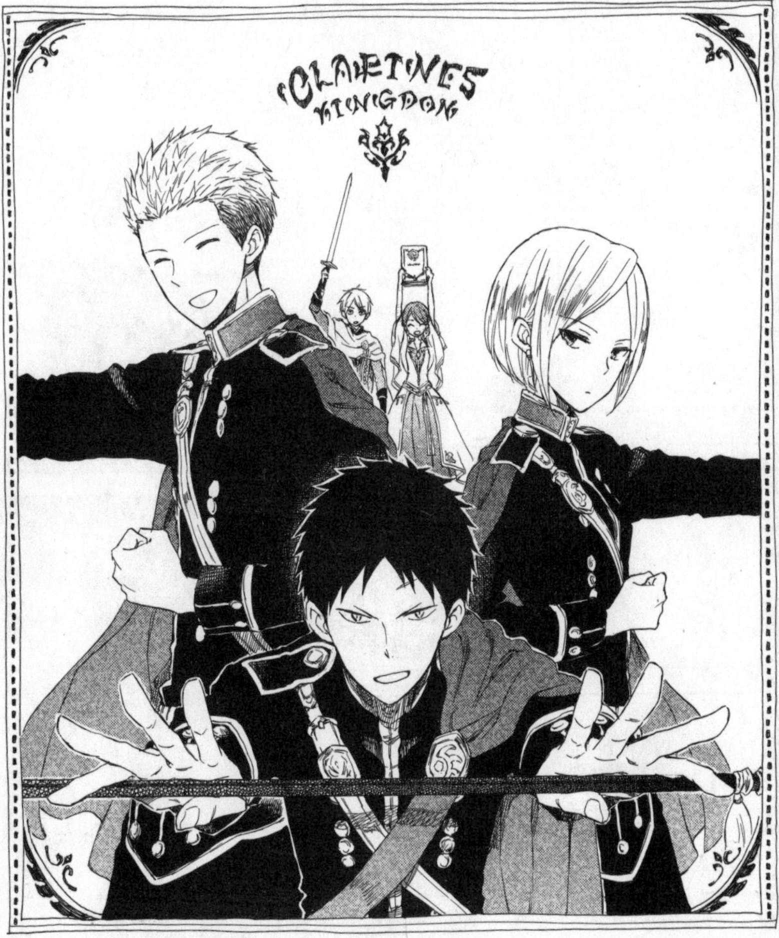
CLARINES
KINGDOM

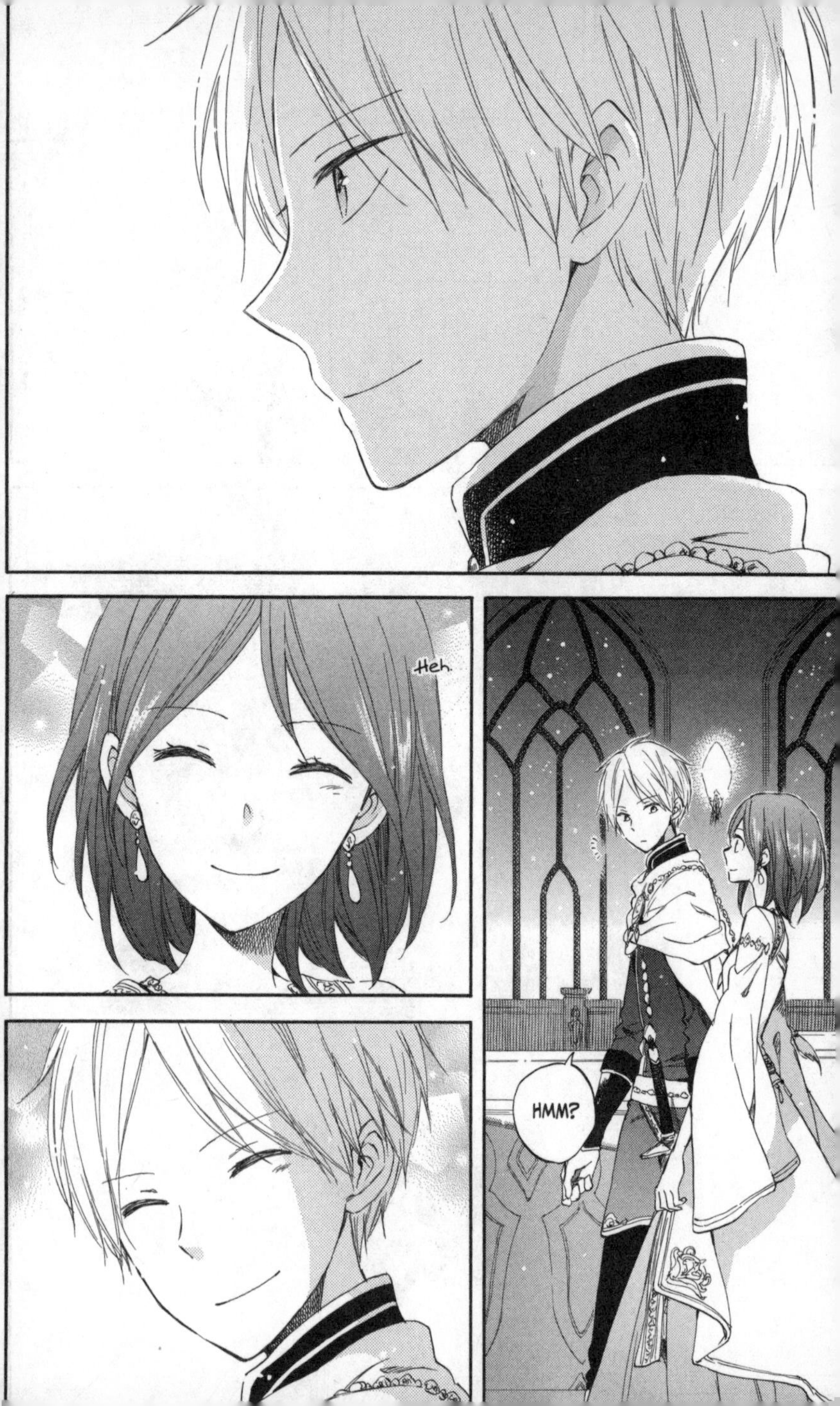
HMM?
Heh.

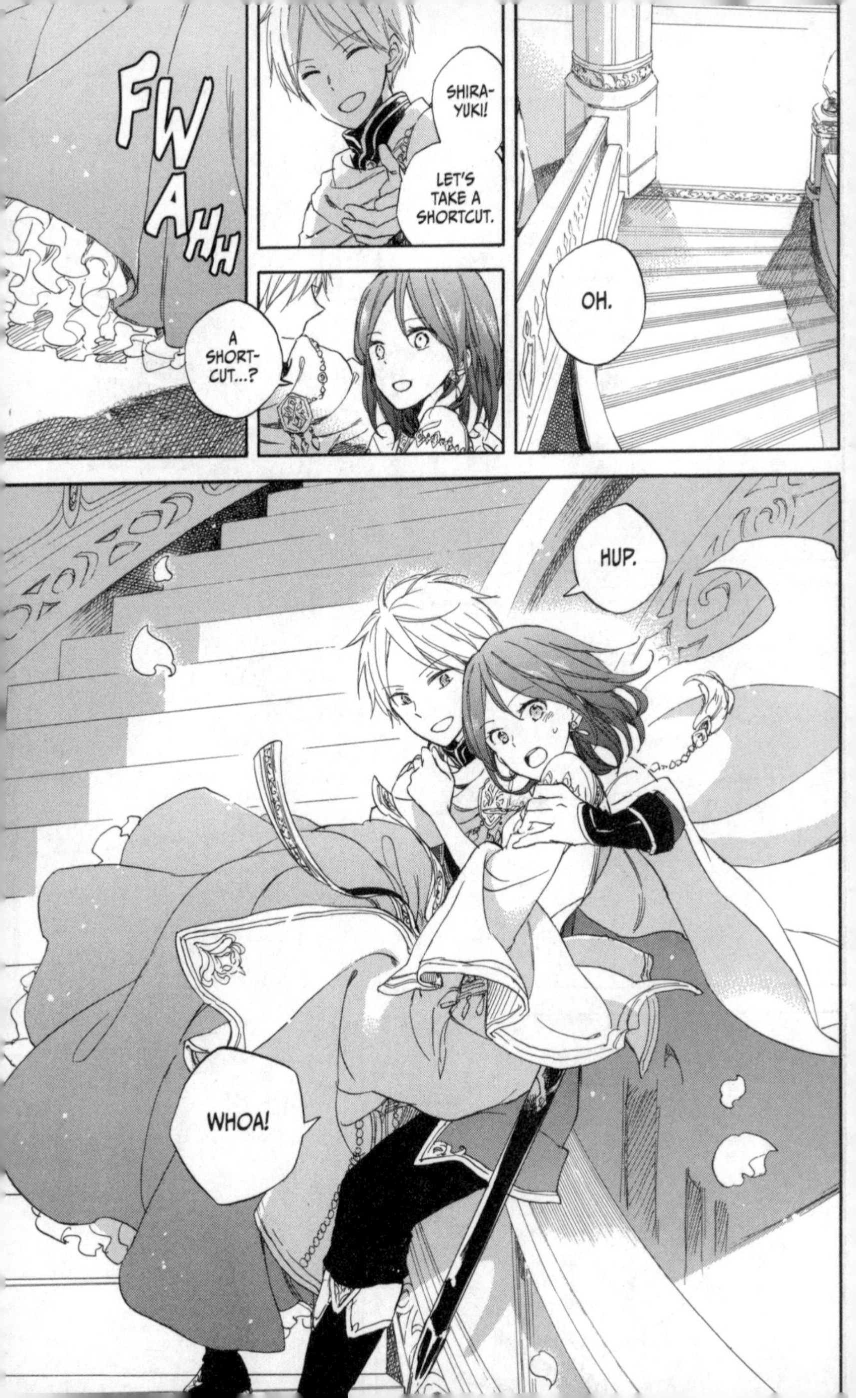
OH.
SHIRA-YUKI!
LET'S TAKE A SHORTCUT.
A SHORT-CUT...?
FWAHH
HUP.
WHOA!

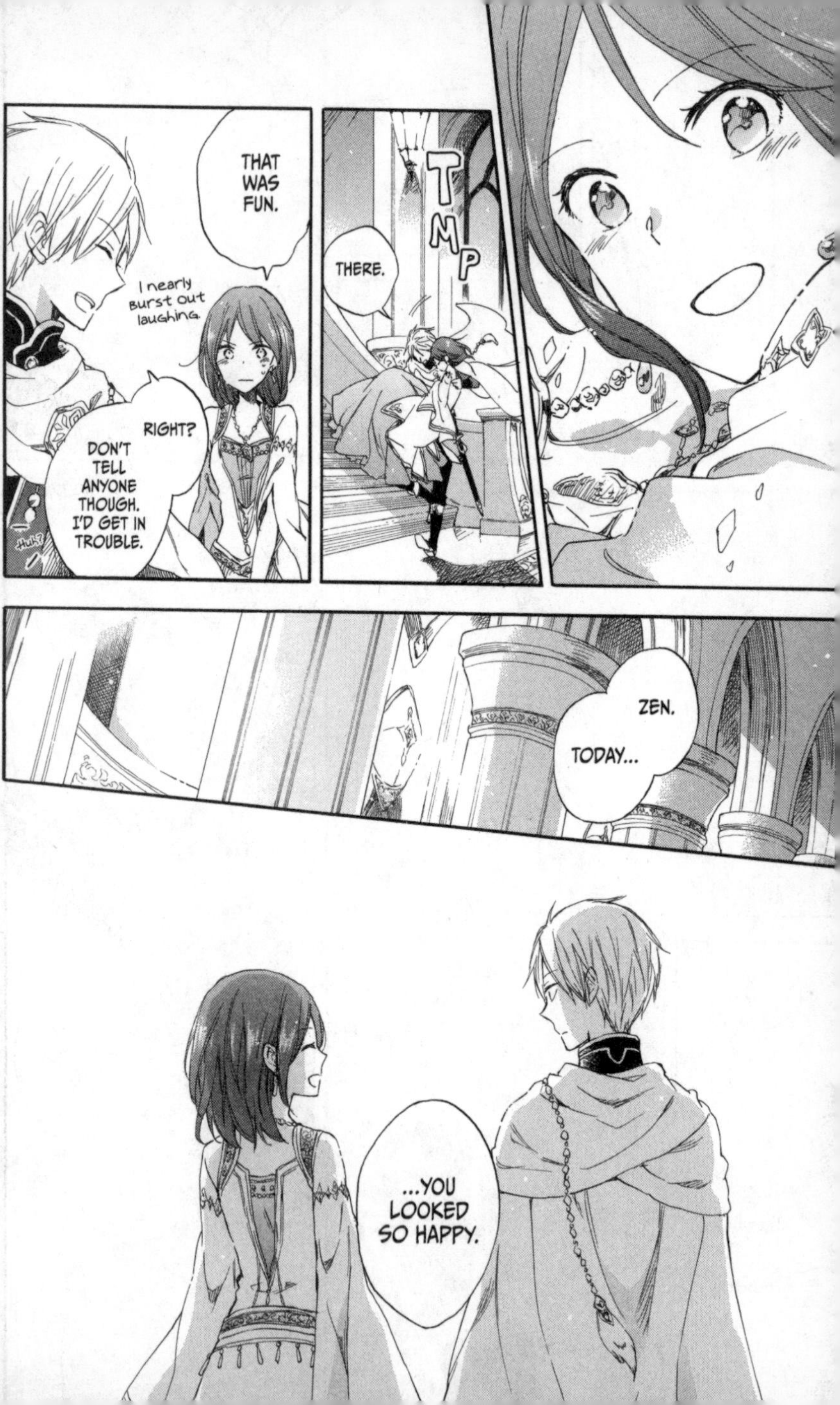
TMP
THERE.
THAT WAS FUN.
I nearly burst out laughing.
RIGHT? DON'T TELL ANYONE THOUGH. I'D GET IN TROUBLE.
Huh?
ZEN.
TODAY...
...YOU LOOKED SO HAPPY.

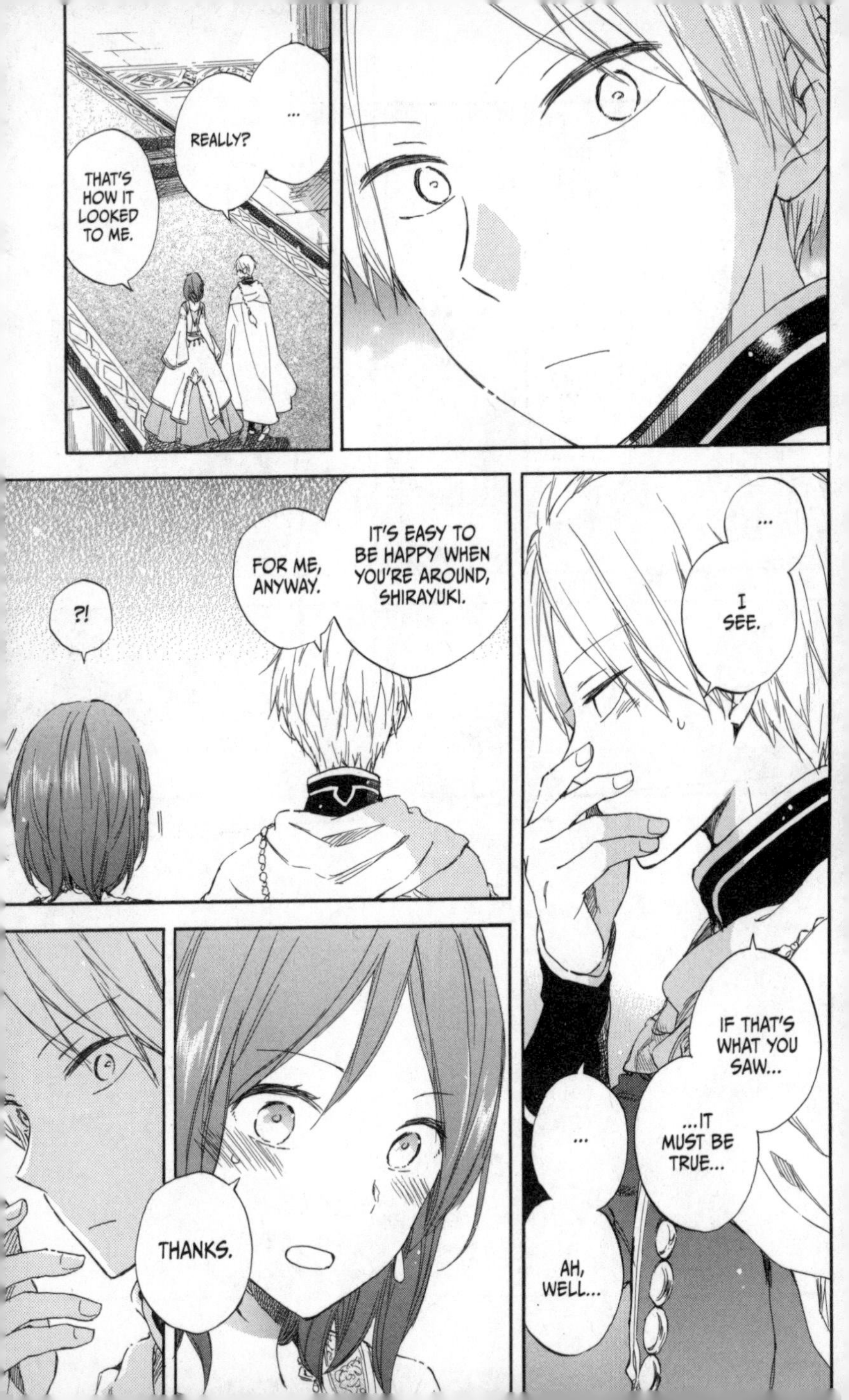
...
REALLY?
THAT'S HOW IT LOOKED TO ME.
...
I SEE.
IF THAT'S WHAT YOU SAW...
...IT MUST BE TRUE...
...
AH, WELL...
IT'S EASY TO BE HAPPY WHEN YOU'RE AROUND, SHIRAYUKI.
FOR ME, ANYWAY.
?!
THANKS.

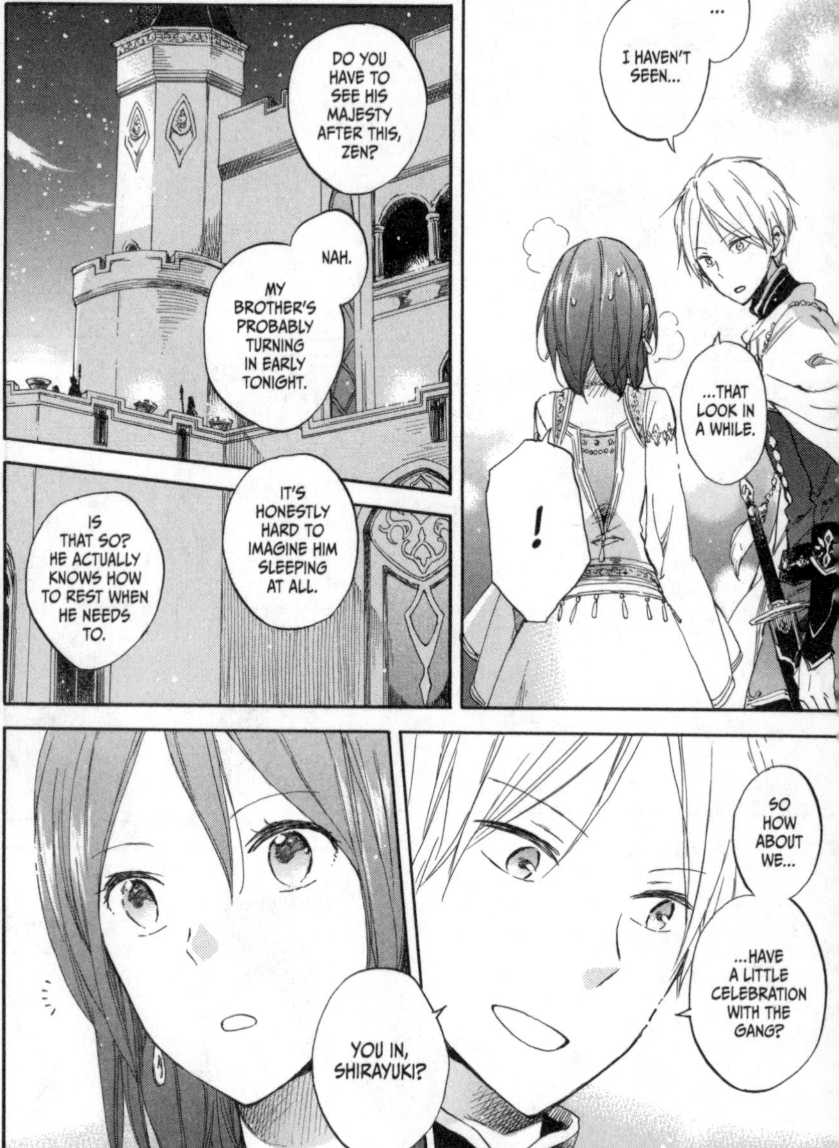
...
I HAVEN'T SEEN...
...THAT LOOK IN A WHILE.
!
DO YOU HAVE TO SEE HIS MAJESTY AFTER THIS, ZEN?
NAH.
MY BROTHER'S PROBABLY TURNING IN EARLY TONIGHT.
IT'S HONESTLY HARD TO IMAGINE HIM SLEEPING AT ALL.
IS THAT SO? HE ACTUALLY KNOWS HOW TO REST WHEN HE NEEDS TO.
SO HOW ABOUT WE...
...HAVE A LITTLE CELEBRATION WITH THE GANG?
YOU IN, SHIRAYUKI?

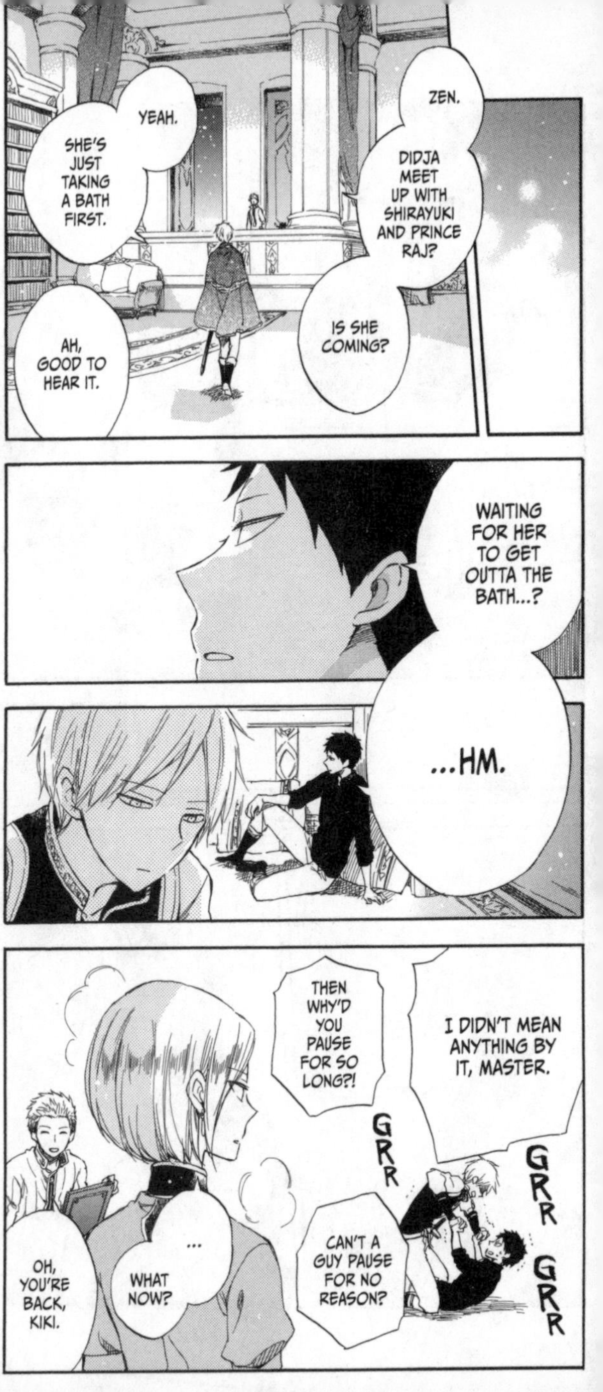
ZEN.
DIDJA MEET UP WITH SHIRAYUKI AND PRINCE RAJ?
IS SHE COMING?
YEAH.
SHE'S JUST TAKING A BATH FIRST.
AH, GOOD TO HEAR IT.
WAITING FOR HER TO GET OUTTA THE BATH...?
...HM.
I DIDN'T MEAN ANYTHING BY IT, MASTER.
THEN WHY'D YOU PAUSE FOR SO LONG?!
GRR
GRR
GRR
CAN'T A GUY PAUSE FOR NO REASON?
...
WHAT NOW?
OH, YOU'RE BACK, KIKI.

4

CHAPTER 50

A whole lineup of familiar faces.

Sakaki's been playing with Princess Rona since she was born, so he's more than used to it.

I'm worried she'll tear Sakaki away from Raj at some point.

I want a scene where Queen Haruto chats with Mitsuhide and Kiki.

CHAPTER 51

A glimpse at the Wisteria boys' past!

Zen has never told his aides about how he used to sleep in his brother's room when he was little.

I don't think he'd ever tell Shirayuki.

I wish I could tell her.

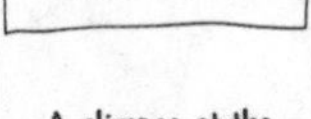
Don't you dare!

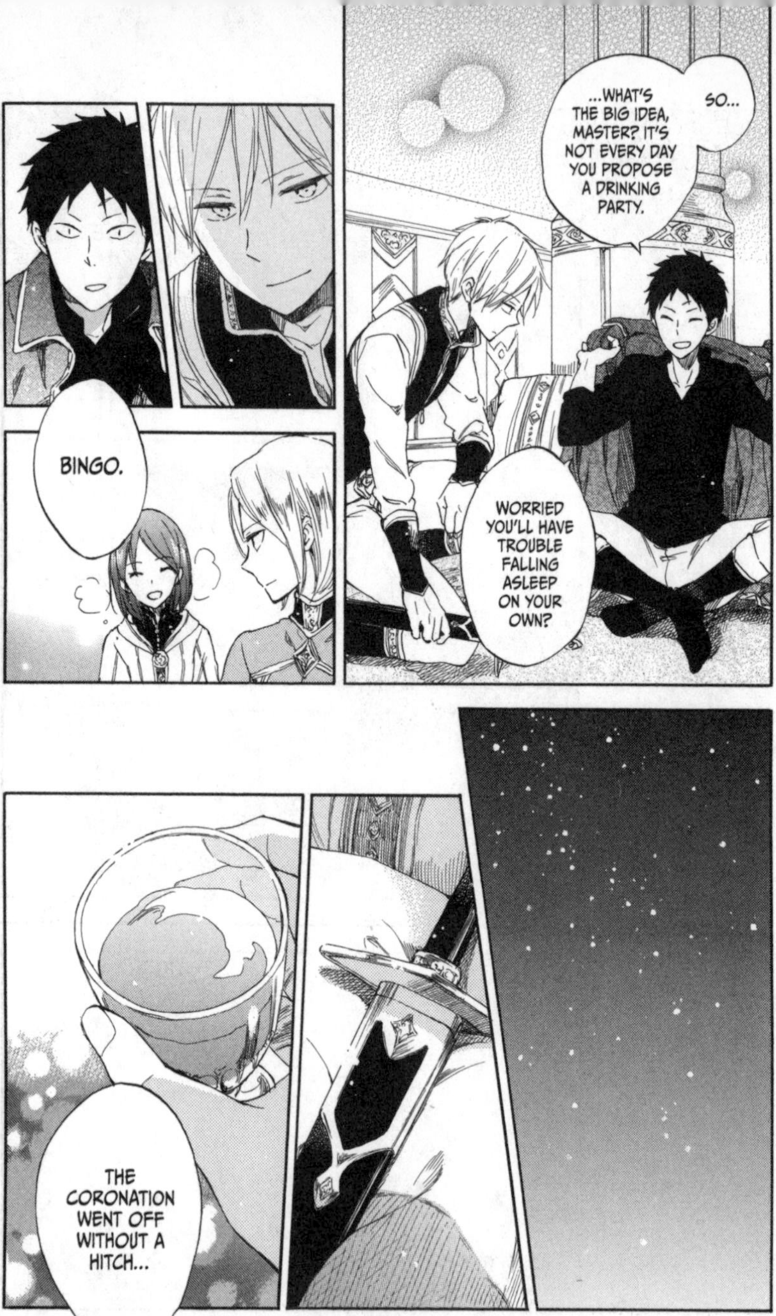
SO...
...WHAT'S THE BIG IDEA, MASTER? IT'S NOT EVERY DAY YOU PROPOSE A DRINKING PARTY.
WORRIED YOU'LL HAVE TROUBLE FALLING ASLEEP ON YOUR OWN?
BINGO.
THE CORONATION WENT OFF WITHOUT A HITCH...

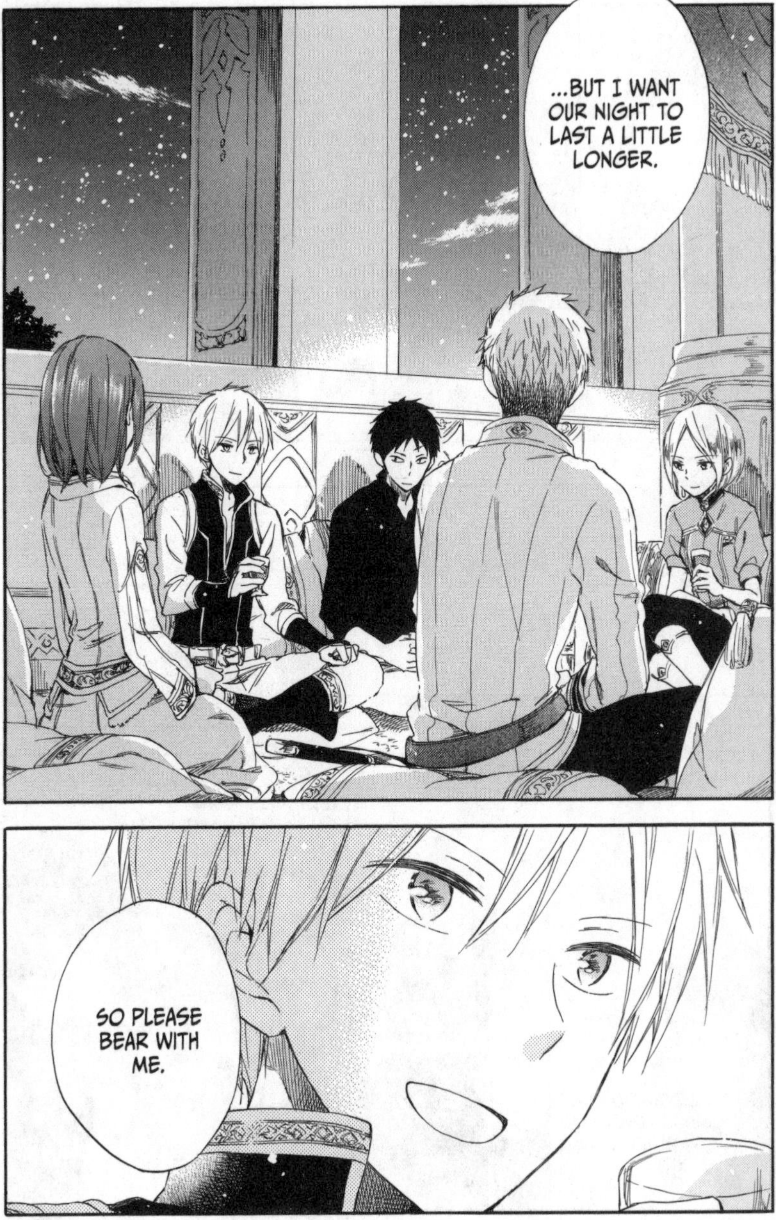
...BUT I WANT OUR NIGHT TO LAST A LITTLE LONGER.
SO PLEASE BEAR WITH ME.

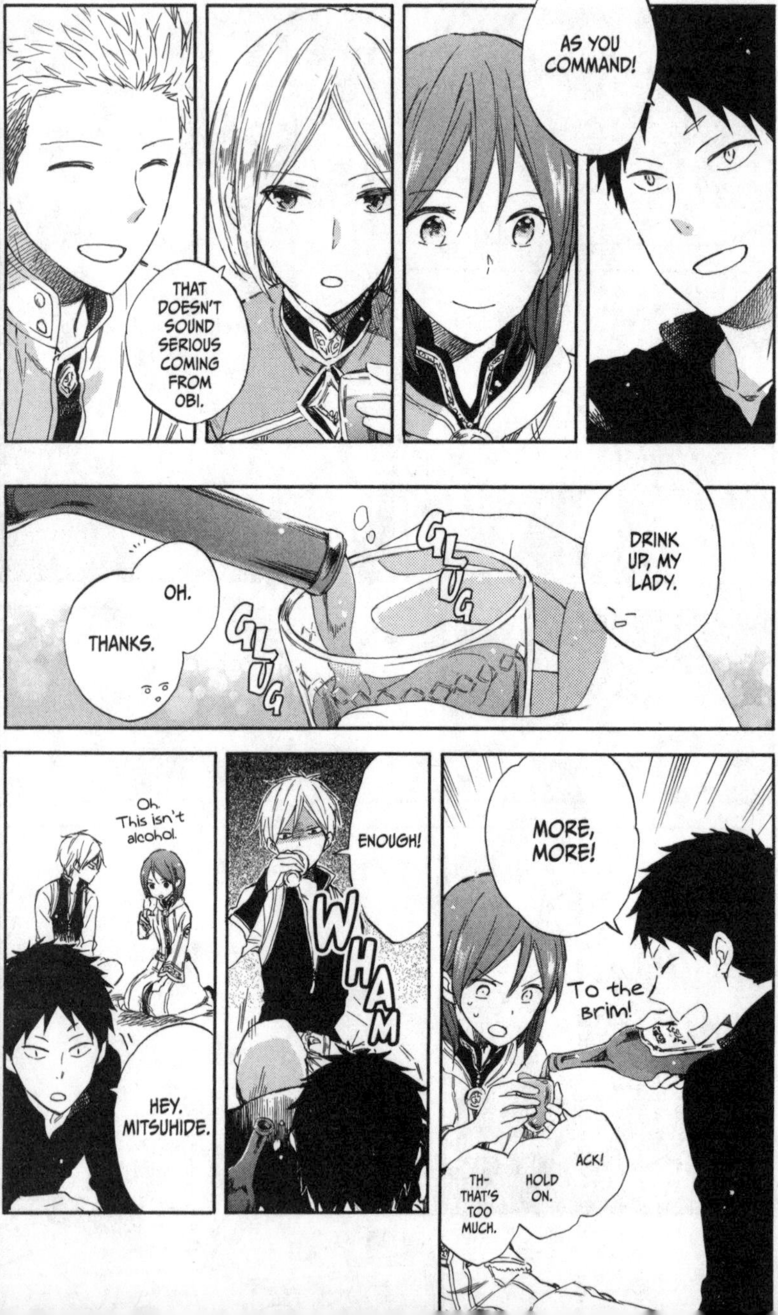
AS YOU COMMAND!
THAT DOESN'T SOUND SERIOUS COMING FROM OBI.
DRINK UP, MY LADY.
GLUG
GLUG
OH.
THANKS.
MORE, MORE!
To the brim!
ACK!
HOLD ON.
TH- THAT'S TOO MUCH.
ENOUGH!
WHAM
Oh. This isn't alcohol.
HEY. MITSUHIDE.

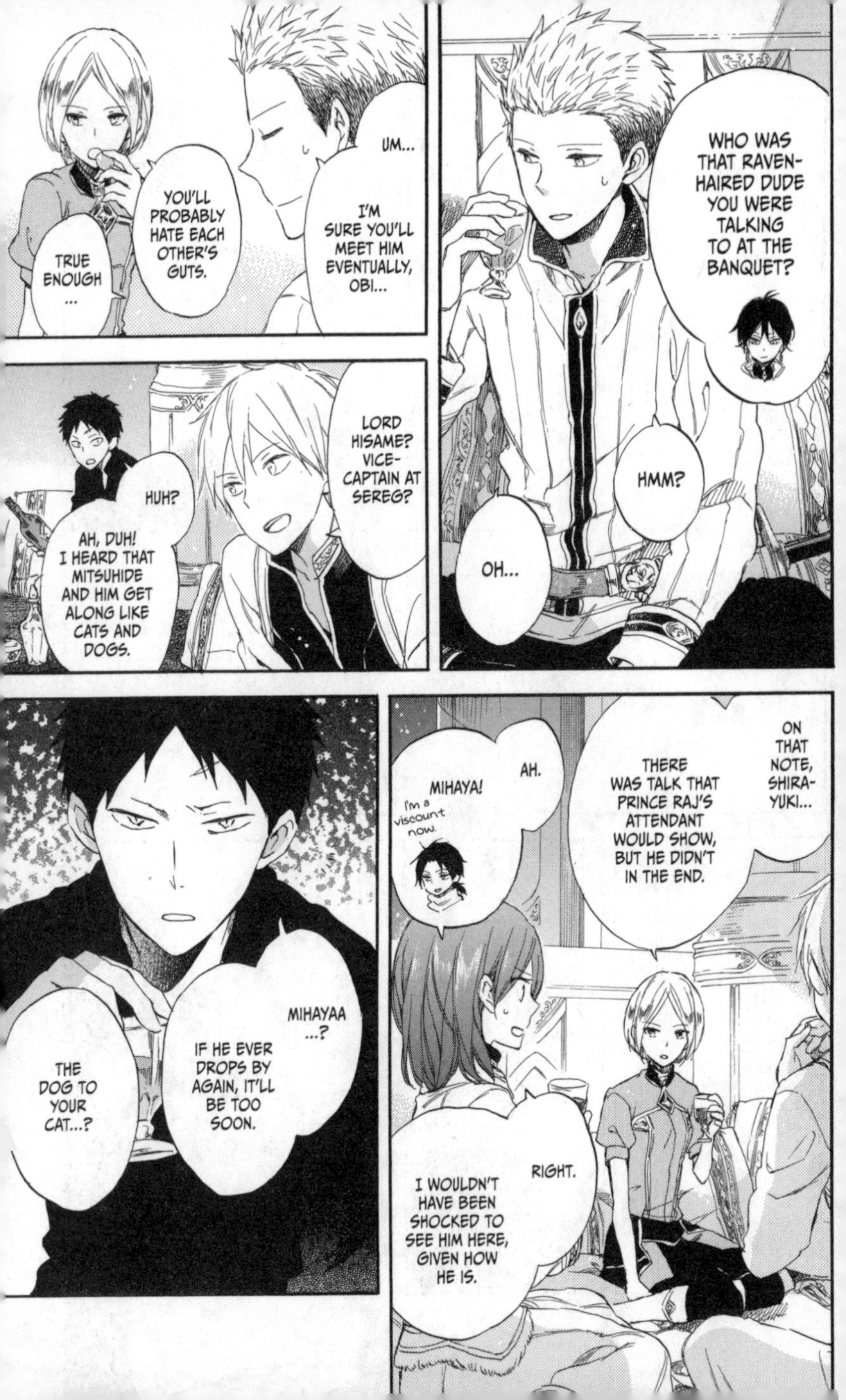
WHO WAS THAT RAVEN-HAIRED DUDE YOU WERE TALKING TO AT THE BANQUET?
HMM?
OH...
UM...
I'M SURE YOU'LL MEET HIM EVENTUALLY, OBI...
YOU'LL PROBABLY HATE EACH OTHER'S GUTS.
TRUE ENOUGH ...
LORD HISAME? VICE-CAPTAIN AT SEREG?
HUH?
AH, DUH! I HEARD THAT MITSUHIDE AND HIM GET ALONG LIKE CATS AND DOGS.
ON THAT NOTE, SHIRAYUKI...
THERE WAS TALK THAT PRINCE RAJ'S ATTENDANT WOULD SHOW, BUT HE DIDN'T IN THE END.
AH.
MIHAYA!
I'm a viscount now.
RIGHT.
I WOULDN'T HAVE BEEN SHOCKED TO SEE HIM HERE, GIVEN HOW HE IS.
MIHAYAA ...?
IF HE EVER DROPS BY AGAIN, IT'LL BE TOO SOON.
THE DOG TO YOUR CAT...?

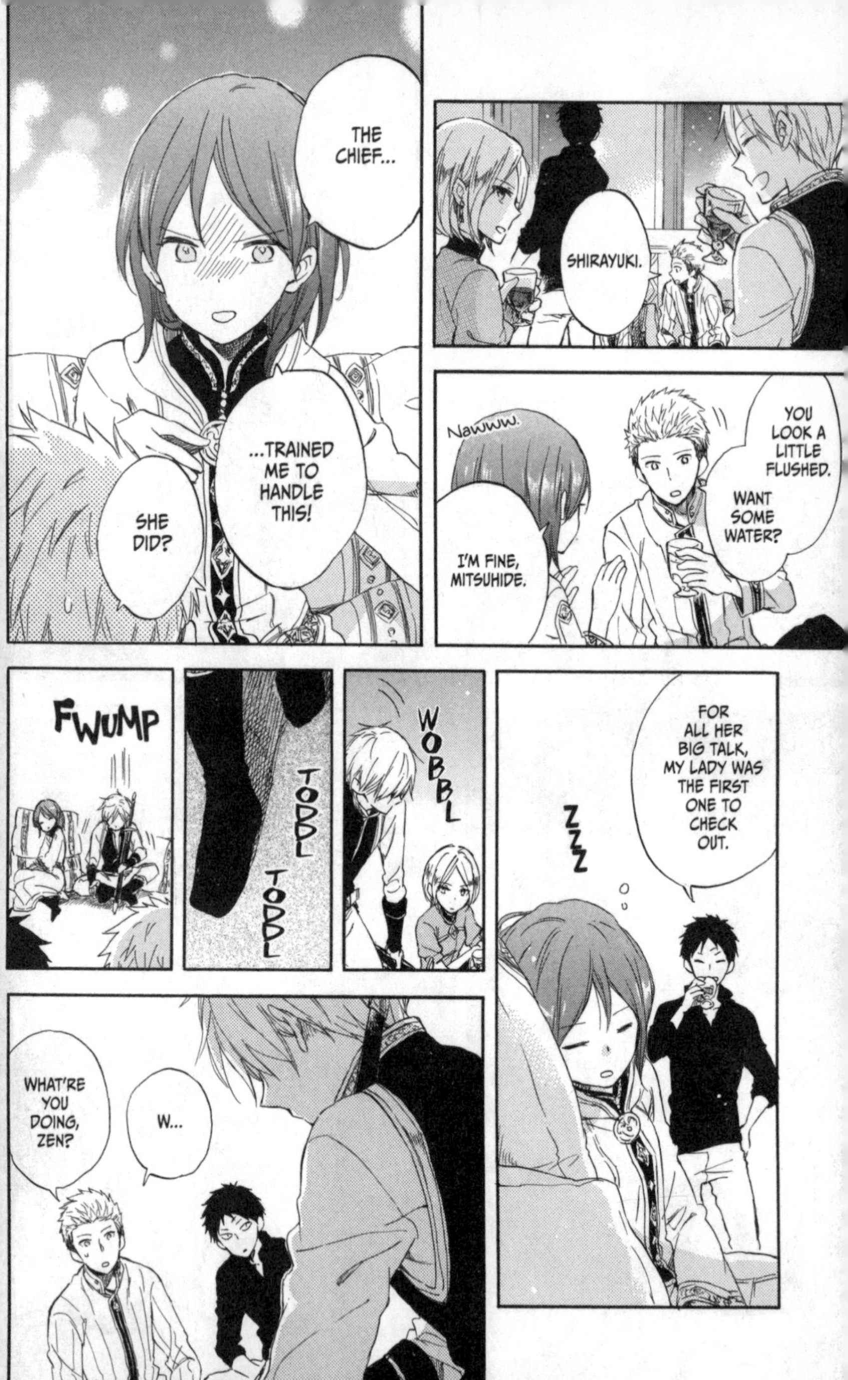
SHIRAYUKI.
YOU LOOK A LITTLE FLUSHED.
WANT SOME WATER?
Nawww.
I'M FINE, MITSUHIDE.
THE CHIEF...
...TRAINED ME TO HANDLE THIS!
SHE DID?
FOR ALL HER BIG TALK, MY LADY WAS THE FIRST ONE TO CHECK OUT.
ZZZ
WOBBL
TODDL TODDL
FWUMP
W...
WHAT'RE YOU DOING, ZEN?

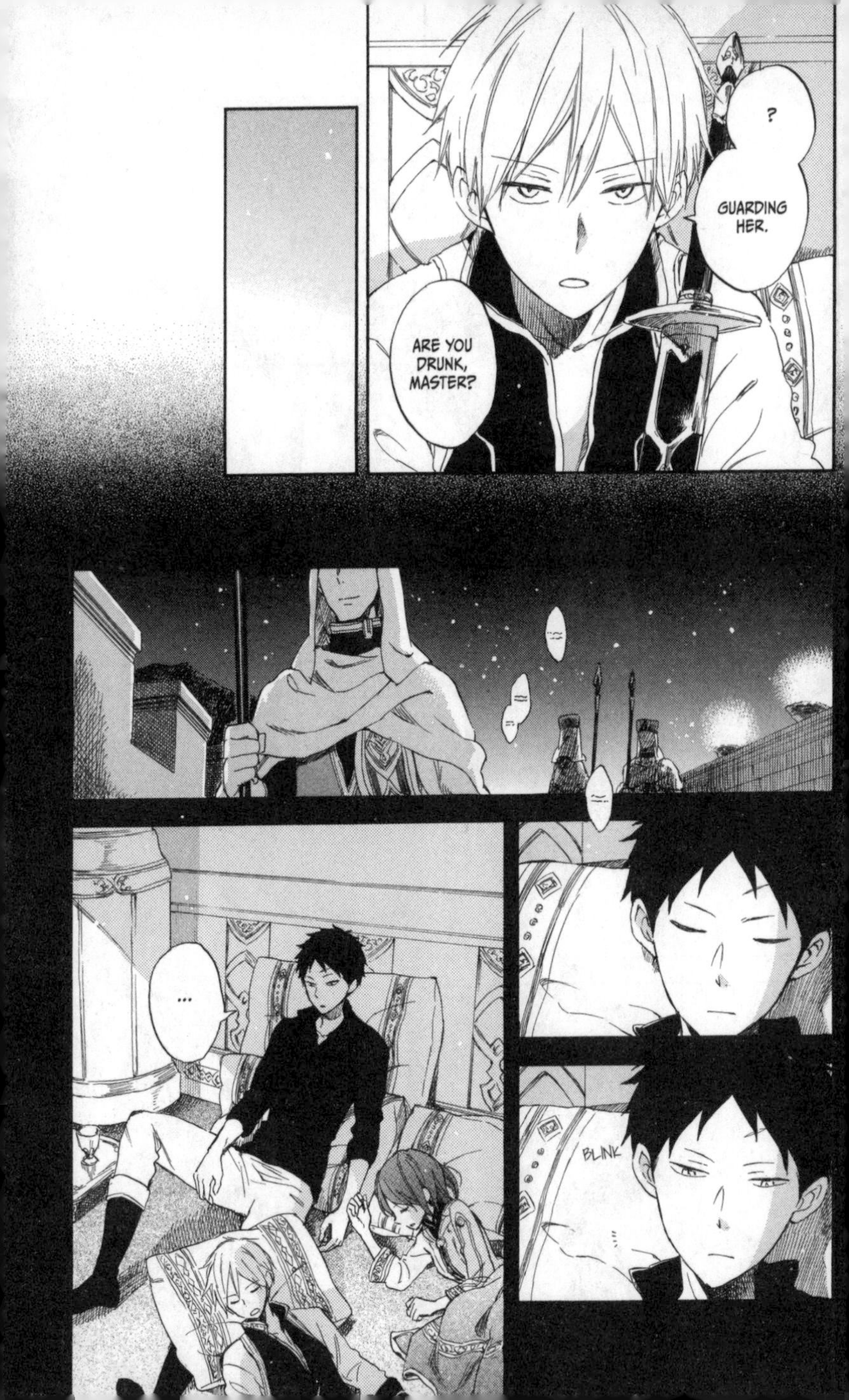
?
GUARDING HER.
ARE YOU DRUNK, MASTER?
...
BLINK

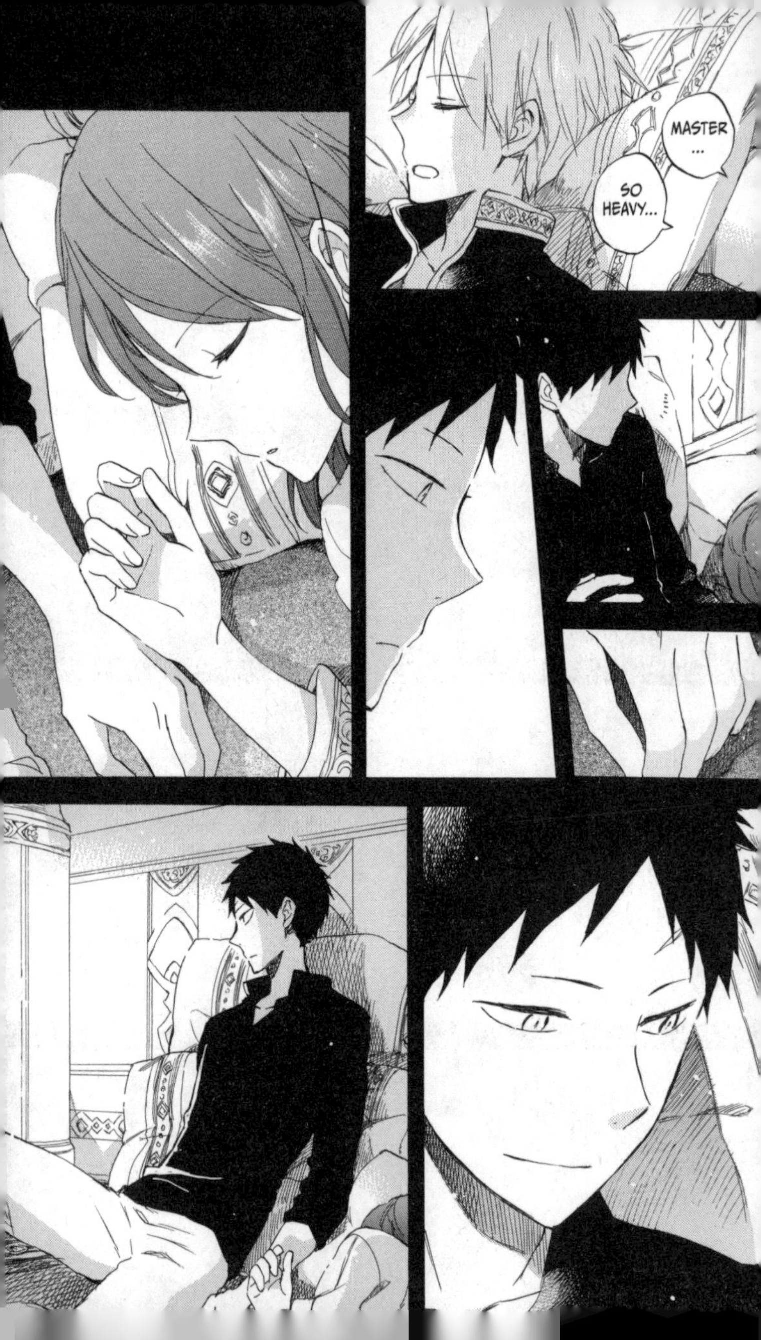
MASTER ...
SO HEAVY...

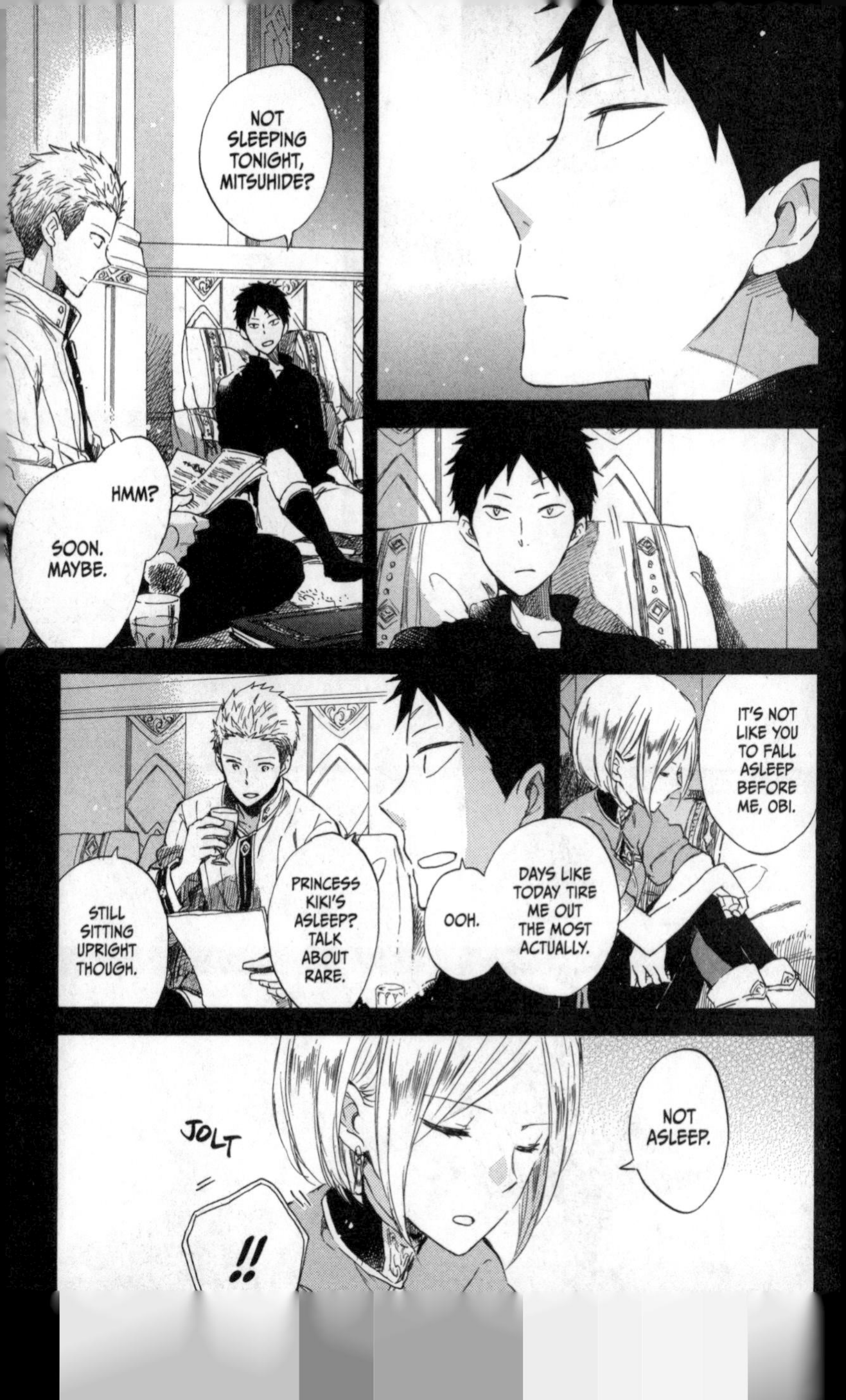
NOT SLEEPING TONIGHT, MITSUHIDE?
HMM?
SOON. MAYBE.
IT'S NOT LIKE YOU TO FALL ASLEEP BEFORE ME, OBI.
DAYS LIKE TODAY TIRE ME OUT THE MOST ACTUALLY.
OOH.
PRINCESS KIKI'S ASLEEP? TALK ABOUT RARE.
STILL SITTING UPRIGHT THOUGH.
NOT ASLEEP.
JOLT
!!

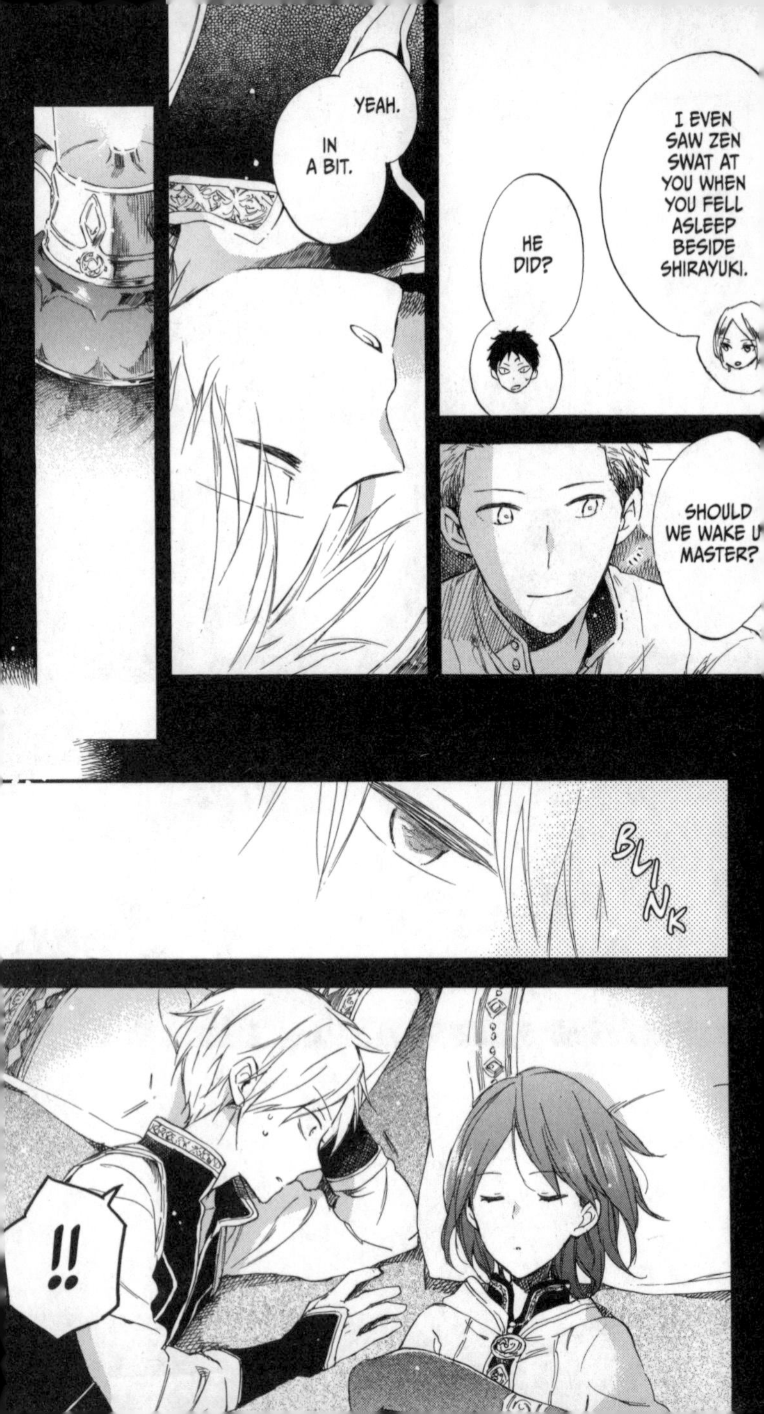
I EVEN SAW ZEN SWAT AT YOU WHEN YOU FELL ASLEEP BESIDE SHIRAYUKI.
HE DID?
SHOULD WE WAKE U MASTER?
YEAH.
IN A BIT.
BLINK
!!

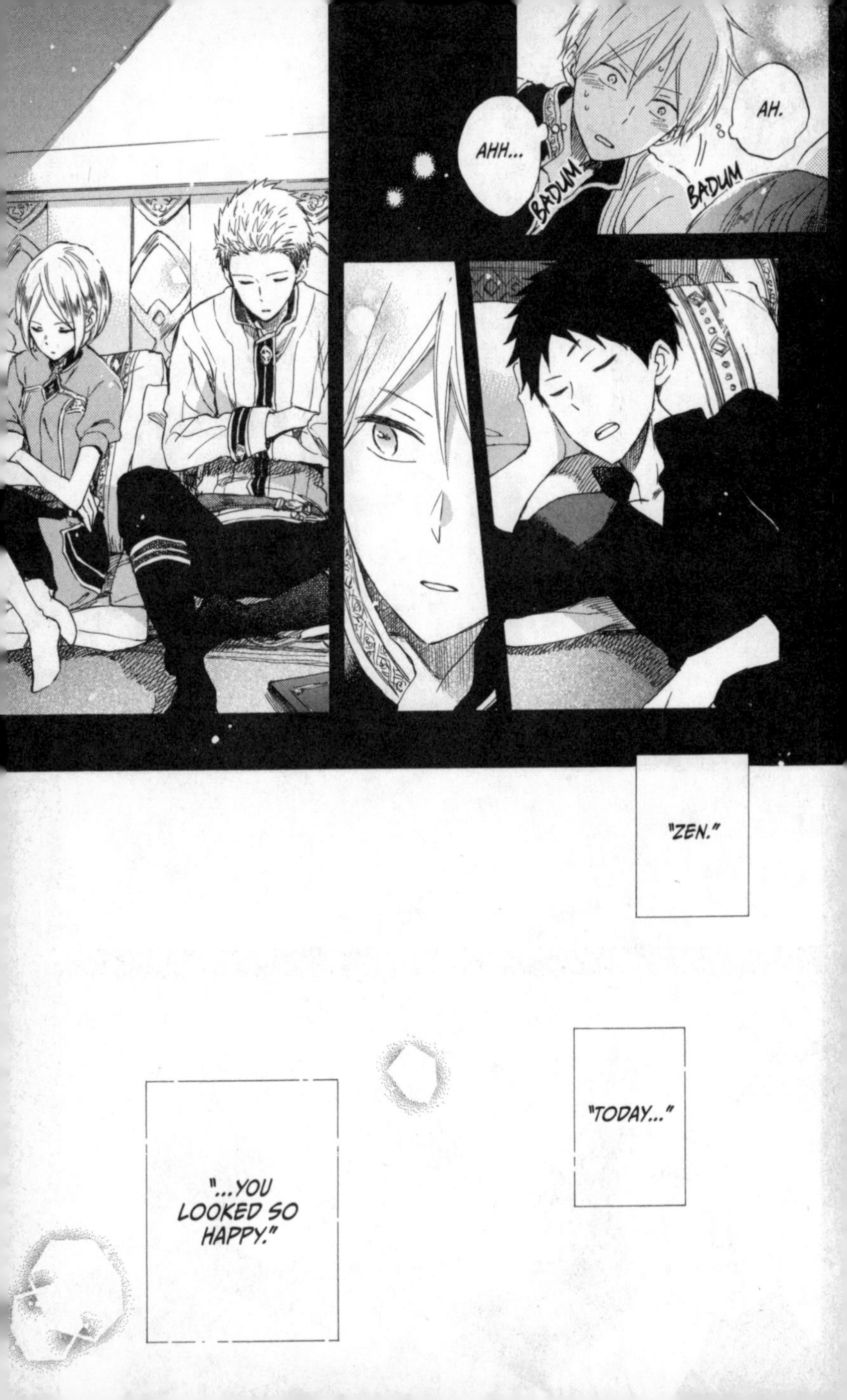
AH.
AHH...
BADUM
BADUM
"ZEN."
"TODAY..."
"...YOU LOOKED SO HAPPY."

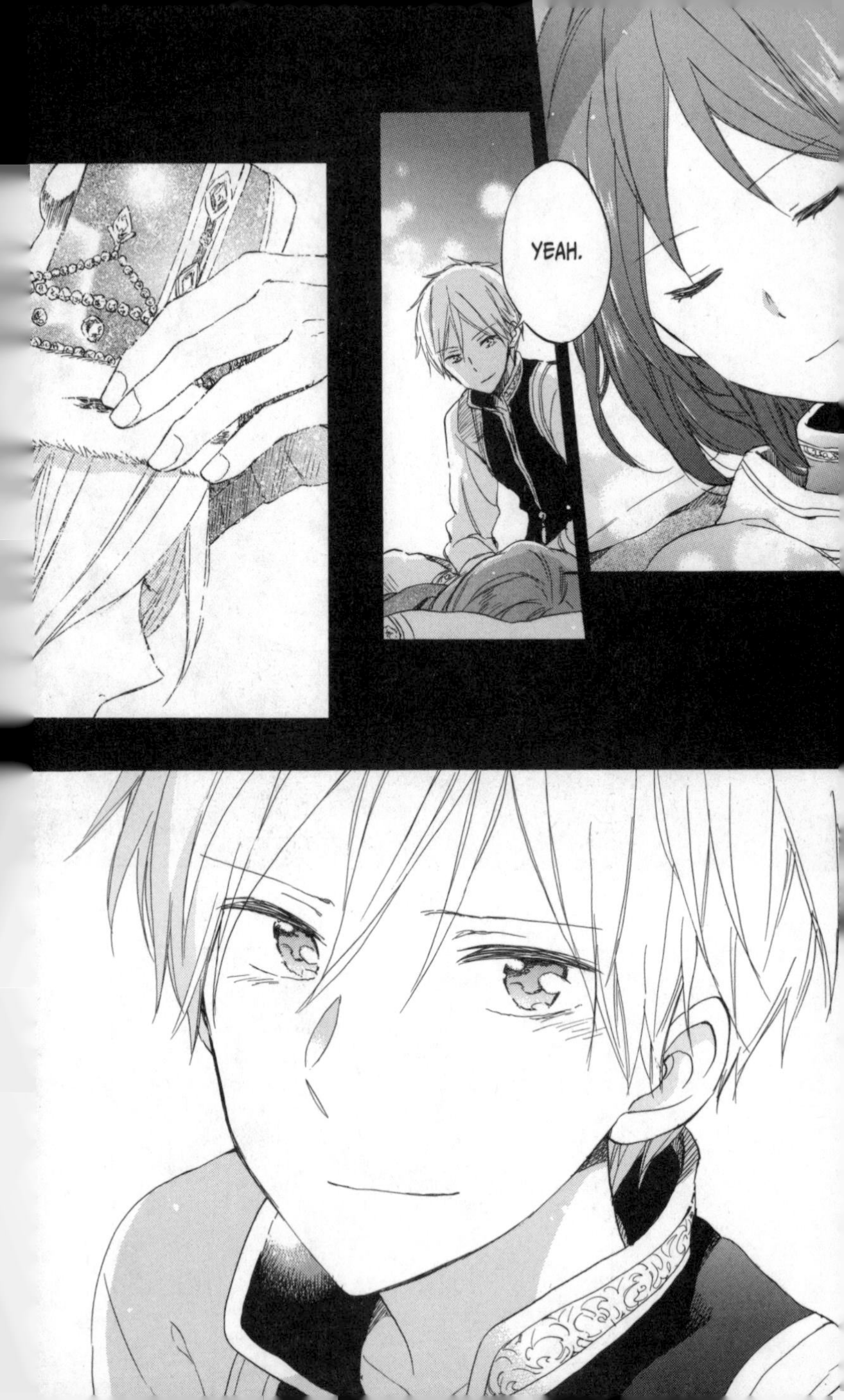
YEAH.

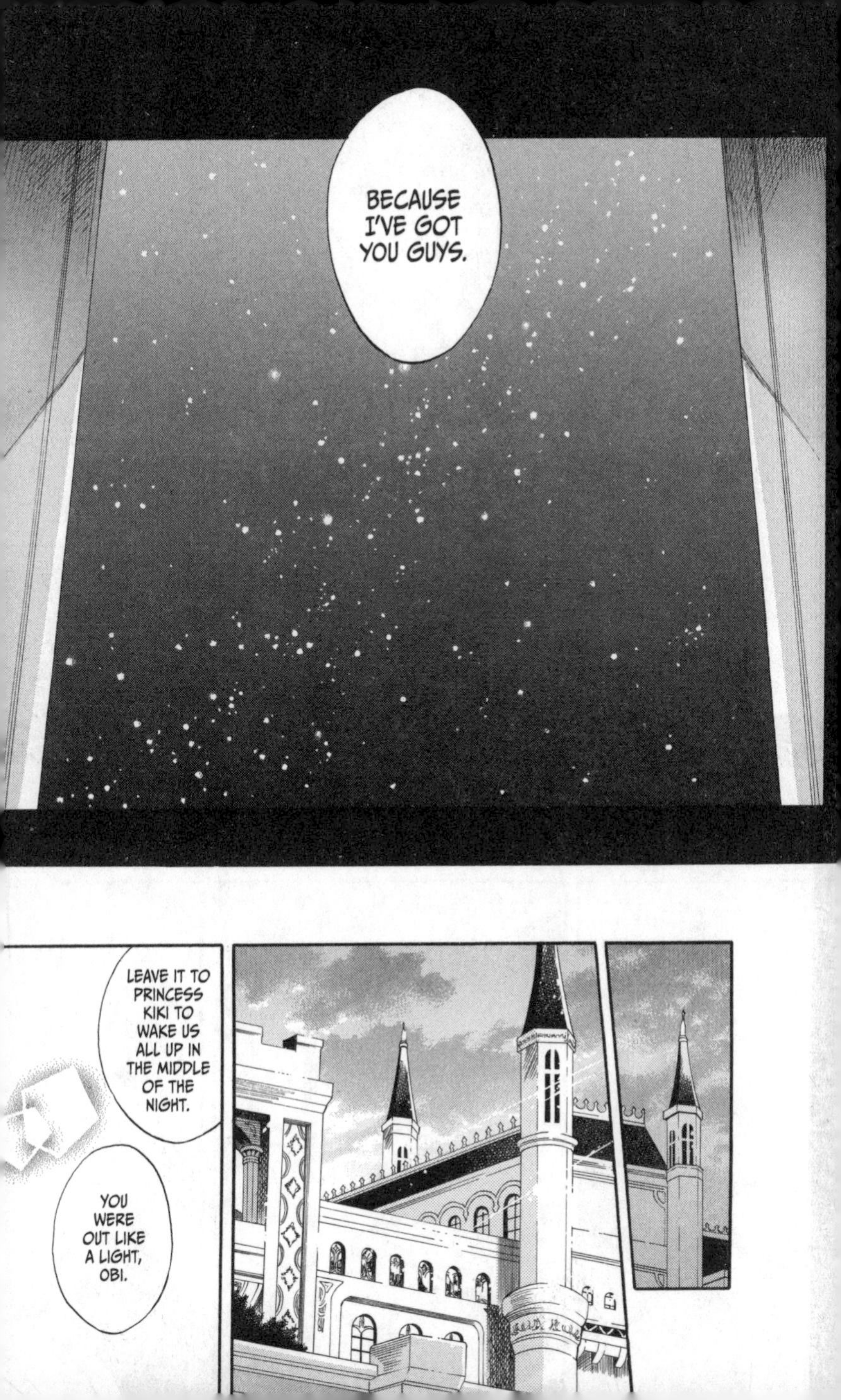
BECAUSE I'VE GOT YOU GUYS.
LEAVE IT TO PRINCESS KIKI TO WAKE US ALL UP IN THE MIDDLE OF THE NIGHT.
YOU WERE OUT LIKE A LIGHT, OBI.

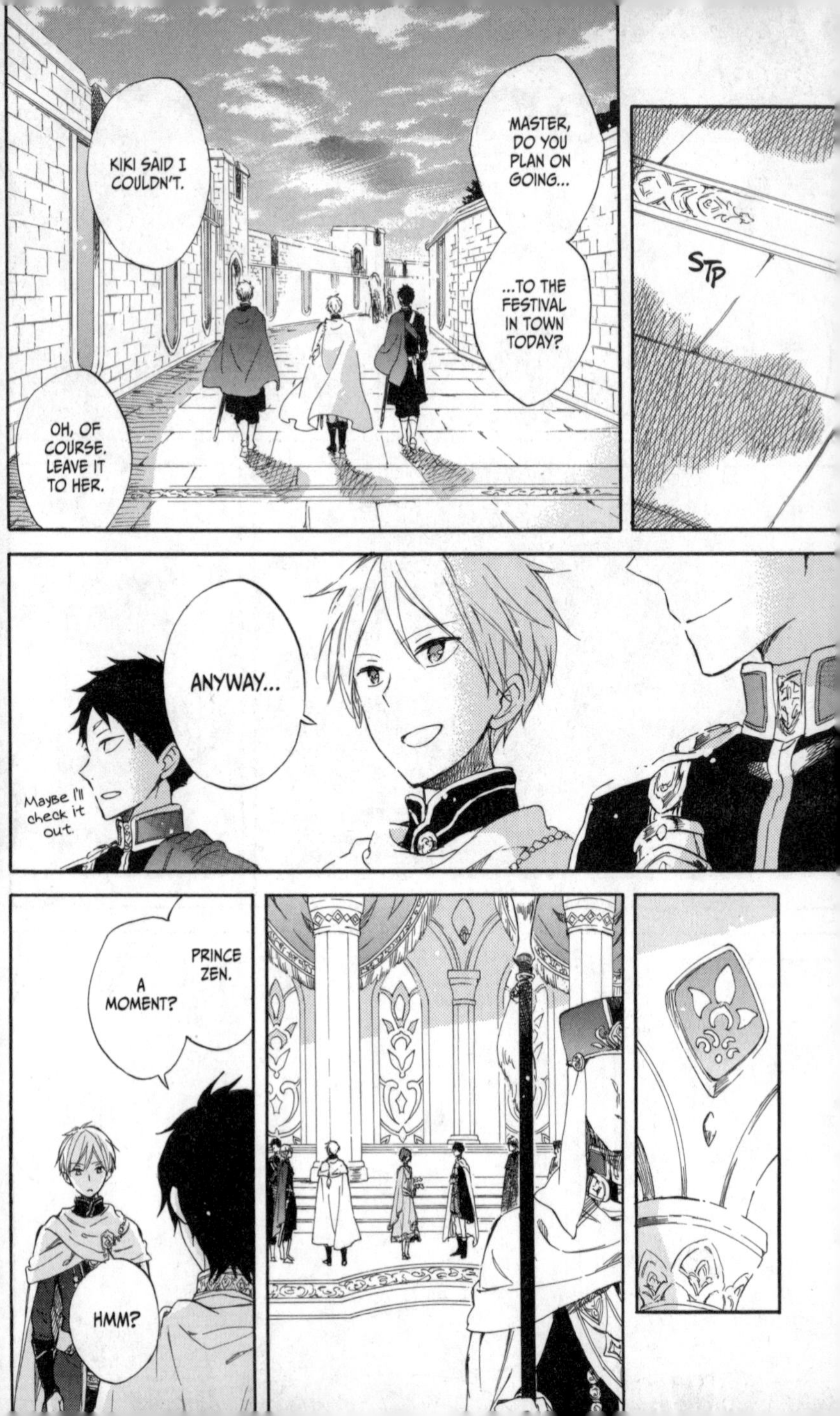
STP
MASTER, DO YOU PLAN ON GOING...
...TO THE FESTIVAL IN TOWN TODAY?
KIKI SAID I COULDN'T.
OH, OF COURSE. LEAVE IT TO HER.
ANYWAY...
Maybe I'll check it out.
PRINCE ZEN. A MOMENT?
HMM?

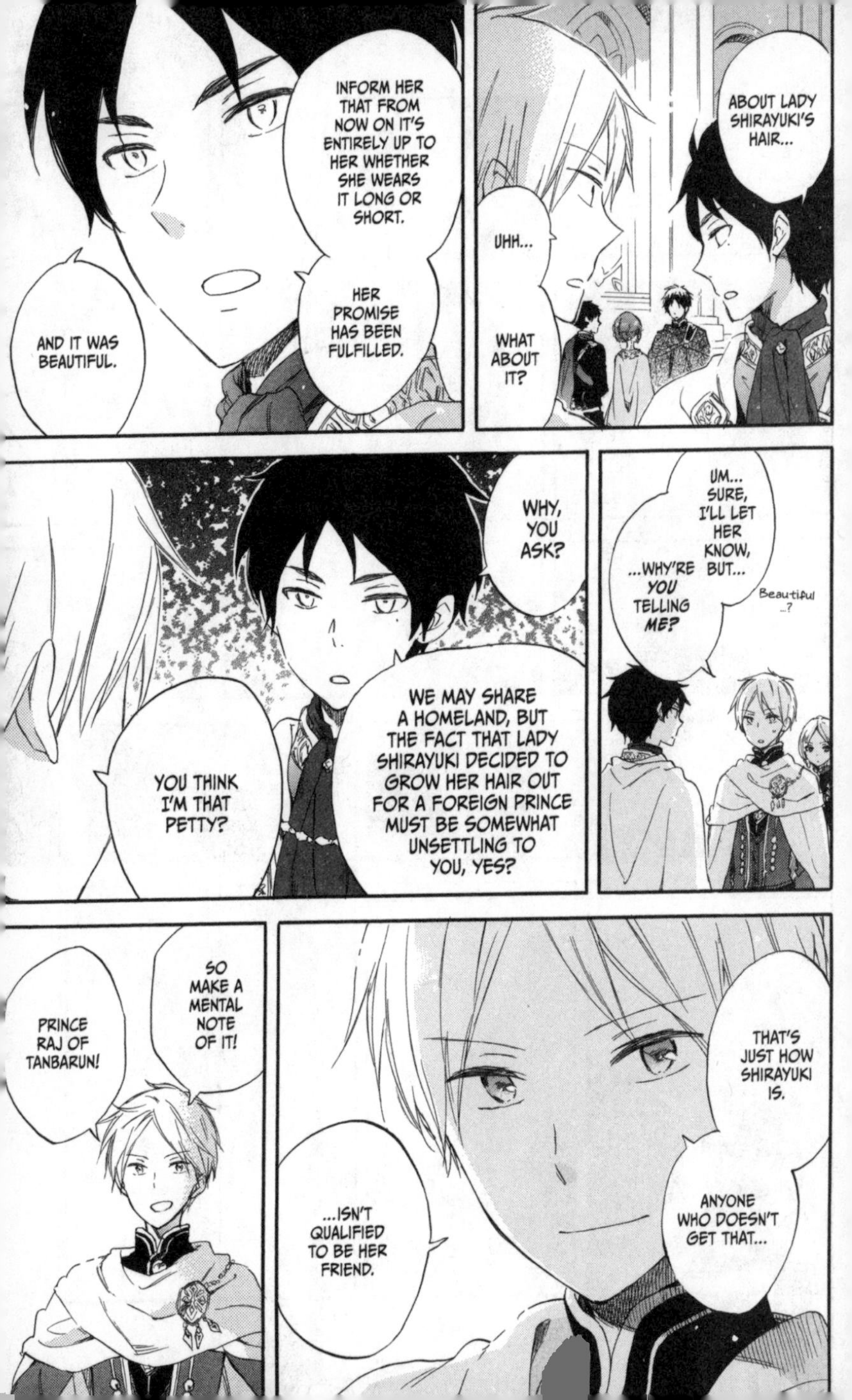
ABOUT LADY SHIRAYUKI'S HAIR...
UHH...
WHAT ABOUT IT?
INFORM HER THAT FROM NOW ON IT'S ENTIRELY UP TO HER WHETHER SHE WEARS IT LONG OR SHORT.
HER PROMISE HAS BEEN FULFILLED.
AND IT WAS BEAUTIFUL.
UM... SURE, I'LL LET HER KNOW, BUT...
...WHY'RE *YOU* TELLING *ME?*
Beautiful ...?
WHY, YOU ASK?
WE MAY SHARE A HOMELAND, BUT THE FACT THAT LADY SHIRAYUKI DECIDED TO GROW HER HAIR OUT FOR A FOREIGN PRINCE MUST BE SOMEWHAT UNSETTLING TO YOU, YES?
YOU THINK I'M THAT PETTY?
THAT'S JUST HOW SHIRAYUKI IS.
ANYONE WHO DOESN'T GET THAT...
...ISN'T QUALIFIED TO BE HER FRIEND.
SO MAKE A MENTAL NOTE OF IT!
PRINCE RAJ OF TANBARUN!

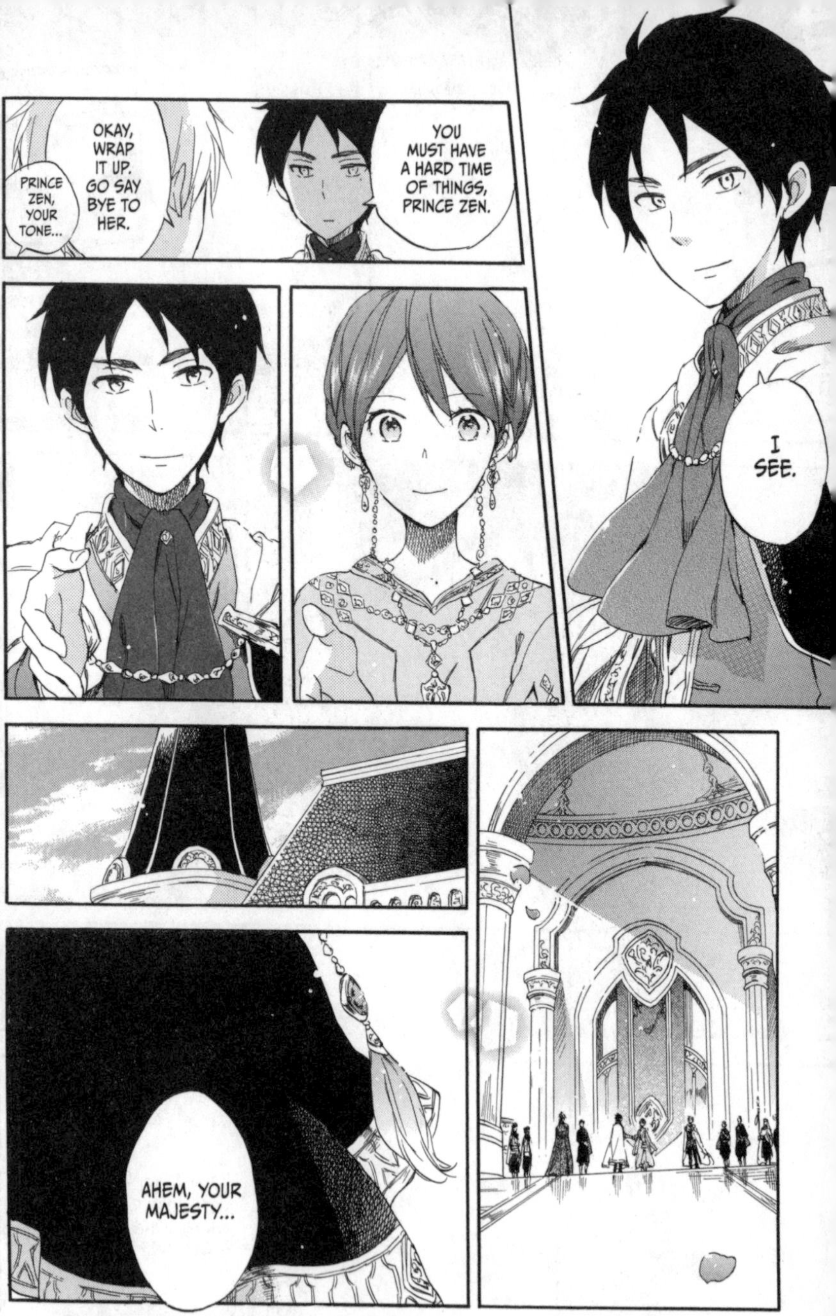
I SEE.
YOU MUST HAVE A HARD TIME OF THINGS, PRINCE ZEN.
OKAY, WRAP IT UP. GO SAY BYE TO HER.
PRINCE ZEN, YOUR TONE...
AHEM, YOUR MAJESTY...

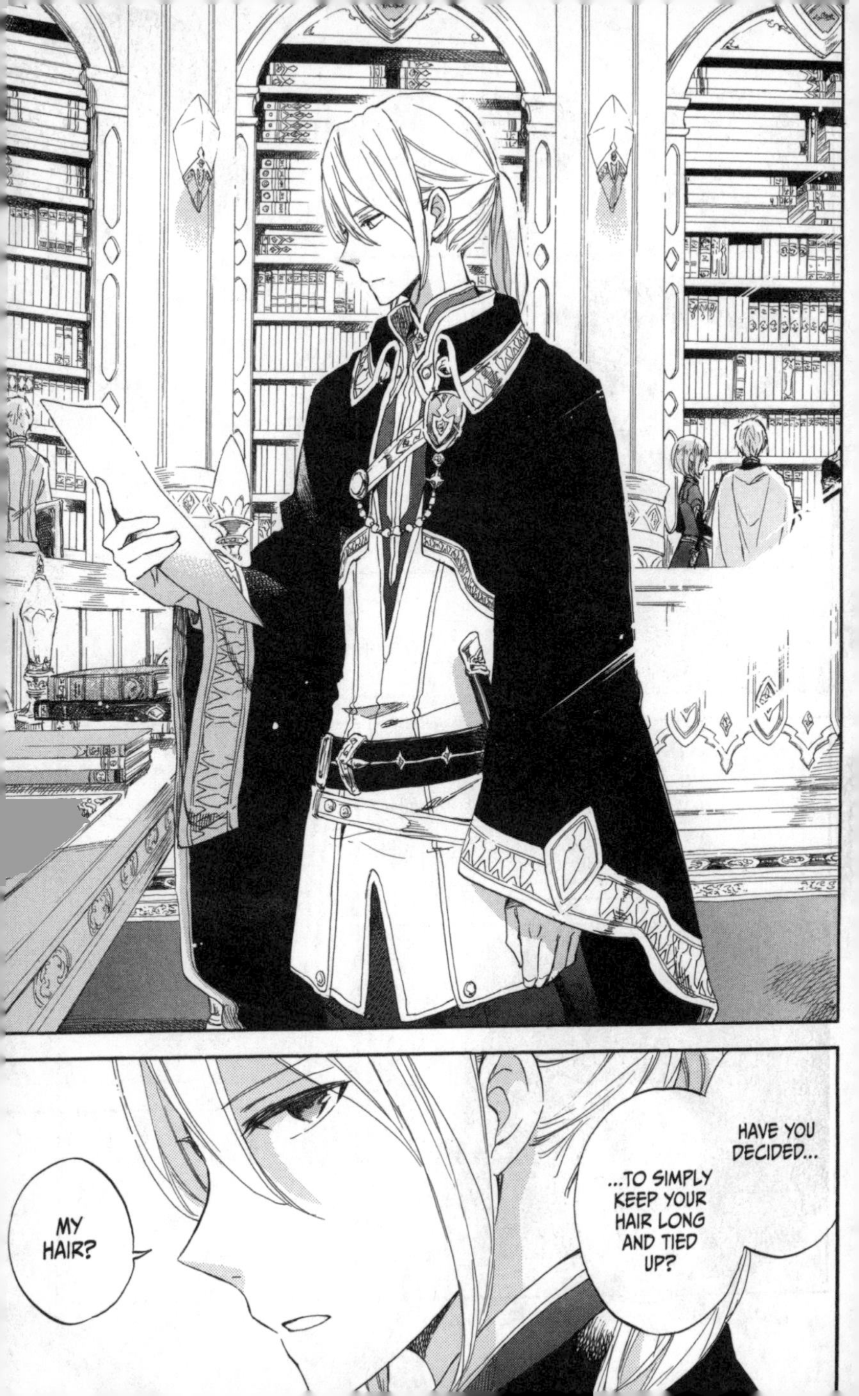
HAVE YOU DECIDED...
...TO SIMPLY KEEP YOUR HAIR LONG AND TIED UP?
MY HAIR?

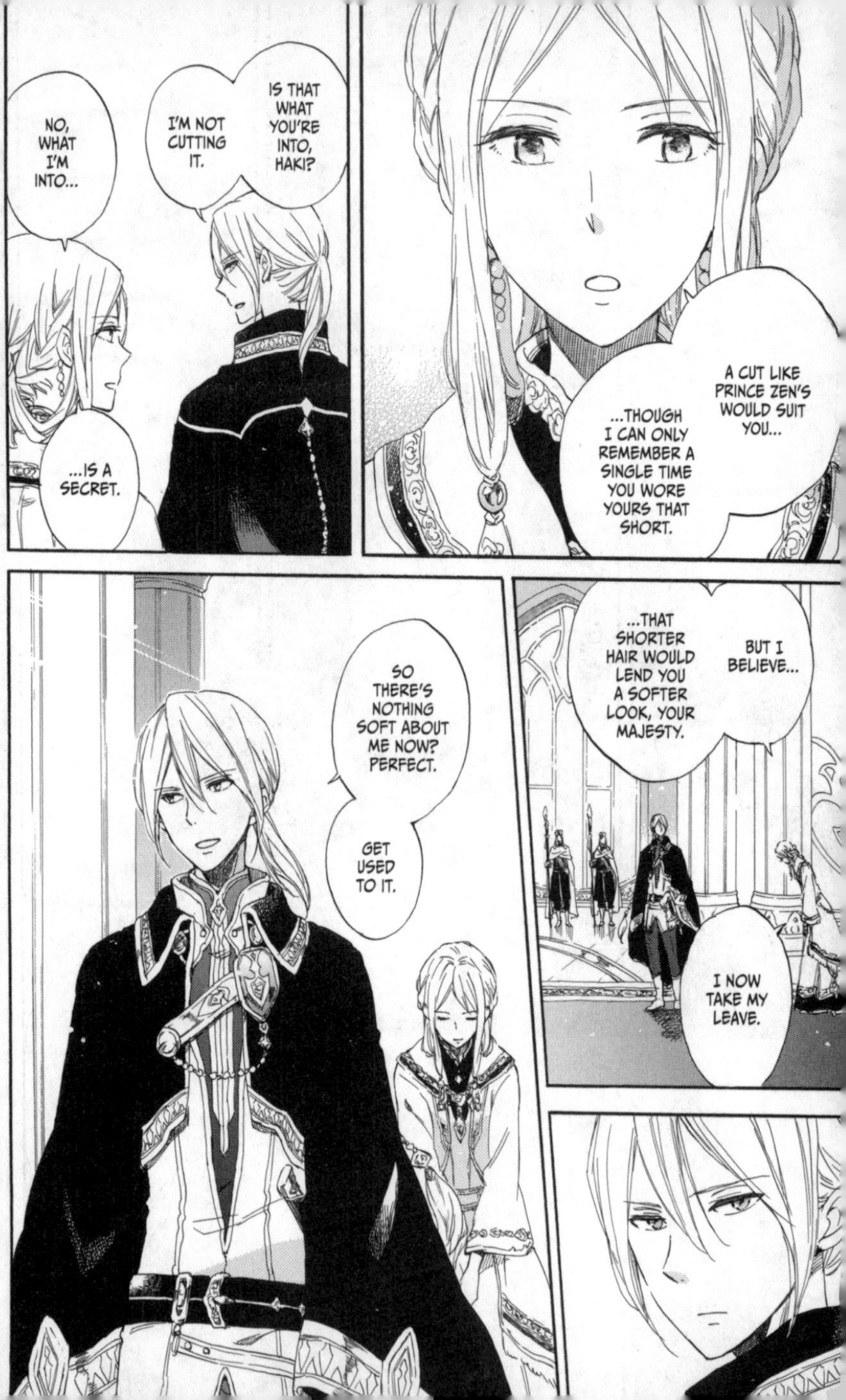
A CUT LIKE PRINCE ZEN'S WOULD SUIT YOU...
...THOUGH I CAN ONLY REMEMBER A SINGLE TIME YOU WORE YOURS THAT SHORT.
IS THAT WHAT YOU'RE INTO, HAKI?
I'M NOT CUTTING IT.
NO, WHAT I'M INTO...
...IS A SECRET.
BUT I BELIEVE...
...THAT SHORTER HAIR WOULD LEND YOU A SOFTER LOOK, YOUR MAJESTY.
I NOW TAKE MY LEAVE.
SO THERE'S NOTHING SOFT ABOUT ME NOW? PERFECT.
GET USED TO IT.

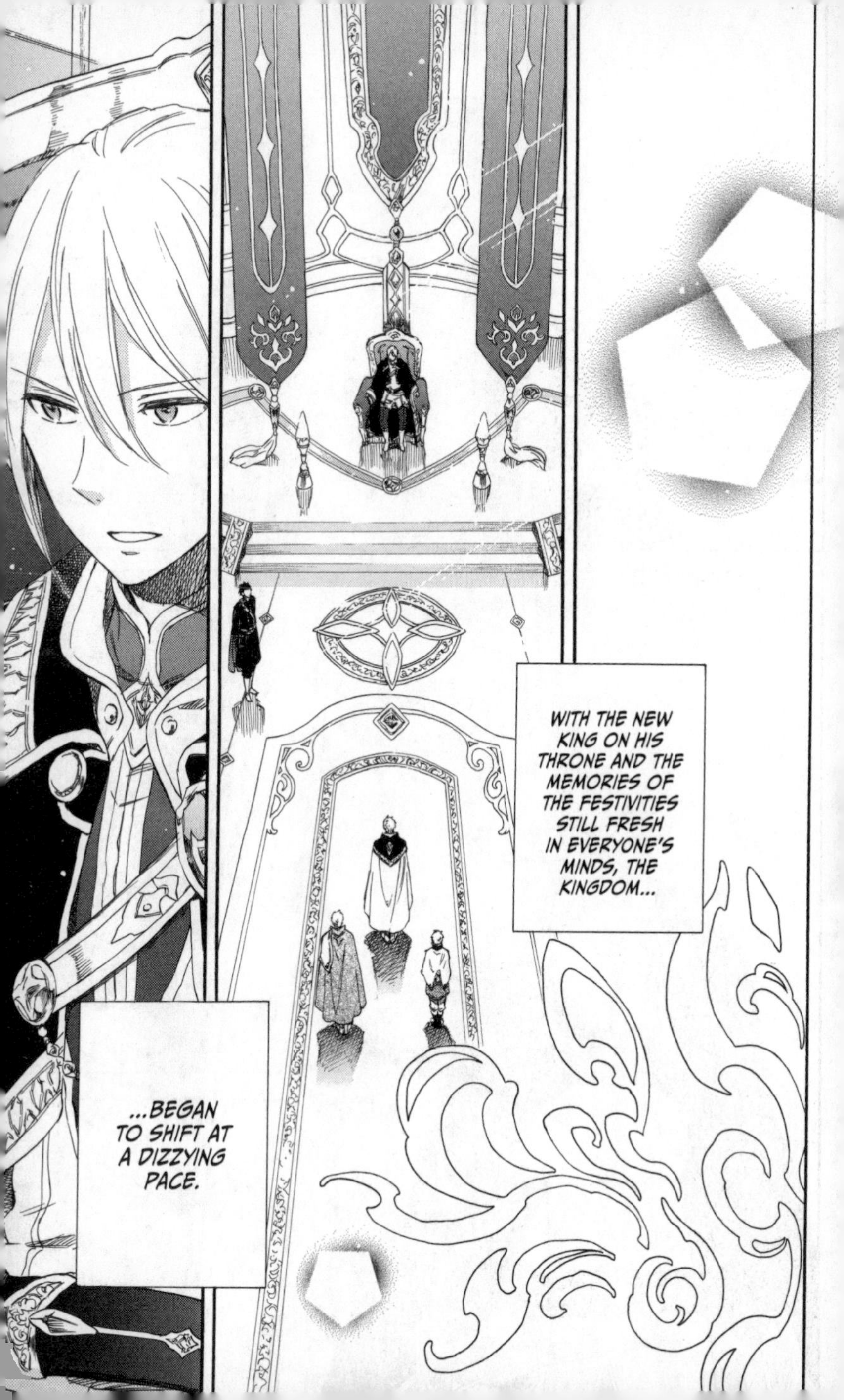
WITH THE NEW KING ON HIS THRONE AND THE MEMORIES OF THE FESTIVITIES STILL FRESH IN EVERYONE'S MINDS, THE KINGDOM...
...BEGAN TO SHIFT AT A DIZZYING PACE.

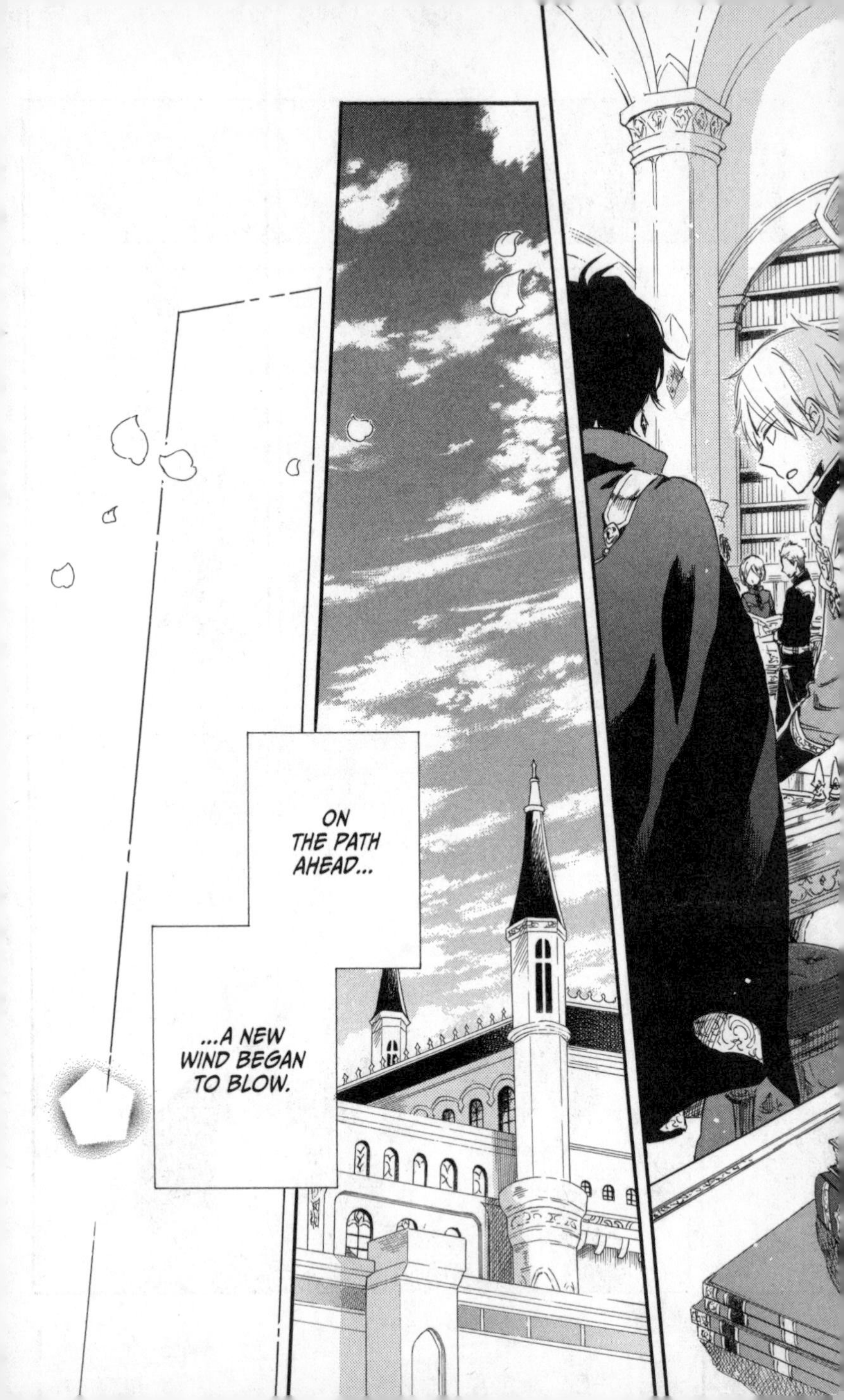
ON THE PATH AHEAD...
...A NEW WIND BEGAN TO BLOW.

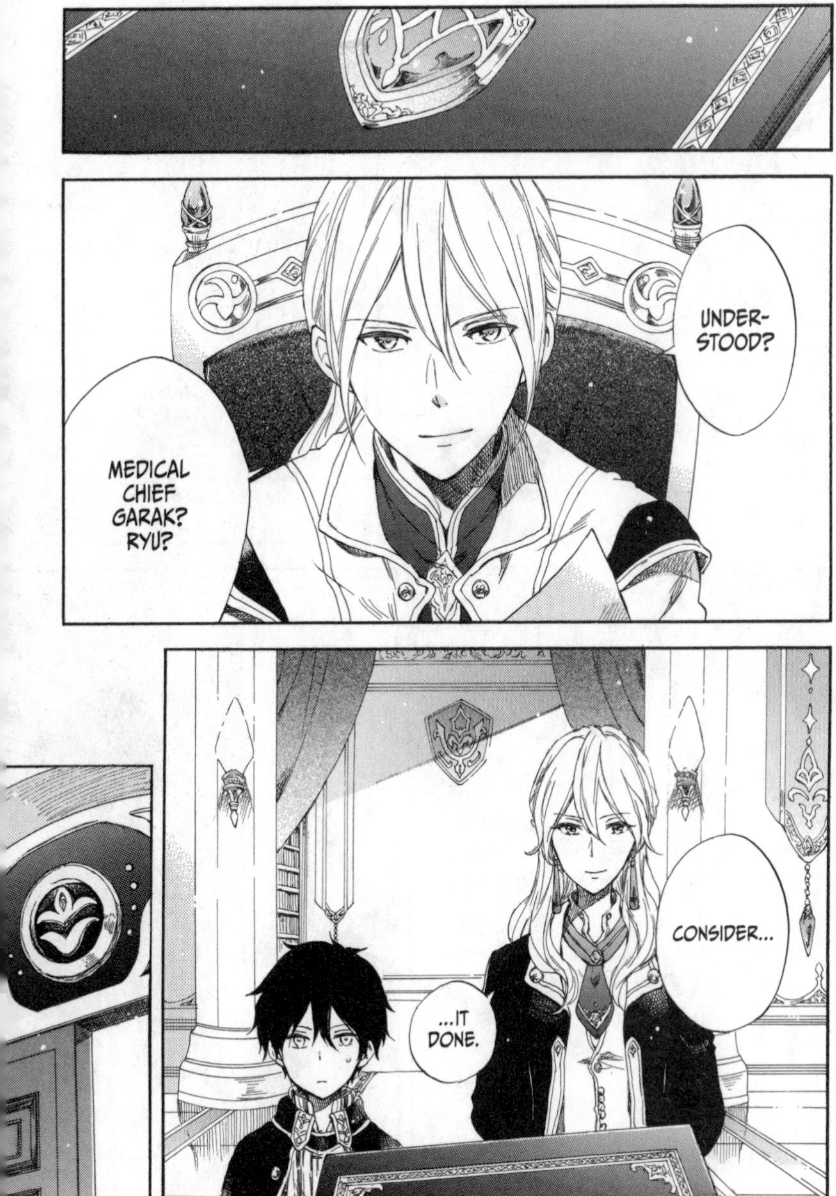
UNDER-STOOD?
MEDICAL CHIEF GARAK? RYU?
CONSIDER...
...IT DONE.

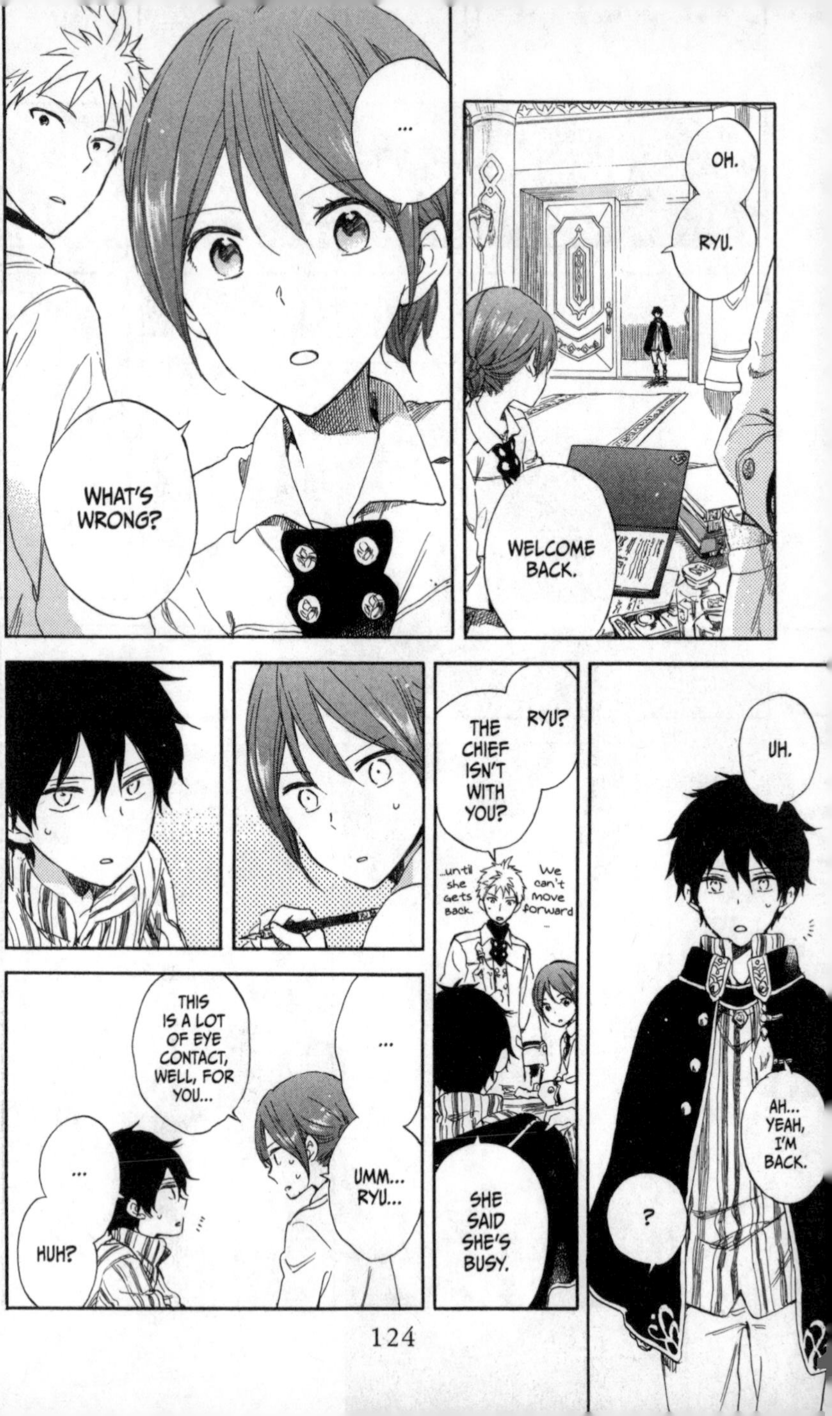
OH.
RYU.
WELCOME BACK.
...
WHAT'S WRONG?
UH.
AH... YEAH, I'M BACK.
?
RYU?
THE CHIEF ISN'T WITH YOU?
We can't move forward ...
...until she gets back.
SHE SAID SHE'S BUSY.
...
UMM... RYU...
THIS IS A LOT OF EYE CONTACT, WELL, FOR YOU...
...
HUH?

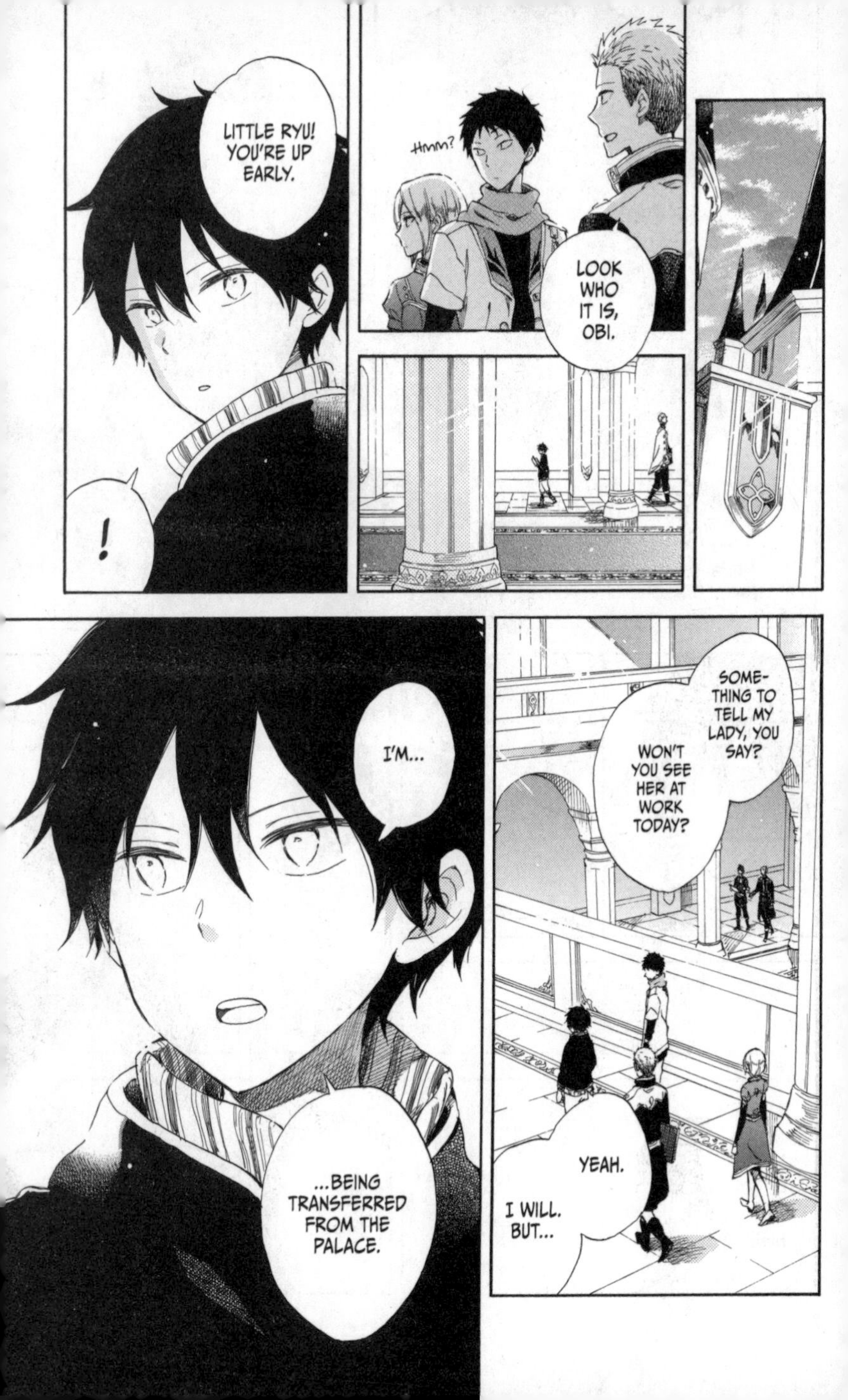
LOOK WHO IT IS, OBI.
Hmm?
LITTLE RYU! YOU'RE UP EARLY.
!
SOME-THING TO TELL MY LADY, YOU SAY?
WON'T YOU SEE HER AT WORK TODAY?
YEAH.
I WILL. BUT...
I'M...
...BEING TRANSFERRED FROM THE PALACE.

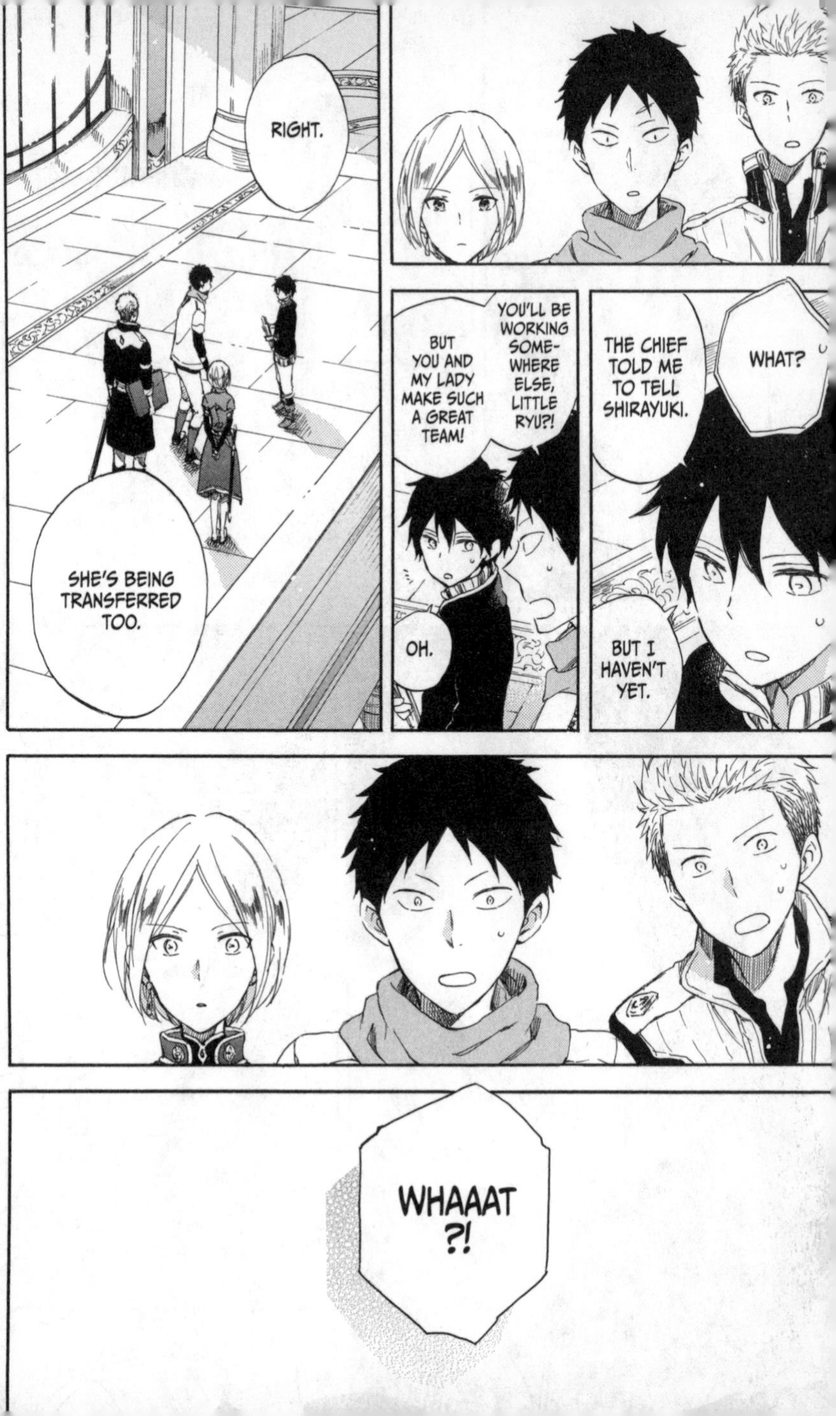
WHAT?
THE CHIEF TOLD ME TO TELL SHIRAYUKI.
BUT I HAVEN'T YET.
YOU'LL BE WORKING SOMEWHERE ELSE, LITTLE RYU?!
BUT YOU AND MY LADY MAKE SUCH A GREAT TEAM!
OH.
RIGHT.
SHE'S BEING TRANSFERRED TOO.
WHAAAT?!

Chapter 54

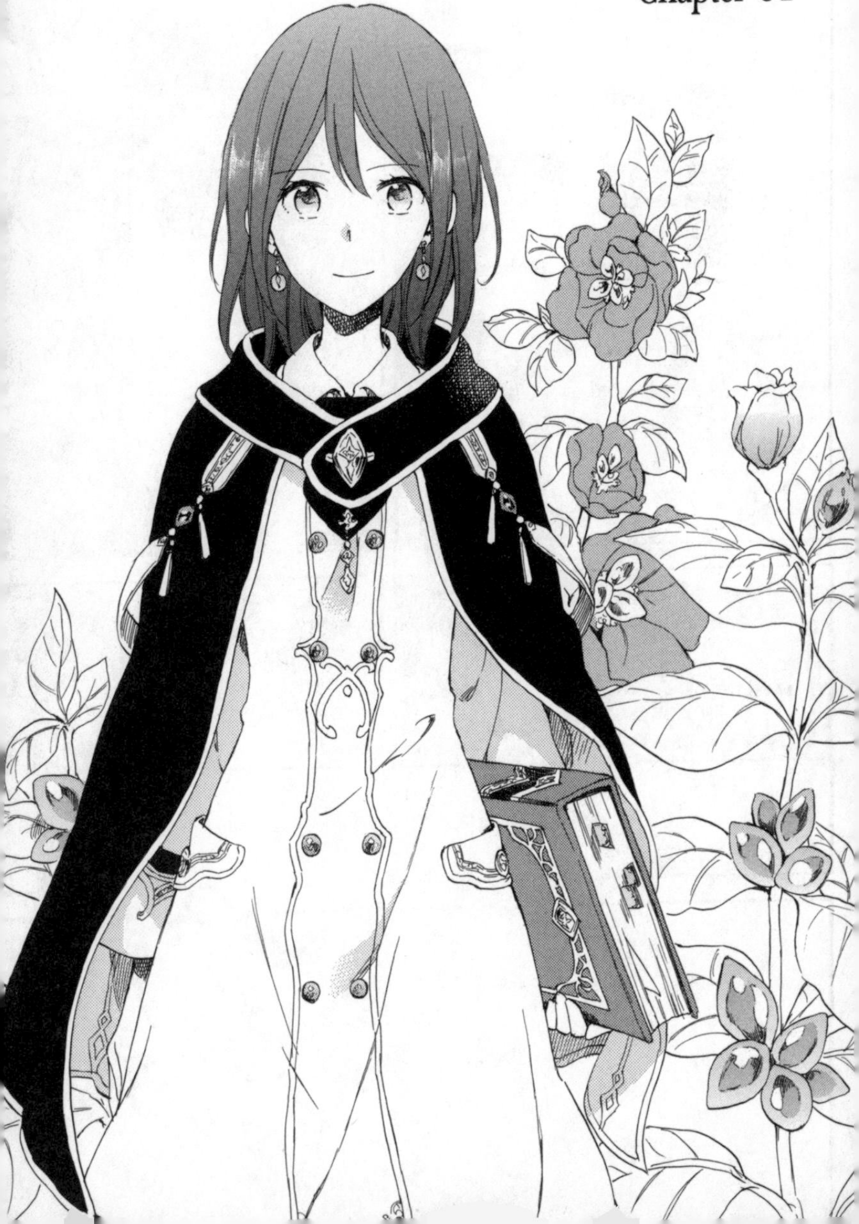

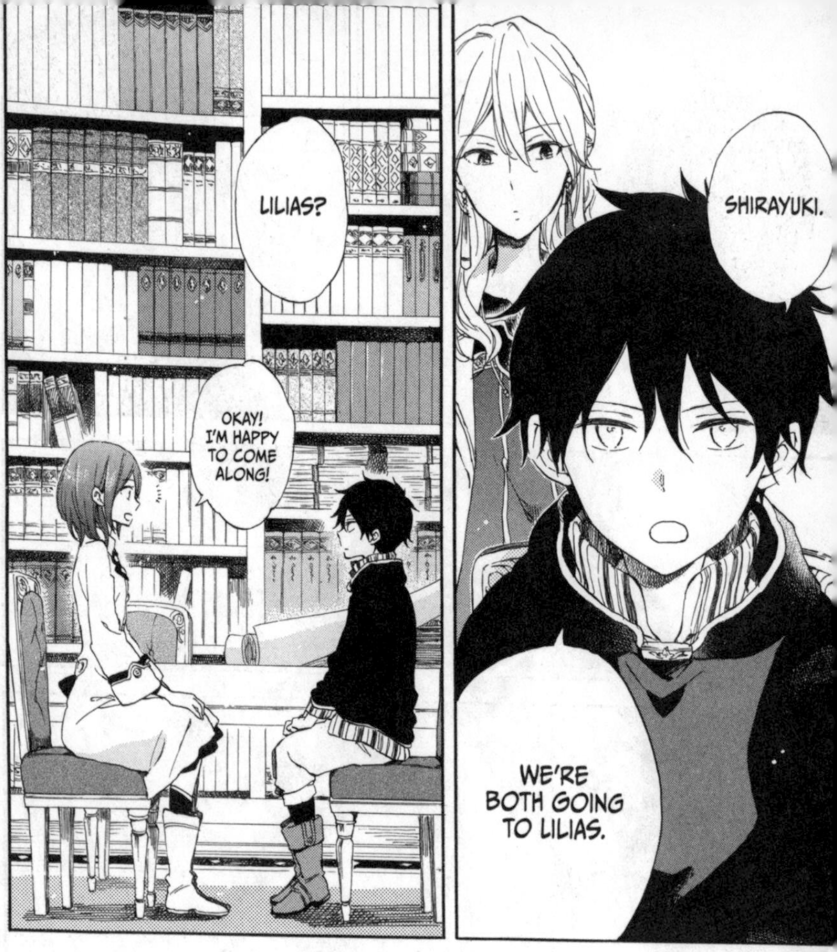
SHIRAYUKI.
WE'RE BOTH GOING TO LILIAS.
LILIAS?
OKAY! I'M HAPPY TO COME ALONG!

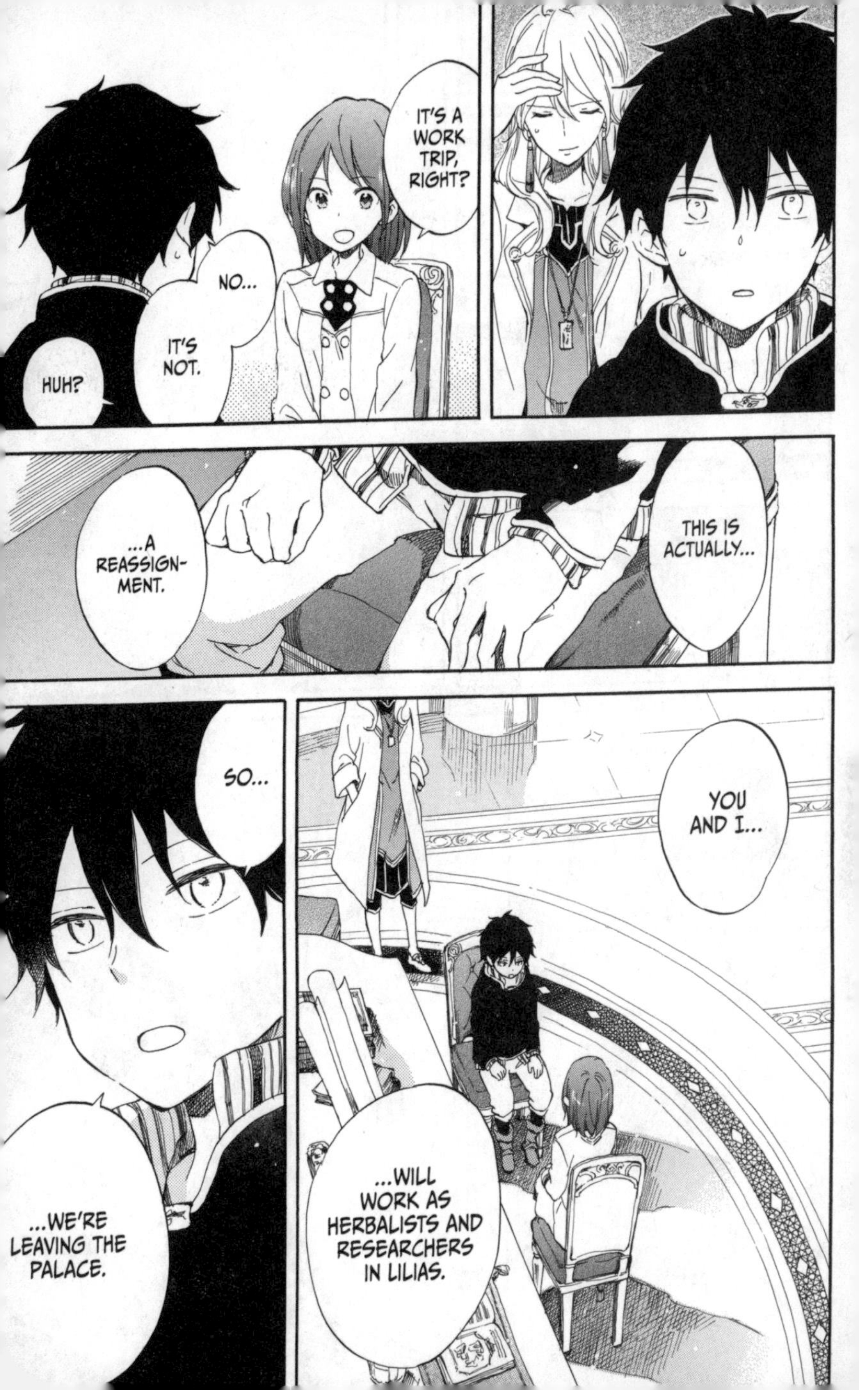
IT'S A WORK TRIP, RIGHT?
NO...
IT'S NOT.
HUH?
THIS IS ACTUALLY...
...A REASSIGNMENT.
YOU AND I...
...WILL WORK AS HERBALISTS AND RESEARCHERS IN LILIAS.
SO...
...WE'RE LEAVING THE PALACE.

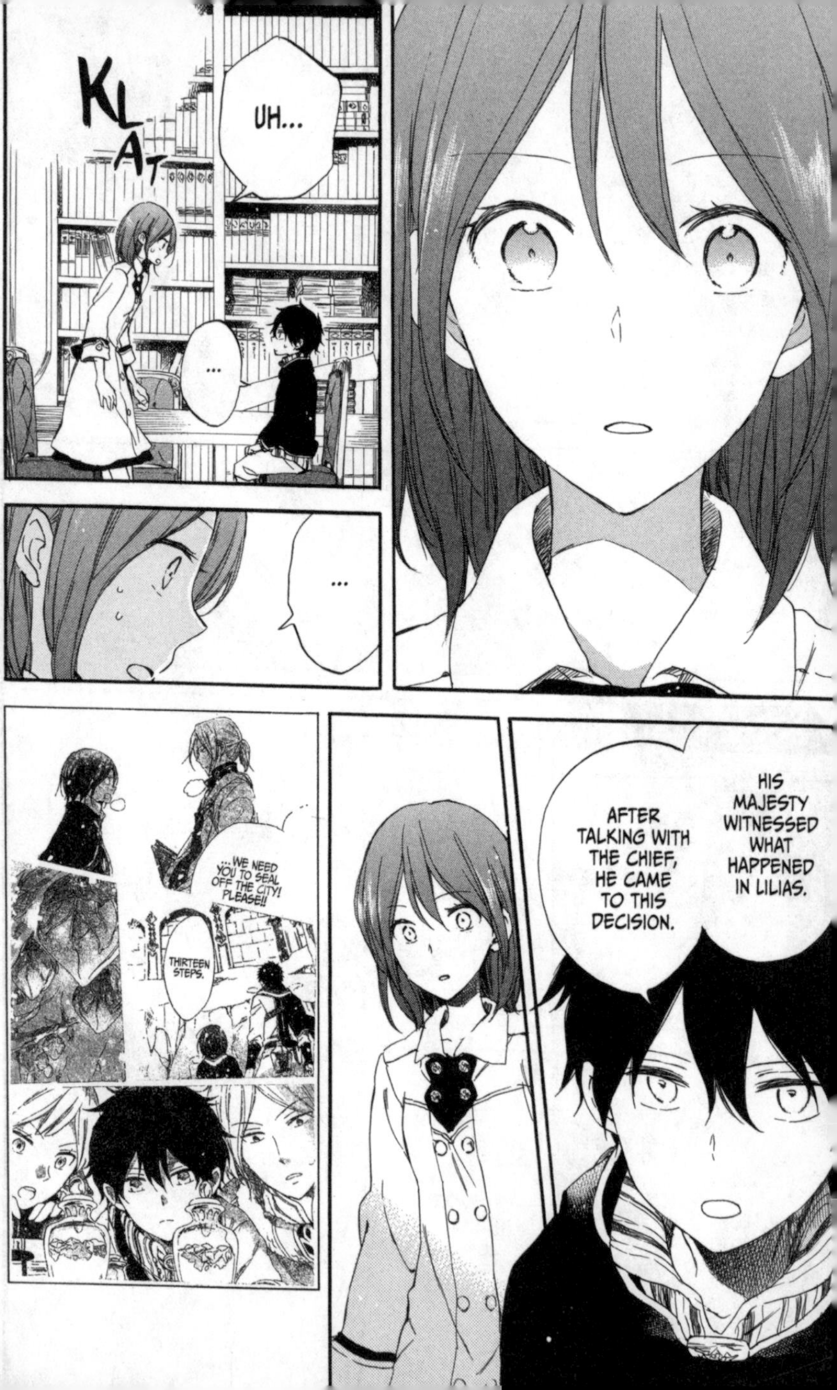
UH...
KLAT
...
...
HIS MAJESTY WITNESSED WHAT HAPPENED IN LILIAS.
AFTER TALKING WITH THE CHIEF, HE CAME TO THIS DECISION.
...WE NEED YOU TO SEAL OFF THE CITY! PLEASE!!
THIRTEEN STEPS.

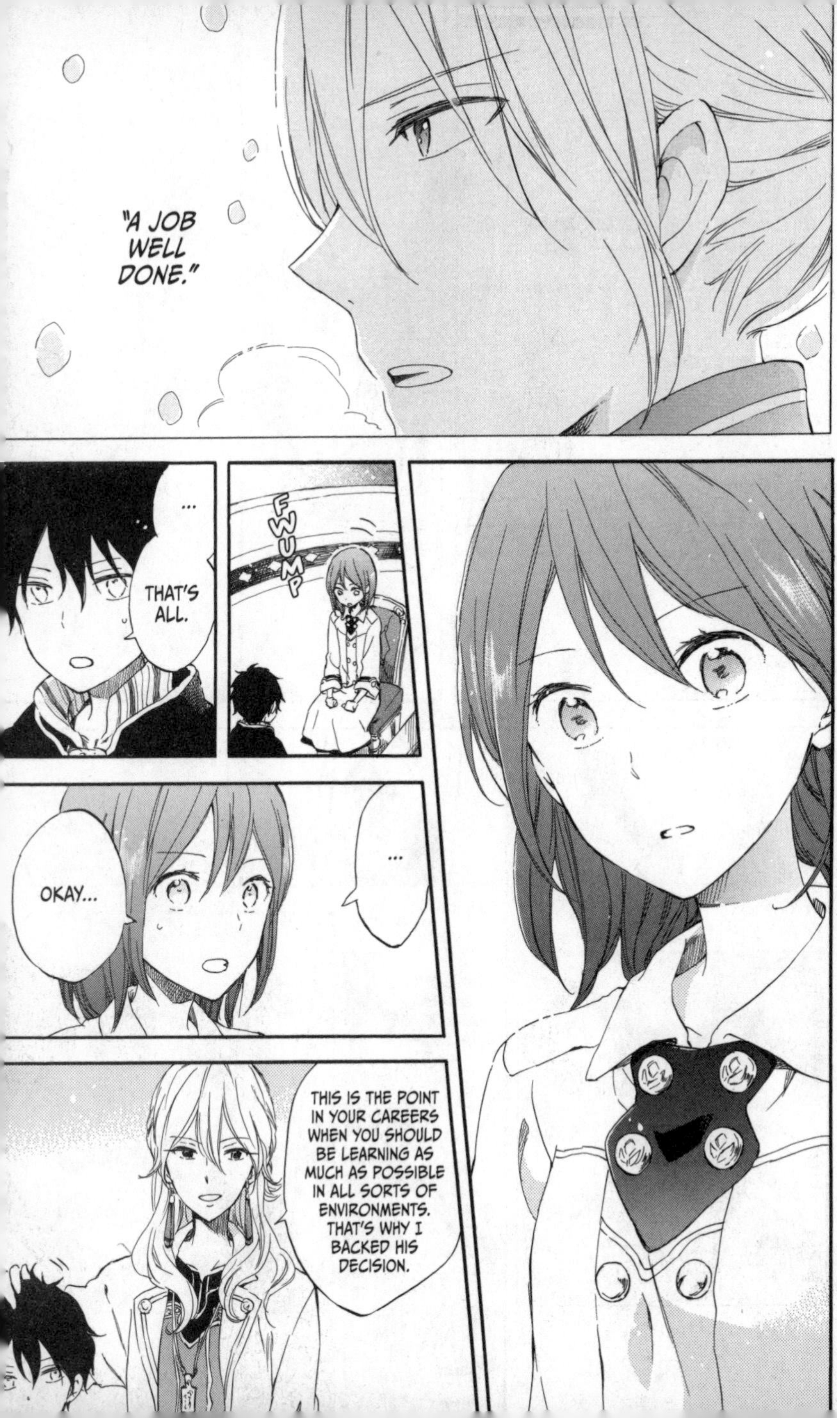
"A JOB WELL DONE."
FWUMP
...
THAT'S ALL.
...
OKAY...
THIS IS THE POINT IN YOUR CAREERS WHEN YOU SHOULD BE LEARNING AS MUCH AS POSSIBLE IN ALL SORTS OF ENVIRONMENTS. THAT'S WHY I BACKED HIS DECISION.

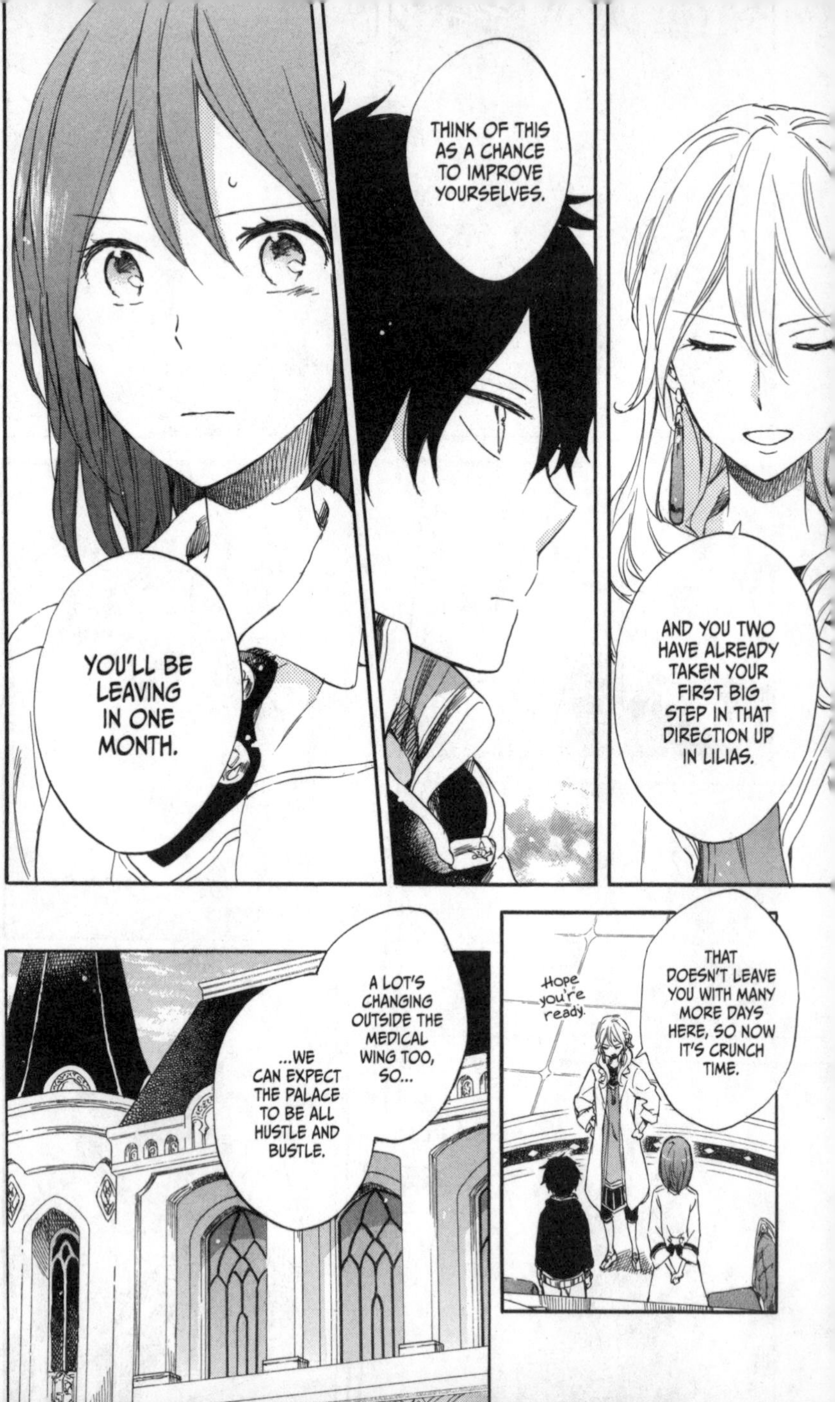
AND YOU TWO HAVE ALREADY TAKEN YOUR FIRST BIG STEP IN THAT DIRECTION UP IN LILIAS.
THINK OF THIS AS A CHANCE TO IMPROVE YOURSELVES.
YOU'LL BE LEAVING IN ONE MONTH.
THAT DOESN'T LEAVE YOU WITH MANY MORE DAYS HERE, SO NOW IT'S CRUNCH TIME.
Hope you're ready.
A LOT'S CHANGING OUTSIDE THE MEDICAL WING TOO, SO...
...WE CAN EXPECT THE PALACE TO BE ALL HUSTLE AND BUSTLE.

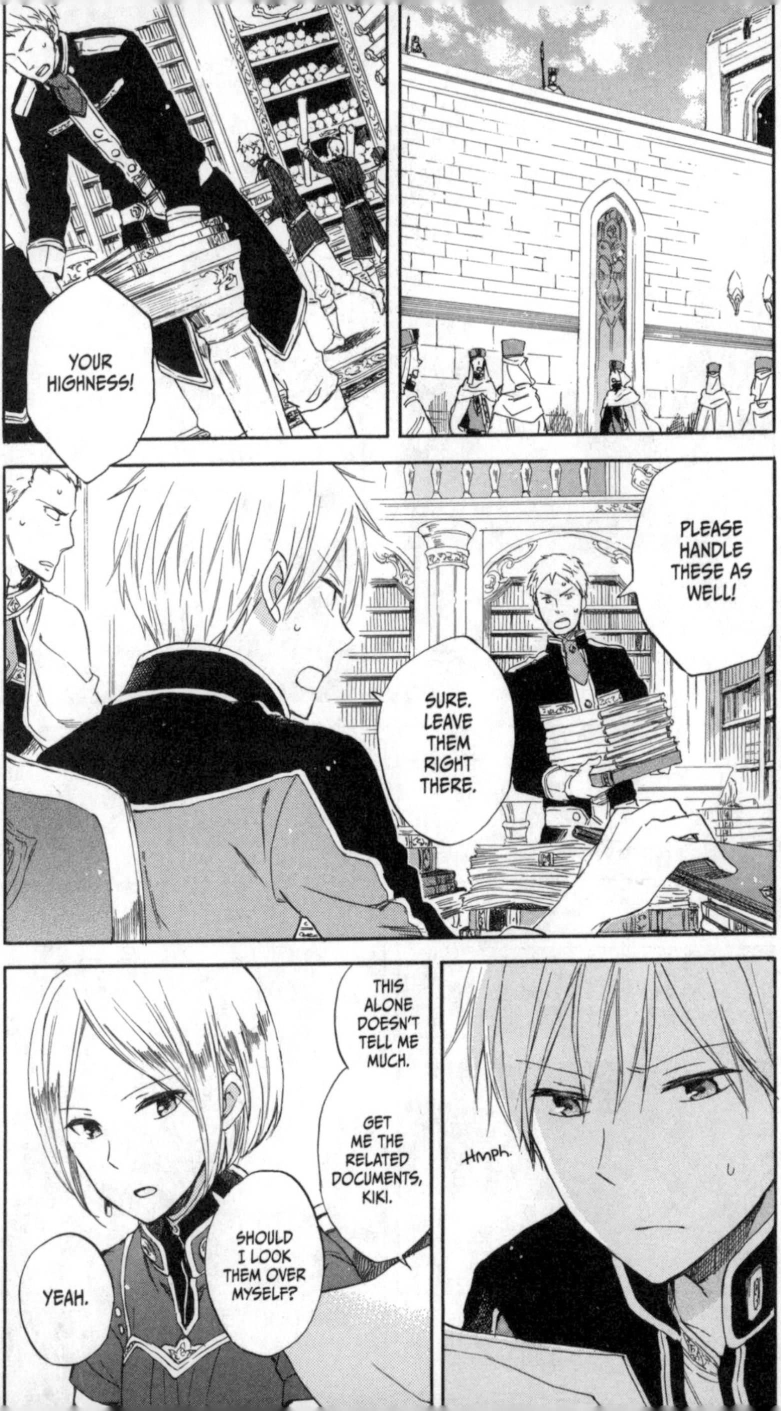
YOUR HIGHNESS!
PLEASE HANDLE THESE AS WELL!
SURE. LEAVE THEM RIGHT THERE.
Hmph.
THIS ALONE DOESN'T TELL ME MUCH.
GET ME THE RELATED DOCUMENTS, KIKI.
SHOULD I LOOK THEM OVER MYSELF?
YEAH.

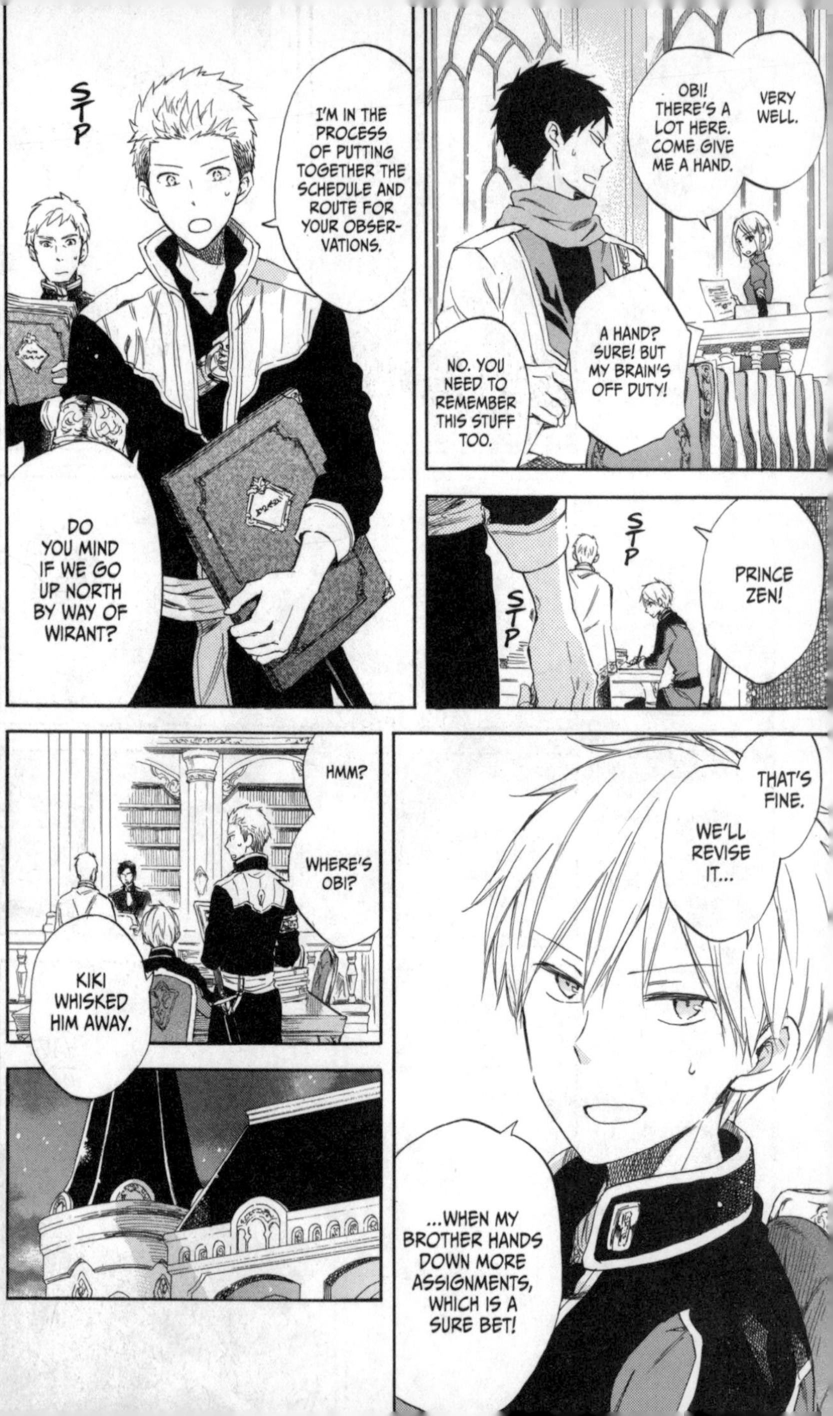
VERY WELL.
OBI! THERE'S A LOT HERE. COME GIVE ME A HAND.
A HAND? SURE! BUT MY BRAIN'S OFF DUTY!
NO. YOU NEED TO REMEMBER THIS STUFF TOO.
PRINCE ZEN!
STP
STP
I'M IN THE PROCESS OF PUTTING TOGETHER THE SCHEDULE AND ROUTE FOR YOUR OBSERVATIONS.
STP
DO YOU MIND IF WE GO UP NORTH BY WAY OF WIRANT?
THAT'S FINE.
WE'LL REVISE IT...
...WHEN MY BROTHER HANDS DOWN MORE ASSIGNMENTS, WHICH IS A SURE BET!
HMM?
WHERE'S OBI?
KIKI WHISKED HIM AWAY.

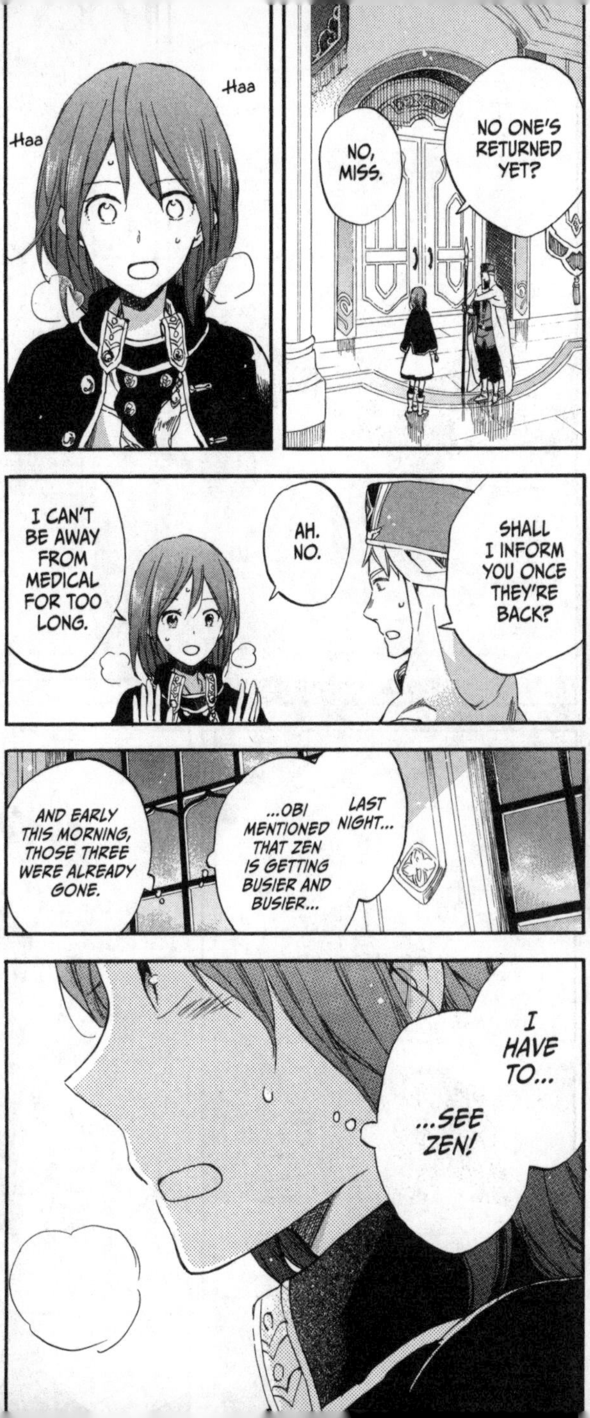
NO ONE'S RETURNED YET?
NO, MISS.
Haa
Haa
SHALL I INFORM YOU ONCE THEY'RE BACK?
AH. NO.
I CAN'T BE AWAY FROM MEDICAL FOR TOO LONG.
LAST NIGHT...
...OBI MENTIONED THAT ZEN IS GETTING BUSIER AND BUSIER...
AND EARLY THIS MORNING, THOSE THREE WERE ALREADY GONE.
I HAVE TO...
...SEE ZEN!

CHAPTER 52

I don't get many chances to draw the castle town, so this was fun. Isn't that bustling restaurant just great?

You've got servers carrying food in both hands! It makes me want to order a heaping plate!

Plus, we got to see the increasingly chilly relationship between Hisame and Mitsuhide, as well as Prince Raj thinking about the meaning of friendship.

Concerning the art—night scenes use a lot of tone. I ask for more and more and more and it never ends. My fingers started to cramp after using all that white to portray lights and stars.

I'm the type who tends to finish strong in a big burst.

CHAPTER 53

It's still nighttime!!

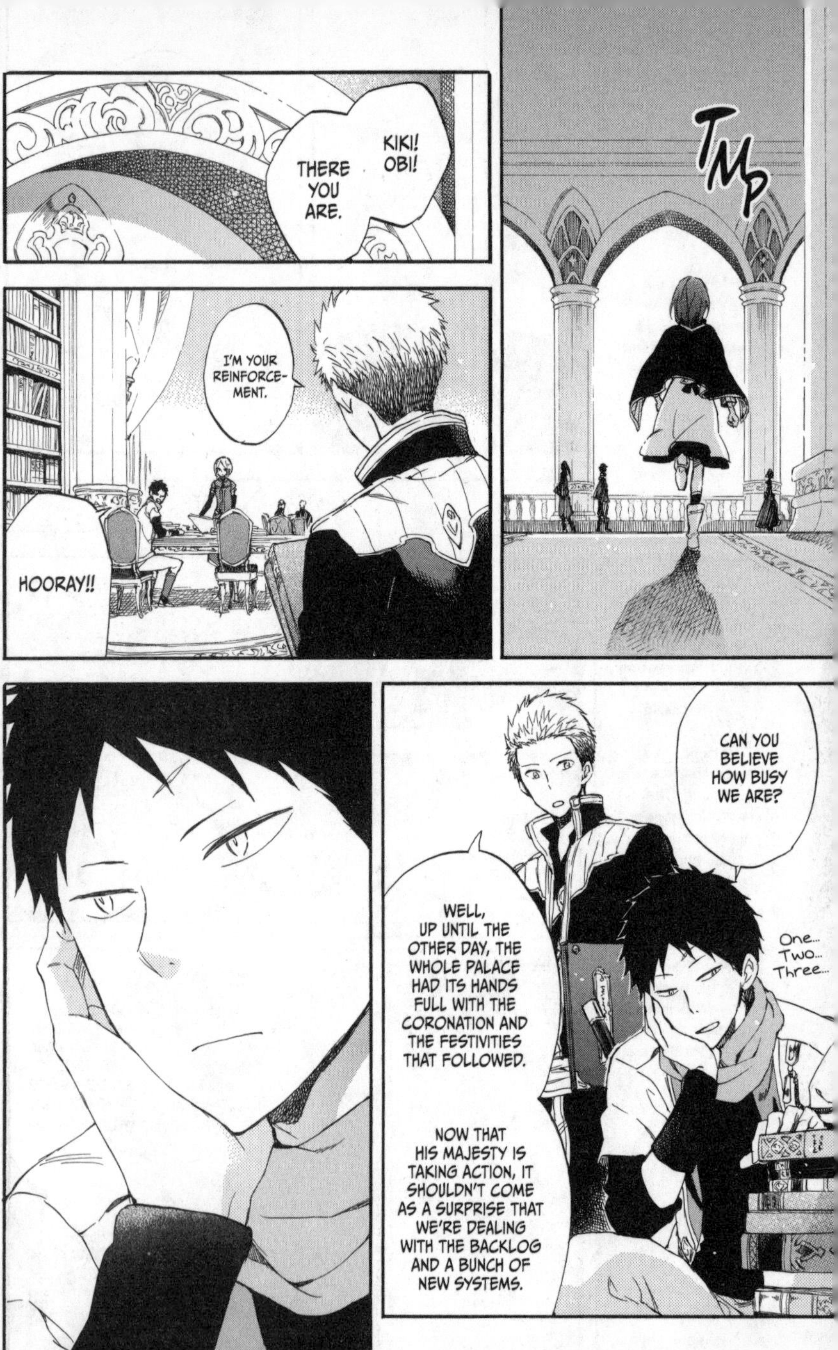
TMP
KIKI! OBI!
THERE YOU ARE.
I'M YOUR REINFORCEMENT.
HOORAY!!
CAN YOU BELIEVE HOW BUSY WE ARE?
WELL, UP UNTIL THE OTHER DAY, THE WHOLE PALACE HAD ITS HANDS FULL WITH THE CORONATION AND THE FESTIVITIES THAT FOLLOWED.
NOW THAT HIS MAJESTY IS TAKING ACTION, IT SHOULDN'T COME AS A SURPRISE THAT WE'RE DEALING WITH THE BACKLOG AND A BUNCH OF NEW SYSTEMS.
One... Two... Three...

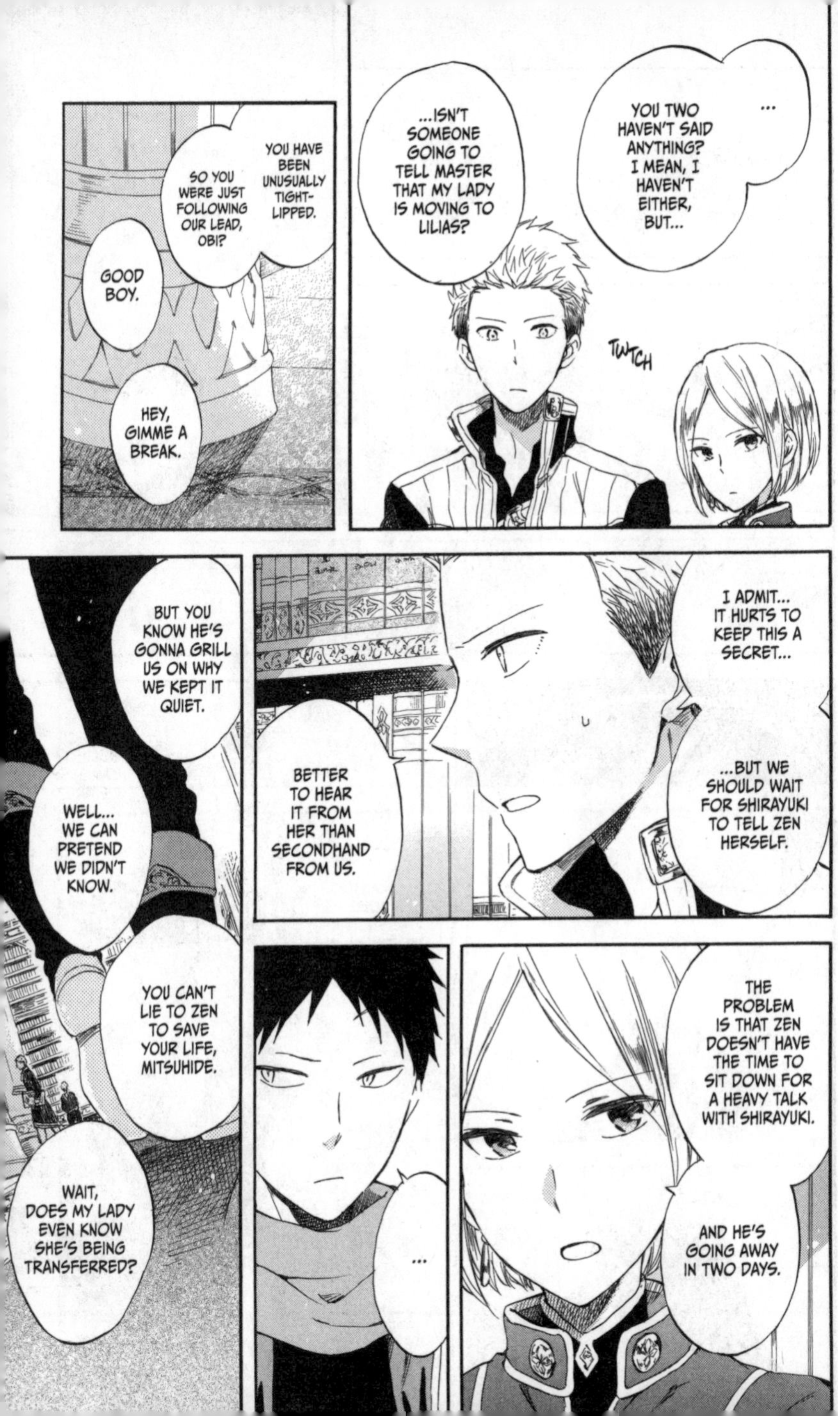
...
YOU TWO HAVEN'T SAID ANYTHING? I MEAN, I HAVEN'T EITHER, BUT...
...ISN'T SOMEONE GOING TO TELL MASTER THAT MY LADY IS MOVING TO LILIAS?
TWTCH
YOU HAVE BEEN UNUSUALLY TIGHT-LIPPED.
SO YOU WERE JUST FOLLOWING OUR LEAD, OBI?
GOOD BOY.
HEY, GIMME A BREAK.
I ADMIT... IT HURTS TO KEEP THIS A SECRET...
...BUT WE SHOULD WAIT FOR SHIRAYUKI TO TELL ZEN HERSELF.
BETTER TO HEAR IT FROM HER THAN SECONDHAND FROM US.
THE PROBLEM IS THAT ZEN DOESN'T HAVE THE TIME TO SIT DOWN FOR A HEAVY TALK WITH SHIRAYUKI.
AND HE'S GOING AWAY IN TWO DAYS.
...
BUT YOU KNOW HE'S GONNA GRILL US ON WHY WE KEPT IT QUIET.
WELL... WE CAN PRETEND WE DIDN'T KNOW.
YOU CAN'T LIE TO ZEN TO SAVE YOUR LIFE, MITSUHIDE.
WAIT, DOES MY LADY EVEN KNOW SHE'S BEING TRANSFERRED?

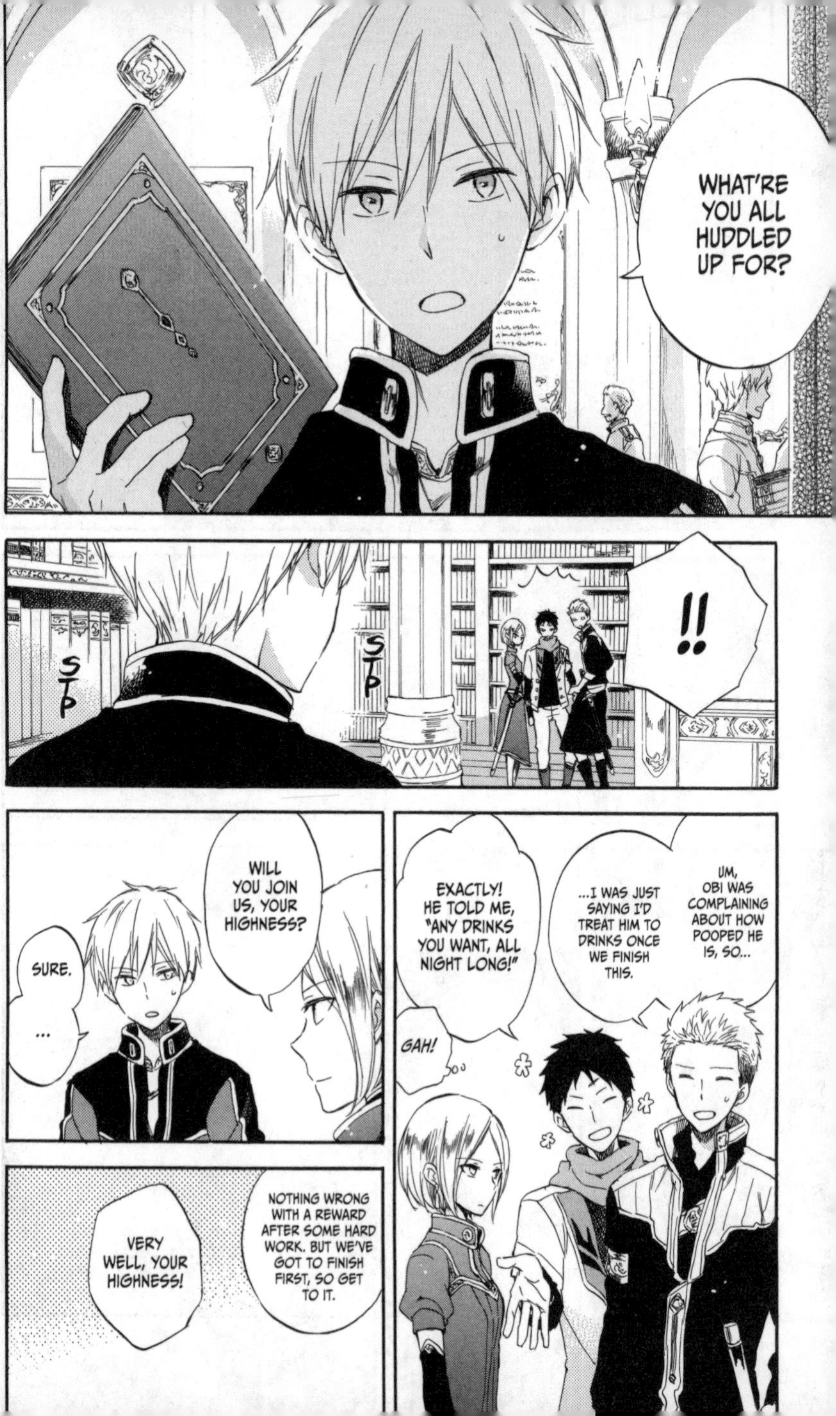
WHAT'RE YOU ALL HUDDLED UP FOR?
STP
STP
!!
UM, OBI WAS COMPLAINING ABOUT HOW POOPED HE IS, SO...
...I WAS JUST SAYING I'D TREAT HIM TO DRINKS ONCE WE FINISH THIS.
EXACTLY! HE TOLD ME, "ANY DRINKS YOU WANT, ALL NIGHT LONG!"
GAH!
WILL YOU JOIN US, YOUR HIGHNESS?
SURE.
...
NOTHING WRONG WITH A REWARD AFTER SOME HARD WORK. BUT WE'VE GOT TO FINISH FIRST, SO GET TO IT.
VERY WELL, YOUR HIGHNESS!

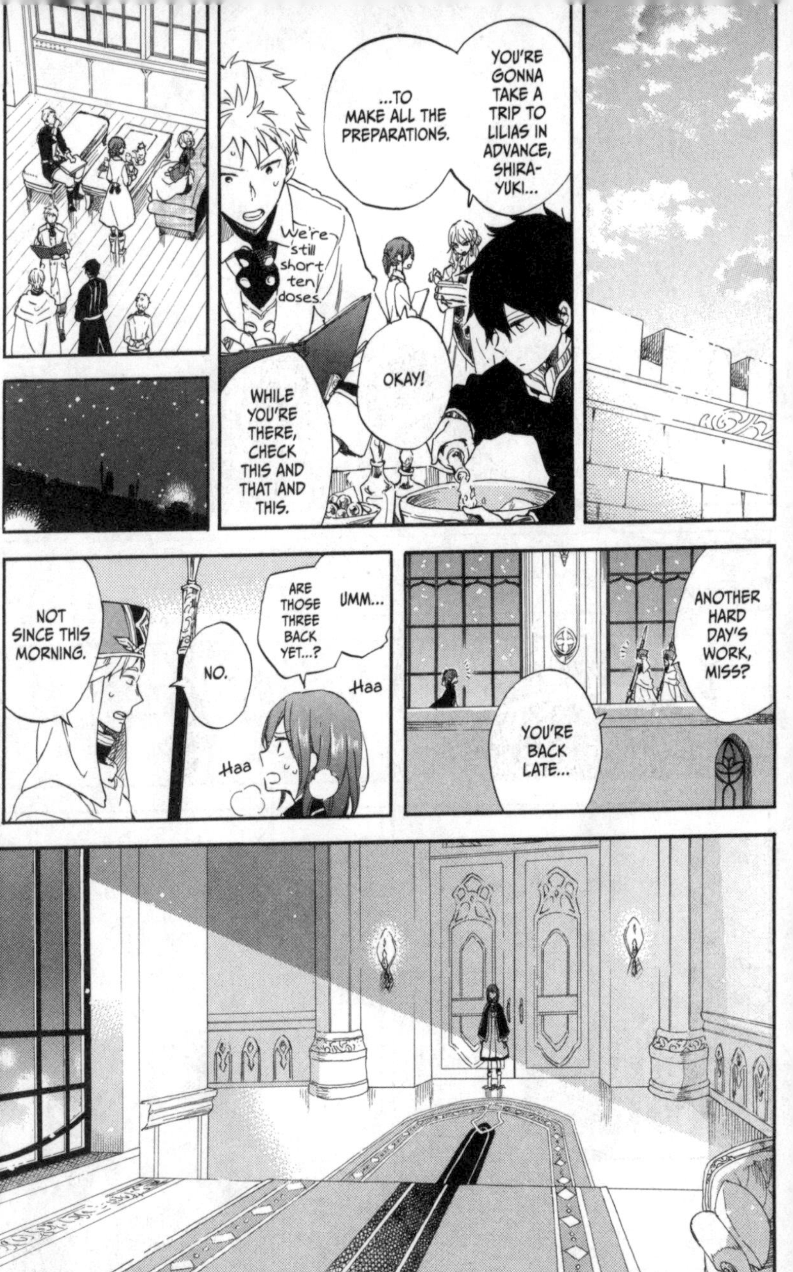
YOU'RE GONNA TAKE A TRIP TO LILIAS IN ADVANCE, SHIRA-YUKI...
...TO MAKE ALL THE PREPARATIONS.
We're still short ten doses.
OKAY!
WHILE YOU'RE THERE, CHECK THIS AND THAT AND THIS.
ANOTHER HARD DAY'S WORK, MISS?
YOU'RE BACK LATE...
UMM...
ARE THOSE THREE BACK YET...?
Haa
Haa
NO.
NOT SINCE THIS MORNING.

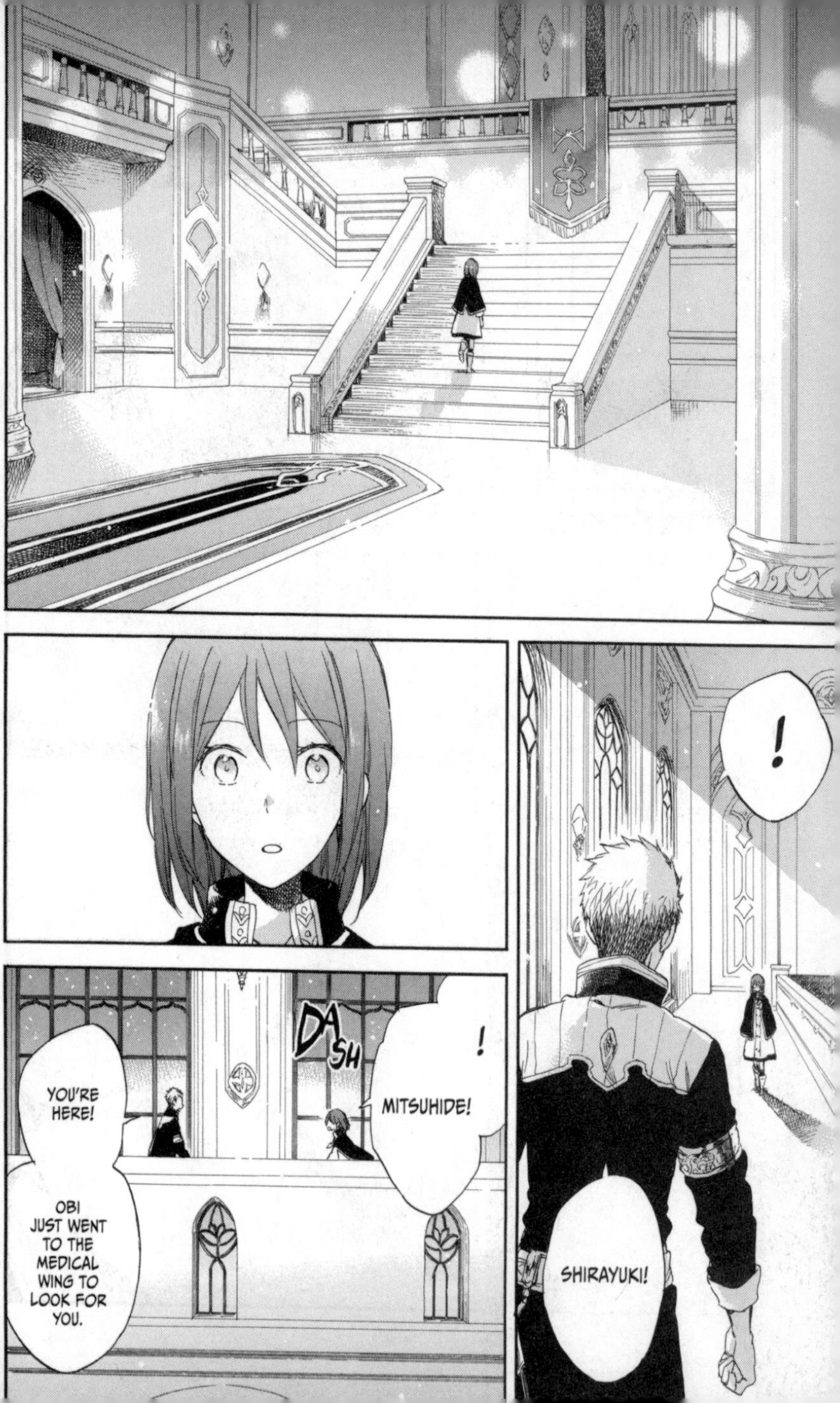
!
SHIRAYUKI!
!
DASH
MITSUHIDE!
YOU'RE HERE!
OBI JUST WENT TO THE MEDICAL WING TO LOOK FOR YOU.

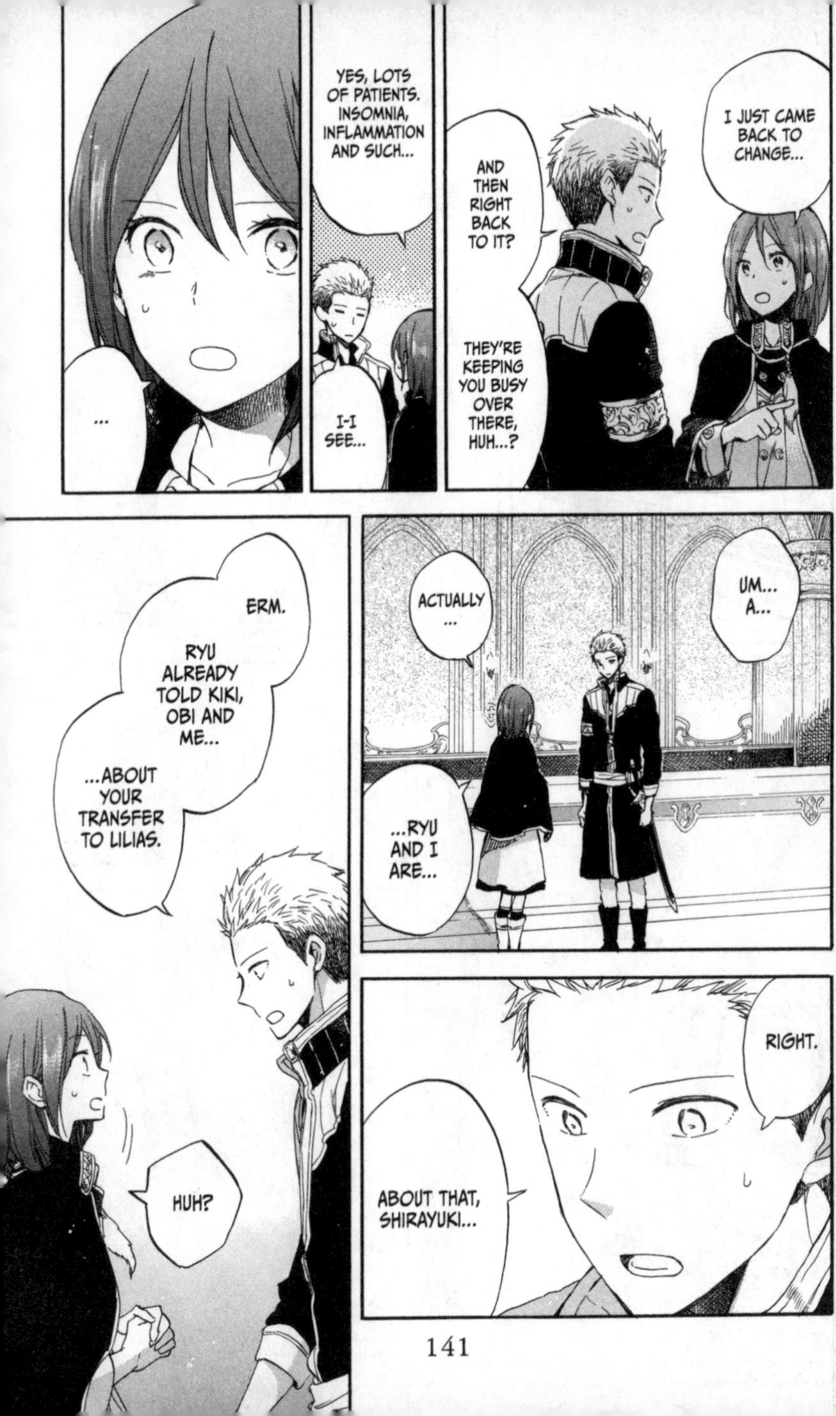
I JUST CAME BACK TO CHANGE...
AND THEN RIGHT BACK TO IT?
THEY'RE KEEPING YOU BUSY OVER THERE, HUH...?
YES, LOTS OF PATIENTS. INSOMNIA, INFLAMMATION AND SUCH...
I-I SEE...
...
UM... A...
ACTUALLY ...
...RYU AND I ARE...
RIGHT.
ABOUT THAT, SHIRAYUKI...
ERM.
RYU ALREADY TOLD KIKI, OBI AND ME...
...ABOUT YOUR TRANSFER TO LILIAS.
HUH?

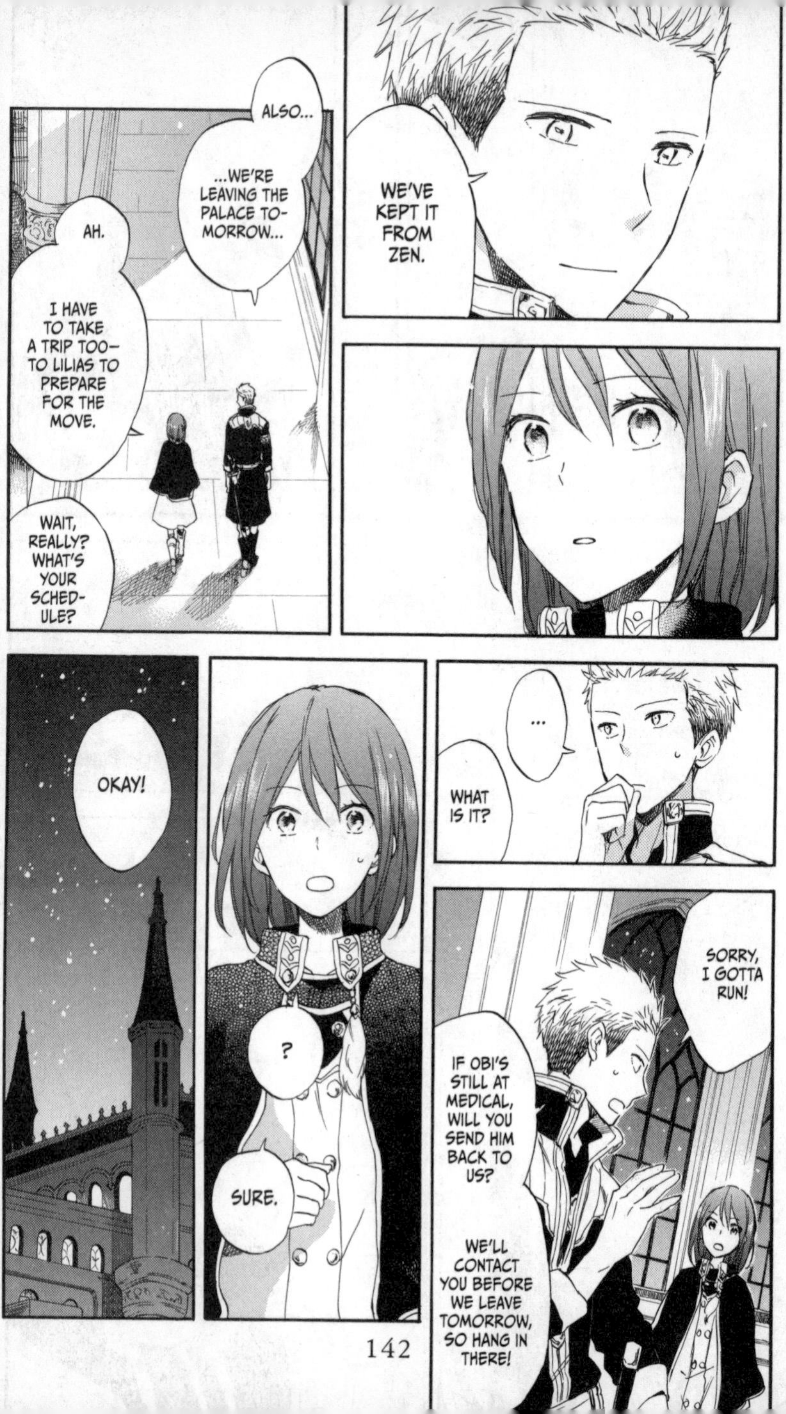
WE'VE KEPT IT FROM ZEN.
ALSO...
...WE'RE LEAVING THE PALACE TO-MORROW...
AH.
I HAVE TO TAKE A TRIP TOO— TO LILIAS TO PREPARE FOR THE MOVE.
WAIT, REALLY? WHAT'S YOUR SCHED-ULE?
...
WHAT IS IT?
SORRY, I GOTTA RUN!
IF OBI'S STILL AT MEDICAL, WILL YOU SEND HIM BACK TO US?
WE'LL CONTACT YOU BEFORE WE LEAVE TOMORROW, SO HANG IN THERE!
?
SURE.
OKAY!

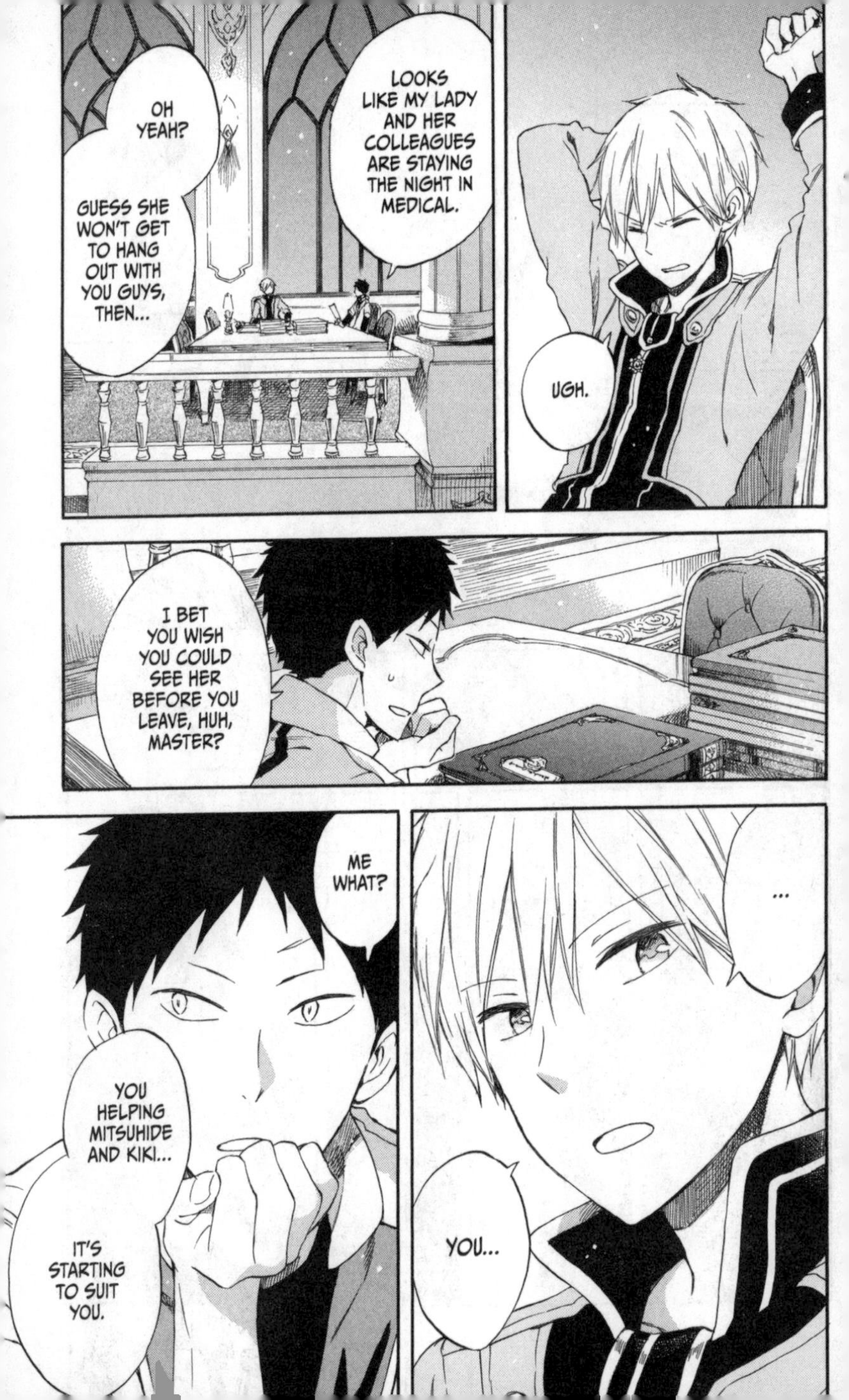
UGH.
LOOKS LIKE MY LADY AND HER COLLEAGUES ARE STAYING THE NIGHT IN MEDICAL.
OH YEAH?
GUESS SHE WON'T GET TO HANG OUT WITH YOU GUYS, THEN...
I BET YOU WISH YOU COULD SEE HER BEFORE YOU LEAVE, HUH, MASTER?
...
YOU...
ME WHAT?
YOU HELPING MITSUHIDE AND KIKI...
IT'S STARTING TO SUIT YOU.

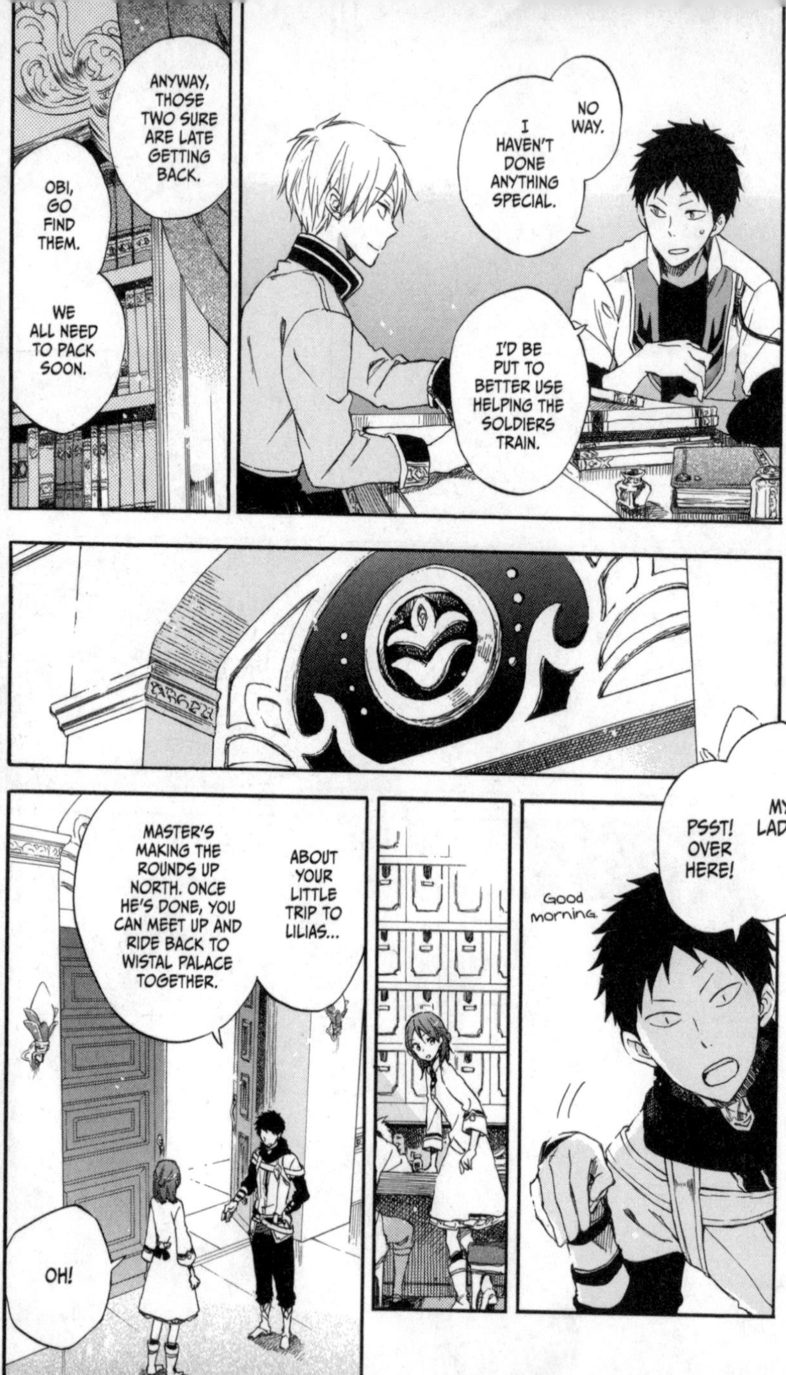
NO WAY.
I HAVEN'T DONE ANYTHING SPECIAL.
I'D BE PUT TO BETTER USE HELPING THE SOLDIERS TRAIN.
ANYWAY, THOSE TWO SURE ARE LATE GETTING BACK.
OBI, GO FIND THEM.
WE ALL NEED TO PACK SOON.
MY LADY!
PSST! OVER HERE!
Good morning.
ABOUT YOUR LITTLE TRIP TO LILIAS...
MASTER'S MAKING THE ROUNDS UP NORTH. ONCE HE'S DONE, YOU CAN MEET UP AND RIDE BACK TO WISTAL PALACE TOGETHER.
OH!

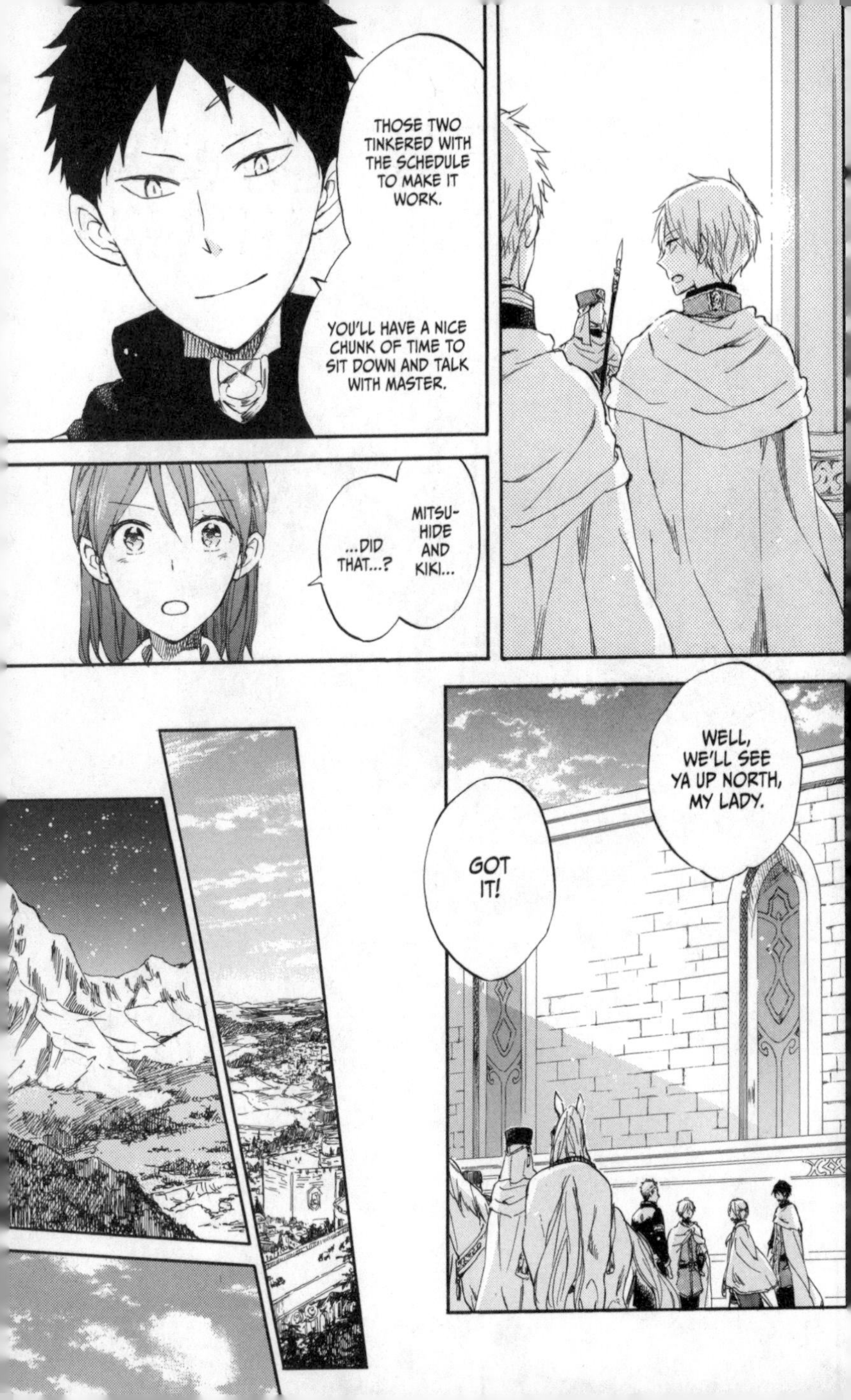
THOSE TWO TINKERED WITH THE SCHEDULE TO MAKE IT WORK.
YOU'LL HAVE A NICE CHUNK OF TIME TO SIT DOWN AND TALK WITH MASTER.
MITSU-HIDE AND KIKI...
...DID THAT...?
WELL, WE'LL SEE YA UP NORTH, MY LADY.
GOT IT!

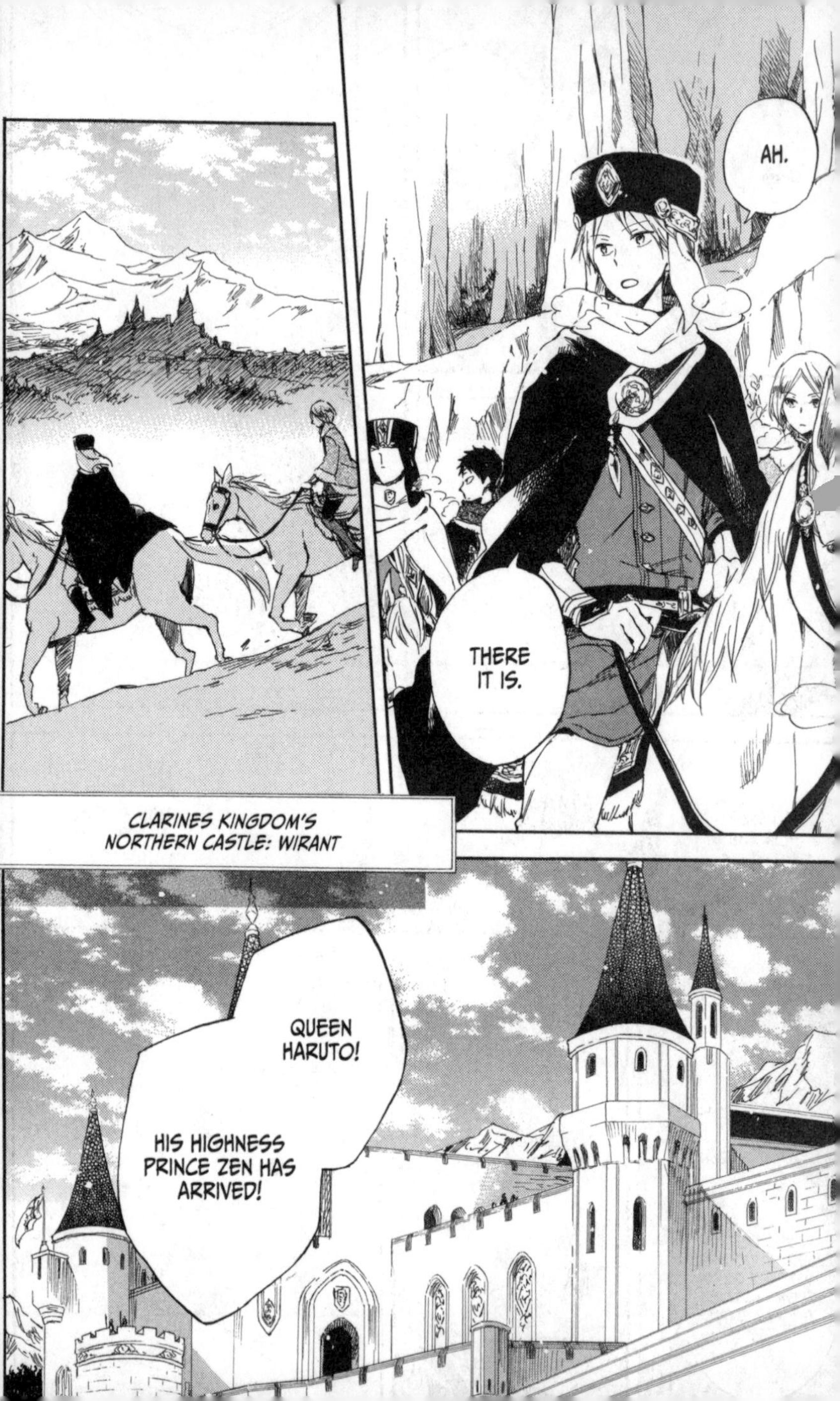
AH.
THERE IT IS.
CLARINES KINGDOM'S NORTHERN CASTLE: WIRANT
QUEEN HARUTO!
HIS HIGHNESS PRINCE ZEN HAS ARRIVED!

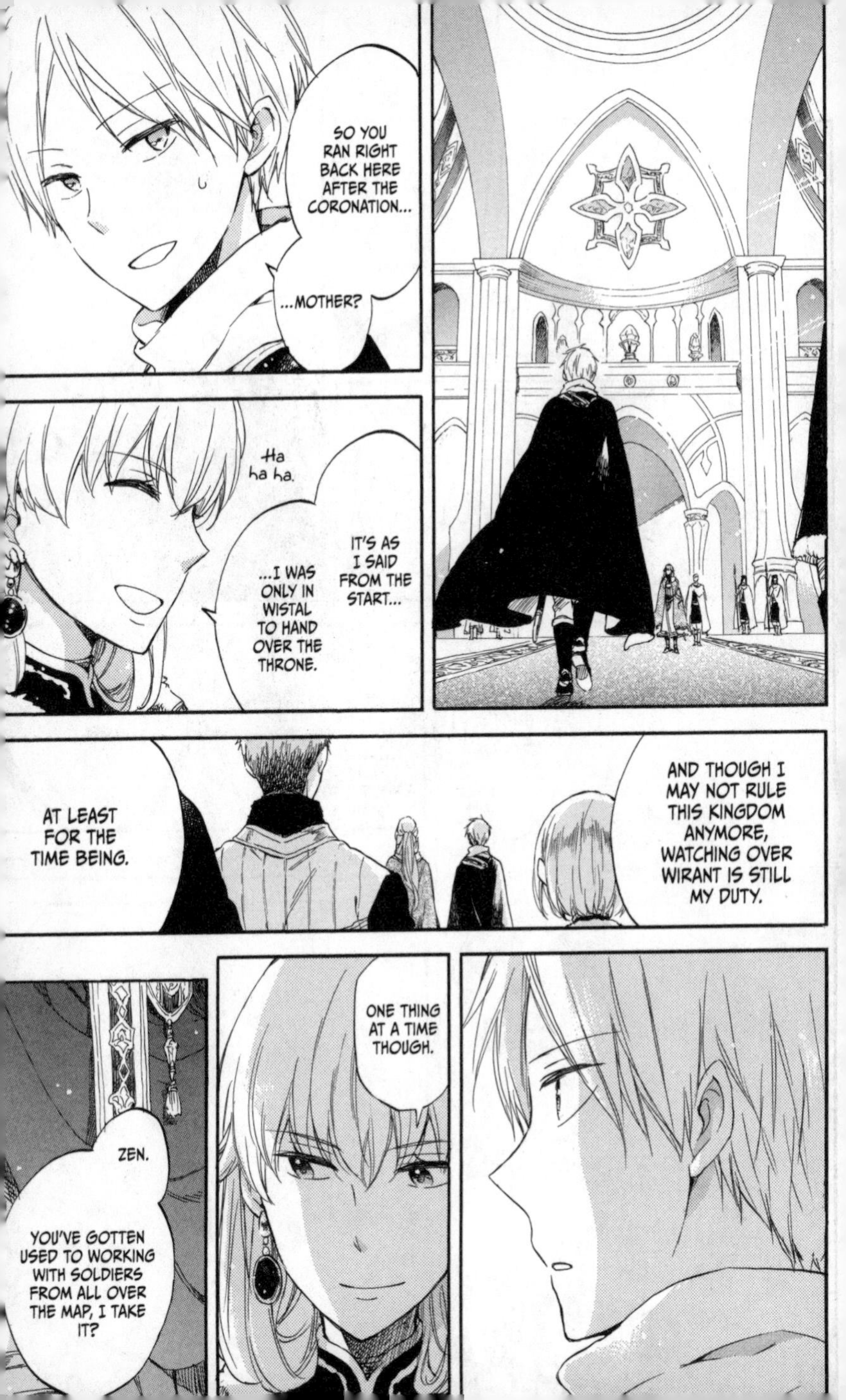
SO YOU RAN RIGHT BACK HERE AFTER THE CORONATION...
...MOTHER?
Ha ha ha.
IT'S AS I SAID FROM THE START...
...I WAS ONLY IN WISTAL TO HAND OVER THE THRONE.
AND THOUGH I MAY NOT RULE THIS KINGDOM ANYMORE, WATCHING OVER WIRANT IS STILL MY DUTY.
AT LEAST FOR THE TIME BEING.
ONE THING AT A TIME THOUGH.
ZEN.
YOU'VE GOTTEN USED TO WORKING WITH SOLDIERS FROM ALL OVER THE MAP, I TAKE IT?

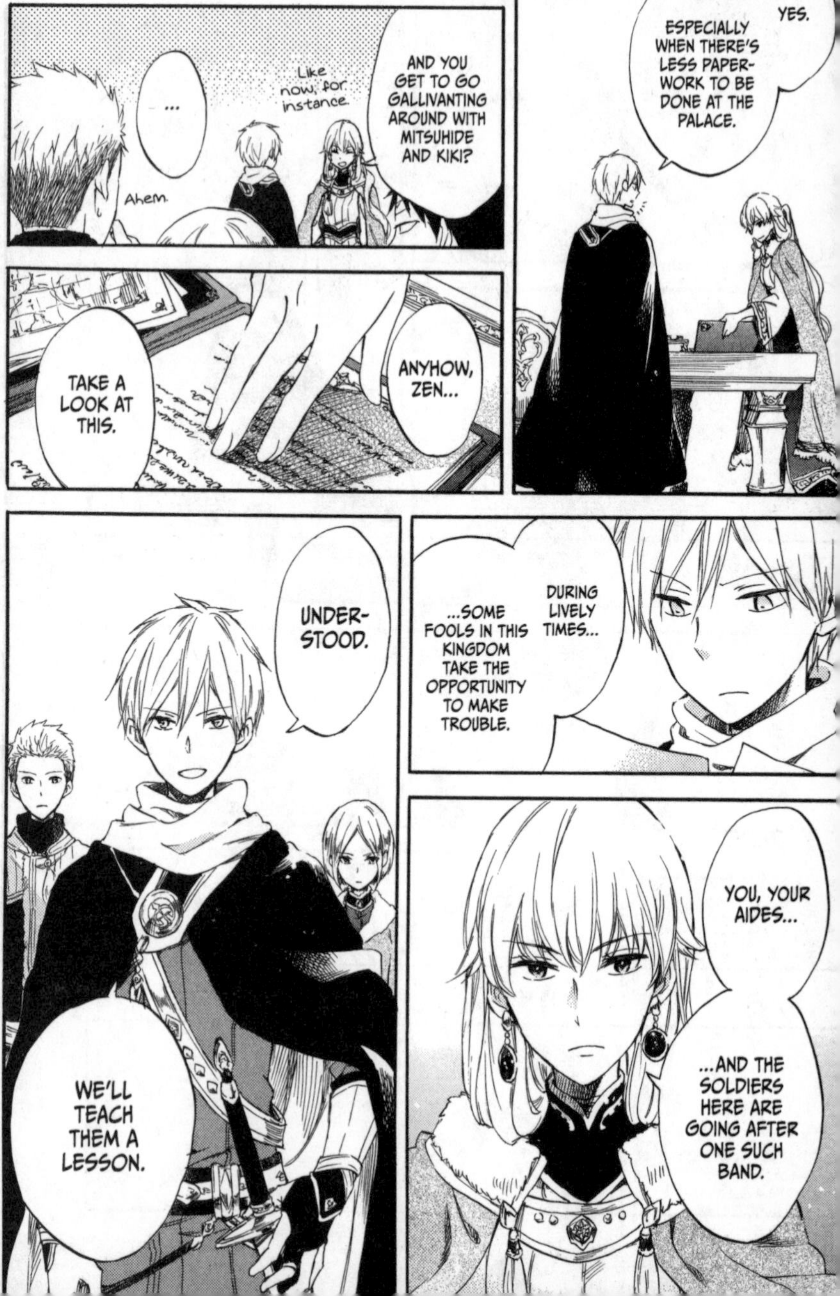
YES.
ESPECIALLY WHEN THERE'S LESS PAPER-WORK TO BE DONE AT THE PALACE.
AND YOU GET TO GO GALLIVANTING AROUND WITH MITSUHIDE AND KIKI?
Like now, for instance.
...
Ahem.
ANYHOW, ZEN...
TAKE A LOOK AT THIS.
DURING LIVELY TIMES...
...SOME FOOLS IN THIS KINGDOM TAKE THE OPPORTUNITY TO MAKE TROUBLE.
YOU, YOUR AIDES...
...AND THE SOLDIERS HERE ARE GOING AFTER ONE SUCH BAND.
UNDER-STOOD.
WE'LL TEACH THEM A LESSON.

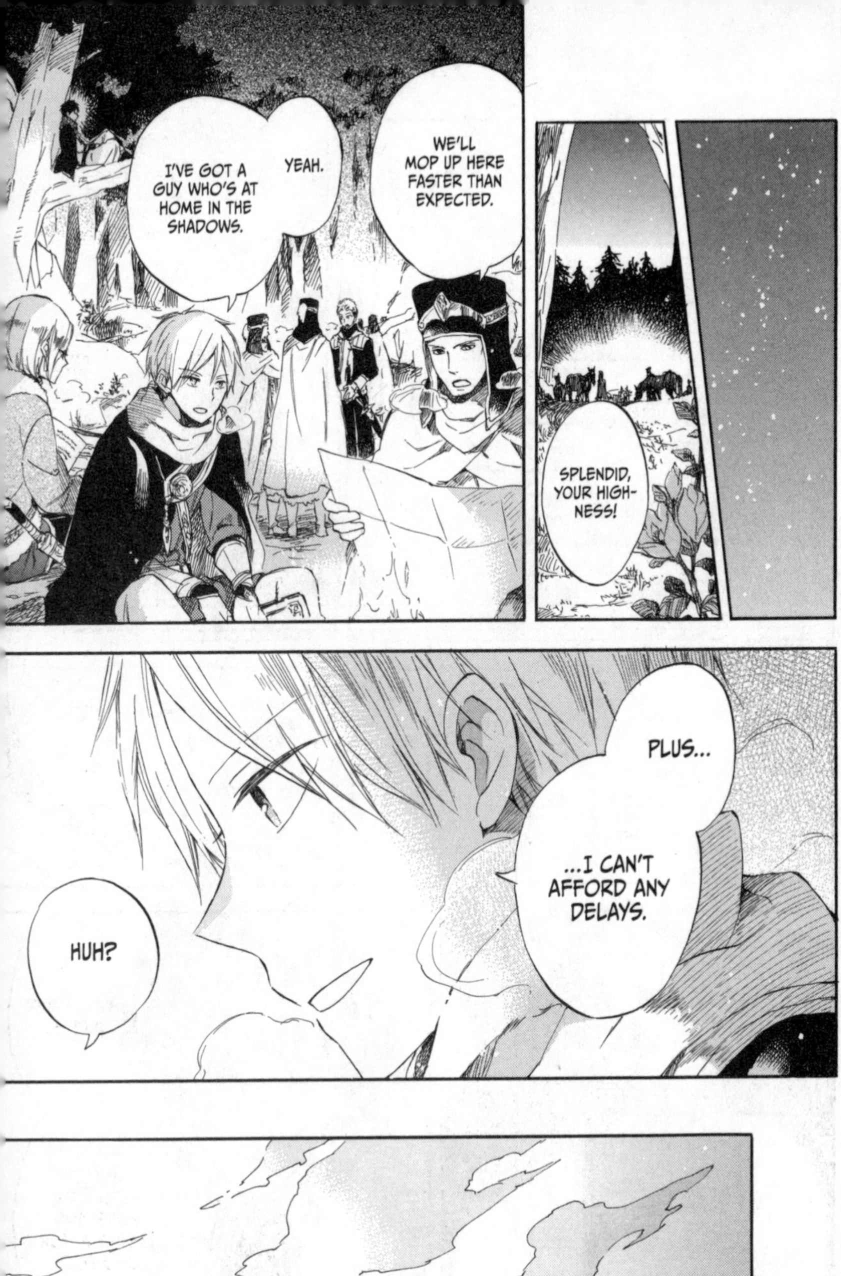
SPLENDID, YOUR HIGHNESS!
WE'LL MOP UP HERE FASTER THAN EXPECTED.
YEAH.
I'VE GOT A GUY WHO'S AT HOME IN THE SHADOWS.
PLUS...
...I CAN'T AFFORD ANY DELAYS.
HUH?

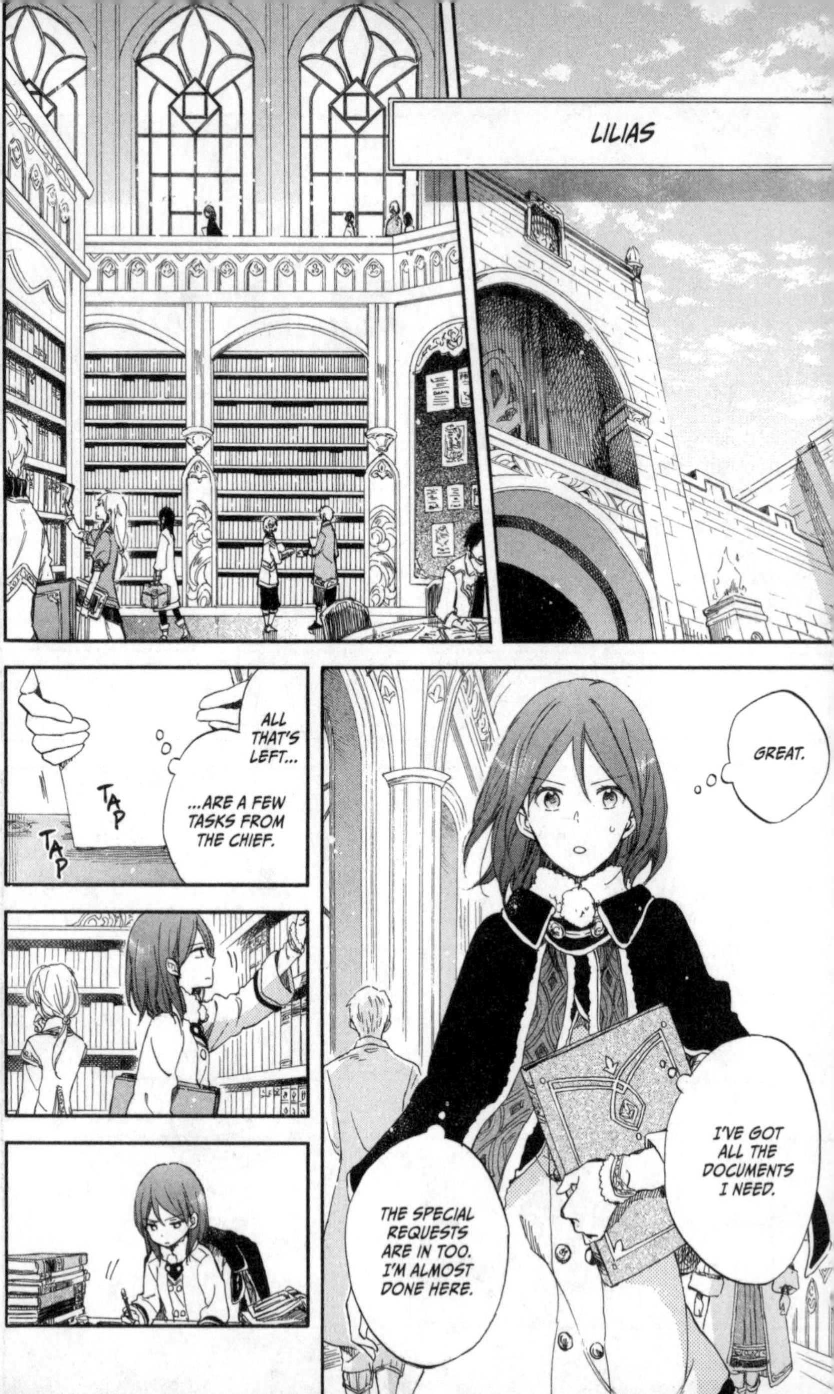
LILIAS
GREAT.
I'VE GOT ALL THE DOCUMENTS I NEED.
THE SPECIAL REQUESTS ARE IN TOO. I'M ALMOST DONE HERE.
ALL THAT'S LEFT...
...ARE A FEW TASKS FROM THE CHIEF.
TAP
TAP

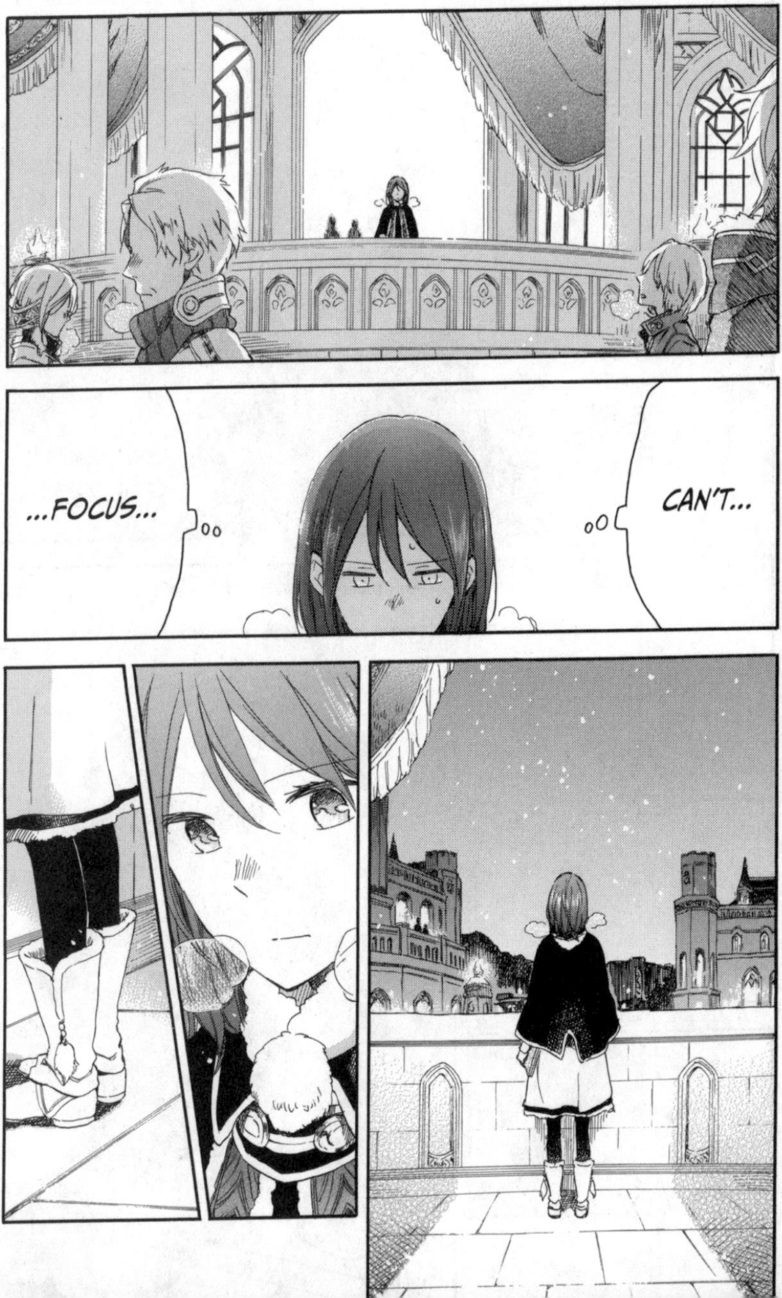
CAN'T...
...FOCUS...

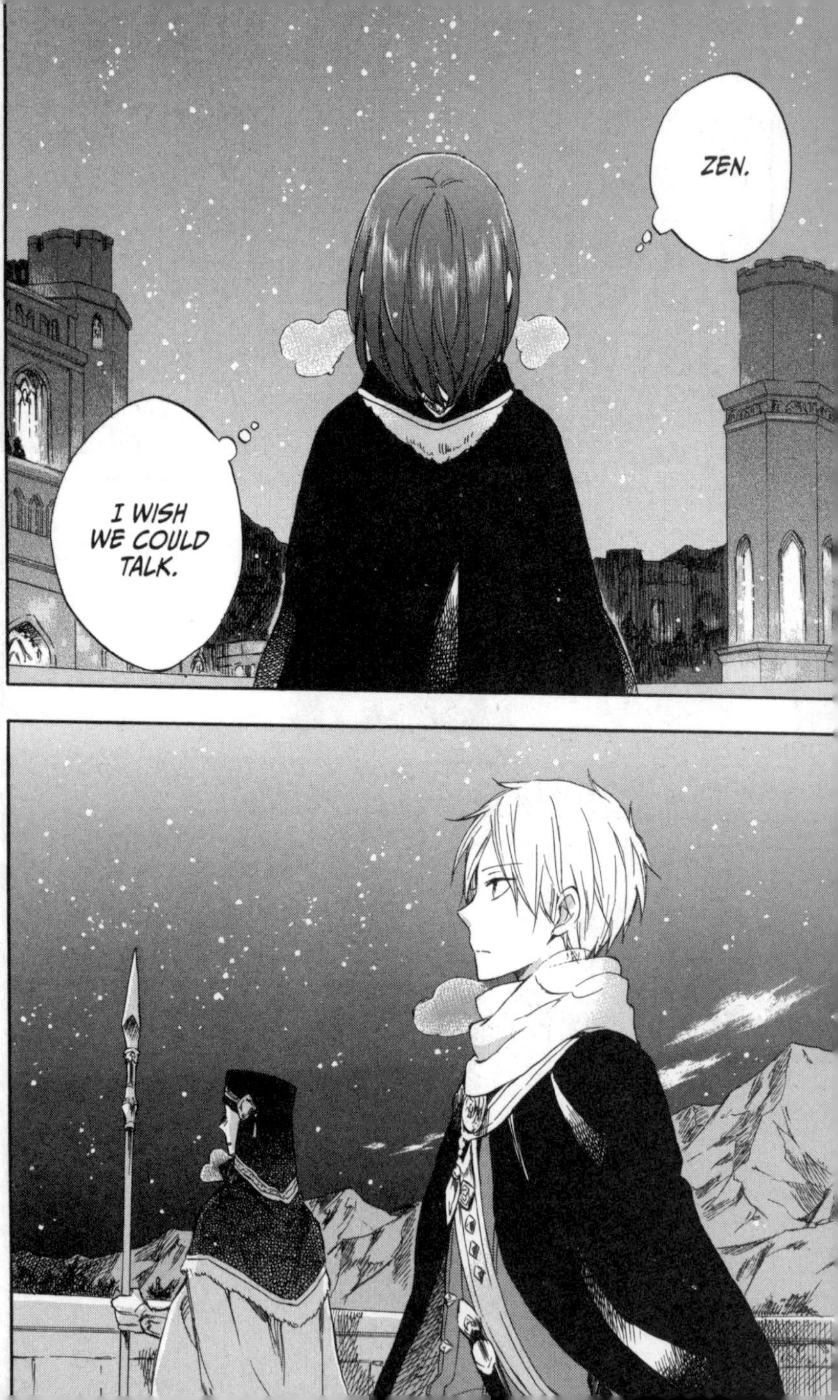
ZEN.
I WISH WE COULD TALK.

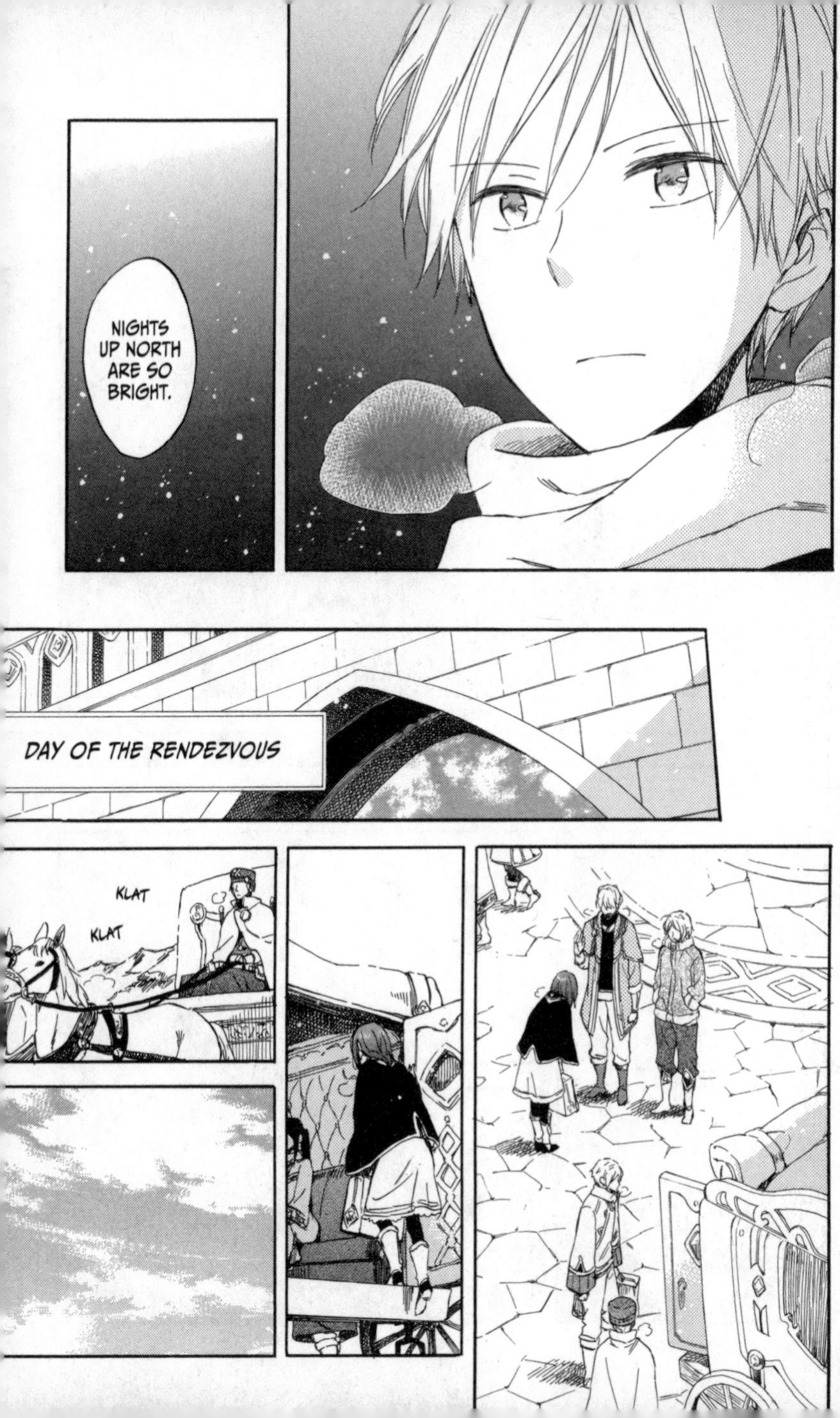
NIGHTS UP NORTH ARE SO BRIGHT.
DAY OF THE RENDEZVOUS
KLAT
KLAT

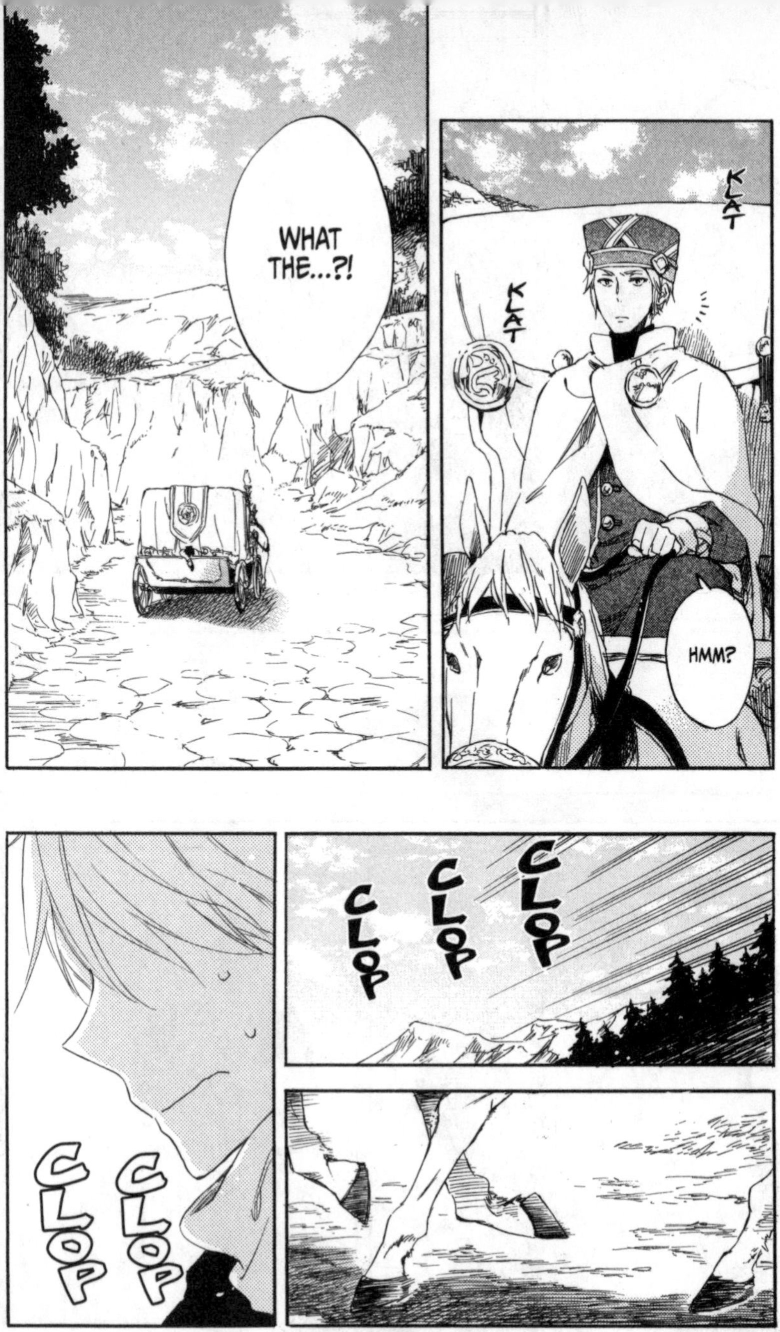
KLAT
KLAT
HMM?
WHAT THE...?!
CLOP CLOP CLOP
CLOP CLOP

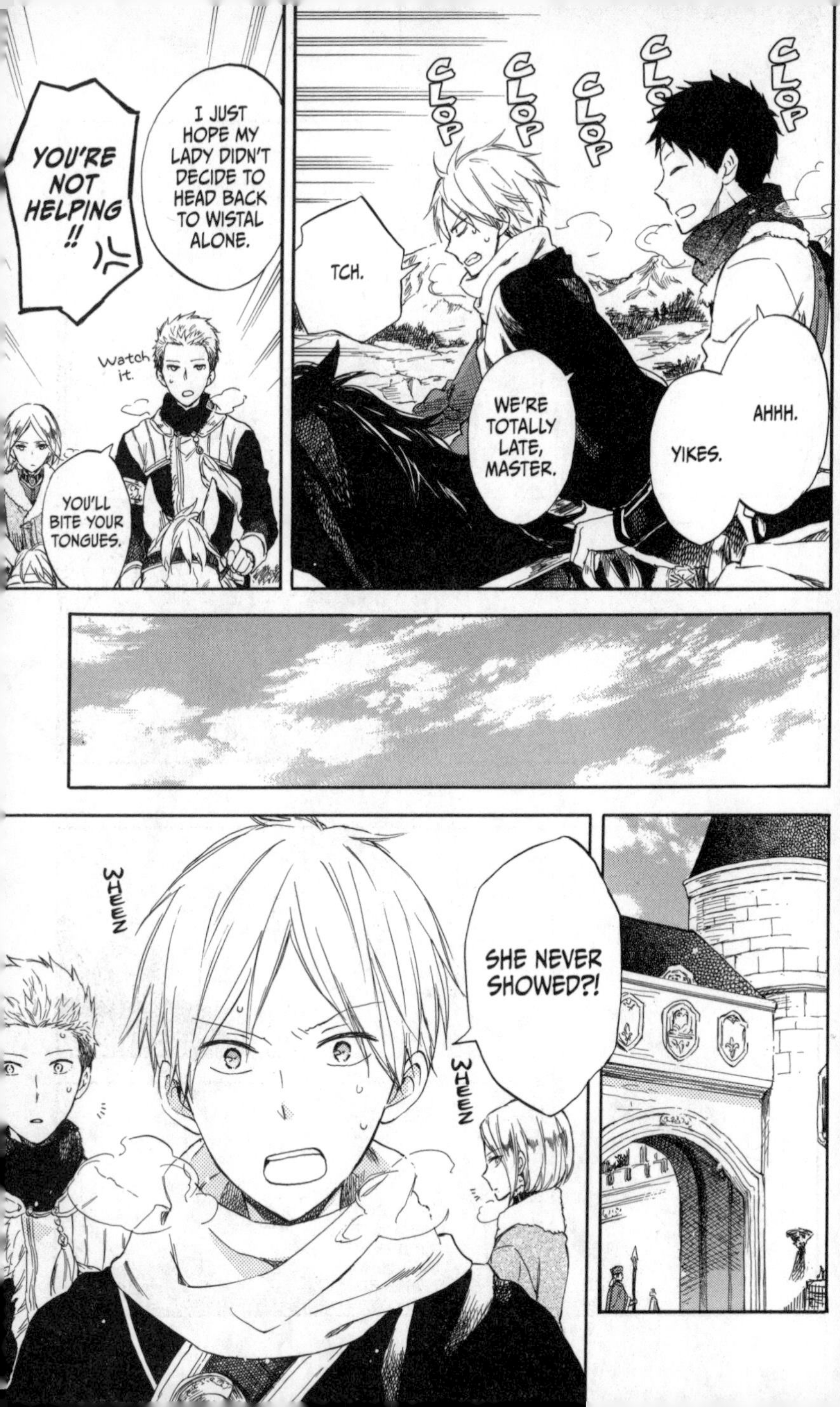
CLOP CLOP CLOP CLOP CLOP
AHHH.
YIKES.
WE'RE TOTALLY LATE, MASTER.
TCH.
I JUST HOPE MY LADY DIDN'T DECIDE TO HEAD BACK TO WISTAL ALONE.
YOU'RE NOT HELPING!!
Watch it.
YOU'LL BITE YOUR TONGUES.
SHE NEVER SHOWED?!
WHEEZ
WHEEZ

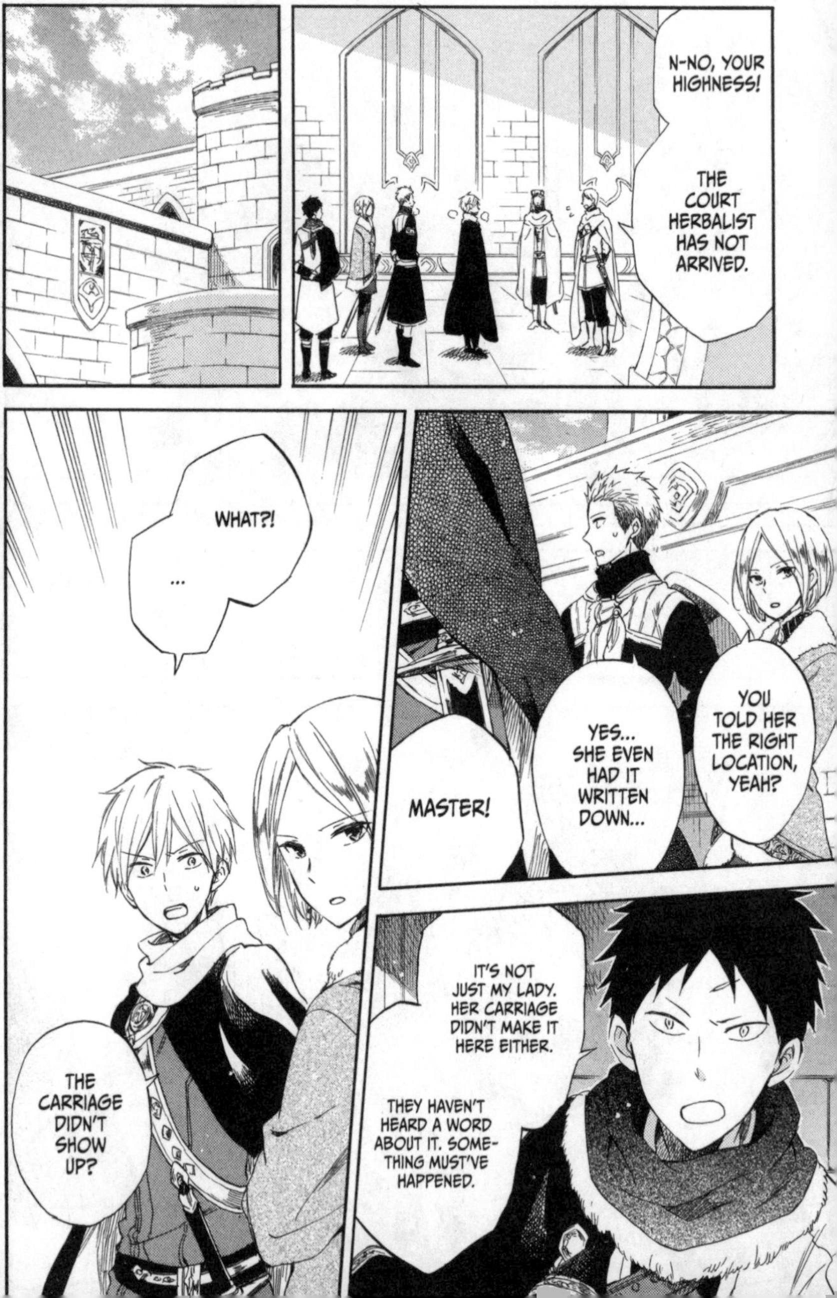
N-NO, YOUR HIGHNESS!
THE COURT HERBALIST HAS NOT ARRIVED.
YOU TOLD HER THE RIGHT LOCATION, YEAH?
YES... SHE EVEN HAD IT WRITTEN DOWN...
MASTER!
IT'S NOT JUST MY LADY. HER CARRIAGE DIDN'T MAKE IT HERE EITHER.
THEY HAVEN'T HEARD A WORD ABOUT IT. SOME-THING MUST'VE HAPPENED.
WHAT?!
...
THE CARRIAGE DIDN'T SHOW UP?

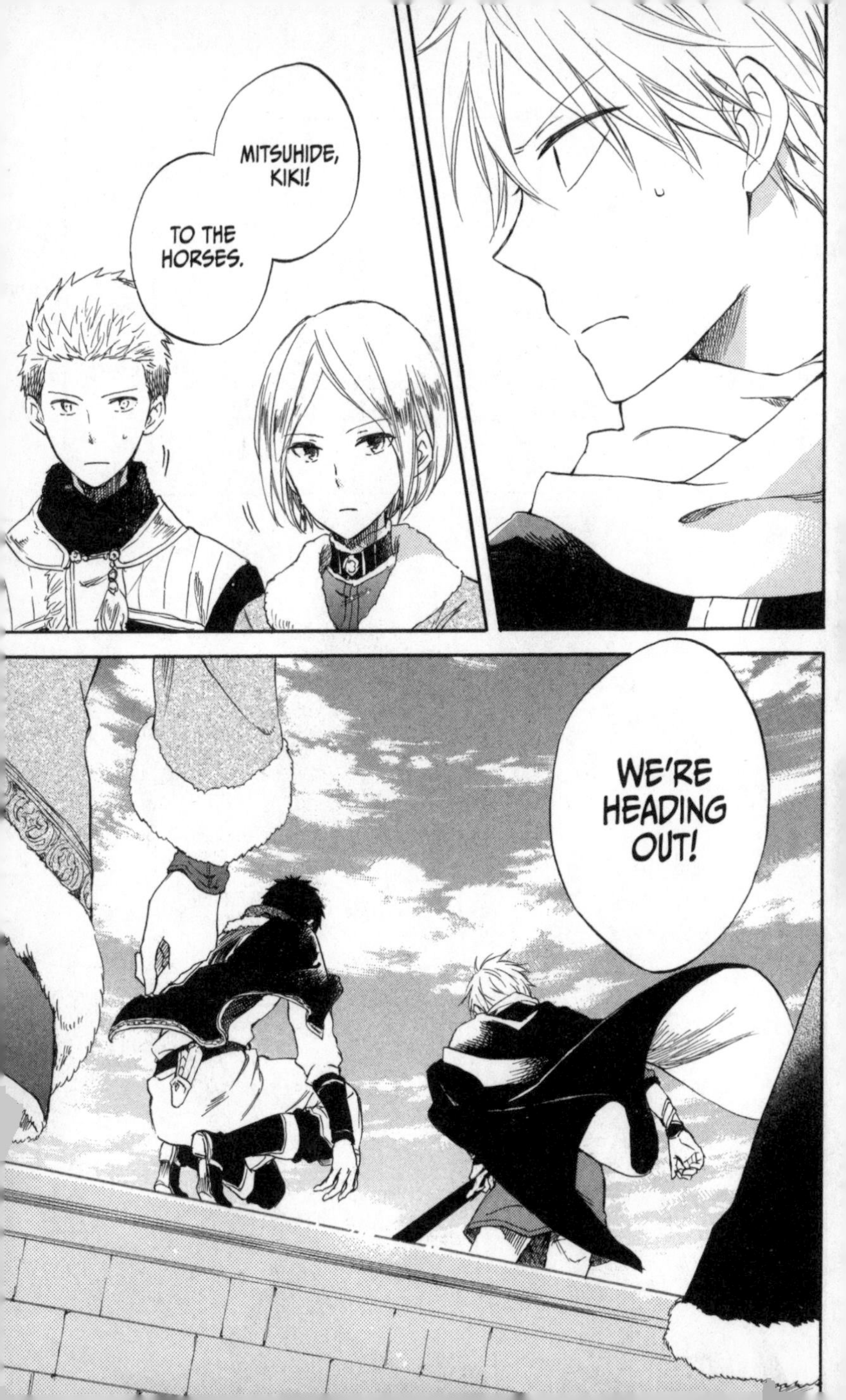
MITSUHIDE, KIKI!
TO THE HORSES.
WE'RE HEADING OUT!

Chapter 55

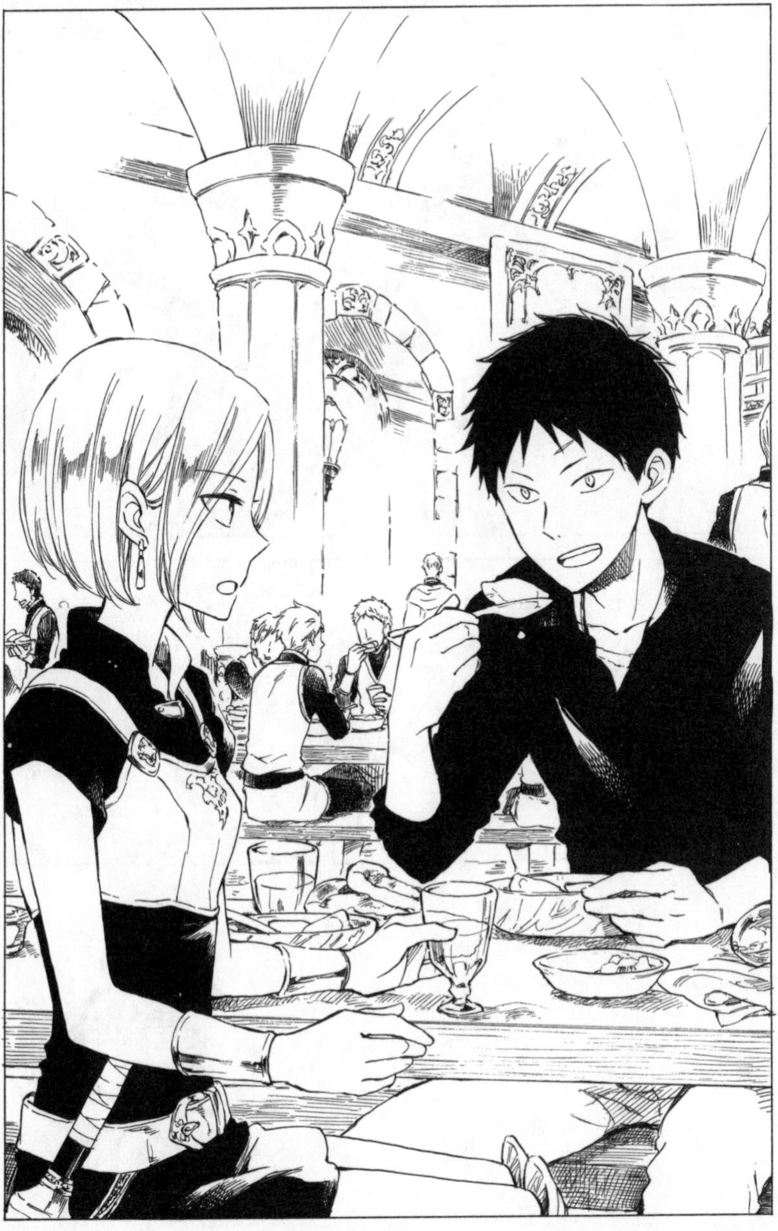

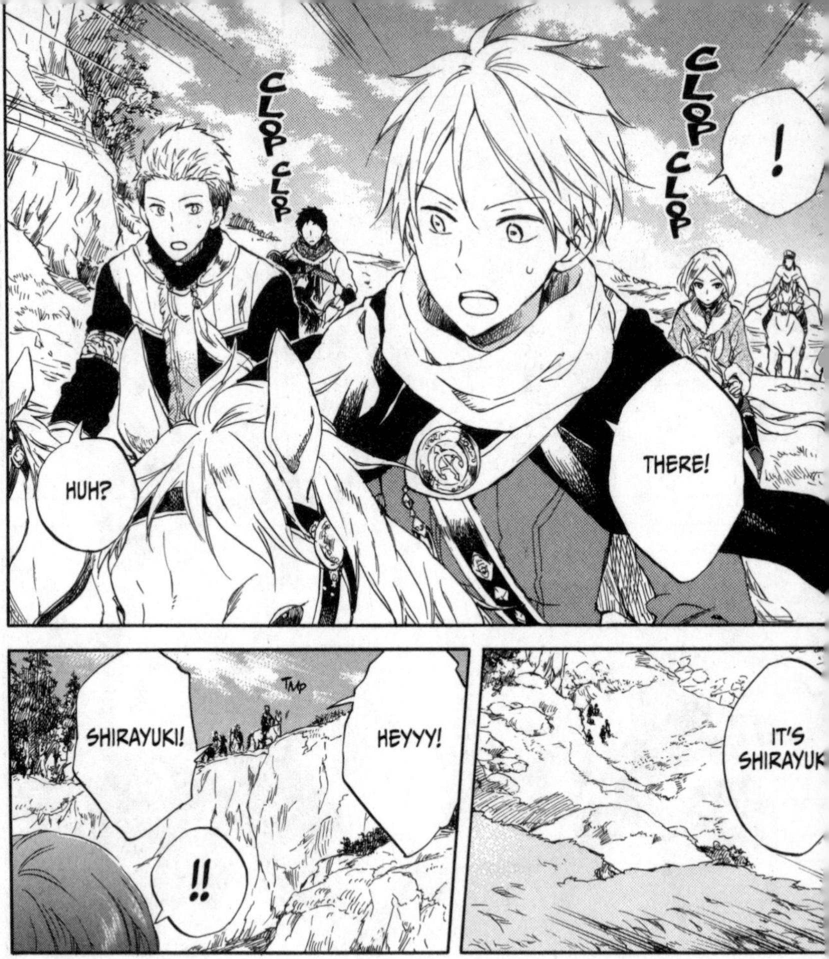
!
CLOP CLOP
THERE!
CLOP CLOP
HUH?
IT'S SHIRAYUK
HEYYY!
TMP
SHIRAYUKI!
!!

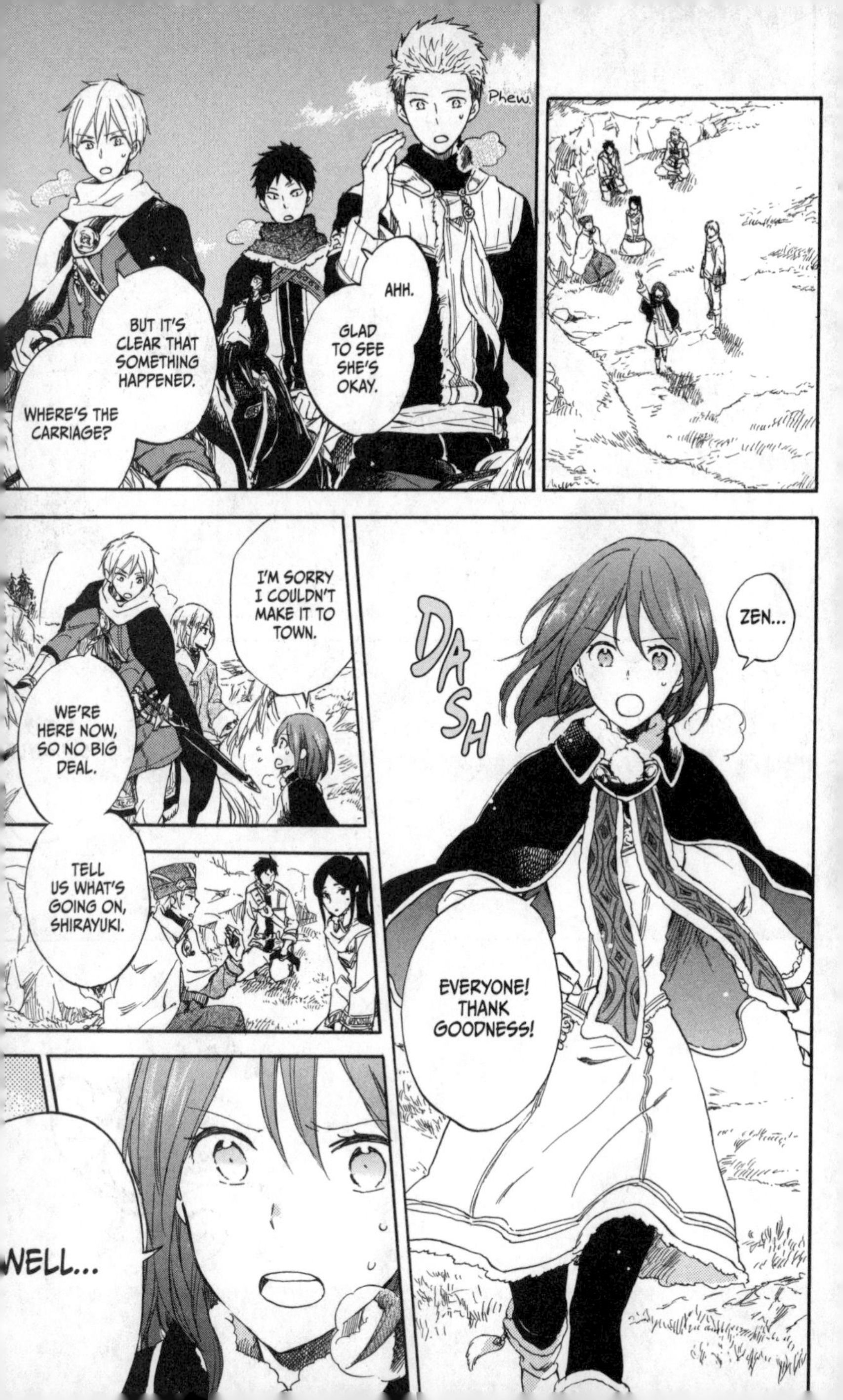
Phew.
AHH.
GLAD TO SEE SHE'S OKAY.
BUT IT'S CLEAR THAT SOMETHING HAPPENED.
WHERE'S THE CARRIAGE?
DASH
ZEN...
EVERYONE! THANK GOODNESS!
I'M SORRY I COULDN'T MAKE IT TO TOWN.
WE'RE HERE NOW, SO NO BIG DEAL.
TELL US WHAT'S GOING ON, SHIRAYUKI.
WELL...

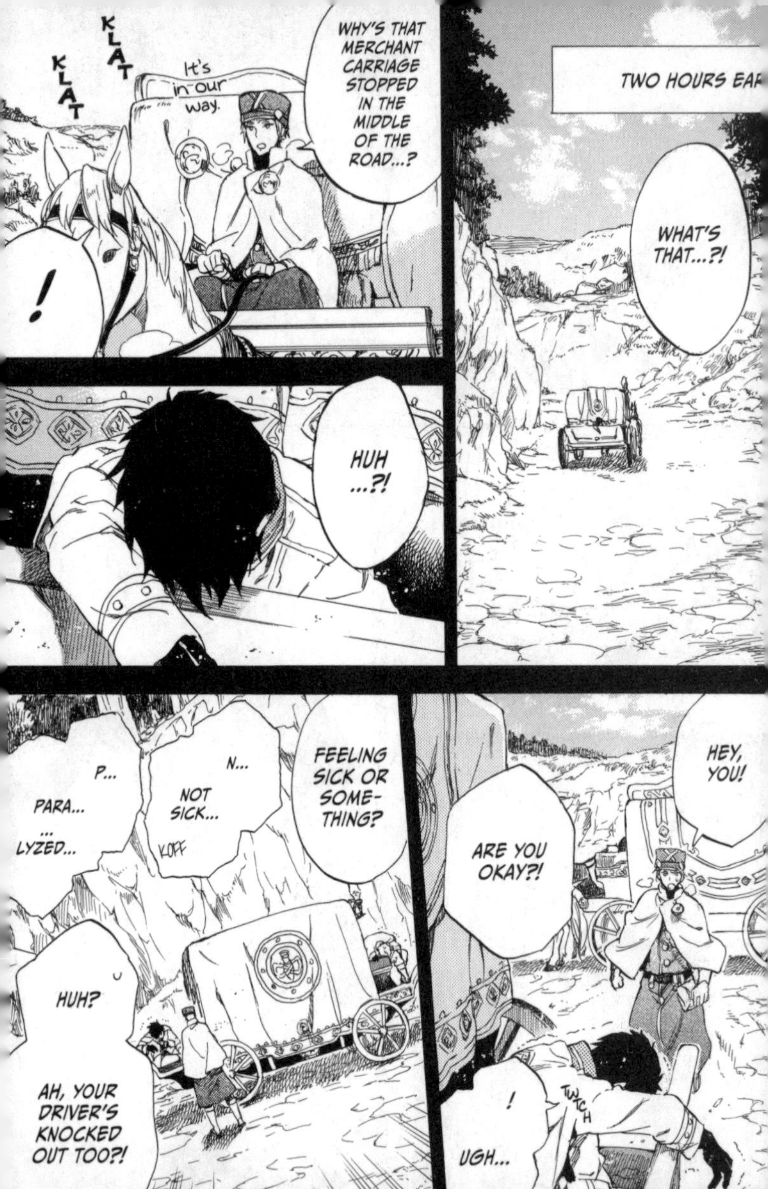

TWO HOURS EAR
WHAT'S THAT...?!
WHY'S THAT MERCHANT CARRIAGE STOPPED IN THE MIDDLE OF THE ROAD...?
It's in our way.
KLAT
KLAT
!
HUH ...?!
HEY, YOU!
ARE YOU OKAY?!
TWITCH
!
UGH...
FEELING SICK OR SOME-THING?
N... NOT SICK...
KOFF
P... PARA... ...LYZED...
HUH?
AH, YOUR DRIVER'S KNOCKED OUT TOO?!

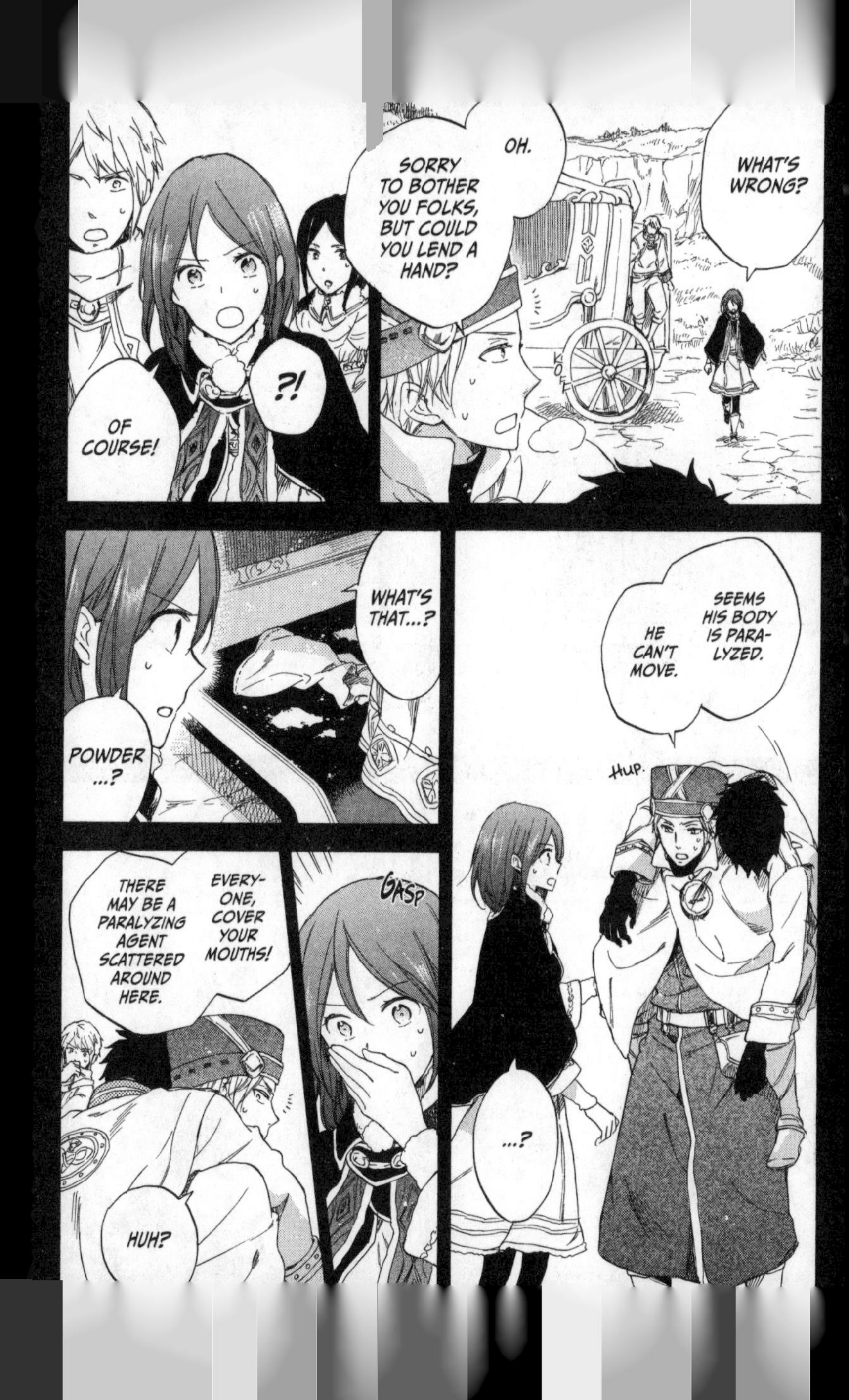
WHAT'S WRONG?
OH.
SORRY TO BOTHER YOU FOLKS, BUT COULD YOU LEND A HAND?
KOFF
?!
OF COURSE!
WHAT'S THAT...?
POWDER ...?
GASP
EVERYONE, COVER YOUR MOUTHS!
THERE MAY BE A PARALYZING AGENT SCATTERED AROUND HERE.
HUH?
SEEMS HIS BODY IS PARALYZED.
HE CAN'T MOVE.
HUP.
...?

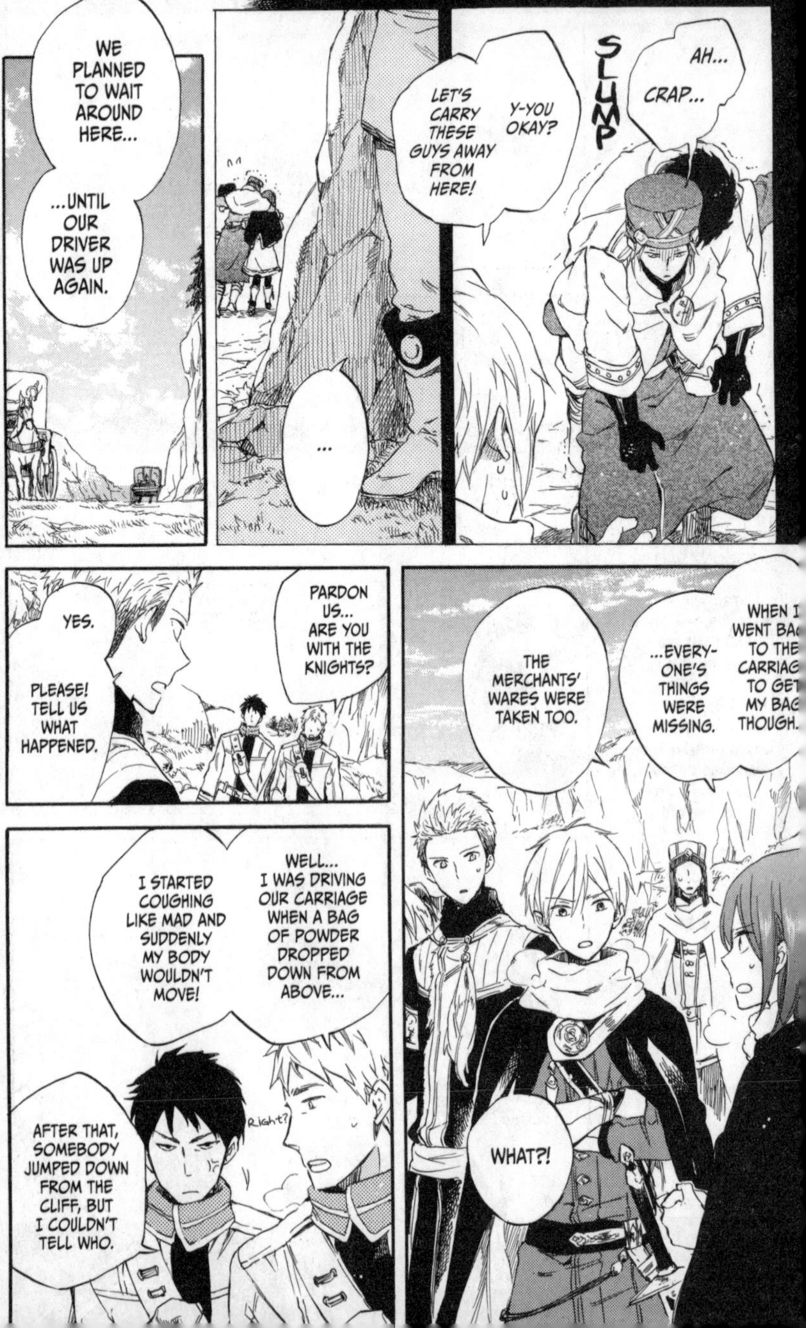
AH... CRAP...
SLUMP
Y-YOU OKAY?
LET'S CARRY THESE GUYS AWAY FROM HERE!
...
WE PLANNED TO WAIT AROUND HERE...
...UNTIL OUR DRIVER WAS UP AGAIN.
WHEN I WENT BAC TO THE CARRIAG TO GET MY BAG THOUGH...
...EVERYONE'S THINGS WERE MISSING.
THE MERCHANTS' WARES WERE TAKEN TOO.
WHAT?!
PARDON US... ARE YOU WITH THE KNIGHTS?
YES.
PLEASE! TELL US WHAT HAPPENED.
WELL... I WAS DRIVING OUR CARRIAGE WHEN A BAG OF POWDER DROPPED DOWN FROM ABOVE...
I STARTED COUGHING LIKE MAD AND SUDDENLY MY BODY WOULDN'T MOVE!
Right?
AFTER THAT, SOMEBODY JUMPED DOWN FROM THE CLIFF, BUT I COULDN'T TELL WHO.

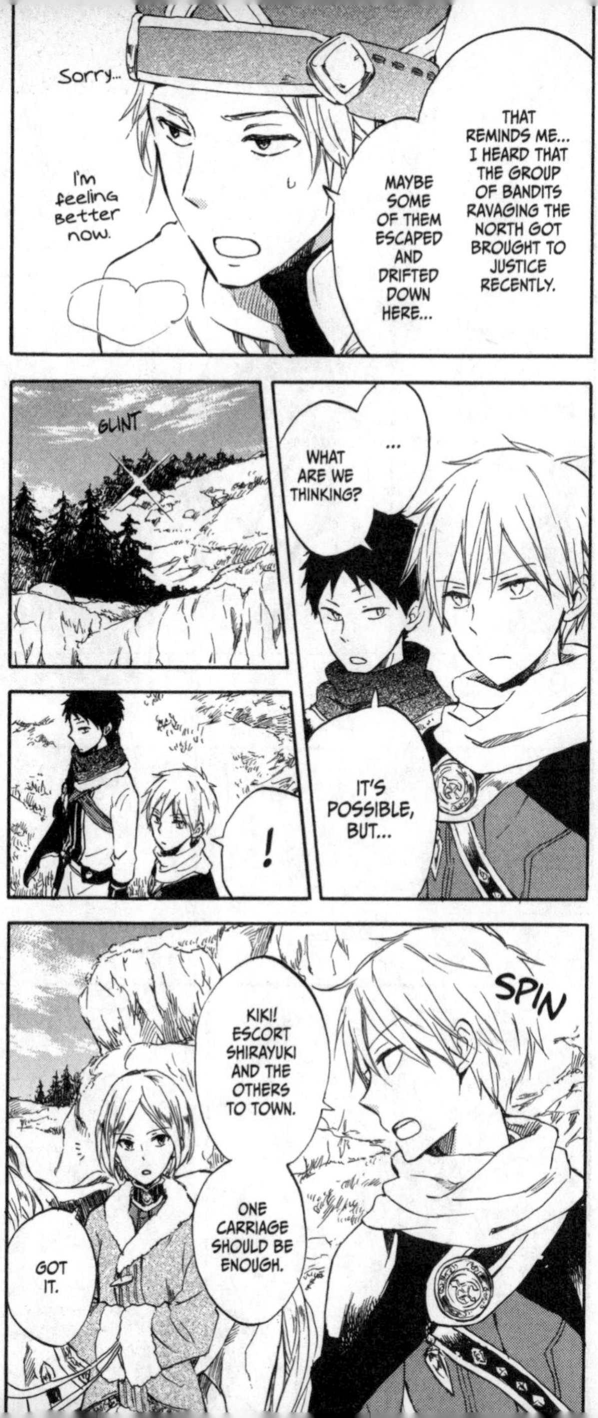
THAT REMINDS ME... I HEARD THAT THE GROUP OF BANDITS RAVAGING THE NORTH GOT BROUGHT TO JUSTICE RECENTLY.
MAYBE SOME OF THEM ESCAPED AND DRIFTED DOWN HERE...
Sorry...
I'm feeling better now.
...
WHAT ARE WE THINKING?
IT'S POSSIBLE, BUT...
GLINT
!
SPIN
KIKI! ESCORT SHIRAYUKI AND THE OTHERS TO TOWN.
ONE CARRIAGE SHOULD BE ENOUGH.
GOT IT.

FINAL SIDEBAR

Moving on into chapters 54, 55 and 56.

This volume ends on a cliffhanger—with Prince Zen completely stunned!

But who will grace the next cover?! Will I talk more about my travels?!

I hope that Izana (on this cover) looked princely before you read the book, but kingly after you finished...

See you in volume 13!

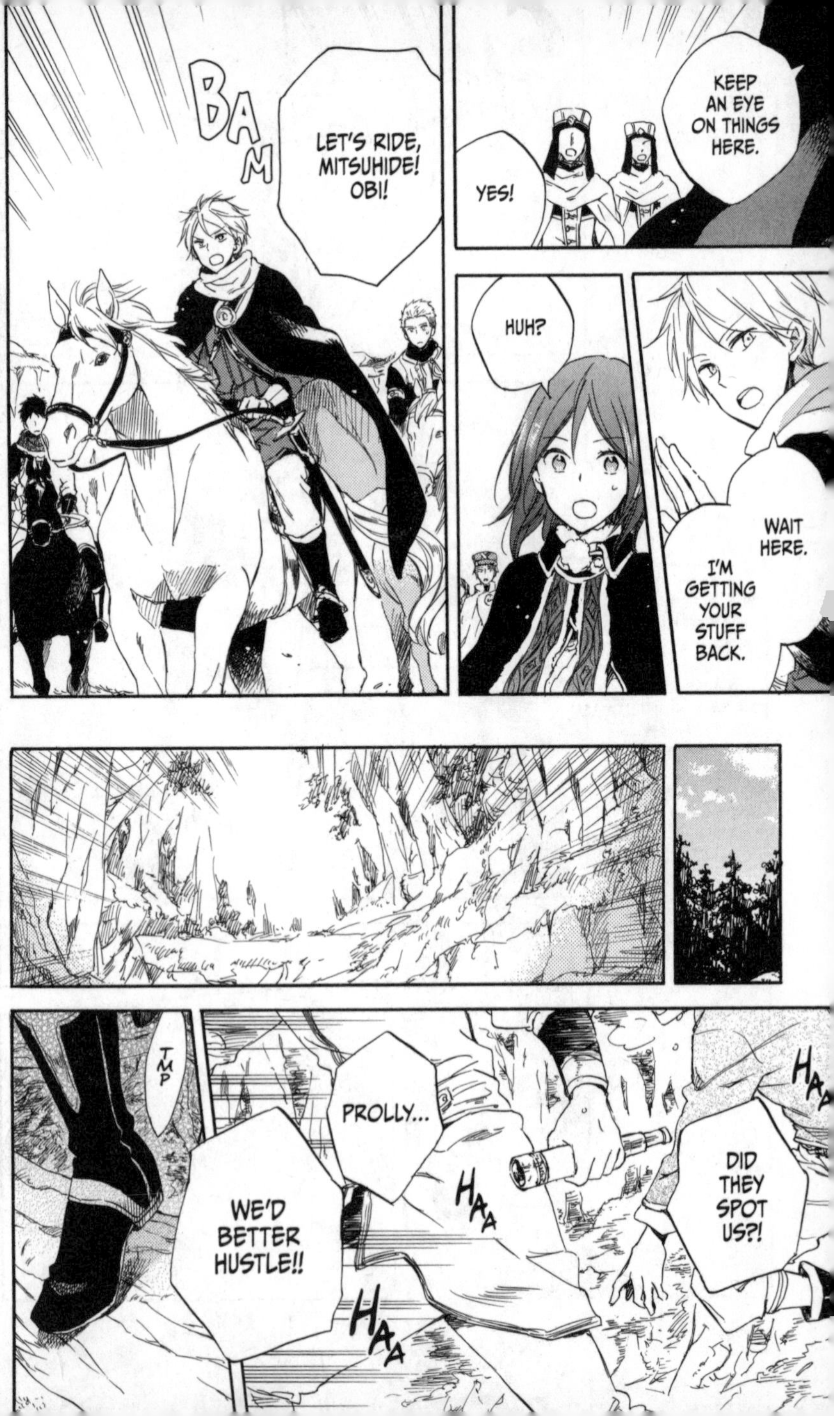
KEEP AN EYE ON THINGS HERE.
YES!
WAIT HERE.
I'M GETTING YOUR STUFF BACK.
HUH?
BAM
LET'S RIDE, MITSUHIDE! OBI!
HAP
DID THEY SPOT US?!
PROLLY...
HAA
WE'D BETTER HUSTLE!!
HAA
TMP

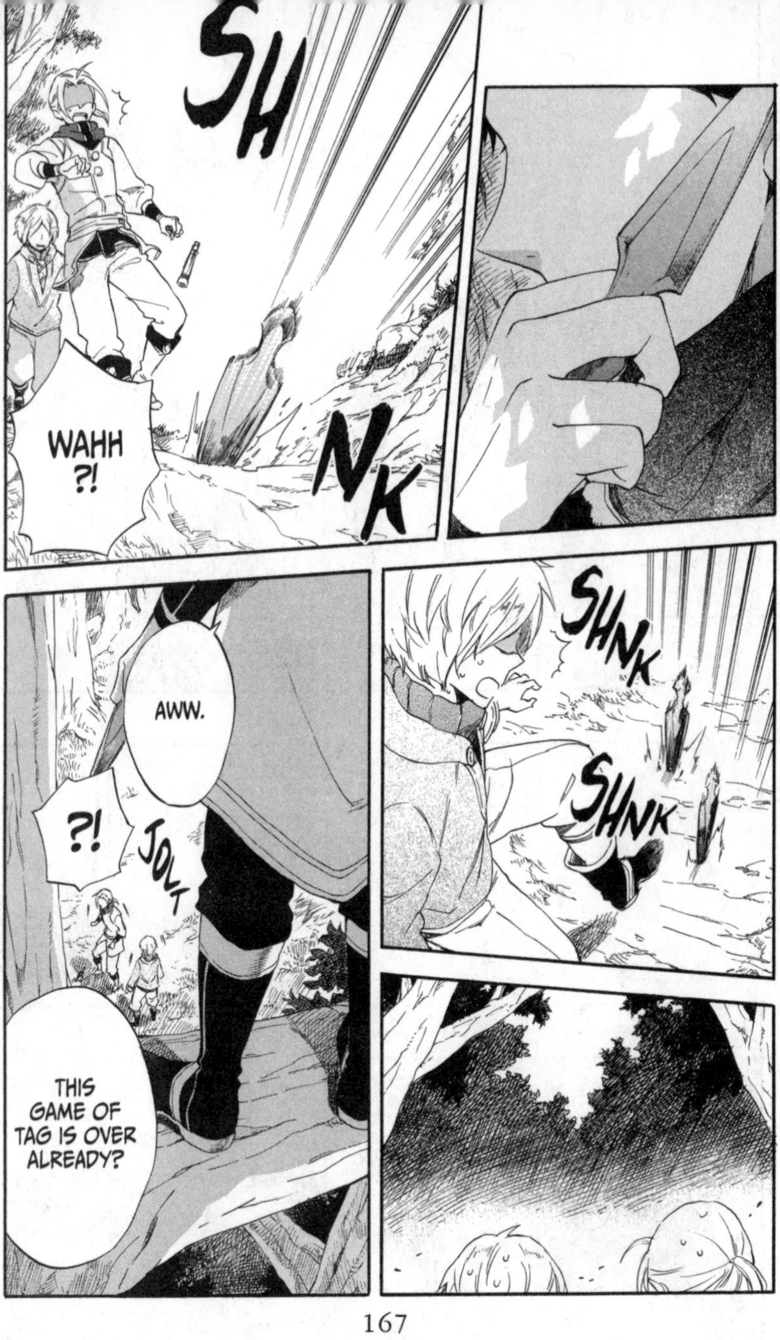
SH
NK
WAHH ?!
SHNK
SHNK
AWW.
?!
JOLT
THIS GAME OF TAG IS OVER ALREADY?

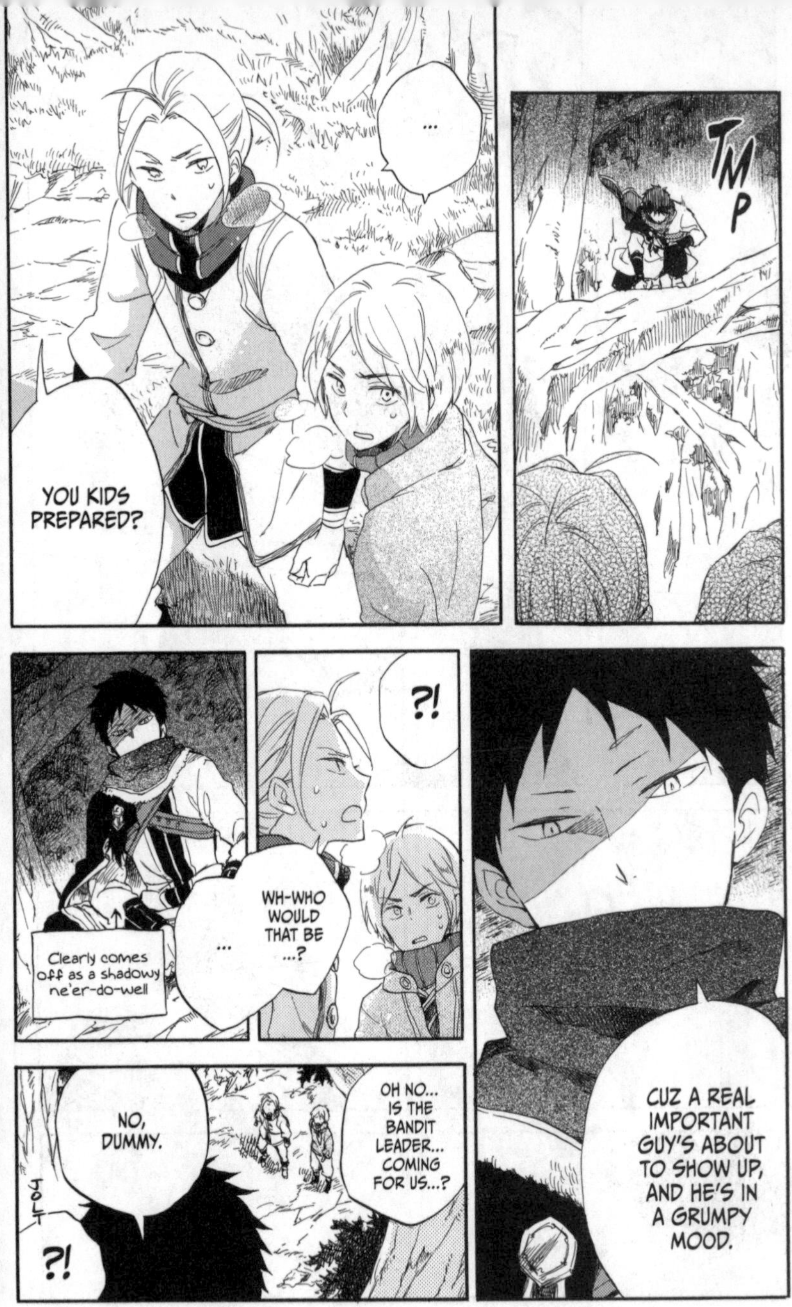
TMP
...
YOU KIDS PREPARED?
CUZ A REAL IMPORTANT GUY'S ABOUT TO SHOW UP, AND HE'S IN A GRUMPY MOOD.
?!
WH-WHO WOULD THAT BE ...?
...
Clearly comes off as a shadowy ne'er-do-well
OH NO... IS THE BANDIT LEADER... COMING FOR US...?
NO, DUMMY.
JOLT
?!

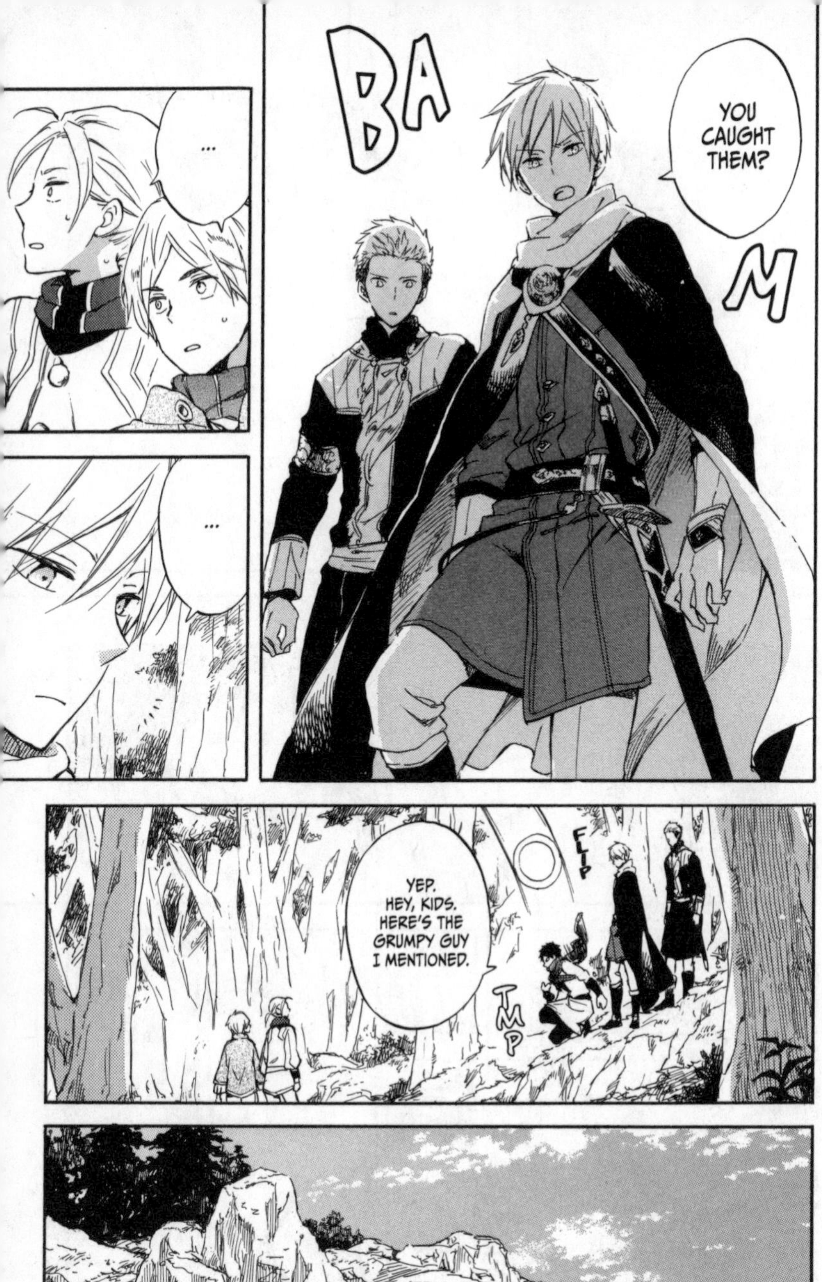
BA
YOU CAUGHT THEM?
M
...
...
FLIP
YEP. HEY, KIDS. HERE'S THE GRUMPY GUY I MENTIONED.
TMP

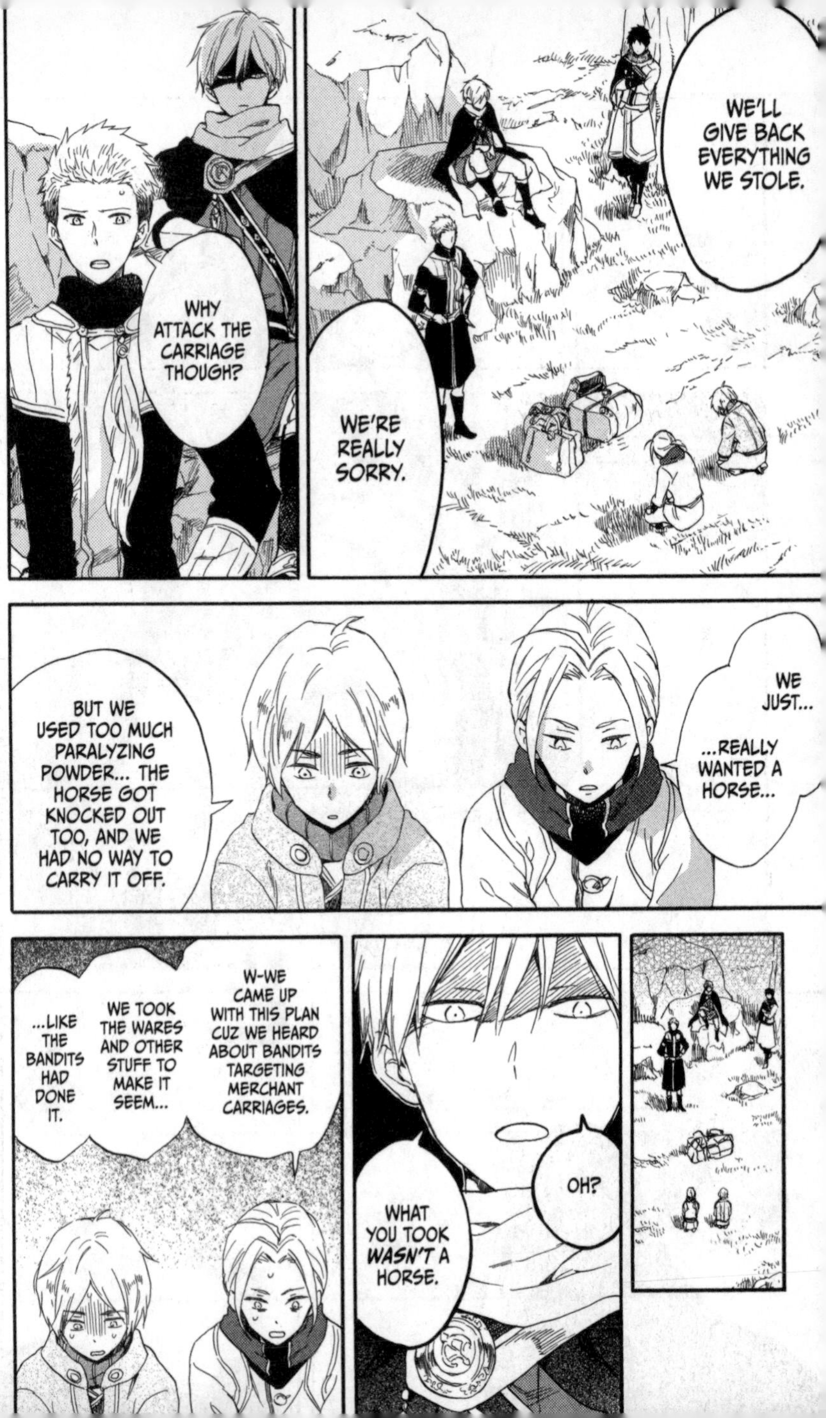
WE'LL GIVE BACK EVERYTHING WE STOLE.
WE'RE REALLY SORRY.
WHY ATTACK THE CARRIAGE THOUGH?
WE JUST...
...REALLY WANTED A HORSE...
BUT WE USED TOO MUCH PARALYZING POWDER... THE HORSE GOT KNOCKED OUT TOO, AND WE HAD NO WAY TO CARRY IT OFF.
OH?
WHAT YOU TOOK *WASN'T* A HORSE.
W-WE CAME UP WITH THIS PLAN CUZ WE HEARD ABOUT BANDITS TARGETING MERCHANT CARRIAGES.
WE TOOK THE WARES AND OTHER STUFF TO MAKE IT SEEM...
...LIKE THE BANDITS HAD DONE IT.

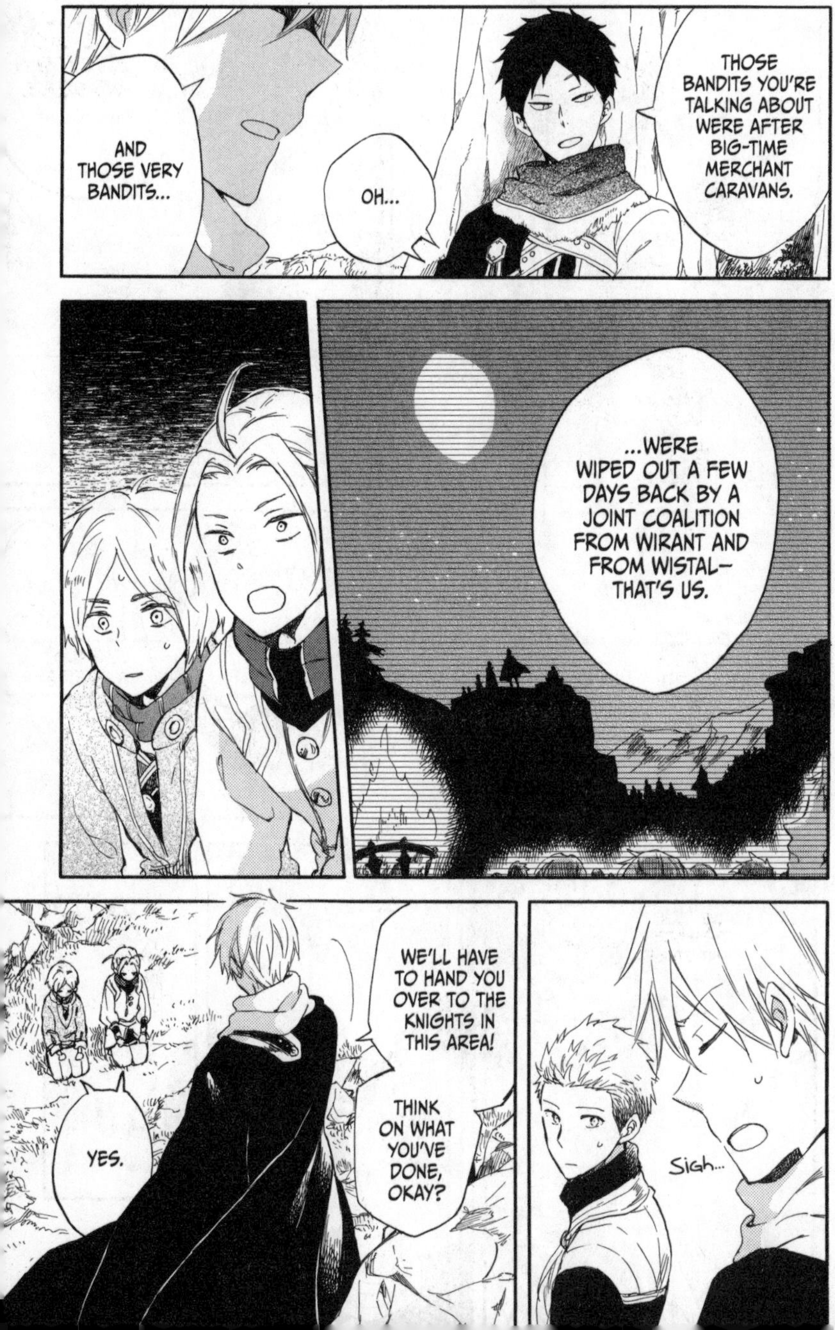
THOSE BANDITS YOU'RE TALKING ABOUT WERE AFTER BIG-TIME MERCHANT CARAVANS.
OH...
AND THOSE VERY BANDITS...
...WERE WIPED OUT A FEW DAYS BACK BY A JOINT COALITION FROM WIRANT AND FROM WISTAL—THAT'S US.
Sigh...
WE'LL HAVE TO HAND YOU OVER TO THE KNIGHTS IN THIS AREA!
THINK ON WHAT YOU'VE DONE, OKAY?
YES.

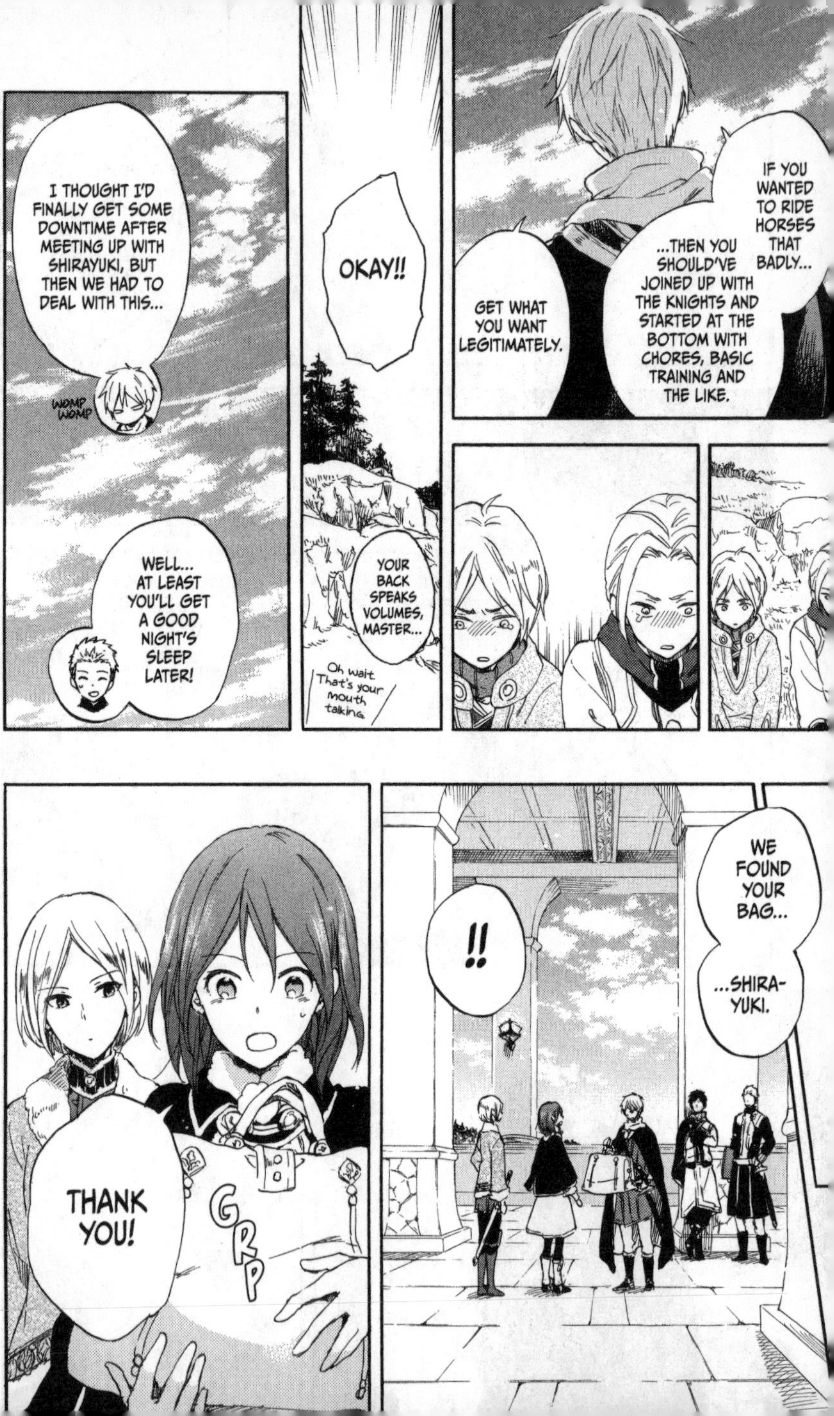
IF YOU WANTED TO RIDE HORSES THAT BADLY...
...THEN YOU SHOULD'VE JOINED UP WITH THE KNIGHTS AND STARTED AT THE BOTTOM WITH CHORES, BASIC TRAINING AND THE LIKE.
GET WHAT YOU WANT LEGITIMATELY.
OKAY!!
YOUR BACK SPEAKS VOLUMES, MASTER...
Oh wait. That's your mouth talking.
I THOUGHT I'D FINALLY GET SOME DOWNTIME AFTER MEETING UP WITH SHIRAYUKI, BUT THEN WE HAD TO DEAL WITH THIS...
WOMP WOMP
WELL... AT LEAST YOU'LL GET A GOOD NIGHT'S SLEEP LATER!
WE FOUND YOUR BAG...
...SHIRA-YUKI.
!!
THANK YOU!
GRP

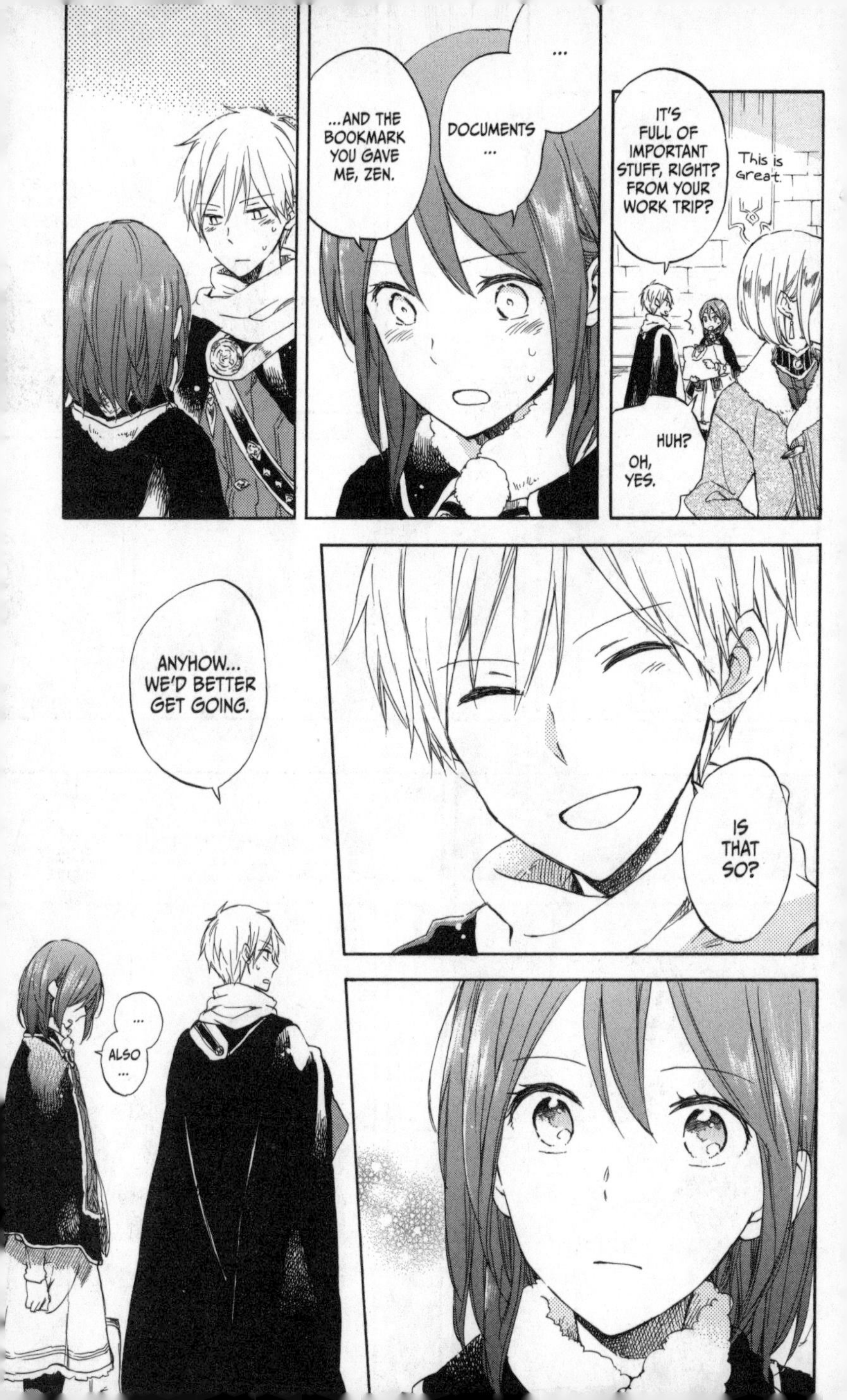
IT'S FULL OF IMPORTANT STUFF, RIGHT? FROM YOUR WORK TRIP?
This is Great.
HUH? OH, YES.
...
DOCUMENTS ...
...AND THE BOOKMARK YOU GAVE ME, ZEN.
IS THAT SO?
ANYHOW... WE'D BETTER GET GOING.
... ALSO ...

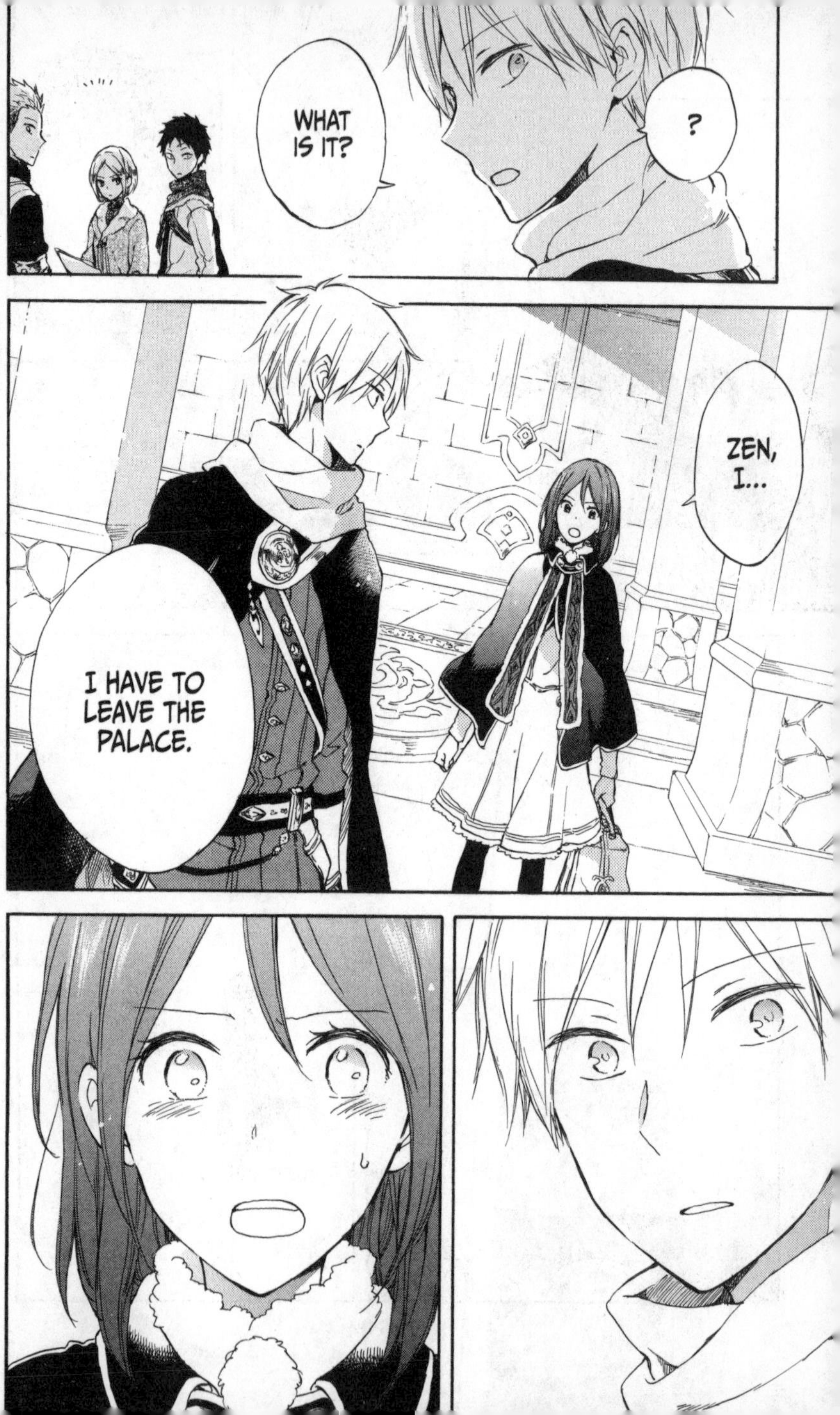
?
WHAT IS IT?
ZEN, I...
I HAVE TO LEAVE THE PALACE.

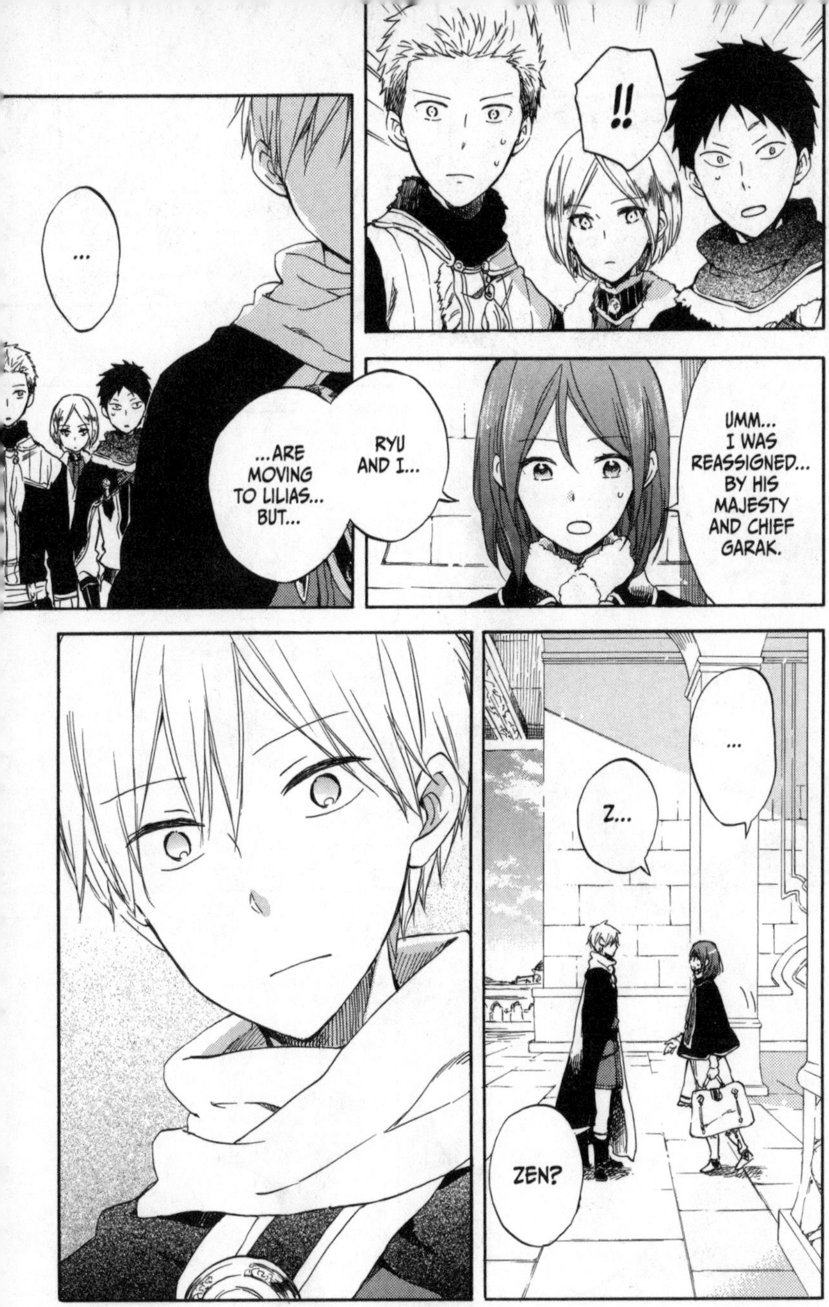
!!
UMM... I WAS REASSIGNED... BY HIS MAJESTY AND CHIEF GARAK.
RYU AND I...
...ARE MOVING TO LILIAS... BUT...
...
...
Z...
ZEN?

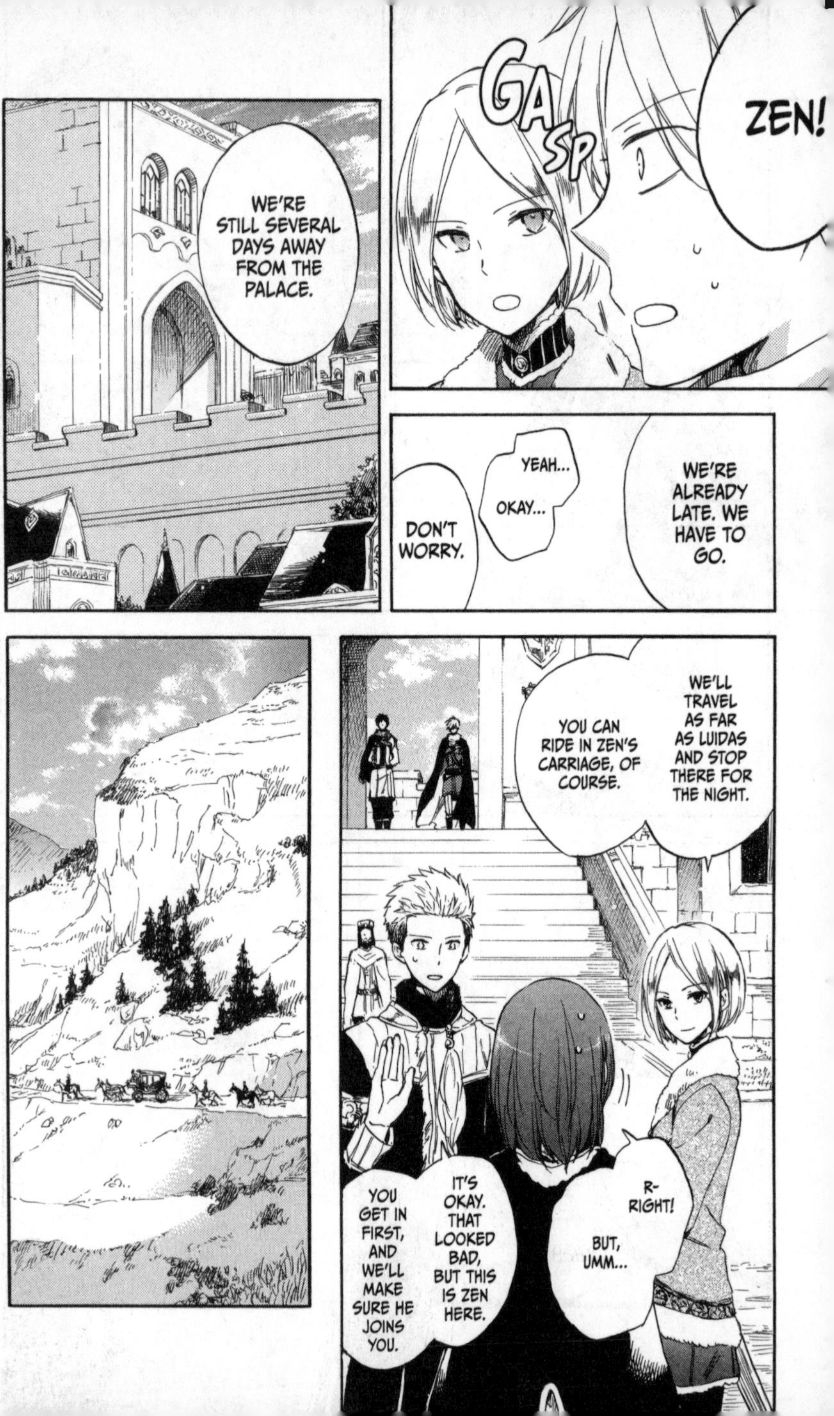
ZEN!
GASP
WE'RE ALREADY LATE. WE HAVE TO GO.
YEAH...
OKAY...
DON'T WORRY.
WE'RE STILL SEVERAL DAYS AWAY FROM THE PALACE.
WE'LL TRAVEL AS FAR AS LUIDAS AND STOP THERE FOR THE NIGHT.
YOU CAN RIDE IN ZEN'S CARRIAGE, OF COURSE.
R-RIGHT!
BUT, UMM...
IT'S OKAY. THAT LOOKED BAD, BUT THIS IS ZEN HERE.
YOU GET IN FIRST, AND WE'LL MAKE SURE HE JOINS YOU.

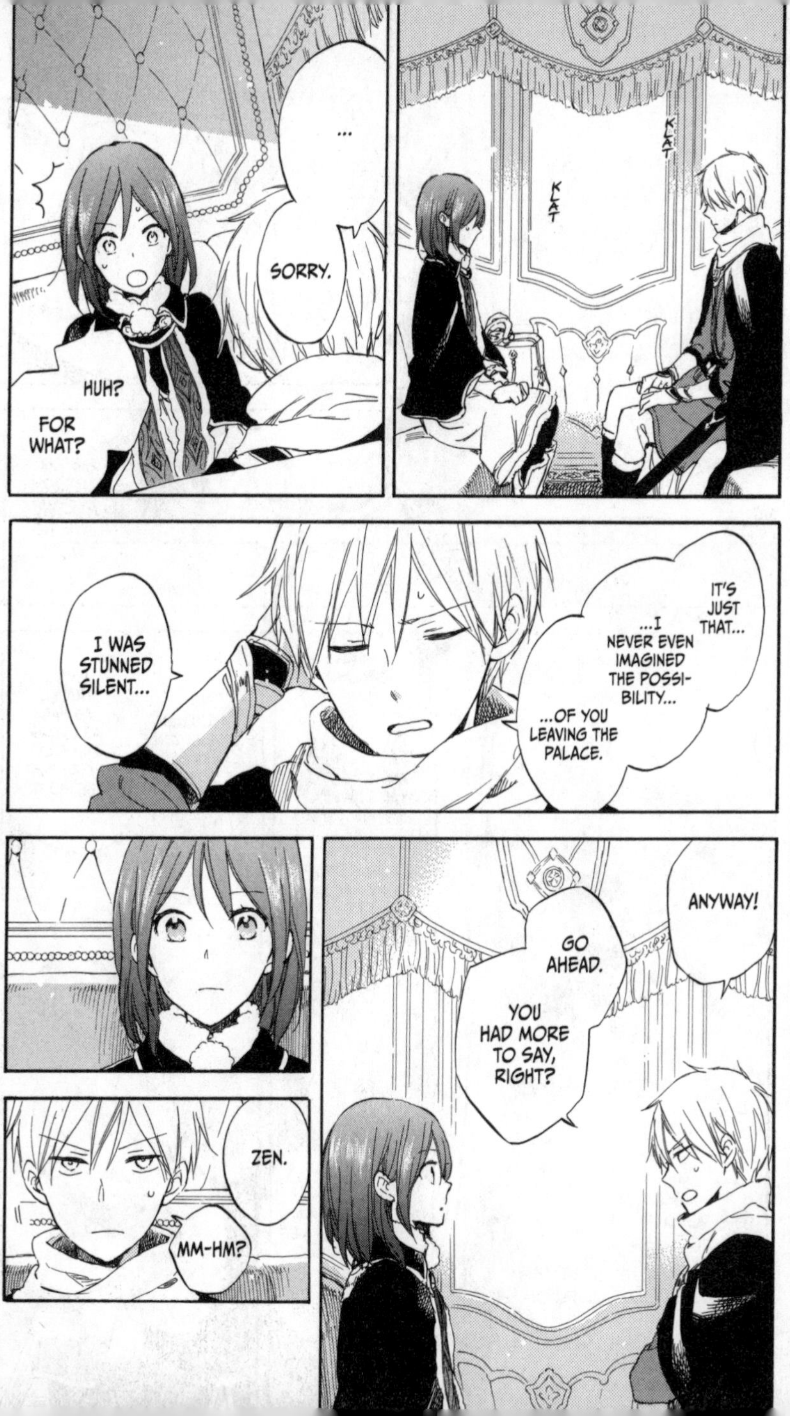
KLAT
KLAT
...
SORRY.
HUH?
FOR WHAT?
IT'S JUST THAT...
...I NEVER EVEN IMAGINED THE POSSI-BILITY...
...OF YOU LEAVING THE PALACE.
I WAS STUNNED SILENT...
ANYWAY!
GO AHEAD.
YOU HAD MORE TO SAY, RIGHT?
ZEN.
MM-HM?

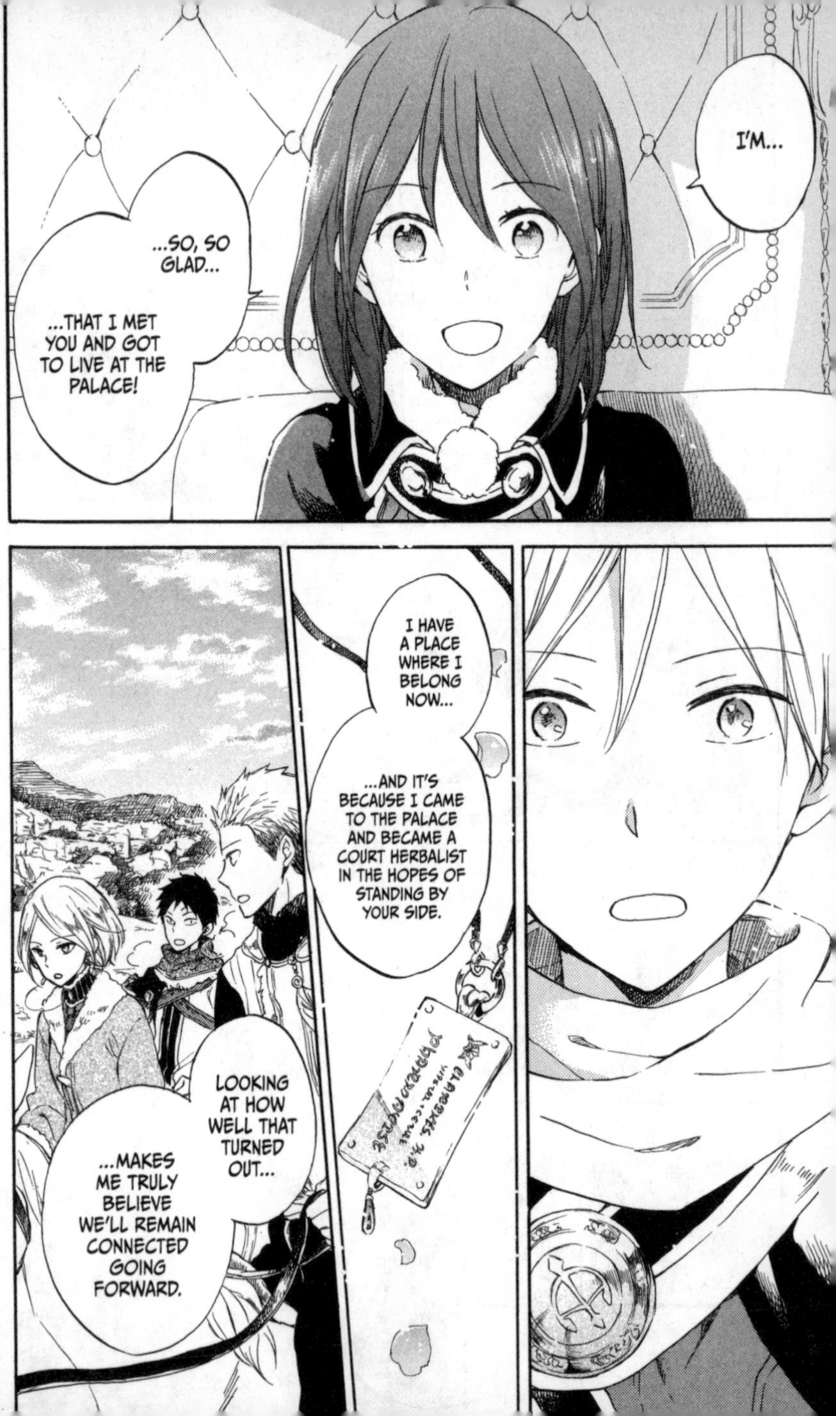
I'M...
...SO, SO GLAD...
...THAT I MET YOU AND GOT TO LIVE AT THE PALACE!
I HAVE A PLACE WHERE I BELONG NOW...
...AND IT'S BECAUSE I CAME TO THE PALACE AND BECAME A COURT HERBALIST IN THE HOPES OF STANDING BY YOUR SIDE.
LOOKING AT HOW WELL THAT TURNED OUT...
...MAKES ME TRULY BELIEVE WE'LL REMAIN CONNECTED GOING FORWARD.

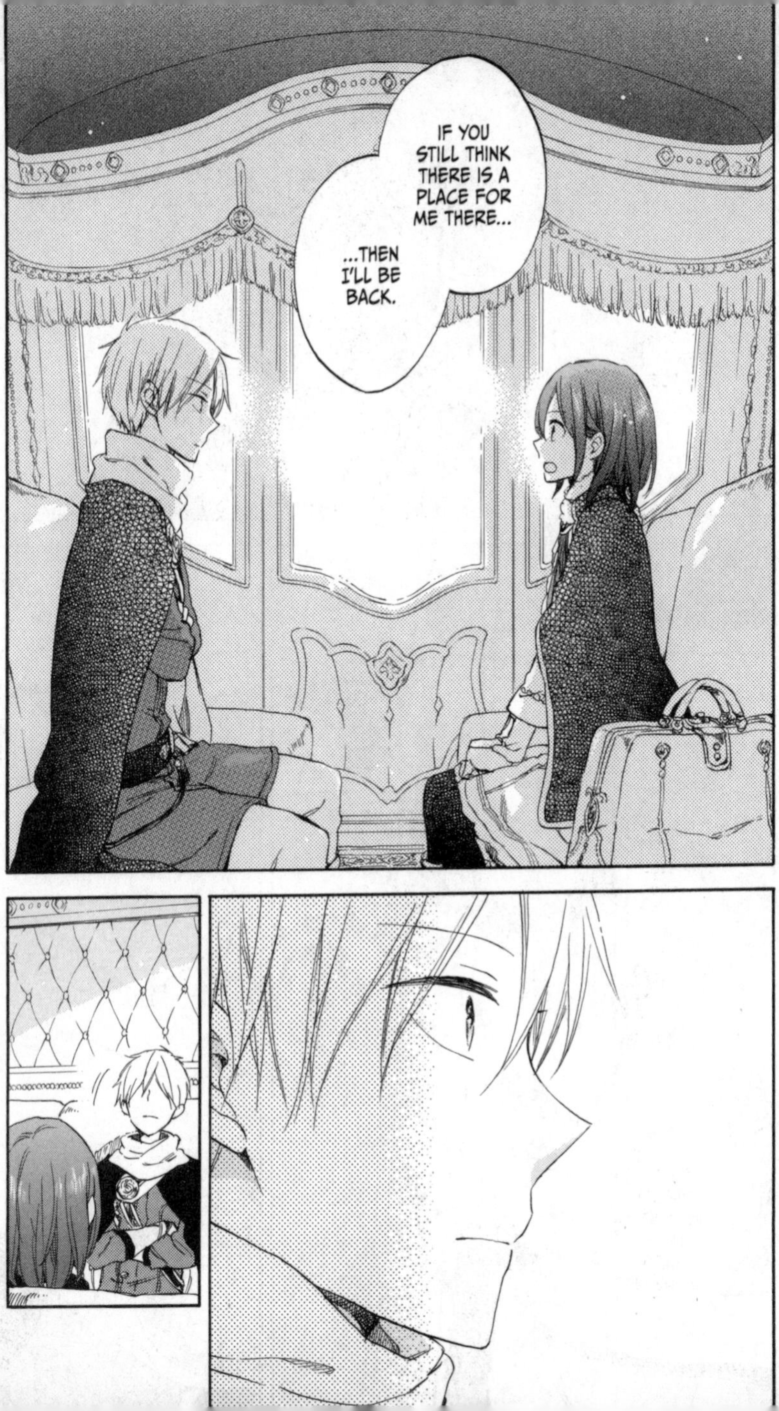
IF YOU STILL THINK THERE IS A PLACE FOR ME THERE...
...THEN I'LL BE BACK.

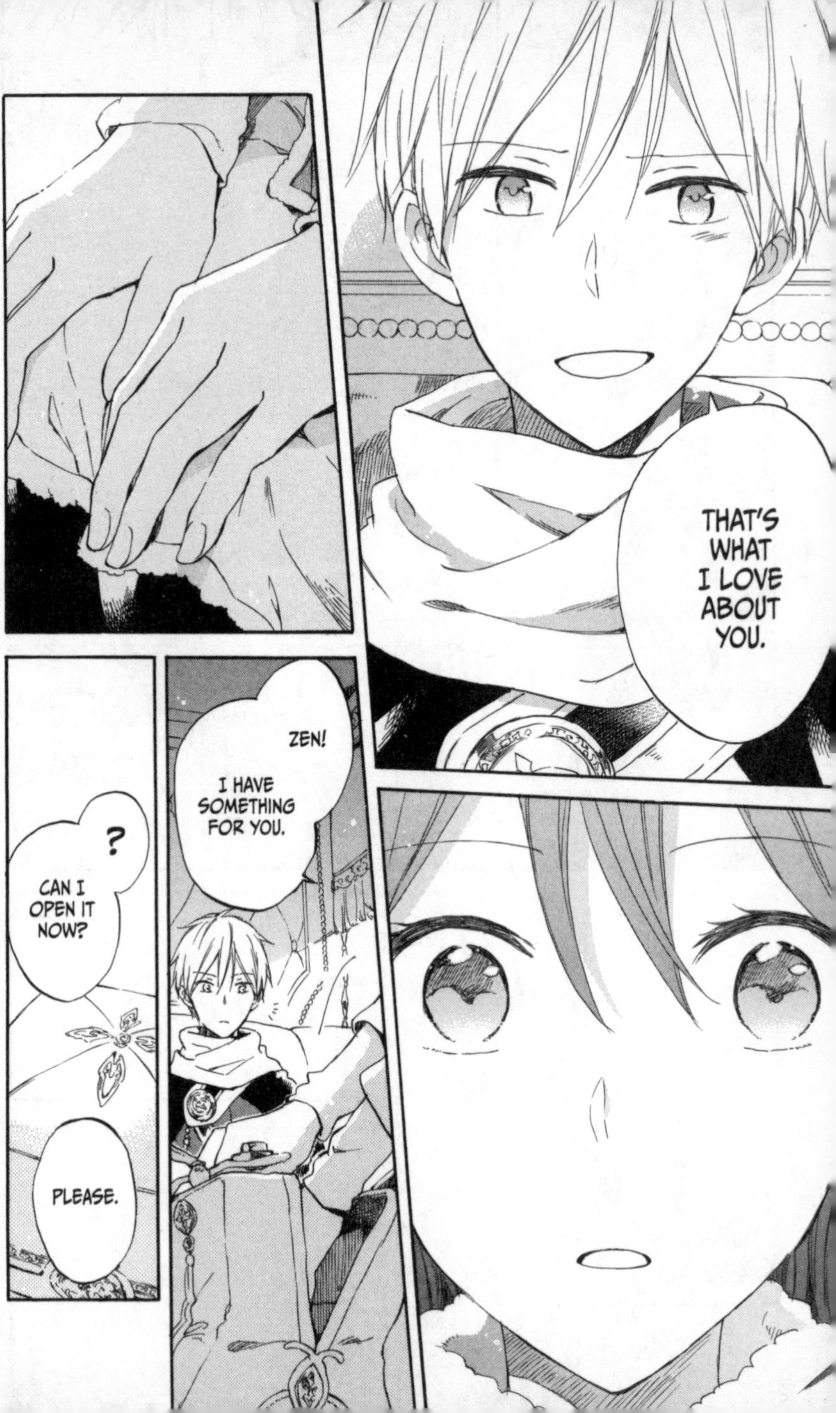
THAT'S WHAT I LOVE ABOUT YOU.
ZEN!
I HAVE SOMETHING FOR YOU.
?
CAN I OPEN IT NOW?
PLEASE.

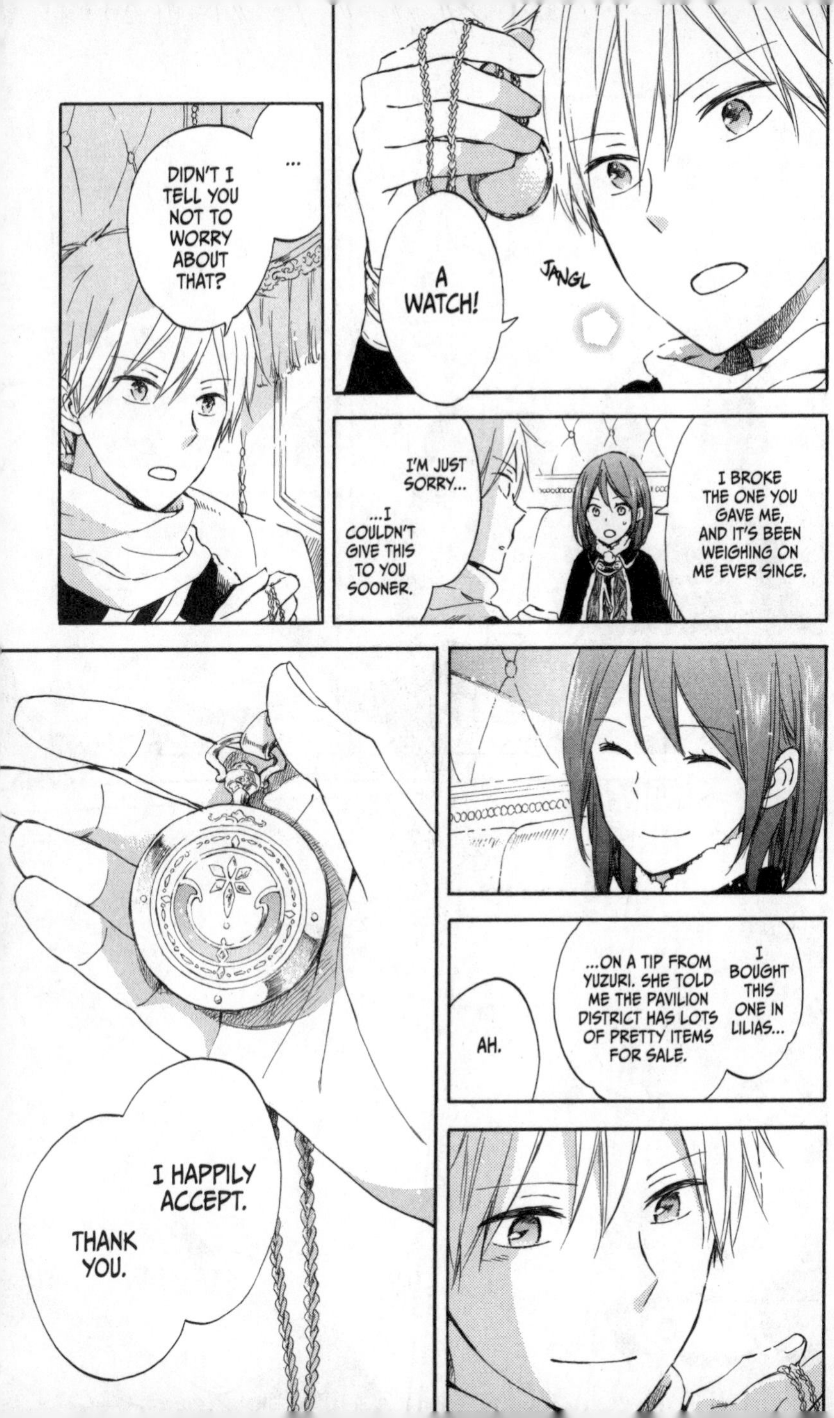
JANGL
A WATCH!
I BROKE THE ONE YOU GAVE ME, AND IT'S BEEN WEIGHING ON ME EVER SINCE.
I'M JUST SORRY...
...I COULDN'T GIVE THIS TO YOU SOONER.
...
DIDN'T I TELL YOU NOT TO WORRY ABOUT THAT?
I BOUGHT THIS ONE IN LILIAS...
...ON A TIP FROM YUZURI. SHE TOLD ME THE PAVILION DISTRICT HAS LOTS OF PRETTY ITEMS FOR SALE.
AH.
I HAPPILY ACCEPT.
THANK YOU.

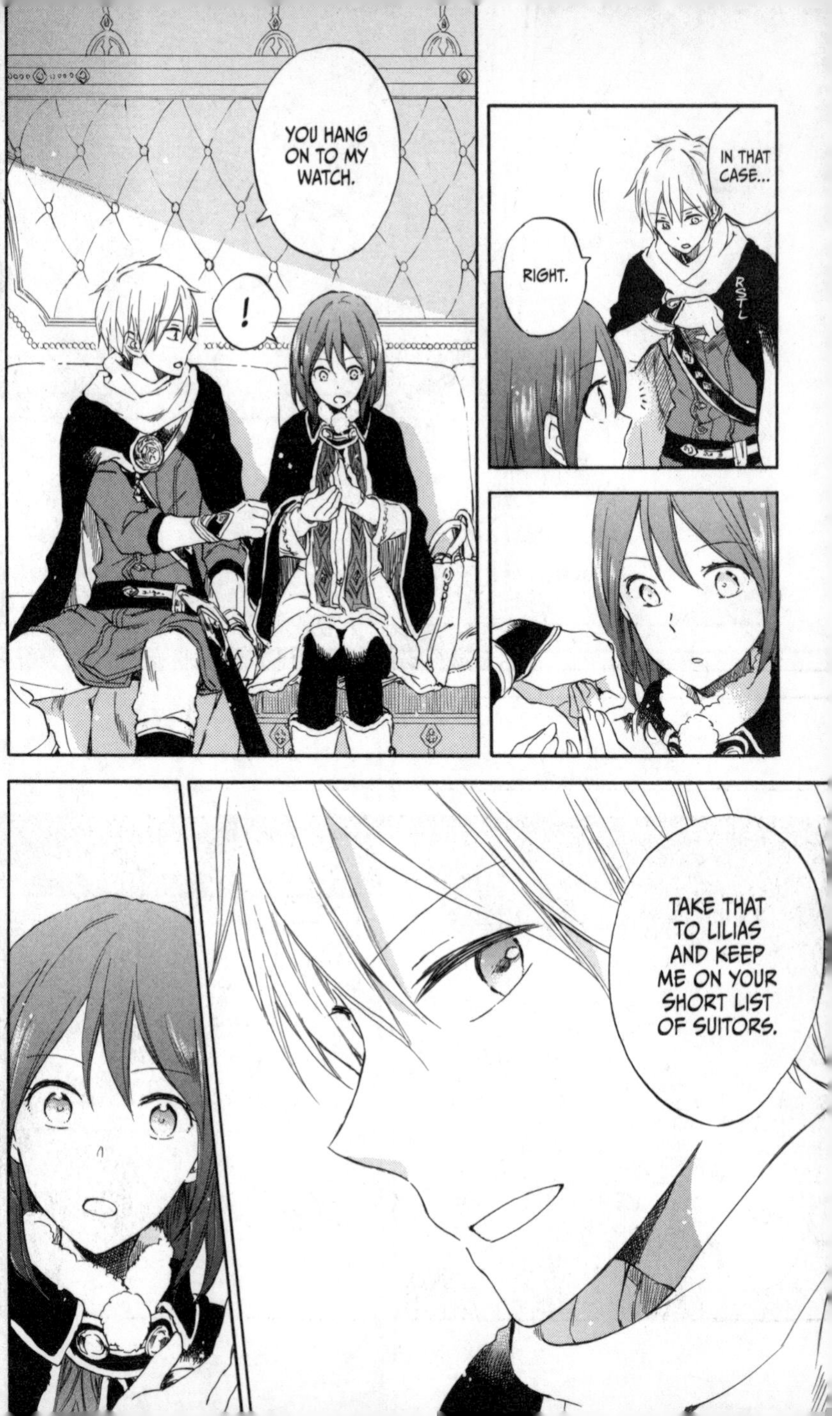
IN THAT CASE...
RIGHT.
RSTL
YOU HANG ON TO MY WATCH.
!
TAKE THAT TO LILIAS AND KEEP ME ON YOUR SHORT LIST OF SUITORS.

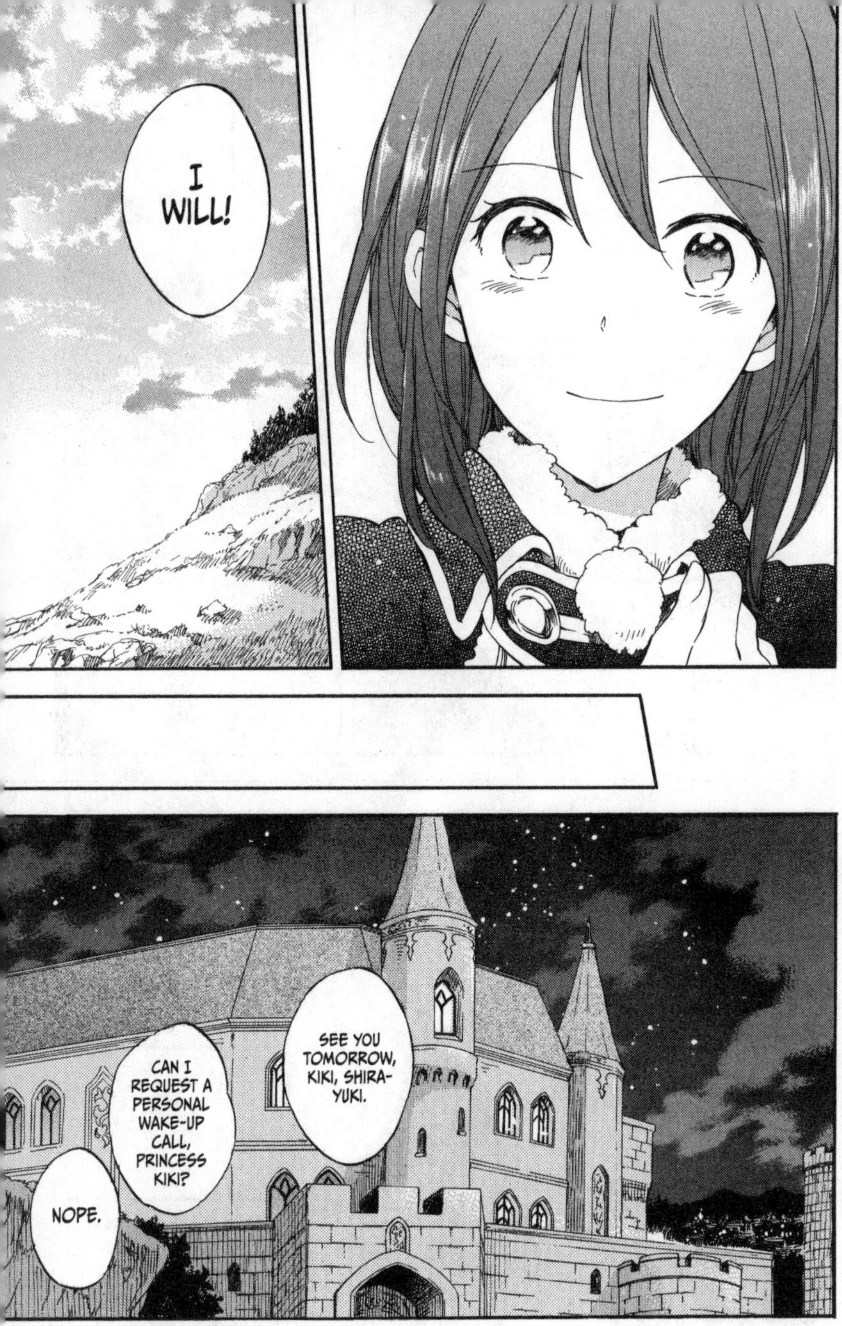
I WILL!
SEE YOU TOMORROW, KIKI, SHIRA-YUKI.
CAN I REQUEST A PERSONAL WAKE-UP CALL, PRINCESS KIKI?
NOPE.

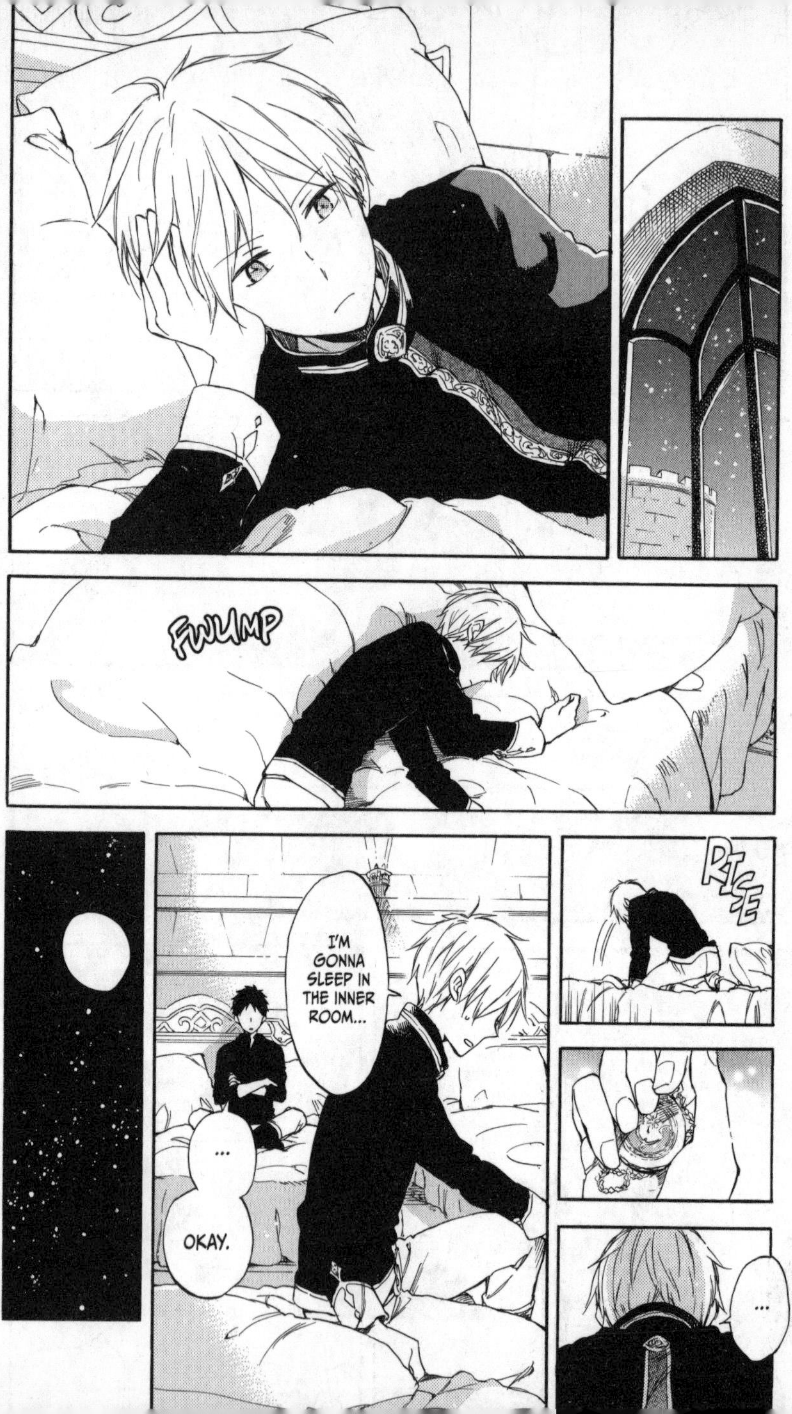
FWUMP
RISE
...
I'M GONNA SLEEP IN THE INNER ROOM...
...
OKAY.

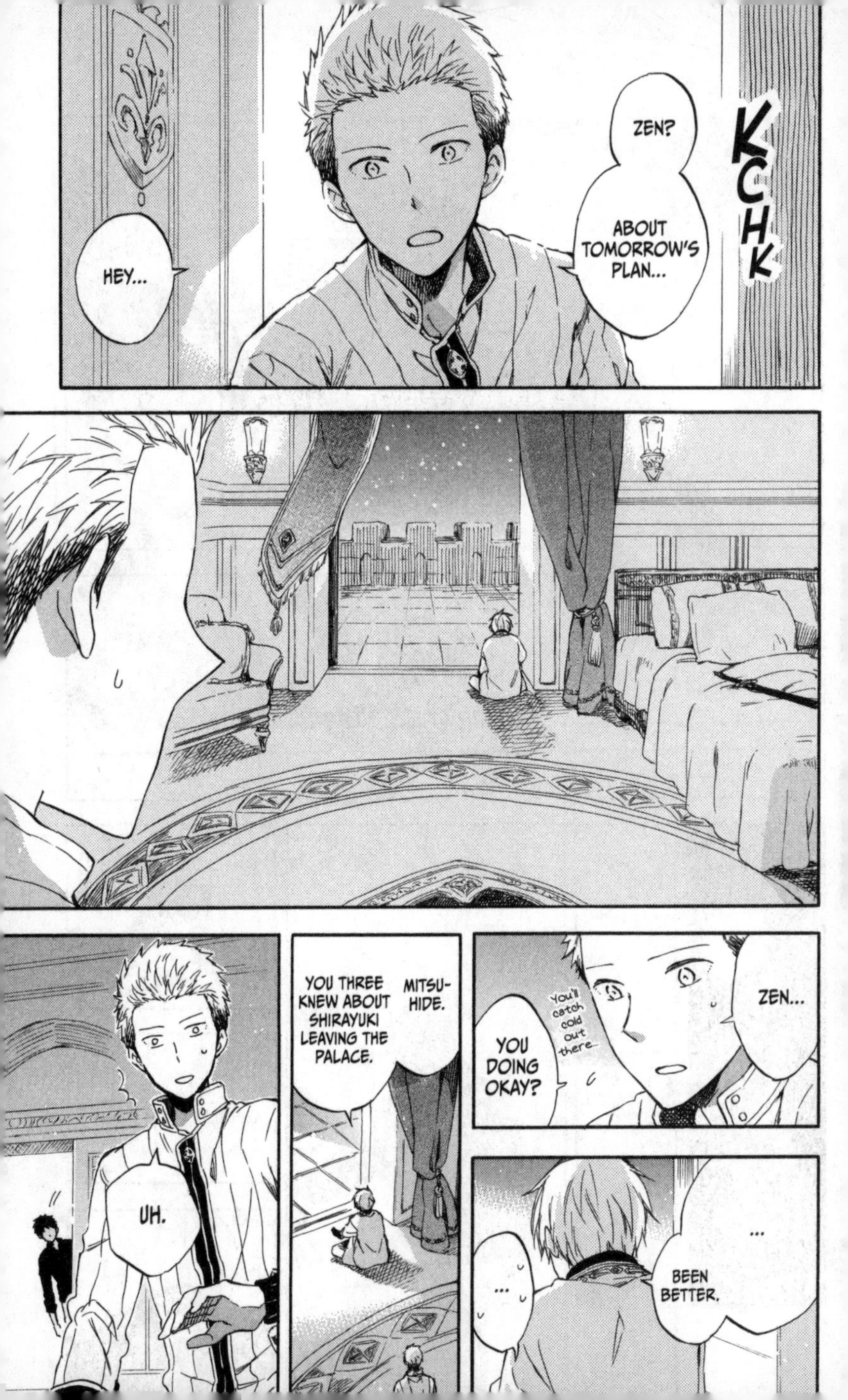
KCHK
ZEN?
ABOUT TOMORROW'S PLAN...
HEY...
ZEN...
YOU DOING OKAY?
You'll catch cold out there.
...
BEEN BETTER.
...
MITSU-HIDE.
YOU THREE KNEW ABOUT SHIRAYUKI LEAVING THE PALACE.
UH.

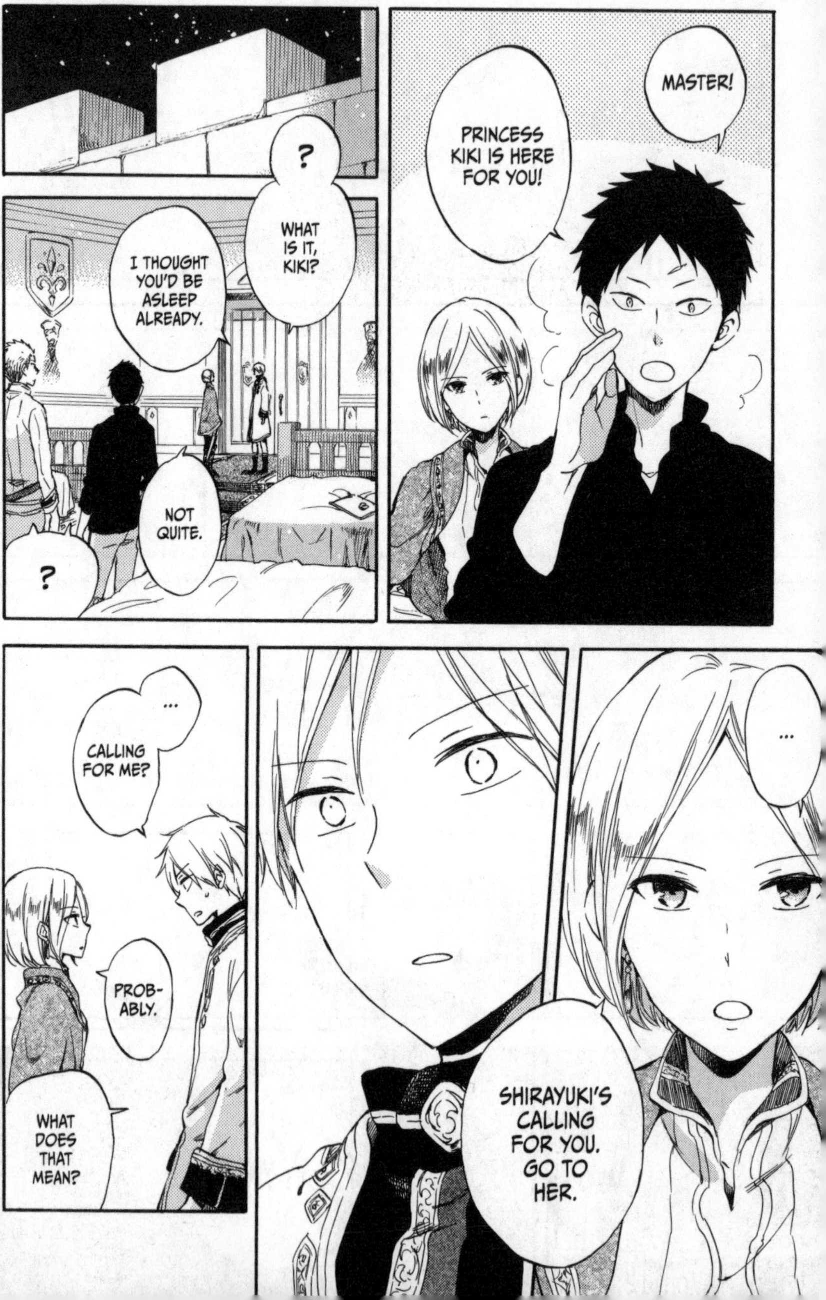
MASTER!
PRINCESS KIKI IS HERE FOR YOU!
?
WHAT IS IT, KIKI?
I THOUGHT YOU'D BE ASLEEP ALREADY.
NOT QUITE.
?
...
SHIRAYUKI'S CALLING FOR YOU. GO TO HER.
...
CALLING FOR ME?
PROB-ABLY.
WHAT DOES THAT MEAN?

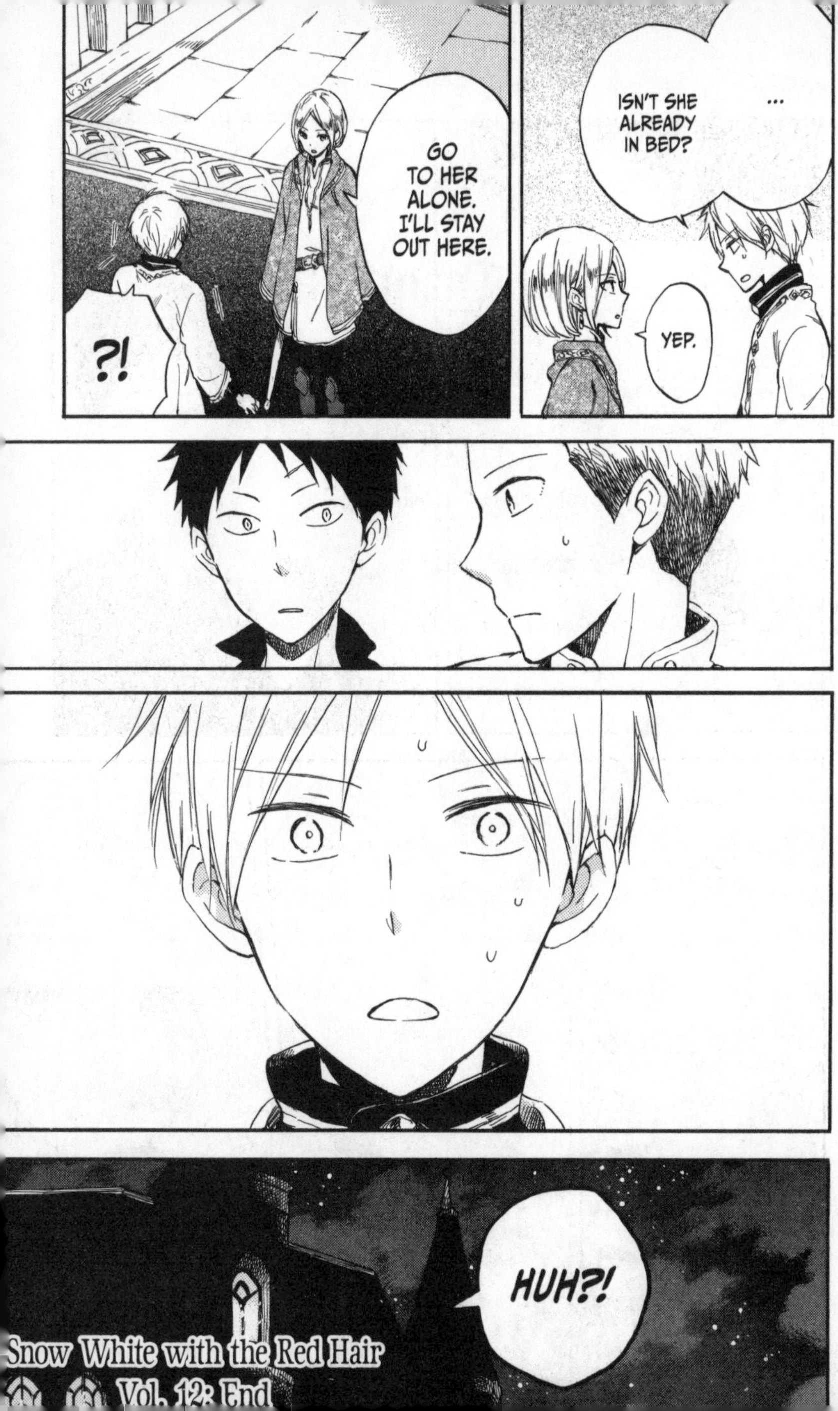
...
ISN'T SHE ALREADY IN BED?
YEP.
GO TO HER ALONE. I'LL STAY OUT HERE.
?!
HUH?!
Snow White with the Red Hair
Vol. 12: End

✦Big Thanks To:✦

- My editor

- The editorial staff at *LaLa*

- Everyone in Publishing/Sales

- Yamashita-sama

- Noro-sama

- Akatsuki-sama

- My mother, father and sister

- All the readers out there!

Sorata Akiduki

Sorata Akiduki was born on March 21 and is an accomplished shojo manga author. She made her debut in January 2002 with a one-shot titled "Utopia." Her previous works include *Vahlia no Hanamuko* (Vahlia's Bridegroom), *Seishun Kouryakubon* (Youth Strategy Guide) and *Natsu Yasumi Zero Zero Nichime* (00 Days of Summer Vacation). *Snow White with the Red Hair* began serialization in August 2006 in *LaLa DX* in Japan and has since moved to *LaLa*.

Snow White
with the Red Hair

SHOJO BEAT EDITION

STORY AND ART BY
Sorata Akiduki

TRANSLATION **Caleb Cook**
TOUCH-UP ART & LETTERING **Brandon Bovia**
DESIGN **Alice Lewis**
EDITOR **Karla Clark**

Akagami no Shirayukihime by Sorata Akiduki
© Sorata Akiduki 2014
All rights reserved.
First published in Japan in 2014 by HAKUSENSHA, Inc., Tokyo.
English language translation rights arranged with HAKUSENSHA, Inc., Tokyo.

The stories, characters and incidents mentioned
in this publication are entirely fictional.

Printed in Canada

Published by VIZ Media, LLC
P.O. Box 77010
San Francisco, CA 94107

10 9 8 7 6 5 4 3 2 1
First printing, March 2021

PARENTAL ADVISORY
SNOW WHITE WITH THE RED HAIR is
rated T for Teen and is recommended
for ages 13 and up for mild language.

 MEDIA
viz.com

shojobeat.com

YOU'RE READING THE WRONG WAY!

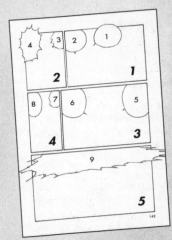

Snow White with the Red Hair reads from right to left, starting in the upper-right corner. Japanese is read from right to left, meaning that action, sound effects and word-balloon order are completely reversed from English order.

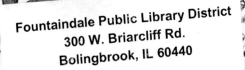